A Sense of Place

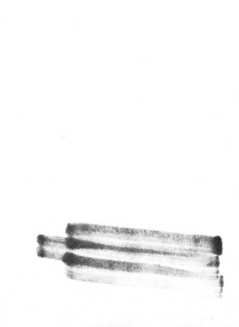

A Sense of Place

Birmingham's Black Middle-Class Community, 1890–1930

Lynne B. Feldman

THE UNIVERSITY OF ALABAMA PRESS

Tuscaloosa and London

Copyright © 1999
The University of Alabama Press
Tuscaloosa, Alabama 35487-0380
All rights reserved
Manufactured in the United States of America

1 2 3 4 5 6 7 8 9 / 07 06 05 04 03 02 01 00 99

Cover design by Shari DeGraw

∞

The paper on which this book is printed meets the minimum requirements
of American National Standard for Information Science–Permanence of
Paper for Printed Library Materials, ANSI Z39.48-1984.

Library of Congress Cataloging-in-Publication Data

Feldman, Lynne B.
    A sense of place : Birmingham's Black middle-class community,
1890–1930 / Lynne B. Feldman.
        p.   cm.
    Includes bibliographical references (p. 281) and index.

    ISBN 0–8173–0967–5 (alk. paper)
    ISBN 0–8173–0969–1 (paper: alk. paper)
    1. Afro-Americans—Alabama—Birmingham—History.   2. Middle
class—Alabama—Birmingham—History.   3. Birmingham (Ala.)—
History.   I. Title.
    F334.B69 N437 1999
    976.1'7810496073—dc21   98–58027

British Library Cataloguing-in-Publication Data available

*To John and in memory of
Rosetta Clarke Young*

"Can a people . . . live and develop for over three hundred years simply by *reacting*? Are American Negroes simply the creation of white men, or have they at least helped to create themselves out of what they found around them? Men have made a way of life in caves and upon cliffs, why cannot Negroes have made a life upon the horns of the white man's dilemma?"

—Ralph Ellison, *Shadow and Act*

Contents

Acknowledgments

The idea for this book originated from seeds that were planted several years ago. Although I did not begin to conceptualize clearly this project until I was a graduate student at Florida State University, I was inspired during an earlier research trip to Nashville for a volume written by John N. Ingham and me. While there, I spent time reviewing the Frost-Bell Papers, at the E. C. Dargan Research Library at the Sunday School Board Library. The richness of the information held in the papers and the impact of legislative decisions on individuals moved me to reconsider my future. I have not looked back since.

I found a perhaps somewhat unusual niche for myself at Florida State University, where my major field was American history and my minor field was in urban planning. Professors Maxine Jones, Joe Richardson, and Valerie J. Connor guided me through their courses in American and African American history, each with their unique perspective. Charles E. Connerly, however, gave me something I never expected to find at Florida State. Although I had an interest in black history from an urban and social perspective, I never expected to find what I did in the Urban and Regional Planning Department at Florida State. Unbeknownst to me until midway through my first semester, Professor Connerly, an urban planner with a strong background in American history, had an office one floor below that of the History Department. Professor Connerly, as I learned, and I share a passion for Birmingham, Alabama, a passion shared with few other people. Our first informal meeting solidified a relationship that has allowed me to express my confusion, interest, frustration, and obsession with a city that has long been overlooked by social historians.

With support from Charles Connerly to pursue themes that combined the disciplines of history and urban planning, I was able to arrive at a thesis topic that satisfied the criteria of both the History and Urban and Regional Planning Departments. Maxine Jones agreed to assume the role of major professor in this unconventional pursuit and exhibited her support throughout the process. Despite my enthusiasm in graduate school, I would not have pursued expanding my thesis into a book without her encouragement. She took the initiative to send my thesis to Malcolm MacDonald, then director at The University of Alabama Press. With some reluctance I began to consider the possibility of entering into a "very long-term" commitment. Mr. MacDonald suggested that I forward a copy of the thesis to Leah Rawls Atkins, former director of the Arts and Humanities Center at Auburn University. A complete stranger to me at this time, Leah went far beyond the call of duty as a new and fresh pair of eyes. Her knowledge of the city of Birmingham combined with her keen enthusiasm propelled me to move ahead. She has become a constant cheerleader, not without criticism, of my endeavor to recreate a sector of the black community at the turn of the century.

Although I was not completely unfamiliar with Birmingham, having visited the city several times for earlier research projects, I still entered the environment with some trepidation. How would I be received as an outsider digging into the closely guarded secrets of Birmingham's black community? With only a few exceptions, I was received graciously and hospitably by the individuals with whom I had personal and professional contact. From the time I entered the doors of the Jefferson County courthouse to the time I completed the research several years later, I met with a professionalism combined with a hospitality that I have not experienced anywhere else.

The staff at the courthouse exhibited unmatched patience. Bennie Dodd always made me feel welcome at the Probate Record Room. From the first time I arrived there with little knowledge of the organization of property records, Bennie methodically instructed me how to use the indices and mortgage and deed records. He always inquired into the progress of my work and exhibited a sincere interest in Canada, Toronto (where I live), and the Toronto Blue Jays. One floor above the Probate Record Room is the Tax Assessor's Office where I first met Charles Crim. Mr. Crim went to great lengths to help me access tax records that were difficult to find and perhaps more difficult to use. With good humor, he directed me to the records and cautioned me about the difficulties involved in interpreting old tax forms. He and his staff were always available to assist me and expressed an interest in the research I was conducting in their department.

The personnel at the Southern History Collection in the Birmingham Public Library made me feel as if I were coming home. Yvonne

Crumpler, Jim Pate, Roger Torbert, Francine Cooper, and Felita Lewis responded to my numerous queries with expediency. Yvonne has helped me through numerous research projects, and without fail, she has located whatever I have requested. Jim Pate has responded to my numerous e-mail queries promptly and professionally. The staff in the Department of Archives and Manuscript at the Birmingham Public Library have exhibited a professionalism combined with good humor that has been a relief during difficult times. Marvin Whiting assisted me during the earlier stages of my research, and Jim Baggett, current director of the department, has responded promptly to my numerous queries in person, by mail, by telephone, by fax, and most especially by e-mail. His sense of humor is refreshing and welcomed all the time. Don Veasey has proved very helpful and has assisted me without exception during my visits to the archives. Ms. Earline Grigsby's assistance at the Smithfield Public Library provided me with valuable materials connected to Industrial High School and the community.

Other facilities within Birmingham proved repositories of valuable information. The Birmingham City Hall staff directed me to the unwieldy volumes that contained the Graymont City and the Board of Alderman minutes. And the staff at the Board of Education assisted me in locating the early Board of Education minutes. Pat Fox allowed me to move into her Chamber of Commerce office to use volumes of city directories that are missing from the Birmingham Public Library. Francis Muir granted me permission to use a tape recorder to record tax information held at the Lawyer's Title Insurance Corp. The cost of using this material is prohibitively high and without her permission I would have been unable to document the transfer of property as I did. Wayne Coleman, archivist at the Civil Rights Institute, ably provided guidance to the Institute's archival collection that is in the process of being catalogued. Elizabeth Wells, curator at the Special Collection of Samford University helped me to locate useful records and numerous master's theses on related topics.

Beyond Birmingham, several collections proved unmatchable in their usefulness. Cynthia Wilson and Dan Williams at the Hollis Burke Frissell Library, Special Collection, at Tuskegee University gave me free reign to peruse the valuable Robert Moton Papers and the National Negro Business League Papers. Clark Center, archivist at W. S. Hoole Special Collections at The University of Alabama, and Norwood Kerr, archivist at the State of Alabama Department of Archives and History each directed me toward critical materials, including maps, newspapers, and company records. Outside of Alabama, Diana

Lachatanere, curator at the New York Public Library's Schomburg Center, and Kevin Proffitt, Archivist at the American Jewish Archives in Cincinnati, helped me to access material without having to travel the distance.

Despite my lack of affiliation with an academic institution I received assistance and guidance from academics who exhibited exceptional professionalism. During the earlier stages of this project, as I was floundering around trying to determine a clearer focus, several individuals shared their expertise. Professor Glenn Eskew of Georgia State University did more than I imagined possible. His careful reading of the manuscript and his keen insight forced me to completely rework the focus into something more meaningful and relevant. Professor Andrew Wiese of Barnard College provided insight into black suburbs, while Richard Harris at McMaster University and Bruce Leslie at SUNY Brockport each took the time to review a significant amount of material and offer suggestions with relation to the chapters on homeownership and education respectively. Other academics who provided suggestions and guidance were Edward LaMonte, Jeff Norrell, and Bruce Stave.

Numerous Birmingham residents gave me a morning or afternoon to share ideas, provide leads and exchange ideas. Otis Dismuke, Odessa Woolfolk, and J. Mason Davis all have very strong ties to and deep roots in Birmingham and they were kind enough to share information with me. Their "leads" took me to Smithfield residents who helped me to unravel the mystery of the black middle class. Other longtime Birmingham residents who gave of their time were John Butler, Verna Kennon, Dr. Dannetta K. Thornton Owen, Barbara Young, Woodrow Young, Richard Charles Young, Norma Walton, Ruth Hawkins, Joe Woodall, James Armstrong, Emma Lamar, Myrtle Lumpkin, Mary Alice Stollenwerck, Reverend Christopher Hamlin, Joe Spencer, and William Battle of the NAACP, and Willie Goodson and Meyer Newfield. Henley Jordan Smith, an ancestor of Joseph Riley Smith, proudly shared his family histories with me.

Ellen Tarry, who left Birmingham many years ago, still feels a strong connection to the city. She extended herself to me in many ways. We corresponded by mail for a time and met for an afternoon at the Smithfield Library. Miss Tarry worked very hard on my behalf. She not only granted me an interview but also searched her home for family photographs that she reproduced and shared with me. They appear in the pages of this book.

The friends I have made along the way are a bonus I never expected to receive when I decided to write about Birmingham. People I met during my work have become good friends. They have extended themselves to me in the tradition of southern hospitality that I no longer believe is a myth. Barbara and Phil Watts, Kathy and Steve Sexton, Cedric and Cynthia Thomas have all become friends as a result of my numerous trips to Birmingham. Francine Cooper is a lifelong friend that I made during the hours I spent in the microfilm reading room at the Birmingham Public Library. Despite the differences in our life experiences, she and I are kindred spirits, and I treasure our friendship deeply. My friends in Birmingham have an understanding about what I am doing in their city that far surpasses the understanding of my friends in Toronto. Over the years I have had nothing to show for the hours I have spent writing and rewriting this manuscript. The absence of tangible evidence further confounded my friends in Toronto. So, for all those people who wondered what I have been doing all this time, here it is.

The staff at The University of Alabama Press has been unquestionably patient. From the first time that Malcolm MacDonald contacted me, many years have passed. Director Nicole Mitchell has shown her faith in me as she followed me with faxes and letters and phone calls during a year of globe trotting. She respected my requests and allowed me ample time for rewrites. Mindy Wilson and Suzette Griffith have capably guided me through the necessary steps of the editing and copy-editing process.

These final paragraphs are the most difficult to write. How does one quantify relationships that cannot be put into words? Rosetta Clarke Young was a unique individual who I knew for far too few years. She was the daughter of Peter Clarke, a black businessman who figures in my story. Miss Young and I met in 1993 when I interviewed her at her home. She could not wait to help me in my research. Her exuberance and enthusiasm, her zest for life and her sarcasm were all embodied in this woman who was well into her seventies when I first met her. She escorted me to people's homes, she took me on a tour of Smithfield, she took me as a guest to her church—the Sixteenth Street Baptist Church—and she insisted that I call her when I returned to my hotel room at night! Rosetta Clarke Young was an exceptional human being.

There is an obvious luxury in being an independent scholar, but there is a liability that is not readily apparent—the absence of intellectual interaction. I have restrained myself from mentioning my husband, John, before this time, but he fills in those gaps and much more.

He has played a role in every part of the creation of this book. From the very moment that I decided I wanted to pursue an education in Black history—at the Sunday School Board in Nashville—to this final stage. In his own inimitable way, John has urged me to do what he knew I could do, but I didn't. He never questioned why I left home to study, though everyone else did, and he never asked me when I would be finished. He encouraged the passion I exhibit with respect to my work and tolerated in stride the frustration and threats of giving up. As a historian who works in Black history, John could offer insight, suggestions, criticisms, and support whenever the need arose. He recognized the danger of being a little too close to the project and pulled back at the appropriate time. He has not yet read this completed manuscript. When he opens the pages of the book he will see that it is dedicated to him—no one deserves it more.

Introduction

Vulcan, the iron statue that symbolizes Birmingham's industrial progress, sits atop Red Mountain. From this vantage point he observed the city's violent struggle to maintain the racial status quo. The Civil Rights movement literally exploded in this New South city, where a reactionary and seemingly omnipotent police commissioner ruled. The *New York Times* reported on April 12, 1960, "Every channel of communication, every medium of mutual interest, every reasoned approach, every inch of middle ground has been fragmented by the emotional dynamite of racism, reinforced by the whip, the razor, the gun, the bomb, the torch, the club, the knife, the mob, the police and many branches of 'the state's apparatus.' " Reputations die hard.

Yet, there was another Birmingham long before it received national recognition as a hateful city. In the late nineteenth century, city boosters who were striving to improve Birmingham's national status and encourage outside investment, initiated drives promoting the creation of healthy communities. Smithfield, a five hundred-acre area that once was a cornfield, was one of the earliest suburbs that caught the attention of these boosters. Sitting west of Birmingham's original city limits, Smithfield offered alternative housing to the city's black and white residents who wanted to escape from cramped living conditions. For African Americans particularly, this was a unique opportunity to participate in the development of a new community away from the congested housing that had become home for them. Many community-oriented residents engaged in activities designed to create a comfortable world for themselves as Smithfield began to take shape. Physical separation from the city allowed them to assert considerable influence over their home environment. Consequently, they gained their greatest sense of self-esteem where they exerted the greatest control—in the home sphere.[1]

Smithfield provides an ideal backdrop against which to examine the lives of a black economic elite who are also called the black middle class.[2] Upon its founding, Smithfield was not segregated by race or class, rather it represented a broad cross-section of individuals and families, both black and white. Their geographic separateness allowed the black residents particularly to remove themselves physically and psychologically from the broader society, where they encountered myriad experiences that shaped their perceptions. They constructed a community that allowed them to temporarily ignore the hostilities of the outside world. It also provided them with the opportunity to partially separate themselves along class lines, as they sought to protect themselves from association with the black masses. Many black families who shared an elevated status relocated to Smithfield where they created a world that provided them with a measure of recognition and harmony and where they nurtured intimate relationships that contributed to their prestige and their personal fulfillment. Seretha Jackson settled in Smithfield when she migrated from Columbia, South Carolina, in 1927. She remembered having "such a good time. I think we had a better time than they have now." Ellen Tarry, the daughter of barber John Barber "Bob" Tarry, shared Seretha Jackson's fond memories when she declared that "those were happy times. . . . These were the years our people were disfranchised. I wasn't aware of it. Our parents kept us in a cocoon."[3]

By examining Smithfield's early settlement and the lives of its emerging black middle-class residents, this study will attempt to uncover the facets that contribute to the creation of an elite black middle class. Many of the older blacks interviewed recall their younger years with fondness. How did they or their families establish a world in which they moved freely without the overbearing restrictions of segregated life in Birmingham? If their memories are selective, there had to be sufficient distractions and positive experiences to counteract humiliations and disappointments. What types of institutions did they construct, and what kinds of social activities did they engage in? In answering these questions, the community of Smithfield takes on greater meaning, for it was here that middle-class blacks achieved a sense of place.

In the late nineteenth century, African Americans were adopting a strategy of self-segregation that had its roots in black nationalism. With its emphasis on self-reliance, black nationalism emphasized the need for African Americans to independently develop vital areas of life—economics, politics, religious, and intellectual—in order to effect their liberation.[4] Increased segregation and discrimination in the late nineteenth and early twentieth centuries helped to create what August Meier calls a "petit bourgeoisie of business and professional men" who were dependent on the perpetuation of a self-segregated economy.[5] Booker T. Washington shared the philosophy of black nationalists when he, as Meier points out, declared that "we are a nation within a nation."[6] In doing so, he urged racial solidarity and a separate black economy. The creation of his National Negro Business League was instrumental in promoting this ideology nationally among African American entrepreneurs and those aspiring to participate in the growing black economy and the derivative black pride associated with self-help activities. In his distinct style, Marcus Garvey's appeal for economic chauvinism and race pride struck a chord with the black masses, many of whom adopted his rhetoric. During the early twentieth century, as blacks across America began to internalize these messages, they exhibited an increasing sense of racial solidarity and pride.

Many African Americans in Birmingham demonstrated their increasing race consciousness and solidarity when they adopted the Washington philosophy of self-help and precepts of economic chauvinism and created their own separate economy. In doing so, they created a viable community and a sense of place through self-segregation. The development of black businesses, private clubs, and private institutions promoted race pride and provided refuge from racial discrimination. The following chapters demonstrate how blacks created an infrastructure of organizations designed to serve their needs and desires. Their efforts at creating a protective environment in which they could assert their independence, nurture interpersonal relationships, and develop strategies to implement race progress also reveal the multifaceted character of the black community. The material reveals not only how some African Americans actively pursued improvements for themselves and for the larger black community but equally important it illustrates class distinctions and class conflict within the black community. When an elite class of blacks staged a fund-raising play at the Jefferson Theatre, dissension between the different classes surfaced as members of the "better" class condemned others for their unrefined behavior. The infrequency of their interaction and their intolerance of lower-class African Americans, who they sometimes referred to as "the other class of Negroes" or "the less fortunate," is revealed in Ellen Tarry's recollection that there were "Negroes we refused to know socially."[7] The story of how Birmingham's elite blacks moved within their own community and among members of mainstream society to effect change is also documented in the following chapters.

A growing black elite class in Birmingham was beginning to take shape as African Americans flocked to the city. This broadly based group recognized its own distinctiveness and sought to perpetuate itself through group solidarity and cohesion. They clustered together in their home environment where they could maintain close contact and develop a supportive network. Members of this group shared core values that they sought to pass on to the larger black community. Public deportment was among the defining features of membership in this class. Refined behavior coupled with other signs of ambition or modest accomplishment were avenues toward acceptance. Although most recognized the value of education, some members were well educated, whereas others were not. With few exceptions, most worked within the separate black economy, although a few owned businesses that served a large white clientele. A few held professional positions as lawyers, doctors, and dentists, and others were businessmen, ministers, or artisans.[8] Many had the financial means to become homeowners while fewer remained renters. Several owned personal property, such as pianos and jewelry, that highlighted their station in life, and a few families even owned automobiles. Numerous elite blacks shared membership in fraternal organizations and churches, while others pursued different avenues of association. Despite these disparities, they shared an interest in not only improving themselves but also in uplifting the race. Among them were individuals who periodically spoke out against the injustices of racism and who organized protests and signed petitions to effect change.

In Birmingham, the complicated race relations under segregation enabled some middle-class leaders to secure important improvements for African Americans. The paternalistic relationship between several black leaders and white benefactors was clearly responsible for some of these changes. William Pettiford could not have elicited support for Industrial High School without adopting a carefully planned posture with white power brokers. White businessmen and philanthropists did not believe that blacks were equal to whites, but they did feel a sense of noblesse oblige and wanted a stable work force. The high school, they believed, would provide them with properly trained workers who would not agitate for change.[9] Welfare capitalism in Birmingham was adopted to elicit worker loyalty, and William Pettiford also played a key role in securing these benefits for black workers.[10] Although the philosophies that leaders promoted were not always accepted by blacks who belonged to the working or lower classes, Pettiford's influence among middle-class blacks assisted him in gaining credibility and support for civic improvements. Largely, class distinctions within the African American community were becoming invisible to whites who insisted on categorizing the black community as monolithic. Yet there were a few whites who recognized the differences and realized the benefits of manipulating relationships with the middle-class leaders. The class divisions within the black community actually helped the leaders elicit white assistance.

The leaders and their middle-class supporters represented the potential achievements of blacks who were not yet uplifted. Their refined public behavior earned them the possibility of winning an audience among those who could make a difference. Carefully crafted strategies were essential for black leaders to maintain black support while developing a workable relationship with sympathetic whites. The civic improvements that the black community sought were intended to uplift the neediest to a level where they could appreciate and adopt the values of the middle class. With limited finances and power, African Americans coordinated their efforts and entered into relationships designed to create an infrastructure of civic organizations that was designed solely to serve black people. To understand their strategies and subsequent achievements, it is necessary to first explore the broader society of Birmingham.

1

The Birth of a Community

In 1871, when Birmingham emerged as a city of the New South, the ravages of the Civil War were still fresh in the minds of all Americans. Yet, the southerners who founded Birmingham looked to the future. They placed their confidence in industrialization as the answer to establishing a secure foothold in the American economy. They were lured into the area by the possibility of economic wealth that lay in the Jones Valley. Rich mineral deposits of iron ore lay buried beneath Jefferson County's imposing Red Mountain, which sat on the southern edge of the valley. Coal and limestone lay nearby. Together these resources were the necessary raw materials to make steel and pig iron. With this knowledge neatly tucked under their belts, their appetites for wealth and distinction were whetted. Without looking back, ambitious Americans readied themselves to participate in the creation of greatness.

Foundries, rolling mills, blast furnaces, coke ovens, and other industrial concerns emerged in the Birmingham District in the early period. The major blast furnaces lay to the east and west of the center city, and the foundries and factories were located within a two-mile radius of the downtown core. Thousands of black and white migrants flocked to the city looking for economic opportunities with such companies as Tennessee Coal, Iron and Railroad Company (TCI), the American Cast Iron Pipe Company (ACIPCO), and the Continental Gin Company. The small city was becoming increasingly crowded as new residents sought a place for themselves within the city boundaries. Municipal and county governments were unable to provide even such basic services as uncontaminated water, and welfare services were also in short supply. The city's residents were feeling the impact of a financial crisis. As long as the furnaces remained outside the city limits, industries lay beyond the reach of Birmingham's tax system. As Ethel Armes stated, "Many of these successful money makers have been still more successful money keepers. Few dollars of theirs have gone to boost along any public welfare moves. 'Before God,' said one of these, 'I will be damned before I will put my hand in my pocket for anything!' "[1] This socially irresponsible attitude resulted in trash-lined streets, a high mortality rate from scarlet fever and small pox, particularly among African Americans, and the absence of an efficient and widespread sewage system.[2] As late as 1910, Birmingham had neither a central library building nor a first-class hotel; yet it aspired to be ranked with Chicago, Pittsburgh, and Atlanta—its southern rival.[3]

Outside investors were a significant factor in the development of the young city, although they were by no means the sole energy behind Birmingham's growth. At least before the 1890s, both Alabamians and other entrepreneurial-spirited southerners relied upon their own resources to industrialize the area, and "they industrialized in their own way, on their own terms."[4] Birmingham was in southern hands until its industries showed a profit and northern money moved in to take control. This happened in 1907 when U.S. Steel purchased TCI;[5] but greatness did not follow. U.S. Steel's discriminatory pricing policies of Alabama steel, combined with less-advanced technology, an unstable work force, and inferior resources (when compared to the rich iron ore fields of the Mesabi range in Minnesota) contributed to Birmingham's slow and disappointing growth as an industrial city. Furthermore, its tenuous position on the national scene and the frequent shifting of management personnel and strategies, contributed to its instability.[6]

The city's boosters had aggressively sought to expand the geographic boundaries of Birmingham when they concluded that the city's prestige was dependent on a large population base. Birmingham had extended its city limits in 1873, 1889, and 1893 but experienced only moderate population growth when compared to Jefferson County's. In 1890, 20,000 people lived outside the city limits in company towns and in areas under development by numerous real estate companies, including the Smithfield Land Company and the Avondale Land Company.[7] The county's population grew more rapidly because of factors directly related to the presence of industry capital invested in the suburbs, which lay beyond Birmingham's boundaries and its jurisdiction.[8] In 1870, Birmingham's population was 3,086, and in 1880 it increased to only 3,800. Ten years later, in 1890, it boasted a population of 26,501, and by 1910, through annexation and migration, the population of the city had exceeded 130,000.[9] During the first decade of the twentieth century, the city organized an ambitious annexation movement that drew thousands of people into the district. The growth of the steel, iron, and coal industries provided the strongest inducement for economic opportunity, and a broad cross-section of newcomers converged on the city. White-collar and professional men arrived to establish service- and retail-oriented businesses or to engage in speculative activities.[10] But their numbers paled in comparison to the numbers of black and white laborers who migrated from the rural regions of Alabama and other southern states. First- and second-generation European immigrants relocated from northern industrial cities when new employment opportunities became available.[11]

Rural workers who had lost their land or who had encountered insurmountable difficulties migrated to the city, where they expected to find employment. Birmingham promised to be a marked improvement to their experiences as sharecroppers, and according to one historian, improvements in living standards were realized.[12] In the earliest years of Birmingham's development, workers' dreams outweighed the inconveniences they were forced to endure. As one early settler recalled: "We arrived September 2, 1871. There was no shelter to be had for love or money so we camped in tents on Village Creek. . . . We waited there two weeks for a house to be near enough completed that we might be sheltered."[13] For many, Birmingham was the first urban stop on their way to the North; for others it was their final destination. These migrants changed the racial composition of the city. Before the founding of the Birmingham District, only 10 percent of the population of Jefferson County was black, but by 1890, blacks constituted 43 percent of Birmingham's population. In 1900, the African American population increased by 47 percent and constituted 43 percent of Birmingham's population. In 1910, the black population grew by 216 percent, whereas the white population grew by 268 percent. At that time, blacks constituted 39 percent of the population—the highest black percentage of any American city with a population of more than 100,000—at which point it stabilized for the following decade.[14] Although a small percentage were members of the middle class who sought employment as teachers, lawyers, and white-collar professionals, the bulk of African American migrants were employed as unskilled laborers. By 1900, more than one-half of Alabama's miners were black, and in the state's iron and steel industry, black workers constituted 65 percent of the work force.[15] Despite the racial implications of attracting large numbers of African American workers into the district, black labor was eagerly sought because it was cheap. Technological advancements had created additional unskilled jobs that blacks were hired to fill despite employers' complaints that they were lazy or undependable. Employers willingly hired blacks because they perceived them to be suitable "to the heavy, hot work about blast furnaces."[16] Not all African Americans were unskilled laborers; some held positions as semi- and skilled workers.

African Americans who migrated to Birmingham in the late nineteenth century encountered an unfamiliar environment with a strikingly familiar tone: White supremacy reigned, and blacks were relegated to an inferior status. Yet, for a brief time during Birmingham's formative years, some blacks participated in a limited way in the mainstream society. Some African Americans who migrated in the 1870s and 1880s partook in the burgeoning business and political arenas.

As Birmingham was beginning to take shape, the bulk of activity was in the downtown core. The early seeds of a retail-financial center were planted along North 20th and North 21st Streets, where buildings were quickly erected and businesses were established. Both black and white entrepreneurs located their shops in what was becoming the Central Business District (CBD). Small African American businesses shared space and customers with the white-owned businesses. Black businesses in the CBD were service-oriented concerns in which African Americans tended to exhibit a strong representation: blacksmithing, shoemaking, and barbering. Bob Tarry and Frank McCree were among the earliest African American barbers who served white customers in shops in the CBD. As Ellen Tarry remembered, "Papa's customers were all white. Most of them were wealthy, too."[17] Black-owned businesses contributed to the city's economy and to the character of the city's business district. Their optimal location in the CBD, however, was only temporary. As property values increased and competition for prime real estate intensified, discrimination against black businesses in the CBD forced the owners to relocate to a segregated environment adjacent to the CBD. Initially the spatial arrangement of black business in the CBD was one of integration and dispersion; by the turn of the century, black businesses displayed a pattern of segregation and concentration.[18]

On the political scene, African Americans living in Birmingham exercised their constitutional rights according to the Alabama constitutions of 1868 and 1875. In the 1870s, approximately 30 percent of registered voters in Birmingham city elections were black, and in the 1880s, the figure ranged from 45 to 48 percent. Although no African Americans in Birmingham held public office, they exercised their political rights. This involvement came to an end when, in 1888, an all-white city Democratic primary was organized to remove blacks from the decision-making process. This move was the forerunner of complete African American disfranchisement in the state. In 1901, the new state constitution effectively disfranchised roughly 33 percent of Birmingham's black population. Within five months of the constitution's ratification, Birmingham's black population of eighteen thousand had only thirty registered voters. This legislation sent reverberations throughout Alabama's African American communities, whose leaders moved to reinstate their rights. Through the Colored Man's Suffrage Association, they tested the constitutionality of the disfranchising provision. But when they filed suit in the U.S. Supreme Court in 1902, the court decided against them.[19]

African Americans were feeling the effects of disfranchisement and its social, economic, and political consequences. Representation throughout the state had significantly dropped: only one black, Eugene Stewart, was elected to an Alabama office during this period. The governor appointed two blacks as notaries public, and the Deputy of Mobile County was African American Calvin Childs.[20] A few blacks continued to challenge the constitution and organized Negro Suffrage Leagues around the state.[21] Birmingham residents Dr. Ulysses G. Mason and J. O. Diffay organized the Negro Republican party in opposition to the revitalization of the Lily-white Republican party, which had refused to seat any of twenty-five African American delegates present at the Republican Convention in Birmingham. Two hundred blacks attended the Negro Republican Convention, which was also held in Birmingham, where speakers denounced the Lily whites and their racist platform. Despite this early showing of support, their momentum soon languished; the organization was short-lived, and it failed to materialize into anything substantial. Their obvious powerlessness to effect change probably contributed to their overall apathy. Yet, some African Americans continued to wage protest against their disfranchisement, and they organized subsequent campaigns against the Lily whites who refused to acknowledge them.[22] After the passage of the new constitution, even African Americans who continued to pay the poll tax were disfranchised.[23] The pattern of denying blacks the vote proved static. Legal and extra-legal forces defeated any challenges blacks organized to overturn their disfranchisement. Next to the poll tax, the Ku Klux Klan (KKK) was the most effective deterrent against black suffrage after 1921.

Coinciding with disfranchisement were other events that transformed Birmingham's political and social environment and directly affected the quality of life for all African Americans. Southern states passed Jim Crow laws to codify the separation of the races. The 1880s set off a segregation drive that rapidly spread throughout the South. State legislatures and city councils mandated racial separation in virtually all public facilities and institutions and imposed similar policies on employment and residential neighborhoods. Alabama waited until 1891 before it used *legal* means to subordinate African Americans by passing the state's first Jim Crow law.[24] On January 20, 1891, the Alabama House of Representatives passed H. 119, the "Separate But Equal Accommodation Bill," and despite the efforts of a black conference to challenge this proposed law, it quickly passed without dissent on February 5. As fast as the conference moved to challenge the legislation, the House moved even faster. The *Huntsville Gazette* declared the law "A Shameful Injustice." Little could be done to reverse the trend toward further racial separation.[25]

In 1896, *Plessy v. Ferguson* encouraged legal work to enforce racial segregation. Jim Crow laws were imposed at varying rates in different facilities throughout Alabama. Soon segregation touched all aspects of social life for African Americans in the state. Blacks initially favored segregation over exclusion because "they believed, or at least hoped, that separate treatment could be truly equal." When blacks protested against segregation, they primarily targeted public accommodations; their chief goal was equal access rather than integration.[26] By 1902, Jim Crow applied to railroad stations where separate waiting rooms were provided for blacks and whites. Birmingham practices exhibited little variation of this trend. In 1902 the city jail was segregated, and in the same year, Will Mathis, a white man who was scheduled to be hanged at the same time as a black man, requested that his hanging take place "at a different hour from the time that the negro, Orlando Lester, will be hanged, and also that he be hanged from a different set of gallows." The city complied. Although Birmingham officials were probably caught up in the climate of the times and shared the hostility toward and fear of blacks that many other white southerners felt, they were also reacting against the city's swelling black population. African American migration continued into the early decades, and by 1930, the black racial composition of Birmingham was the highest of any major American city.[27]

As Jim Crow laws became increasingly restrictive, some blacks challenged the injustices imposed on their daily lives.[28] Blacks in Birmingham attempted to develop their own strategies to dismantle the rigid social arrangement of segregation. In 1905, the *Birmingham Wide-Awake* challenged streetcar ordinances: "We advise Afro-Americans in every section of the south where an attempt is made to separate the races on the street cars to boycott the street railways. This policy has been successfully pursued in many cities of the south, with the result that 'Jim Crowism' has been practically discredited— notably so in Montgomery, Houston and one or two cities in Mississippi. We advise the people never to get on a street car where the color line is drawn."[29]

Although some blacks lived close enough to walk to their places of employment and others lived in company housing, many blacks lived far from their jobs and had no other choice but to ride on the street-cars. A boycott was not a viable option. On occasion, a few sympathetic whites would speak publicly in their defense. B. F. Riley, a Birmingham minister and reformer, supported black challenges against the inferiority of Jim Crow accommodations and the discriminatory fee schedules. He declared that blacks were just in protesting "the un-just discrimination of certain corporations by declining to provide equal facilities of comfort for a uniform rate of travel." He recognized the injustices of Jim Crow and stated that blacks were not attempting to achieve what whites most feared—social equality: "Possibly no ap-prehension is more far-fetched and strained than this one."[30]

In 1906, an incident involving Rev. T. W. Walker, entrepreneur and pastor of the Shiloh Baptist Church, moved him to protest inadequate and inferior accommodations on the Birmingham Railway, Light and Power Company's street cars.[31] Walker was arrested and charged with refusing to pay carfare, disorderly conduct, and resisting arrest, all of which he claimed were false. The *Birmingham Truth,* a local black newspaper, rallied to Walker's defense and found the accommodations "ridiculous and its empoyes [*sic*] are insulting in the extreme."[32] Birmingham's Mayor George Ward responded to the incident when he acknowledged the "inadequate street car accommodations for colored people" and recognized the city council's duty that "more seats, or more trailers, or larger cars are put into service at once." The case was followed in both black and white newspapers, and according to the *Birmingham Ledger,* a white paper, "the case promises to be the start-ing point for the agitation to have the Jim Crow law instituted in Bir-mingham." The paper correctly forecast what lay ahead for the city's African Americans.[33]

The issue of imposing Jim Crow statutes on public accommoda-tions hung like a dark cloud over Birmingham for several years after Walker's case. When the Birmingham Railway, Light and Power Company introduced a "Pay-as-You-Enter" policy, it appeased African Americans who had been victimized by conductors accusing them of not paying their fares. Blacks wanted the company to adopt the policy used by the Tidewater lines, where blacks and whites used separate doors at the middle of the car, but used the common receptacle for depositing fares. When the system was introduced on one or two lines that were largely patronized by African Americans, no separate entrances were supplied. Consequently, whites and blacks shared the same entrances; blacks had to stand back and allow white passengers to enter first, and whites on their way to their seats had to pass by seated blacks. Whites objected to the arrangement and pointed out the possibility of race friction, while the *Birmingham Reporter*, representing black riders, also challenged the arrangement for different reasons: "Why should not the black man, who is paying the same fare as the white man, enter when he can and take a seat as all street car passengers do? . . . By all means do away with the Pay-as-You-Enter system, or introduce separate entrances and exits for white and colored passengers."[34]

Abuses of the system persisted, and although African Americans had to ride the streetcars, they continued to publicly voice their protest. Black newspapers with the support of some ministers, including Revs. John Goodgame and A. C. Williams, provided the forum through which to detail their grievances. The *Reporter* faithfully documented and railed against the injustices committed against blacks by the Birmingham Railway, Light and Power Company: "Yes, the colored people are aroused, and why should they not be aroused, when it is hardly possible for them to live in Birmingham without riding on the cars, and when they ride they are almost smothered to death in many instances because of the sandwich way in which they must ride? And, this is not because of the lack of space in the cars, it is because a cruel and ignorant conductor refuses to move a little hickory board marked 'Colored.'"[35]

The Birmingham Railway, Light and Power Company came under fire from both whites and blacks who articulated their unique grievances. Conflicts mounted throughout the 1910s and peaked by the early 1920s. In March 1923, later than in many other southern cities, Birmingham adopted an ordinance requiring partitions and separate entrances for blacks and whites on all streetcars in Birmingham. Despite the Chamber of Commerce's opposition to the law, and the Birmingham Railway, Light and Power Company's reluctance to comply because of the expense incurred to make the necessary changes, the decision was finalized when the City Commission voted unanimously for separation.[36] In late May 1924, the *New Era*, a black newspaper, issued a complaint against the inferior conditions for blacks but not against the policy of segregation. African Americans opposed the accommodations but did not develop a collective strategy to challenge the new policy. In 1930, Birmingham passed another city ordinance that introduced Jim Crow taxis.[37]

Separation of blacks and whites applied to most other public facilities—schools, parks, theaters, zoos, and even elevators. Blacks were allowed to share elevators with whites in department stores where they were customers but were forced to use the freight elevators in office buildings. The Lincoln Reserve Life Insurance Company, an interracial company, refused to continue to occupy its offices in the Jefferson County Bank Building as a protest against these restrictions.[38] The city's one skating rink became the backdrop for racial conflict. During Birmingham's initial growth, blacks enjoyed skating at Union Hall.[39] Their enjoyment was short-lived when Jim Crow excluded them from the facility. And in 1907, when they were on the verge of getting their own rink, they encountered opposition from local businessmen who protested against the proposed site for the new rink. The city council had granted them permission to construct a rink, but a snag occurred when the aldermen withdrew their support after learning that the site was across the street from the Jefferson Theatre and near to the Hippodrome and the Bijou Theatre. These were places of amusement where large numbers of whites assembled.

The city council commissioners insisted that they had not been notified of the site when they granted permission. A businessman's petition was responsible for the city's reversal: "Observation and experience teach us that the best way to maintain peace and quiet, law and order, between white people, and negroes is to keep them separate and apart in social life, and we believe it best for the negroes that they should not be encouraged to assemble together in large numbers too frequently." The petition pointed out how blacks would congregate "not only for innocent amusement and pleasure," but it would provide space where they would hold political and other meetings, and under "the heat of passion and excitement be moved to do unlawful acts."[40] The petitioners urged that an alternate site be selected away from the downtown core. Downtown property owners were opposed to blacks assembling in their district for fear of unrest between the races; they were likely concerned about property values, although they never publicly declared so, and they feared unruly blacks spilling onto the streets and threatening whites who in the future might stay away from the theaters altogether. The scenario was becoming all too familiar to blacks.

African Americans occasionally resorted to collective action when new barriers were erected to impede their mobility. They had enjoyed access to public parks until 1903, when the superintendent of parks began to restrict black access. Members of the Sixteenth Street Baptist Church appealed to the City Commission for permission to use Avondale Park for a special event. When the Commission granted them permission on one occasion, the Avondale Civic League objected. "It never once occurred to the people of the Sixteenth Street Baptist Church that any of the citizens of Birmingham would offer the least objection to one day's outing at the Avondale Park for the negro people. . . . Is it asking too much for one day's outing in the park where the animals are on exhibition for every day in the year?"[41] Newspapers cried out for fair treatment. The *Reporter* railed against the fact that "Negroes of Birmingham are to be taxed for the support of Avondale Park and the Zoological Garden, and then denied any permission to use it." The editor challenged the city's white taxpayers when it wagered that "the membership of the Sixteenth Street Baptist Church pays more taxes than the members of the Avondale Civic League."[42] Another paper took up the fight and demanded that "Negroes should either have admission to the park, or a part of them, or there should be parks set aside for the Negroes, just as acceptable in every way as other public parks."[43] The white *Ledger* also supported the fight: "If the public parks, public libraries, public playgrounds for children . . . are necessary for the moral, social and educational uplift of the white man, they are necessary for the uplift of the Negro."[44] The *Ledger* did not support social integration, but rather noted the need to create public space for blacks.[45]

When they encountered discrimination on a more personal level, middle-class individuals who might otherwise have remained silent reacted. Peter F. Clarke, a Birmingham resident and taxpayer for more than thirty years, could remember when he was allowed to share parks with whites. Yet, in 1919, when he took his son to the Avondale Park Zoo, Clarke was reminded about how his status as an African American had changed. Clarke was instructed by a police officer to leave the park immediately without his son, who had wandered away. Clarke had avoided such confrontations during his long tenure in the city. He held a highly esteemed position among elite blacks. His early

A Matriarch of the Clarke Family, c. 1910 (Courtesy of Barbara Young)

migration from Hale County to Birmingham enabled him to participate in the founding of several race institutions. He served as vice
president of the Alabama Penny Savings and Loan Company during
its early years and remained in the bank's employ until it closed.
Clarke was a founding member of the short-lived North Alabama
Colored Land Company that was incorporated in 1887; he owned
P. F. Clarke and Company, a real estate firm housed in the Pythian
Temple in the Black Business District (BBD); and he sat on the Board
of Directors of the Alabama Colored Orphans and Old Folks Home.
He was a Prince Hall Mason and a layleader at the Sixteenth Street
Baptist Church, where he contributed to the church's high visibility
and reputation.[46] But his status did not transcend the boundaries of
black recognition. The incident moved him to reflect, "This kind of
treatment will make me or any other decent man leave his home. . . .
I don't know how others are treated, but this is too much for me."
Clarke had deep roots in Birmingham, and he remained in the city
until his death.[47]

Blacks worked toward bringing about change by forging alliances
in structured frameworks with sympathetic whites. In 1919, more
than two hundred well-positioned African Americans organized a
meeting in Montgomery with the Alabama legislators and Governor Thomas E. Kilby to present their grievances in a memorial. The
committee was comprised of mostly middle-class blacks who represented the Interdenominational Ministerial Alliance and the Negro
Betterment League. Oscar Adams, spokesman for the Birmingham
delegates, Rev. John Goodgame, pastor of the Sixth Avenue Baptist Church and Rev. J. A. Bray of the Colored Methodist Episcopal
Church constituted the Birmingham contingent. They took issue
where African Americans felt the sharpest stings of discrimination:
education, lynching, the franchise, wages, living conditions, and Jim
Crow practices on public accommodations, specifically on railroad
cars and in waiting rooms. Their petition was never enacted into law,
and the inequities persisted.[48] Again African Americans looked forward to eliciting change by working with whites in the Birmingham
Commission on Interracial Cooperation (CIC). Although the CIC had
a presence in the city in the early 1920s, by 1926 James Burton, interstate secretary of the national organization, reported that "The situation [in Birmingham] is far from satisfactory, though I believe the interracial forces will eventually win out." When he conducted a series
of interviews in Birmingham, he found there to be a rather mixed response about the city's racial environment. African Americans could

Rosetta Clarke, c. 1930, youngest daughter of Peter F.
Clarke (Courtesy of Barbara Young)

not depend on the CIC to work toward altering the city's social order
or to aggressively tackle problems that plagued the black community.
Largely, the CIC remained quiet until the next decade when the organization was moved to adopt a visible role during the Scottsboro
trial.[49]

African Americans were not free from discrimination in employment. Job opportunities had been responsible for their relocation, and
some realized modest economic and occupational mobility. But, most
did not. Birmingham's coal and iron industries depended on large
numbers of skilled workers, most of whom were white, and large
numbers of unskilled black laborers.[50] The need for unskilled laborers
drove up the black population in Birmingham, as whites refused low-

level jobs that they called "nigger work." Although their manpower kept the industrial machine running, blacks were faced with limitations that inhibited their job mobility. Henry M. McKiven's study of labor in the iron and steel industries illustrates the nature of the labor force hierarchy and how skilled whites workers particularly exhibited patterns of job protectionism and how they played an integral part "in shaping the town's system of industrial segregation."[51] In coal mining, "the color line remained deliberate and pronounced in each group, most visibly in the UMW."[52] In 1880, approximately 60 percent of the unskilled work force was black; by 1910, according to one estimate, blacks held 75 percent of the jobs at the iron furnaces and steel mills.[53] Two decades later, one historian was moved to conclude that "mining as a whole in Alabama is slowly becoming a Negro occupation."[54] Consequently, as the majority of blacks were systematically excluded from union activity, they were relegated to the unskilled positions in the large industries. African American leaders were not unified in their reactions to blacks role in labor unions, and many black workers saw promise in the open shop movement.[55] Booker T. Washington had appeared in Birmingham to denounce unionism, and such local figures as William Pettiford, William McGill, and P. Colfax Rameau all stood behind him. All were in the pay of industry leaders.[56] In the 1894 coal strike, industrialist Henry DeBardelben used Pettiford among other black preachers to counteract the influence of union organizers. In 1908, TCI's chief executive officer George Crawford consulted Pettiford, whom he perceived to be "a man of high character, greatly interested in the improvement of his race." Pettiford was rewarded for his complicity. With TCI funds, Pettiford employed lecturers to visit the company mining camps and give group and individual instruction in domestic science, sewing, and housekeeping. Others like Benjamin L. Greer, vice president of District 20, and Rev. W. M. Storrs strongly advocated the benefits of union affiliation.[57] Ultimately, the message from management was the clearest and most definitive: Birmingham was not a union city.[58]

Abuses against African Americans were mounting. Closely tied to management's ability to squash the unions was its ability to exploit the convict lease system.[59] Convict leasing provided a cheap and reliable source of labor while it reinforced the racial divide in labor.[60] Despite the combined efforts of African Americans and Dr. Thomas Parke and Julia Tutwiler, two white reformers, to eradicate the system, change was slow to come. Alabama was the last southern state to abolish convict leasing when it finally legislated it out of its penal system in 1928.[61] From 1890 to 1918 African Americans constituted between 80 and 92 percent of the city's chain gangs, and after 1915 *only* blacks worked on the streets in clear visibility of the city's residents. Despite organized labor's objection to the system, convict leasing helped to build Birmingham's infrastructure of roadways.[62]

In the late 1890s, African Americans found their freedom to move about Birmingham increasingly restricted with the introduction of the fee system, which put a premium on arrests.[63] Officers did not only target black male adults who could be leased as convicts: In 1895, an officer killed a thirteen-year-old black girl who was taking coal near a railroad car. Incensed blacks held a mass meeting at the Shiloh Baptist Church and "issued a stirring protest and appeal to the white people of Birmingham." Some whites recognized the injustices of the act, and the Birmingham Trade Council urged state officials to conduct an investigation into the child's murder.[64] Middle-class blacks challenged the fee system on another occasion, and this was one of the few times that their claims brought about a reversal of charges. In 1918, Oscar Adams wrote a letter to the *Birmingham Age-Herald* in response to the actions of law enforcement officers who had arrested and charged over a hundred blacks who were selling sandwiches to a large crowd at the circus. Adams criticized the fee system and declared that the humiliations suffered and the fines imposed "have hindered our progress and shaken the morale of Negro people in almost every section of the city."[65] The *Age-Herald* joined the *Reporter's* criticism: "The wholesale arrest of Negroes on trivial charges, when the arrests are prompted chiefly from a desire to secure the fees resulting therefrom, is a practice that is repugnant to all ideas of right and justice."[66] The *Reporter* declared a victory when the judge dismissed the cases from the municipal court and refused to allow the collection of costs.

In 1919, the Bessie Jones Affair highlighted the abuses of the system when blacks issued a rallying cry of opposition to the wholesale arrest of black women charged with vagrancy.[67] Bessie Jones was a young child who, according to the *Birmingham Voice of the People,* was arrested "on the streets of Birmingham for nothing." African Americans pulled together and raised funds both to reimburse the money spent by her mother to secure her daughter's release and to send the child to school. The *Voice of the People* covered the story and printed letters from indignant whites and blacks who called for justice. The *Voice* called for the immediate discharge of "officers who deliberately arrest innocent persons whether through racial prejudice or for the getting of commissions."[68] The fee system persisted until

1919 because it "was firmly entrenched in the legal and political system of Alabama."[69] Yet, as one system that victimized blacks was dismantled, another began that purported to be a legitimate means of reinforcing the status quo.

The Ku Klux Klan embodied the most heinous elements of racism, using intimidation and violence to achieve its goals. Mob violence and lynching were rare in Birmingham, but some incidents did occur.[70] During the early 1920s, the Klan enjoyed a resurgence of popularity in the urban Southeast, particularly in the larger cities where industrialization and immigration were perceived threats to the established social order.[71]

Racial tension was on the increase in Birmingham in the early twentieth century as the city's population was becoming more diverse with immigrants who remained outside the strong southern traditions of most Birmingham residents.[72] Under a progressive agenda, in 1916 William Simmons organized Birmingham's Robert E. Lee Klan as the first Klavern in Alabama and possibly the most powerful one in the Southeast.[73] By 1924, the Klan claimed 18,000 members and 15,000 of the city's 32,000 registered voters.[74] Although the KKK acts of aggression in the early 1920s were directed less frequently against African Americans than against whites who violated the accepted norms, all blacks were justified in exercising caution. In 1922 Klansmen dressed in white robes and cowls and paraded through several black residential districts. No one was injured during the incident, but the threat of violence was implicit by their very presence. When the proposed construction of a black high school in 1923 wrought the ire of Klansmen, African Americans were reminded of widespread opposition to black progress.[75]

Black and white citizens moved to eradicate the Klan's influence. The Birmingham Bar Association and the Chamber of Commerce denounced the Klan and sought to undermine its credibility and curb its activities in the city.[76] Their opposition achieved little. In 1925, a spate of floggings occurred, which targeted African Americans, Italians, and others for threatening the city's moral fabric. In 1926, a North Carolina Mutual Insurance Company district manager asked the Durham head office to forego investigation of a black youth killed by the Birmingham police and pay the death claim. In his letter he said, "We know that these 'cracker officers' are likely to shoot any of us down for no cause in the world."[77] The city failed to convict any of the perpetrators of these crimes until 1927 when a nineteen-year-old male orphan was beaten for drinking in public. Charges were brought against seven men, and two were found guilty. The *Age-Herald* recognized the importance of the decision and compared it to the fall of the Bastille.[78]

Although the decision marked a turning point for the Klan—its influence was on the decline as membership rolls reflected attrition in the ranks—they continued to exert influence. In 1928, a police officer killed a black school teacher after he had attended the Teacher's Association meeting in Birmingham. According to the officer, he was acting in self-defense when the teacher drew a gun. Lillian Shortridge, a member of "one of Ensley's oldest and most respected families," was beaten by a white man. The assailant was let off when the police arrived, and Miss Shortridge and her friends were charged with disorderly conduct. According to the *Truth*, in response to the police force's "reign of terror," more than fifteen families departed Birmingham in search of a safer environment, and numerous homes were up for sale. The hostile environment did not victimize local residents exclusively. Oscar De Priest, an Alabama native and the first northern black to become a U.S. congressman, was denied the opportunity to speak from the platform of Birmingham's city auditorium. The KKK burned him in effigy as a way of symbolizing its opposition to black political power. This reaction resonated beyond Birmingham. After the incident, the committee of management of the Mosaic Templars of America decided against holding its national grand lodge meeting in Birmingham as scheduled and moved it to Little Rock.[79] Apart from verbal outcries, African Americans could not counteract the violence through legal means, and they were unprepared to adopt extralegal strategies. Rather, they exercised greater caution, or they left the city.[80] The lives of middle-class blacks and the masses were distinctly separate in their home environment, but when they left their private sphere and entered into the public domain, they shared the experience of being black in a white world.

After the turn of the century, African Americans found their mobility increasingly restricted. Traveling to and from work became more challenging as the city changed entrances to and seating arrangements on streetcars so that the races could travel in complete isolation from each other. Public places that were once accessible became out of bounds. And the freedom to move freely was also removed as the convict lease and fee systems were widely practiced. Furthermore, the presence of the KKK intensified blacks' uneasiness and fear in their own city. African Americans were unable to eradicate the abuses, and their allies in the white community were too few and uncommitted to challenge the status quo. Responding to the intensified racial hostility, African Americans embraced self-segregation to create for themselves a better world without whites. Jim Crow and other social control mechanisms did more than negatively impact on the black community. These forces acted as cohesive elements drawing blacks together in building their own institutions and socioeconomic foundations; it also moved many blacks to turn toward their home environment for self-definition and comfort. Smithfield was one place where they found solace in their surroundings.

2

Smithfield

The Suburb

Smithfield was originally the plantation of Doctor Joseph Smith. It consisted of 500 acres of fertile land and productive soil. At one time it was enclosed with a white-washed board fence with gates at advantageous places. Picnics were held in the wooded areas, where sparkling springs flowed and where at a later date the circuses always pitched their tents, following their parade up town.

—*Union Labor News,* April 30, 1953

Sentiments such as the ones above are shared by many African Americans when questioned about Smithfield. They paint a utopian picture as they reflect on the community that many blacks held in high esteem. One longtime resident of Smithfield articulated it most succinctly when he declared that "if you were in Smithfield, you were an 'A Number One Black.'"[1] A common thread runs through the memories of many middle-class Smithfield residents—that Smithfield was a very desirable place to live. It was a community where blacks achieved a feeling of belonging and a sense of identity.

Smithfield was among the earliest Birmingham suburbs that realized rapid settlement as blacks and whites sought refuge from the crowded city. The city's boosters aggressively sought to incorporate these areas and expand the city's boundaries over the decades. They pushed ahead with their Greater Birmingham Movement from 1898 to 1910 as a means to achieve a national status for their city. Birmingham was growing rapidly, and optimism filled the air. The *Silent Eye,* a local newspaper, proudly boasted: "She is undoubtedly the steel magnet of industry and progress, outrivaling the world in commercial push and progress. . . . [N]one can resist the power of her great magnetism, and her unbounded store of steel, iron and coal productions continually draws toward her increasing population and wealth that will eventually make her the center of throbbing commerce."[2] To fulfill these goals, boosters had set their sites on a grand scheme that

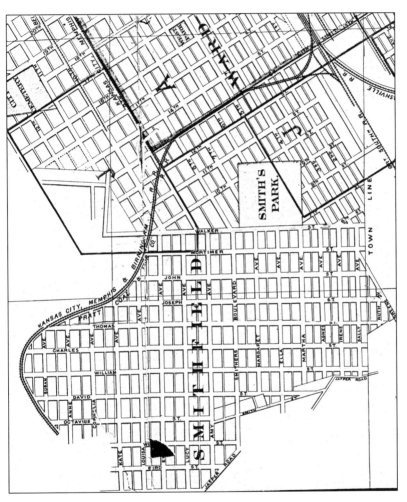

Street layout of Smithfield, c. 1888. The area to the east of Walker Street is the city of Birmingham. Notice that Smithfield had its own grid pattern at an angle to Birmingham. (From the *Atlas of City of Birmingham and Suburbs, 1887–88*, Ellis Beers and Co., New York, courtesy of Agee Map Collection, Birmingham Public Library)

would annex its incorporated neighbors by 1900. By that year, however, Birmingham was nothing more than "the largest of a cluster of 16 independent communities, 'touching elbow' in Jones Valley and having a combined population of over 100,000."[3] Smithfield Village found itself caught in this aggressive annexation campaign. This budding community was an unincorporated area that was included within the boundaries of the Town of Graymont. Graymont, which in 1907 officially changed its status to the City of Graymont, was one of nine municipalities targeted for annexation. It had an independent police, fire, and educational system and its own mayor and Board of Aldermen.[4] The residents of Smithfield initially opposed incorporation as a separate district in 1902. Its opposition fell in line with the other municipalities, all of which initially chose to maintain their independent status primarily to avoid paying higher taxes. Gradually, they all altered their stance and moved to support annexation as a means to receive improved city services and realize an increase in property values.[5] When Graymont and thus Smithfield were annexed into the city of Birmingham in 1910, Smithfield lost its independent political status but maintained its separate identity.

Birmingham's pursuit for broadened city limits was not unique. Boosterism was a national phenomenon as cities sought to improve their economic position relative to other competing cities. They vied to increase their populations as a means to attract outside investment. The boosters' campaign to enhance Birmingham's national status benefited the city directly. For example, in 1905, the Birmingham Real Estate Association lent their support to improving the sanitary conditions of the city and suburbs: "We as business men foresee the great advantage in proving to the world that we have a clean city—so clean that we may thereafter throw our doors open and say to the people in other Sections, to come and enjoy the greatest of all blessings—good health."[6] The twenty-year battle for annexation was finally laid to rest when the Alabama Supreme Court ruled that the annexation bill was constitutional.[7] On January 1, 1910, Birmingham's boundaries were officially expanded when it added nearly forty-eight square miles and 70,000 people through its "Greater Birmingham Plan." It had moved into the major league as a southern city, and it had become Alabama's largest city, with a population of 132,685. Never again would Birmingham engage in another annexation campaign this successful.

Prior to annexation, the official area of the city remained small, and neighborhoods were characterized by their heterogeneity. Commercial districts and residential areas coexisted, not yet controlled by land-use ordinances. On the city's south side, "foundries, lumber mills, factories, and breweries mingled with homes." The residents themselves reflected an occupational, racial and class mix: "The city tax collector lived on the same block with a railroad flagman, a black gardener, a civil engineer, and a carpenter."[8] As Blaine Brownell noted, "Negro residential settlement in Birmingham reflected, however, the same pattern of dispersal of most southern cities in this period."[9] Residential clustering occurred. Blacks and whites lived in close proximity to each other as spatial limitations restricted movement and choice. Despite the self-segregation that occurred on many streets, city directories reveal that some black families and white families lived side by side. Other streets and blocks reflected a pattern of micro-segregation, whereby a racial separation of residence by lot or block-segment occurred.[10] For whites, the residential mixing of the races became increasingly intolerable as the black population expanded. By 1910, there were 52,305 blacks living in the city, and their numbers were increasing. In 1915, the Alabama legislature conferred upon the city of Birmingham the authority to prevent conflict between the races. This empowered the city to impose General Zoning Code provisions that prohibited blacks from living in areas designated for whites.[11] In 1919, a Birmingham city ordinance declared it to be "a misdemeanor for a member of the colored race to move into . . . or having moved into, to continue to reside in, an area in the city of Birmingham generally and historically recognized at the time as an area for occupancy by members of the white race."[12] The effectiveness of this legislation secured the best housing opportunities for whites while it also reinforced the priority of racially homogeneous neighborhoods. In 1923, members of the African American community sent a petition to the city council to protest the zoning ordinances that so successfully kept the races apart.[13] Their grievances were ignored. In 1926, Birmingham adopted a comprehensive zoning ordinance that provided for rigid residential segregation, after whites had protested against the construction of black housing near white neighborhoods.[14] With the introduction of each legal measure, residential segregation increased and resulted in the emergence of all-white and all-black neighborhoods.

The severe housing shortage prompted real estate development of unprecedented dimensions in the young city.[15] In 1884, the Elyton Land Company initiated a suburban movement when it developed residential areas north of the business district and south of the railroads. The new districts were intended to attract well-heeled Birmingham residents. The South Highlands area, annexed into Birmingham in 1895, was where the most affluent white residents of Birmingham relocated. There they purchased stately homes on the broad avenues that characterized the neighborhood. Their favorable response to new housing moved speculators to follow the lead of the Elyton Land Company. In 1886, Henry Caldwell, the president of the company wrote, "Wilder and wilder the excitement grew. Stranger and resident alike plunged into the market. . . . In many instances the purchaser would seize his receipt and rush out on the street to resell the property at a handsome profit before his bond for title could be executed."[16] They established land companies to develop communities laying just beyond the city limits but still near enough to provide easy accessibility to places of employment. The Smithfield Land Company participated in the rush to develop land.

The response was none too soon. Migration continued apace, and the demand for housing reached crisis proportions. Although the more affluent or middle-income families had some alternatives, the poor had little choice of residency. Many poor blacks and white migrants settled into low-amenity residential areas on the eastern and western edges of Birmingham.[17] Their homes were overcrowded and crudely constructed and were lacking in basic services. The high mortality rate among the black population revealed their vulnerability to diseases such as tuberculosis, typhoid, and cholera caused by unsanitary conditions and an impure water supply. In the first decade of the twentieth century, death among blacks from tuberculosis was two and one-half times as great as among the white population. One study conducted for the Birmingham area characterized black housing as "nests of infection."[18] Other blacks and whites lived in segregated company housing built by the corporate giants who wanted to control all aspects of their workers' lives.[19] Apart from the blacks who lived in company towns and from those who lived in cramped and unsanitary quarters, was a small number of elite blacks who created a community for themselves in the city's core on Sixth Avenue North. Ellen Tarry remembered her first childhood home fondly: "With flowers blooming in the yard and the vines so shiny and green, it did not matter too much that the houses never were painted. . . . [T]he houses were well-kept, since that was the fashionable section of town for our people in those days."[20] Within a block or two of their small homes were St. Paul's AME and the First Congregational Church with its highbrow congregation. Residents cooperated in making this area a tightly knit community. Yet, as better housing became available, the Tarry's and their friends and neighbors moved on.

Smithfield was the first suburban development to respond to the city's housing crisis.[21] Although a multitude of land companies had scrambled for financial gain in Birmingham real estate, very few weathered the unstable nature of the market. The Smithfield Land Company, not the omnipresent Elyton Land Company, stands out as one such company that cautiously developed residential properties during the late 1880s and 1890s. The directors of the organization not only developed property but also established a lucrative relationship with a prominent member of Birmingham society. The key player in the success of the Smithfield Land Company was not a member of its board of directors nor a founding member of the company. It was Joseph Riley Smith, an entrepreneur who parlayed his keen business sense into a sizable fortune.[22]

John Smith, Joseph Smith's father, migrated from Union District, South Carolina, and first arrived in Blount County (a portion of which became Jefferson County in 1819) via Lincoln County, Tennessee, in 1816. Over time, he acquired two thousand acres of rich farmlands along Valley Creek in Elyton, west of Birmingham. There he engaged in large-scale cotton and corn production, with the labor of about sixty slaves. His agricultural operations were ripped apart during the Civil War, when Union soldiers confiscated his crops for their personal use and after the war when his slaves were set free. Despite these setbacks, Smith reestablished his farming and real estate activities. Prior to his death, he had amassed considerable wealth. Smith transferred much of his property holdings to his children, who inherited the remainder of Smith's estate when he died in 1878.[23] Smith was also active in politics, serving as magistrate in 1824 and county commissioner at the county seat of Elyton.[24]

John Smith established himself as a member of the Elyton elite. He and his clan busied themselves with social affairs and engaged in nurturing their ties with other prominent families. One early resident recalled about her own family that "there were few days through any summer that their house was not full of company. . . . They had fine cooks and house maids, abundance of fruit, melons, chickens, vegetables, pigs and everything to be thought of."[25] His wife, Sally Riley, who descended from one of the original Virginia families, added to the family's place in society. One undocumented family history concluded that the Smith family members were "conspicuous factors in [Jefferson County's] history. It has furnished brains, muscle, energy and capital to the advancement of the county in larger proportion perhaps than has any other connection."[26] It was upon this foundation that Joseph Smith built his own business empire.

The eldest of John Smith's twelve children, Joseph Riley Smith was born on February 6, 1818. He received his education at Union Seminary in Tennessee and graduated from the medical department of Transylvania University in Lexington, Kentucky. Upon returning to Elyton, he practiced medicine and surgery from 1843 to 1870, when he left the medical profession and pursued a vocation in the mercantile business. He founded, in association with Baylis E. Grace, Sr., the first newspaper in Jefferson County, the *Central Alabamian*. Smith also served as director of the Birmingham Insurance Company, was a stockholder in the First National Bank, a director of the Birmingham and Pratt Mines Street Railroad, and a member of the Masonic order.[27] Although Joseph Smith was engaged as a physician, editor, and real estate developer, his education did not cleanse him of his rugged character or his "quick Irish temper."[28] He continued to operate a farm in the tradition of his father. The 1850 Agricultural census reveals that he owned forty-five acres of improved land and fifteen hundred acres of unimproved land that were assessed at $1,200. He also owned several pieces of machinery and close to one hundred animals, including sheep, swine, and cattle. The value of livestock was assessed at $700. He raised such crops as Indian corn, oats, and rice. Considerable growth had taken place over the following decade. By 1860, the acres of improved land had increased to four hundred, and the unimproved property stood at six hundred acres. The cash value of the farm increased to $18,000. A significant increase in production with the labor of twenty-two slaves had also occurred as evidenced by the bushels of wheat, corn, and oats produced.[29] Up until at least 1880, Smith continued to produce crops on his land. However, the turn of events during the 1880s prompted Smith to adopt a different strategy. Land values were increasing exponentially, and Birmingham was showing signs of promise as a New South city.

Smith became one of the largest land developers in the area when he took advantage of the late-nineteenth-century real estate boom. He further enhanced his holdings when he inherited six hundred acres of worn-out flat plantation land that lay nearby the antebellum community of Elyton, then the county seat. Smith subdivided the plantation to form a suburban community when land prices skyrocketed. His ownership of commercial and residential real estate made him a rich man. Initially, his commercial holdings were the most profitable, since

Birmingham's early growth was centered in the downtown core where he owned a sizable acreage of increasingly valuable land. Smith acted more prudently than other land speculators who were drawn to Birmingham's booming real estate market. Rather than quickly selling his holdings to turn a profit on the inflated prices, Smith divested some of his holding and retained ownership of other properties that he proceeded to rent. When questioned on why he held on to his property for so long, he replied, "I have found that real estate is the best way for a man to keep money. He has only to get his board and clothes and home comforts. What good will it do him besides that?"[30] He cautiously protected his real estate investments, and by the first decade of the twentieth century, he could boast a Smith domain of sorts in downtown Birmingham. In 1903, the combined tax assessed value of his vast property amounted to $126,564.00. His county property was assessed at $2,400.00, his Birmingham property at $103,950.00, and his Elyton holdings at $500.00. His Smithfield property, including what was then designated as North and South Smithfield, amounted to 1,012 lots valued at a total assessed value of $19,714.00.[31] He was one of the largest landowners in Jefferson County at the time and is rumored to have been the largest taxpayer.

The Smith farm, which was located on the rise above Valley Creek, extended from Third Avenue on the south, to the Pratt City carline on the north, and from the Greene estate (now Elyton Village) on the west to Walker (Sixth Street) on the east. This addition to the Birmingham District first appeared in a deed dated July 9, 1882, although in March of the same year, Smith had already sold the first lots of what became Smithfield. In 1883, Joseph Smith also laid out a private forty-acre park that he had purchased from James M. Ware for $1,600 in 1879. It became known as "Smith's Park" as he cleared the land, which was nothing more than a briar thicket, and laid out a private racing track. It cost $1,250 to grade and finish, and the track cost $750. He later deeded this land to the City of Birmingham as a park, where traveling circuses performed and where at one time the state fair was held. In 1925, the forty-acre tract was surveyed and subdivided. Streets, sidewalks, and sewers were built, and lots were put up for sale. The gross receipts from the land sale at this time was estimated at $1,000,000.[32]

Joseph Smith first began to sell off his property in 1856. He owned all the land from the Linn Foundry to Elyton and sold it for $15 an acre in 1858. He recalled that he had "cultivated all the tract from the gas house to Elyton in corn up to 1871. I sold the land to W. P.

Hickman who sold it afterward to Judge J. C. Morrow. He afterward sold it to W. A. Walker, Sr., including a tract of 160 acres."[33] He admitted that he had "no idea of selling the land, but one day Mr. William Berney said he would give me $1,000 for two blocks of about 80 acres. I sold it, and in less time than six months I sold very much of the land. I think I sold as much as $20,000 worth in the past three years."[34] These few transactions provided the momentum that began the development of a new suburb known as Smithfield.[35]

Smith created a utopian setting for his family in Smithfield, when he built a large two-storied, New England–style house, "with red brick chimneys and interesting ells and porches. The residence was set in an extensive acreage, and surrounded by orchard, gardens, fields and farm buildings." It was bounded on the North by Martha Avenue, on the South by Sallie Avenue, on the east by Joseph Street, and on the west by William Street. Later on, a small cottage was erected on the front grounds. After the death of his first wife, Margaret Harvie Jordan, his second wife, Mary Smithers, redecorated their homestead and built an addition.[36] Smith not only provided generously for his family; his philanthropy extended beyond his relations. He gave liberally to charities that benefited the indigent, the infirm, and black and white children. In 1887, Dr. Joseph Smith deeded a Smithfield lot for the building of the Hospital of the United Charities, and he contributed $5,000 in 1899 toward the construction of the 200-bed St. Vincent's Hospital. He also donated Smithfield lots and buildings for the Joseph R. Smith Schools, one for white children the other for black children. Beyond furnishing the buildings, he also paid all the expenses of the schools, except for a fund from the state, which only amounted to $950 per session. In the city proper, he contributed to uplifting Birmingham from the long-lasting effects of the 1893 Panic. In 1896, Joseph Smith, his agent T. H. Molton, and the community-spirited citizens promoted the concept of a larger public auditorium than O'Brien's Opera House.[37] The Birmingham Auditorium Company was organized on September 15, 1896, and Smith deeded his lots to the company for $9,000 worth of auditorium stock. Clearly, Smith played a key role in the civic life of Birmingham.

While Joseph Smith was divesting some of his wealth, other players who were interested in Smithfield entered the picture. On November 3, 1886, nine Birmingham investors incorporated the Smithfield Land Company with a capital stock of $850,000 and bought approximately two hundred acres of North and South Smithfield property, calculated at about $1,200 per acre.[38] Smith also sold smaller plots of land to independent investors looking to take advantage of a promising new residential development. Several prominent families who were intimately associated with the Smith family reaped the benefits of early investment. The land was strategically located between the Pratt Mines to the northwest and their nearly completed furnaces, which offered abundant employment opportunities. Nearer to Smithfield, on the same side, was the Pioneer Mining and Manufacturing Company (which was absorbed by the Republic Iron and Steel Company in 1899), with its mines and blast furnaces. To the southwest was the emerging iron manufacturing village of Oxmoor, and to the east lay Birmingham. The new community was well located within the boundaries of Jefferson County.[39]

The Smithfield Land Company improved the property when it laid out broad eighty-foot-wide streets and avenues in a grid pattern that met the Birmingham grid at a forty-five-degree angle, giving one the sense of entering a new community.[40] These roads immortalized the Smith genealogy (until the names were changed to coincide with those of the city) when they were named after Smith's family members and close friends. The first map to identify the new district with highway names affixed went on record on December 8, 1887. A sample of streets, named after men, and avenues, named for women, provides an illustration of the naming process. Smithers Avenue was the family name of Dr. Smith's second wife, Mary Smithers of Kentucky; Margaret was named for his first wife, Margaret Jordan; Martha was chosen for a daughter who died in childhood. Samples of street names are as follows: John Street was named for John Fleming Smith, a son, and Mortimer Street for Dr. Smith's father-in-law, Mortimer Jordan. Walker Street, the most easterly boundary, was named for the William A. Walker family, who were friends and neighbors of the Smith family.[41]

A variety of interested parties introduced services to the area. In addition to laying out streets, in 1887 the Smithfield Land Company began construction of the Smithfield Railway to serve the new Smithfield development.[42] Although the road was only a few blocks long and the tracks were never used before the company was dissolved, the effort to bring transportation to Smithfield illustrates efforts to unite this new district with the city. It appears that the rights to this line were acquired by the Bessemer and Birmingham Dummy line, which made the Smithfield line redundant.[43] Thus, Smithfield was provided with direct access to Birmingham probably as early as 1890. This transportation system stimulated the rapid residential growth of

Smithfield, which continued to attract new residents as additional lines went into the city and reached out to the furnaces. Smithfield also received other essential services. In 1907, a contract was entered into between the City of Graymont and Joseph R. Smith, Jr., Thomas O. Smith and Charles J. Smith, sons of J. R. Smith, Sr., and executors of his estate to construct sewers for the area.[44] City officials acknowledged the need for additional water closets and introduced a regulation that required "every householder, manufacturer, merchant, or other persons desiring to maintain a water closet or closets, privy or privies . . . to obtain a permit from the sanitary inspector." Bureaucratization and regulation was their solution to the sanitation problem. Although there is no direct evidence that reveals who received these services, related documentation suggests that many black and whites families benefited from these improvements. Mortgage records offer insight: those who wanted the service had to pay for it. When individuals purchased or occupied homes, they were responsible for financing pipe installation and sewage connections, while Smith's estate assumed responsibility for the cost of constructing these sewers. Another alluring feature of this area was the availability of good water, that was made accessible by sinking wells from twenty-five to seventy-five feet beneath the surface. Such wells remained suitable as long as the area remained lightly populated; however changes in the water system were required when the area's population increased.

Smithfield's early success hinged on attracting investors. This occurred rapidly as individuals and businesses assessed the advantages of participating in the district's development. Joseph Riley Smith subdivided his vast property holdings, which he then sold to individuals, male and female, black and white, and to the Smithfield Land Company. The real estate company then sold the property to individuals and families who were eager to become homeowners and tenants in a promising new suburb. The earliest residents of North and South Smithfield filtered into the new development and settled into a pattern of living that reflected the racial and economic diversity of the area. During its earliest development, the district was a community whose residents belonged to different racial, ethnic, and class groups: African Americans lived alongside recent immigrants from Italy, England, and Germany, who also shared space with native-born whites. The area's racial mix reflected the absence of strict zoning ordinances that were not yet in effect. As black and white residents relocated to Smithfield, they, too, sorted themselves as city dwellers had done. Some blocks reflected a pattern of race-based micro-segregation, whereas others exhibited a checkerboard of white and black residences.[45] Class differences as well as race differences were apparent among the households. Numerous unskilled workers lived in Smithfield, among them Patrick Kennedy, an Irish migrant who worked as a day laborer, and Christian Morrow, an African American railroad worker. Several skilled workers also lived in Smithfield including W. Schlegle, a white migrant from Illinois who worked as a machinist, L. Miller, a white pattern maker, and Alfred Baylor, a black brick mason. Although fewer in number, there were also professionally employed residents: A. B. Perdue was a white lawyer from Georgia and Arthur Parker was an African American educator from Springfield, Ohio.[46]

Waves of migrants relocated to Smithfield and other parts of the Birmingham District primarily from the rural Black Belt of Alabama— the strip of black prairie soil that curves from the eastern part of Alabama into Mississippi on the west.[47] It is spotted by towns: Montgomery, Selma, Linden, Marion, Greensboro, Eutaw, Livingston, Camden, and Union Springs. Here cotton was king. Slavery supported a robust economy. After the Civil War, most emancipated blacks were unable to escape the deeply entrenched caste system.[48] When economic opportunities abounded with the birth of Birmingham, African Americans of varied backgrounds descended on the city. The *Christian Hope,* among several other race papers, issued strong encouragement to its readers with stories of improved living conditions and abundant jobs. As word spread throughout the black communities, migrants flocked to the Magic City. Between 1900 and 1930, the African American population decreased substantially in the Black Belt and nearly tripled in the Mineral District where Birmingham sat. Their exodus from the fields created a labor problem that moved plantation owners to restrict black mobility.[49] The boll weevil, poverty, racial oppression, and the exploitative sharecropping system were pushing many blacks away from their rural roots. Others who were not sharecroppers abandoned their homes and jobs in small towns for improved economic and social opportunities in an urban environment. They all took a risk and entered into the fabric of urban life where there was greater possibility to realize their potential and enhance their position in the political economy.[50]

Besides the vast numbers of poor rural blacks who migrated from the Black Belt, well-positioned and well-educated blacks were drawn to Birmingham. These were African Americans who had the means to create a more comfortable community for themselves in one of many small Alabama cities that lay southwest of Jefferson County. One such city was Marion, which was located in Perry County. According to Weymouth Jordan, antebellum Marion typified other small towns in the Black Belt. Many wealthy planters settled in Marion, where they built palatial homes and transformed the city into a bustling trade center. Several African Americans rose to prominent positions in the region shortly after the close of the Civil War.[51] A small number of black families achieved middle-class status in Marion. W. E. B. Du Bois visited Marion in 1899 and reported that nearly all of the thirty-three better-class black families and a number of others owned their own homes. Du Bois also reported that among the better-class families, there were seven farmers, six ministers, five barbers, five carpenters, three masons, two undertakers, and so forth. The Congregational Church was their preferred church, although there was a Methodist and a Baptist church. The American Missionary Association's Marion Normal and its Lincoln schools offered many African Americans a solid secondary education. The institutions also trained teachers, ministers, doctors, and business men and women to become leaders.[52] Some black families who had satisfied their goals and had established deep roots in the Black Belt remained.[53] Others left the area, including several community leaders who took their skills beyond the boundaries of Marion and relocated to places where they could improve their lives and rise to influential positions in other black communities. William R. Pettiford resided for a time in Marion before moving on to Birmingham where he preached the merits of racial uplift, homeownership, and economic independence. Middle-class blacks who migrated to Birmingham joined forces with black leaders already entrenched in the city. Together they constituted the leadership class and helped to shape the environment for Birmingham's diverse black communities.

Several interviews of early Smithfield residents revealed that their families migrated from Perry County and specifically from Marion as well as from neighboring counties within Alabama. James Whitehead, a former resident of Smithfield, recalled that his father's friend helped him find a place to live as a boarder in Smithfield when he migrated from Marion with his wife and young son. He recalled, "I guess they just wouldn't let anybody live there."[54] Hale County was another source of enterprising blacks who relocated to the area. One columnist at the *Truth* reported that "Few communities and counties have sent up to Birmingham quite so many 'hustling, bustling' Negro citizens possessing thrift and integrity as Greensboro and Hale County."[55] Birmingham's well-heeled blacks also came from several

John Barber "Bob" Tarry (1867–1921), one of the first black barbers in Birmingham and a respected citizen within the black community and among his prominent white customers. (Courtesy of Ellen Tarry)

northern and southern states, but the vast majority migrated from regions within Alabama. Middle-class blacks often relocated their businesses to a larger urban center where they could expand their client base. Ellen Tarry remembered: "Papa, who was a barber by trade, was born in Athens, Alabama, about 1868. He settled in Birmingham when the Magic City was still a tiny village close to the coal mines and steel mills that were pouring riches into the pockets of Northern industrialists. Mama migrated from the country, in this case, a small

Eula Meadows Tarry with daughters. Standing in the background is Ellen Tarry, left of Eula is Ida Mae, and on the right is Elizabeth. This photograph was taken at Cloud Studio while Bob Tarry was in Chicago. During his visit, he was preparing to move the family there, and he was also arranging to set up a Chicago barber shop with Alonzo Herndon of Atlanta. (Courtesy of Ellen Tarry)

Gone-with-the-Wind community a few miles on the Alabama side of the Georgia-Alabama line."[56]

For most arrivals from Alabama and neighboring states, Birmingham was their final destination. Just as the *Christian Hope* had encouraged migration, so too did earlier migrants and labor recruiters share responsibility for drawing large numbers of new settlers into the city.[57] The population surge in the Birmingham District resulted not only from chain migration. Many large iron, coal, and steel companies employed agents to recruit much-needed workers, irrespective of color, from the rural regions of Alabama, as well as experienced workers from Pittsburgh and other northern industrial centers. The impact of these two forces had a major effect on the racial composition of Birmingham's population in the late nineteenth and early twentieth centuries: In 1870, fewer than 2,500 blacks lived in Jefferson County, and only 5,000 blacks lived in the surrounding area. By 1900, 67,000 blacks lived in the Birmingham District—57,000 in Jefferson County and 16,500 within Birmingham's city limits.[58]

Chain migration drew new migrants into Birmingham.[59] This unfamiliar environment created unforeseen difficulties that a supportive network of friends and family alleviated. Both the community networks and the kinship ties encouraged and assisted migrants upon their arrival in the city. Already-settled residents could offer lodging, emotional support, personal care, and short-term cash, or any combination thereof.[60] When improved housing became available in new areas such as Smithfield, a new arrival was often dependent on personal connections. The large Marion contingent in Birmingham assisted others from the same city.[61] Some individuals and families who lived in Smithfield migrated from other southern states including Georgia, Mississippi, Arkansas, North Carolina, and Florida. Their connections proved valuable. Seretha Jackson was born in 1901 in Columbia, South Carolina. In 1927 when she came to Birmingham, several South Carolinians from Columbia had preceded her. She quickly found employment as a music teacher at the Washington School, and she readily secured accommodations in Smithfield. Initially, she boarded with the Nall family, who lived on Charles Street. When Seretha and Lewis Jackson, a Birmingham native and mail carrier, married in 1929, they lived with his parents in their Smithfield home until they purchased their own home nearby. They remained in Smithfield their entire married life, and Seretha Jackson continued to live there well into the 1990s.[62]

Smithfield also welcomed families who relocated from within the Birmingham District. Some families simply relocated from their dwellings in Birmingham proper to the new and attractive environment. Both A. H. Parker and Edward A. Brown boarded with other tenants at 1602 Avenue H before they relocated to Smithfield, where they participated in the area's development. Other middle-class residents moved from their enclave of several blocks around Sixth Avenue and Fifteenth Street in Birmingham. Smithfield was a vast improvement over their city residences.[63]

After the turn of the century, South Smithfield became predominantly black. New housing developments created alternative housing for whites, who left Smithfield for more homogeneous neighborhoods. As they vacated their dwellings, African Americans moved in. The black population of Smithfield continued to increase as new housing construction continued. In 1898, it was 55.2 percent black; ten years later, it was 83 percent black, and by 1928 few white residents remained.[64] Although their residential choices were limited, African Americans, like other ethnic groups, used it to their advantage. They congregated among those who shared common interests, values, and culture, and in doing so, they derived a sense of security and familiarity that enhanced the quality of life. As Smithfield residents, they engendered a sense of racial solidarity that empowered them to develop a stronger sense of neighborhood cohesiveness.[65] Throughout the neighborhood's transition, many residents embraced middle-class values, which included owning their own home and participating in the creation of a healthy environment.[66] Smithfield offered the chance to realize these dreams. Seretha Jackson recalled that moving to her home on Second Street was "like moving to heaven."[67]

3

Steps toward Building the Home Sphere

Smithfield's early success as a thriving suburb reflected the "national movement of successive waves of people out from the center of the city."[1] It had many of the positive features associated with suburban life: it was serviced by early transportation systems; it was located near jobs; and its wide lots allowed for more spacious living conditions. Its broad streets and avenues that lay at a forty-five-degree angle to the city's roads gave the community a distinct character. It was within commuting distance but sufficiently remote to avoid the city's overcrowded conditions and, at least for a time, the daily political wrangling of Birmingham's municipal government. Smithfield offered a different kind of lifestyle: It offered more spacious environs and the possibility of homeownership.[2]

Smithfield presented a unique opportunity for residents to establish more permanent roots as the district was beginning to take shape. When families settled into Smithfield, their home life took on great importance. Whether the new residents arrived from Birmingham or from Ireland, Italy or from one of the northern or southern states, they looked for a place to build a better life for themselves. Although the new environment was radically different from the one they left, many migrants shared some fundamental values with their new urban neighbors. Their quest for better housing and an improved community life brought them together. For a time, Smithfield exhibited a somewhat different pattern of residential settlement as middle-class black and white families showed a strong interest in the area as did members of the working class.

As racial differences disappeared in Smithfield, class distinctions persisted. African Americans of different backgrounds with similar dreams flocked to Smithfield, and each contributed to the development and character of the new neighborhood where they ultimately dominated the landscape. They chose residential self-segregation to experi-

41

ence the comfort of living close to one another.[3] When residents began to manipulate their environment, Smithfield started to take shape as a community.[4] The sense of community that they developed had a direct impact on their daily lives, and many neighbors shared pride in their common living space apart from the more dominant mainstream society by virtue of its geographic separateness.[5] Smithfield was a place where they could reinforce social networks, erect their own institutions, and participate in homeownership.

Olivier Zunz's classic study of Detroit's immigrant community from 1880 to 1920 reveals that homeownership offered a foundation for community organization and thus was "worth the gamble of tying up their assets to create a world of their own."[6] Smithfield homeowners not only derived comfort and a measure of status but also established a strong connection with the suburb. It was the homeowners who exhibited a stronger identity with community institutions and activities, and they were among those who were more committed to creating and perpetuating a healthy environment.[7] Several studies have suggested that homeownership gives residents a feeling that they have a "stake in the community" and that it gives them a sense of pride. Seretha Jackson, who lived in Smithfield for more than sixty years, revealed these feelings when she declared, "I had never lived in a rented house in my life, believe it or not." Her longtime residency also supports the claim that homeowners exhibit a high rate of stability.

Homeownership was a dream that most Americans held in common. Literature from the mid-nineteenth century forward reveals the importance placed on owning one's own home.[8] Urbanization enhanced the ideal of homeownership as city dwellers sought to portion out a place for themselves in the crowded surroundings. A diverse array of professionals espoused the virtue of homeownership, a Jeffersonian ideal, to the American people. Ministers, writers, politicians, and business-minded individuals almost uniformly urged Americans to embrace the concept of homeownership as a means to achieve greater happiness, to share in social mobility, and to become, over and above all else, better citizens.[9] Independence and self-determination, as well as responsibility, stability, and propriety were promoted as qualities that were either innate to homeowners or derivative from the experience of homeownership.[10] Although the rhetoric had a redundant sameness, the underlying agendas of the various proponents of homeownership differed widely.[11] Nevertheless, homeownership was not a panacea for the nation's ills; however, criticisms of homeownership as an ideal fell on deaf ears because Americans were wary of paternalism. They wanted to be autonomous and have the security of their own homes.[12]

Homeownership was promoted as an appropriate aspiration for all Americans, but African Americans were rarely included in the equation. What administrators failed to realize was that African Americans shared these dreams. One national black paper was moved to declare that perhaps no other group in the United States "believes so thoroughly as does the American Negro in the philosophy of home buying and home owning."[13] Yet, no group faced greater challenges to become homeowners than African Americans. Many black leaders promoted land and homeownership as a means to uplift their people and create a step toward economic independence. Booker T. Washington's philosophy on homeownership was tied into his crusade promoting self-help, thrift, and economic independence in an attempt to continue the process of reinforcing the black community. "I want these coloured farmers and their wives to consult about methods and means of securing homes, of paying taxes, of cultivating habits of thrift, honesty, and virtue, of building school-houses and securing education and higher Christian character." The Southern Federation of Colored Women shared Washington's philosophy, and the Alabama branch was particularly active in this line of work. The organization's officials espoused the value of owning one's own home and conducted discussions about homeownership.[14]

When African American migrants arrived in Birmingham, many aspired to own their own homes. George Brown, an employee for the Sloss Company in 1931, was born in Dallas County just below Selma. He recalled, "When I came to town [Birmingham] I still liked the idea of having my own house. My uncle had his own home and I liked that idea."[15] Some blacks who shared this dream managed to purchase their own homes in spite of the obstacles. But Birmingham was still in its infancy in the late nineteenth century. It was not yet a city of homeowners; according to the U.S. Census, in 1890 only 10 percent of Birmingham families owned their own homes. The rate was below that of other cities with populations of more than twenty-five thousand, primarily because it was a new urban center. In 1910, when the annexation campaign incorporated suburbs where there was a higher incidence of homeownership, 30 percent of Birmingham's population owned their own homes. What emerged was an imbalanced racial and occupational profile of property owners: skilled white workers tended to accumulate property at a higher rate than semi- and unskilled white and black laborers. The real estate developer built the suburb of Avondale with white residents in mind and built the developments of Powderly and East Lake for a racially and occupationally homogeneous population.[16] Nonetheless, some African Americans who remained in the city for any length of time were able to acquire property.[17]

Smithfield grew at a time that Frederick Lewis Allen called the "horse-and-buggy era of Suburbia," because commuters were confined to areas within walking distance of railroad stations and dummy lines.[18] Access to employment was the key factor in determining the success of a new housing development. Smithfield provided adequate though somewhat unreliable public transportation to the mills, mines, furnaces, and other places of employment where many residents worked.[19] Despite the shortage of essential services, new residents were drawn to the area by the large tracts of land that were sectioned off and subdivided into lots. The original lots reflected a uniformity in size: 50 feet wide and 190 feet (and sometimes 200 feet) deep. The 1880s lot prices varied from $200 to $400; the variance reflected the location of the property and the relationship between vendor and purchaser. The increasing demand for housing in Smithfield resulted in the creation of smaller and more expensive lots: Some lots had a width of only $33\frac{1}{3}$ feet, which were then divided further into two lots of only $16\frac{2}{3}$ each. Smaller lot sizes ensured affordability for a larger number of families and greater financial return for the property owner.

Most African Americans in the nation, in Birmingham, and in Smithfield were never able to make the transition from renter status to homeowner. Many families who moved to Smithfield were unable to afford a home. They became tenants and either continued renting or bought a home when they could afford to enter the housing market. Even though some tenants felt a certain commitment to the community as reflected by their long-term residency in the area, others moved beyond the boundaries of the suburb. In Birmingham, many renters exhibited a level of transience that reflected the cyclical nature of their employment in steel mills and coal and iron ore mines. Nevertheless, some tenants who had secured stable employment had greater opportunity to establish permanent residency. Olivier Zunz correctly concluded that a core of stable residents, regardless of the number of transients, provides the neighborhood with a level of stability. Their permanence as Smithfield residents, whether as homeowners or renters, contributed to the development and nature of the community.[20]

Renting offered certain advantages that homeownership did not. These benefits, however, did not prevent some tenants from having their own unique set of problems. Many struggled to maintain their residency in Smithfield.[21] Renters approached their status from different perspectives. Many renters took as much pride in their domiciles as did homeowners. One individual declared, "You know I am this sort of man—if I live in a place, I believe in keeping it clean and doing little things to keep it looking nice around the yard and house, no matter whose house it is."[22] One Smithfield resident recalled the absence of acceptable rental housing stock and found it tolerable only as a temporary stopgap: "Sometimes it might be in houses that you would not think of buying but you would rent. . . . But you bought furniture and you fixed it up. You put up nice draperies, and things. You did the best you could until you could get out of there and find somewhere where you could buy."[23] Some rental properties were not well maintained, but often that was not the fault of the tenants. One former tenant recalled how the landlord failed to maintain her home: "We tried to get him to fix it but he wouldn't. We had a basement, but we couldn't use it; it had water all the time." When asked if she ever dreamed about owning her home, she replied, "I sure did but I wasn't making enough money."[24]

Birmingham residents were being courted to enter the housing market as homeowners. In the 1880s the Birmingham District experienced an "Own Your Home" campaign. Blacks and whites alike were targeted as potential homeowners. In 1886, the *Birmingham Age-Herald* advertised "Valuable property for sale." "City business property, city residential property, Smithfield business and residential property."[25] Black-owned newspapers also urged their readers to become homeowners: "Own Your Home. Be your own landlord and apply your rent toward paying for a home."[26] The *Truth* declared "Bargains for Sale. Two lots—Smithfield $350 per lot."[27] The advertisements reached the people. Early mortgage and deed records reveal the enthusiastic response. Boastful declarations also illustrated the success of advertising campaigns: "The Real Estate and Rental Co. of Messers Deampert [*sic*] informs your correspondent that their business is on a boom especially Smithfield property. [D]uring the past week they sold 1,750 [worth of real estate and] all the purchasers were colored."[28] Advertisements that promoted the possibility of homeownership enhanced Smithfield's appeal.

Beyond the newspapers' campaigns were the businesses founded to endorse homeownership and financially assist potential buyers. The

1887 Birmingham city directory listed more than 150 black and white real estate agents with established offices. In 1886, African Americans organized the Colored Mutual Investment Association to "buy and sell real estate, build houses and to establish homes." The North Alabama Colored Land Company, with A. L. Scott as acting president, was incorporated with a capital stock of $50,000 on January 5, 1887, and offered similar services.[29] Smith & Brown advertised "Bargains for Sale. Two lots in Smithfield," and Julian C. Carlton declared, "We have two very desirable lots on Mortimer St., Ninth Ave." White companies dominated the real estate frenzy. Robert Jemison and two of his associates established the Jefferson County Building and Loan Association with a capital stock of $2,000,000 in 1892. Robert Jemison stated that the purpose of the organization was the "purchase and sale of real estate, building, renting and sale of stores, dwellings and other buildings and in making loans on mortgages of real estate."[30] White real estate firms urging homeownership advertised with scintillating copy in white- and black-owned newspapers: "No Place Like Home," "Own Your Home," and "Buy Now." Jonas Schwab and Company advertised, "We have Desirable Houses for Sale. In city and suburbs on easy terms." The Birmingham Building and Improvement Company urged readers to "Be your own landlord and apply your rent toward paying for a home." And Armstrong and Wheless advertised in the *Age-Herald*, "Valuable property for sale. . . . Smithfield business and residential property." The campaigns were reaching everyone, whether they picked up local race papers such as the *Truth, Hot Shots,* or the *Free Speech,* or the white-owned *News* or *Age-Herald.* The word was spreading and people were responding.[31]

The color of one's skin was not the sole determinant of whether someone owned their own home. Many black and white families in Smithfield did become homeowners whereas others did not. Discrimination in lending practices enabled whites to gain financial assistance more easily than African Americans, but some families overcame this obstacle and accumulated sufficient savings to purchase a home. In 1890, African Americans in Alabama owned a total of 15,736 homes, including both farm homes and other homes. When the statistics for "other homes" are considered separately, blacks owned a total of 6,889 homes. For 1910, comparable statistics are available for specific cities within each state, and Smithfield was included in the Birmingham figures. Birmingham's African American population at this time numbered 52,305 and included a total of 14,229 black-occupied households. The number of black-owned homes was 2,340 or 4.4 percent. By 1930, Birmingham black homeowners numbered 4,709, or 4.75 percent, whereas 10.5 percent of the city's white population, which numbered 160,551, owned their own homes.[32]

Smithfield's middle-class residents displayed a significant rate of homeownership. In 1900, one-third of the residents in Smithfield were white. They comprised 48 percent of the homeowners in the sample of ninety-six white households.[33] Although more African American households occupied rental property, 23.5 percent of black households were homeowners. The sample reveals that whites and blacks were achieving homeowner status, albeit at different rates. Furthermore, it reveals that African Americans in Smithfield were achieving home-owner status at a quicker rate than blacks in Birmingham. In 1900 the number of black homeowners in Smithfield had almost reached the national figures for black homeowners in 1930. In 1910 the number of white households had decreased significantly, comprising only 10 percent of the entire sample; yet of those households 50 percent owned their own homes. Conversely, black households increased markedly over the decade, and of those households, 31.4 percent were homeowners. Clearly the majority of households rented their accom-modations, but some renters had moved into homeownership whereas some new residents bypassed renter status and immediately purchased homes. As white residents moved out of the area, many either sold or rented their property to new black residents.[34] By 1920, African Americans made up close to 97 percent of the households in Smith-field; 19 percent were homeowners. This decline in homeownership among blacks reflects the increasing density of the area with the addi-tion of not only new homes on single lots but also the creation of mul-tiple dwellings on single lots and the creation of alley housing.

Landlords often considered black rental property as one of the best returns on a relatively small investment. Smithfield, with its high pro-portion of black renters, attracted a diverse landlord class that in-cluded many European immigrants. As Sam Finocchio recalled—and the records support his claim: "Jews owned lots of rental property in Smithfield." J(ames) L. Lowe also remembered the presence of Jewish landlords: "The Sirotes, the father Isaac and his son Morris, owned a lot of shotgun homes in Smithfield." Italians who lived in Birmingham and Smithfield also owned several rental properties. In 1904, Phillip Rietta lived in Smithfield and owned nine properties in North Smith-field, which were assessed at $900. Some landlords left Birmingham but retained ownership of their Smithfield investment for a time as the suburb's property increased in value and continued to bring financial gains for landlords. Consequently there was a percentage of absentee owners who were more concerned about rental payments than they were about the community. Jennie Whitehurst held title to a property after her husband's death. She retained ownership for a brief time after she migrated north to Jamestown, New York.[35]

African Americans also profited from real estate investments in the Smithfield area. The purchase of rental properties was one of the few ways that enterprising blacks in the area could make money. The records reveal that some African Americans accumulated sizable holdings beyond their principal residences. Rev. Lewis Steinback was a black landlord who owned several properties in Smithfield and in other areas of Birmingham. He was one of many pastors from the Black Belt who settled in Smithfield. Born into slavery in Marengo County, Steinback recalled, "One year, all the wages I received above my scanty meals and rough clothes, was one dozen apples. Often I was glad to obtain a good meal of parched corn." His ambition propelled him to become educated, and in 1883, he was ordained in the Baptist church. Steinback participated in the twenty-ninth session of the Colored Missionary Baptist Convention of Alabama held at the Shiloh Baptist Church in Birmingham in 1896, which may have piqued his interest in the city. He was the pastor at the African Baptist Church in Tuscaloosa and then moved to Birmingham, where he was the minister at Sardis Baptist Church. Steinback had diverse business interests: he was the publisher of the *Christian Hope* newspaper and second vice-president of the Prudential Savings Bank. He probably realized his greatest financial coup when he invested in real estate.[36] Edward A. Brown was an attorney who also invested in Smithfield real estate before he purchased property for his principal residence on Mortimer Street. Brown was born in North Carolina and was the first African American to be admitted to the Alabama bar. The *State-Herald* described him as "show[ing] very little African blood [and] might be easily mistaken for a white man. He practiced 3 years in Cleveland and was also a notary public in that city. He is intelligent, educated and genteel in appearance and address."[37] Brown held memberships in several fraternal associations and was a member of the First Congregational Church. He was involved in the start-up of a number of black businesses, and he was active in the local chapter of the National Negro Business League. His involvement in these various organizations gave him the necessary skills and connections to invest in Smithfield real estate as a homeowner and investor. Like the white absentee owners, African Americans who lived outside of Alabama also owned Smithfield real estate. Lucius S. Henderson, a black physician who resided in Memphis, owned several rental properties in the suburb. With a first mortgage *without* interest from the Alabama Penny Savings and Loan Company, Henderson financed the construction of homes in 1900. In 1910, Thomas Windham paid $3,500 to Henderson for the deed on his Smithfield property. Henderson also owned properties in Birmingham and had financed them with a mortgage from the former mayor, W. H. Morris. One can only speculate that Henderson probably lived for a time in Birmingham, had established a solid reputation, and had recognized the value of real estate investment.[38]

The *Birmingham Ledger* reported in 1903 that, according to real estate brokers, "The majority of serious inquiries [about home purchasing] are from [the] middle and working class who are continuing to secure residence property for themselves."[39] Neither the paper nor the real estate dealers specified the race of these interested home buyers. It is clear from the rapid development of Smithfield and the increase in African American homeowners, that blacks and whites shared aspirations and successes. The mortgage as a credit instrument enabled them to achieve their goal. And the availability of multiple mortgages, that is, second and third mortgages, offered a further incentive to rush into homeownership. The terms of the mortgages—small monthly payments over many years—made homeownership attractive, affordable, and accessible.[40]

A multitude of financial arrangements were, in theory, available to individuals aspiring to become homeowners in Smithfield. The most fortunate home buyers were those who had purchased Smithfield property directly from Joseph Smith. Smith as the principal landowner offered a choice of properties at reduced rates. In 1886, a flurry of activity took place in the Smithfield real estate market. The transactions, which are recorded in the deed and mortgage records, reveal a rapid succession of ownership of Smithfield properties during its early years of development. Although Smith initially engaged in the largest Smithfield real estate transaction with the Smithfield Land Company, he also divested his property to many individuals, both African American and white. In 1886, Philipp Schillinger, owner of the Philipp Schillinger Brewing Company and proprietor of a saloon that catered to blacks, purchased several vacant lots on Ella and Martha Avenues from Smith for $1,000. Rather than keeping the properties as a long-term investment, seven months later Schillinger sold the same six lots for $3,000 to Emanual Solomon and Emil Levi, Jewish wholesaler dealers in "wines, liquors and cigars," who also owned a downtown retail business. They did not retain ownership of their lots either, but rather divested much of their holdings to the McAllister brothers. In 1899, Levi and Solomon sold the remaining property to William Gage, one of their black employees. Gage's working relationship with his employers had secured him the opportunity to become a homeowner.[41] Robert Terrell, Jr., was a white merchant who also benefited from Joseph Smith's divestment. Terrell owned considerable property in Smithfield, where he also lived for a time. He continued to retain ownership of several Smithfield properties that he developed at different times over the years. Joseph Smith's close associates C. H. and T. H. Molton, also invested in the budding suburb. C. H. Molton owned two lots on Ella Avenue in the late 1880s, which he had purchased from Smith for $425 each. Although T. H. Molton "sold property, made leases and insured buildings for Dr. Smith" for eighteen years, he never invested heavily in Smithfield real estate. William Morris was employed as a real estate broker when he invested in Smithfield property. He was also one of the largest stockholders of the Elyton Land Company, and he served as the third mayor of Birmingham for two years.[42]

Joseph Smith did not only transact business with more established white professionals and businessmen; he also conducted business directly with several African Americans during the 1880s. Joseph Smith's will revealed that he had offered purchase money notes to many black property owners in Smithfield, including many well-positioned families: Richard Blount, R. E. Pharrow, Dr. Arthur M. Brown, and J. O. Diffay. Most of the notes were for $400, but some amounted to $800. Other African Americans engaged in a different financial arrangement with Smith. When Benjamin Webb wanted to buy property in Smithfield, Smith loaned him $50 on a promissory note for the purchase of a lot on Ella Avenue. For an additional $150, Smith granted Webb the deed on the property in 1898. The Webbs retained their property for at least two decades, and by 1921, Luvenia Webb, his second wife and now a widow, secured a mortgage from Windham Brothers Construction Company for $150 plus 8 percent interest. These early residents purchased their lots when Smithfield property first became available. Their relationship with Smith afforded them a unique opportunity: to purchase land at a reduced price.[43] By 1906, after Joseph Smith's death, the executors of his estate rapidly sold the remainder of undeveloped properties. Rev. Lewis Steinback and Hattie and David Upshaw each paid the estate $500 for lots on Margaret Avenue. All these individuals had earned a solid reputation within their own community and had earned at least some recognition from Joseph Smith and his heirs. As prominent African American families purchased land and moved to Smithfield, they were achieving the long sought-after goal of homeownership while they created a middle-class enclave for themselves.[44]

Some blocks were developed and grew dense more quickly than others. Martha Avenue between Mortimer and Walker Streets (identified in tax records as Block 43) and several adjacent blocks experienced rapid growth. At the turn of the century, many property owners and speculators saw the advantage of portioning off lots. In doing so, they were able to realize a financial windfall. Rather than having just two lots to sell, when subdivided they would have four lots to sell at inflated prices. This practice opened additional housing opportunities otherwise unavailable, but it also created denser living conditions. E. A. Brown recognized the value of dividing properties: In 1903, he granted Ed Davis a deed for a quarter of this lot for $200. Alex Evans, like Ed Davis, purchased a portion of the same lot. In 1903, Brown deeded him the property for $575. Alex Evans worked as a barber who maintained his residency in Smithfield from at least as early as 1904 until beyond 1920. Evans learned his trade while working as a porter and apprentice at Frank McCree's downtown shop. For some, barbering provided occupational stability and sufficient status to win the confidence of individuals who held mortgages on Evans' home. He, like many others, carried several mortgages as a homeowner as a means to maintain his home.[45]

The city's African Americans who were looking for financial assistance had the unique opportunity of appealing to the city's three black banks that were operating simultaneously during the early twentieth century. This was a notable achievement, because most U.S. cities did not have even one black bank to serve the city's African American population. In 1911, William Lauderdale founded the Peoples Investment and Savings Bank to "Buy, own, sell, lease and rent and dispose of real estate of any and all kinds."[46] The officers encouraged individuals to open an account with the bank as a means to working toward qualifying for a loan "for investment on a home."[47] It, however, did not enter into any large-scale lending for Smithfield residents. The Prudential Savings Bank helped a few African Americans finance their homes in Smithfield. Among those it helped were Lewis Steinback, the bank's second vice-president, who, in 1911 borrowed $702. Richard Blount also benefited from the bank's services.[48] In contrast, the Alabama Penny Savings and Loan Company played a significant role in increasing the percentage of African American homeowners in Smithfield and elsewhere in Birmingham. Rev. William Pettiford, one of the bank's founders and its president, was a particularly strong advocate of homeownership. His speeches at the National Negro Business League proceedings reveal his commitment to assisting blacks purchase their own homes through the bank's lending policies: "One of the main features of our work has been and is, to teach the art of saving money and of purchasing homes, so that out of the 8000 depositors who have been with us more than a thousand have purchased their homes." In the late 1900s, Pettiford proudly declared that "there are over 1,500 colored people in the city owning their homes, many of which have been fully paid for."[49] His philosophy mirrored that of Booker T. Washington's: homeownership was the means to financial and personal stability and community development. Many of Smithfield's homeowners were able to purchase and maintain their homes through the cooperation of Pettiford's bank, which played the largest role in converting Birmingham's African American renters to homeowners. Frequently the Alabama Penny Savings and Loan Company entered into multiple mortgages with its customers. In 1904, it entered into a mortgage agreement with C. L. Montgomery. The terms required that the debt of $98.57 be paid in four promissory notes. By 1921, the debt was paid in full and satisfied. Circumstances dictated the terms: In 1906, Montgomery refinanced his home. This time the Alabama Penny Savings and Loan Company offered more stringent terms: Montgomery had to repay the debt of $708 in five promissory notes.[50]

African Americans had alternatives to secure financing when the Alabama Penny Savings and Loan denied assistance. A few blacks arranged mortgages through white-owned banks, although most of these exclusively assisted white patrons. The Steiner Brothers Bank was the one white bank that played a significant role in financing black ventures and particularly homeownership in Smithfield. A Jewish-owned banking house, it offered mortgages to several black homeowners. It also assumed several mortgages that the mortgagee no longer cared to hold, purchased property that had foreclosed, and at times its founders gave personal loans.

During the early twentieth century, several private black organizations that operated exclusively as ethnic organizations also assisted blacks who sought to become homeowners. The Afro-American Benevolent Society and the Great Southern Home Industrial Association both offered a multitude of services and engaged in real estate activities. The Certificate of Incorporation of the Afro-American Society listed "borrowing money" among its many purposes. In 1909, the Reverend T. W. Walker and his colleagues founded the Afro-American Land, Improvement and Investment Company to engage in all aspects of real estate development including lending money.[51] However helpful these organizations were in assisting African Americans, there is no evidence that they were instrumental in helping them purchase homes in Smithfield.[52]

Other blacks secured financial assistance from a variety of building and loan associations and real estate companies. The Black Loan Company advertised in the *Age-Herald:* "Money Loaned to salaried people or on anything of value." The W. B. Leedy Real Estate and Investment Company also advertised their services: "We are prepared to make first mortgage loans at 6, 7 and 8 percent on well improved business and residence property in Birmingham. Money in hand; no red tape and no delay." The Jefferson County Building and Loan Association with more solid capitalization offered its services to a diverse clientele. It's advertisements highlighted its reliable record: "Investment 6 percent or 8 percent. This is an old fashioned Building and Loan Association. . . . [It] has never failed to pay an obligation when due or pay cash for stock present for withdrawal."[53] Some African Americans benefited from the Association's services. Alex Evans was one of several Smithfield residents who financed his home improvements through this company.

As property values began to increase, newspaper advertisements reminded prospective owners of prices. In 1913, the Black Belt Land Company advertised several Smithfield properties, including two houses on Emma Avenue and John Street for $2,250, and a six-room house with a three-room servant's house on Seventh Avenue for $5,000. N. B. Smith advertised "24 4- and 5-room houses with hall. Smithfield. $24,000 worth $34,000."[54] Clearly, a variety of housing was available in Smithfield, but only a few black families could afford the limited number of large and more attractive homes.

Individuals interested in purchasing a home sought lenders who offered flexible terms. The lease-sale contract was one popular alternative method of financing that was available to prospective homeowners. The advertisements for this type of financing were enticing: "Home Sweet Home. I have a good number of 3, 4, and 5 Room Houses that you can get as low as $10 down and $10 per month." Essentially the interested homeowner agreed to pay the owner a principal amount divided into monthly payments. Upon completion of the payments, in theory, the owner granted a deed to the renter. During his or her tenancy, the renter was required to pay real estate taxes, insurance, and maintenance expenses. If the renter failed to meet his obligations, which violated the terms of the lease, the owner had the option to "re-enter premises and annul the lease." The money paid by the tenant was then held as rent. The tenant had built no equity in the property until the full conditions of the lease were met and the deed was transferred. It was an exploitative arrangement that undermined the efforts of many aspiring homeowners. In 1914, *Hot Shots* editor William McGill and his wife Sarah sued George McAllister for their deed. After having paid taxes since 1910, the McGills lost their right to the property by 1915. In contrast, O. L. Craig, a black letter carrier, after nine years completed the terms of his 1913 lease-sale contract for a property on John Street. Anthony Binion, a black laborer, also purchased his home after meeting the terms of his contract with N. B. Smith.[55]

A significant amount of home financing occurred at the individual level. Joseph Smith offered mortgages to the whites and blacks who purchased his property. Benjamin Webb and A. M. DeYampert bought their land directly from Smith, and once they were ready to improve on their property, they approached either black or white lenders. Individual lending practices opened avenues otherwise closed to some families aspiring to purchase homes. William Gage worked for Solomon and Levi and clearly earned their respect. They were able to evaluate his character and consequently decided to enter into a business relationship with him.[56] Other white lenders offered mortgages to African Americans over time. In 1900, C. E. Leonard, an executive at J. J. Addington Company, loaned money to A. M. DeYampert and J. O. Diffay. Leonard also granted mortgages to such black organizations as William Lauderdale's Great Southern Home Industrial Association. He had established himself as a reliable lender, and blacks had proved themselves to be responsible borrowers. Several white women conducted business with blacks who needed financial assistance. In 1910, Fannie Herzfeld took out a $850 mortgage on Ed and Mattie Davis's home, and Rosa Starr Granville gave a $1,250 mortgage to Charles T. Mabry.[57]

As Smithfield became increasingly settled, a visible change began to occur. Houses stood on formerly empty lots and residents walked the streets and congregated on the front porches as neighbors socialized. A community began to take shape. Blacks seized the opportunity to make their homes comfortable and attractive and their neighborhood safe. Many families spent large amounts of money to construct their homes and to maintain and improve their living space. Rev. Frederick R. Kennedy was an early Smithfield homeowner who, with his wife Catherine, owned their home at 516 Martha Avenue during the 1890s. The Alabama Penny Savings and Loan Company helped the Kennedys to build a comfortable home for themselves and develop several other properties they owned in North and South Smithfield. In 1910, the bank held a mortgage on Kennedy's two adjacent properties on Martha Avenue for $1,629.55 at 8 percent interest. When Windham Brothers completed the construction, Kennedy sold one of the houses for $2,200. As vacant lots, the Smithfield Land Company had sold them to the George and P. E. McAllister for $700 in 1888.

In 1907, James O. Diffay, his wife Rosa and their children made their new home on 508 Sixth Avenue, where they lived for several decades. In 1906, Diffay had purchased the lot for $500 from Joseph Smith's Estate, and in the following year he began building a home with a mortgage of $2,000 at 8 percent interest from the Alabama Penny Savings and Loan. Six months later he took out another loan for $500. Diffay satisfied both these debts in 1909. The Diffays continued to improve their home, and by 1924 the family home was assessed at $2,400. In addition to their residence they owned another Smithfield property that conceivably supplemented their income. They made a comfortable life for themselves in Smithfield.[58]

J. O. Diffay was a successful barber who was born in 1863 and raised in Jefferson County. As a young man, he was involved in several business ventures and associated with some of the most elite members of Birmingham's black society. Diffay, in partnership with Samuel Roebuck, owned a barbershop. By 1901, Diffay was sole owner of the barbershop located in the Black Business District and had $200 worth of taxable property. He employed several barbers, including other Smithfield residents.[59] In 1902, Diffay was selected to manage the real estate department of the Alabama Penny Savings and Loan Company. Two years later, he was president of the Peoples Mutual Aid Association and served as secretary alongside Joseph Barker, another Smithfield resident who was the bookkeeper at the Alabama Penny Savings and Loan Company. In 1903, the *Truth* recognized Diffay's achievements and declared that his "life is one well worthy of emulation by our young men." The Diffays raised seven children in their new home. Their comfortable financial situation is revealed by the fact that several of their children did not continue to live at home and did not work to supplement the family income. Rather, they attended such prestigious black schools as Atlanta University, Fisk University, and the Pratt Institute in Brooklyn.[60] In 1914, when William Pettiford died, J. O. Diffay assumed the presidency of the Alabama Penny Savings Bank (formerly the Alabama Penny Savings and Loan but renamed in 1909). However, his position did not provide the security that the family had hoped for. When the bank collapsed in 1915, Diffay likely suffered a financial setback that affected his family's living arrangements. In 1920, four female teachers boarded with the Diffay family, whose number had been reduced as a result of the grown children moving out. Although the Diffays may have perceived it as their civic responsibility to board teachers, they may have taken in boarders as a temporary measure to weather their financial difficulties. They made sacrifices to ensure the survival of the family unit, which depended on its economic viability.[61] Despite the likely impact the Bank's closing had on the Diffays, they nonetheless maintained their social position. Diffay continued to operate his barber shop, and the family continued to enjoy the piano and the other personal effects they had accumulated over the years.[62]

Although male heads of households tended to negotiate mortgages, their wives frequently entered into the arrangements. Once their mortgage payments were completed, both spouse's names often appeared on the deed. Occasionally unmarried, divorced, or widowed women managed to purchase property in their own names. Although women were asserting themselves through the suffrage movement during this time and demanding their rights, they were not acknowledged as equal to men, nor were their business skills respected. Consequently, women, and particularly African American women, found it difficult to purchase property or establish a business without the support of a man. Nonetheless, as noted earlier, some white women independently invested in Smithfield real estate. A few black women did the same. Pinky Harris, an officer in several women's orders, and Margaret Jemison were both widows who entered into a lease-sale contract with George McAllister. Jemison occupied the dwelling with several boarders. McAllister deeded them the property when Jemison and Harris paid their $630 debt over a thirty-four-month period. In 1904, Orlean D. Kennedy, a black teacher at Cameron School and later at Industrial High School and librarian at the Washington Library, managed to acquire a sizable mortgage from the Birmingham Building and Improvement Company. In thirteen years she had satisfied her $1,746 debt.[63]

To own one's own home was a shared aspiration. A house with shutters and a small yard with a garden typified the dreams of many. Homeownership was an investment that required careful management of funds and continual upkeep of the property. Yet, the realities of homeownership were rarely mentioned; advertisements and promotions only highlighted the pleasures associated with owning one's own home. Unsuspecting and uninformed individuals and families entered into homeowner status only to discover that it was not all what it appeared to be. Monthly mortgage payments often were all a family could manage. Maintenance expenses and taxes pushed them beyond their means.[64]

Many homeowners lacked the experience necessary to make astute financial decisions and an unexpected turn of events could dramatically alter the course of their lives. J. O. Diffay had handily weathered his economic downturn, but other homeowners were not so lucky. Ed Balls, a tailor, owned two lots in Smithfield. He paid E. A. Brown $200 for a forty-five by one hundred foot undeveloped lot in 1903. Balls and his wife, Ruth, borrowed $1,108.78 from the Alabama Penny Savings and Loan Company in 1906 and $1,074 one year later. Balls satisfied the debts and continued to incur other mortgage debts to improve his property. The couple were establishing themselves in a comfortable home when a problem changed their lives: Ed Balls failed to comply with the terms and conditions of a $1,300 mortgage he executed to S. Leon in 1909. In 1912, "S. Leon offered for sale at public outcry for cash at the county court house, the property conveyed by said mortgage, after giving 30 days notice in the *Labor Advocate*." Carl Steiner, from the Steiner Brothers Bank, offered $1502.35, the highest bid, and assumed ownership of the property. Steiner proceeded to sell a clear title on Ball's former property for $1,500.[65] Personal tragedy could alter one's life situation and drain one's financial resources. The Balls' experience was not unique. The *Age-Herald,* the *Labor Advocate,* and other newspapers often advertised mortgage sales for properties available to the highest bidder when the owner was unable to meet his or her financial obligations. Whites were not immune from this fate: In 1895, Lot 16, Block 39 went on the "block" when C. L. and Sarah Fletcher failed to meet their payment owing to Charles H. Molton. C. R. Sexton's property faced a similar fate, when Sexton failed to satisfy his debt to Joseph Smith.[66] Astute investors reacted to these opportunities and often bought the property for a reduced price. These "fire sales" often enticed local folk who longed to own their own home; the reduced prices of property presented an opportunity. Overwhelmingly, homeowners were physically tied to their community because of the high cost of equity; their financial burden impeded their geographic mobility. Although many homeowners remained in their home for many years, homeownership did not guarantee financial security or stability. Frequently they were burdened with multiple mortgages that they were unable to pay on time. Dicie Brown, once a Smithfield homeowner, struggled to maintain her home with her children's help. Ultimately, she lost her home and was forced into renter status when she failed to meet her financial obligations.[67] Yet, she had secured ties with the community and elected to stay in Smithfield as a renter.

Individual homeowners were not unique in their vulnerability. Businesses or joint ventures also were susceptible to foreclosures. A. M. DeYampert had successfully financed his home and store and lived comfortably on Joseph Street. His solid reputation as a "wide-awake young man of color [who] owns a successful grocery store" enabled him to arrange numerous mortgages with a variety of individuals and agencies.[68] His ambition moved him beyond his grocery store to conduct his own real estate business and, for a time, to operate an art studio located in the Pythian Hall building.[69] After purchasing a lot from Joseph Smith for $200 in 1899, DeYampert appealed to several sources for financial assistance. The Alabama Penny Savings and Loan Company held the first of many mortgages on the property. He continued to improve his properties through refinancing, and in 1929, his four-room frame house and store were assessed at $4,050. DeYampert also owned other property around the corner from his store, which he rented out for a time before selling it. Despite the appearance of financial security with his considerable holdings, he encountered difficulties when he and his business partners, Rev. T. W. Walker and C. A. Howze, were unable to carry their mortgages on several properties in Smithfield and the surrounding Birmingham area. In 1907, when J. S. Kennedy, a Talladega attorney, filed suit against DeYampert et al., and won, he gained title to more than eight properties. DeYampert and his business associates lost their money and their jointly held properties.[70]

The foreclosures and lawsuits presented here are in no way intended as examples of failures. Rather, they are offered as illustrations of the incertitude of homeownership as well as the efforts and sacrifices Smithfield residents made to create a comfortable home environment for themselves. Discriminatory labor practices, mismanagement, and personal tragedy often undermined the efforts of African Americans and whites who aspired to own their own homes. Despite the middle-class profile of many Smithfield homeowners, their status did not guarantee stability in the housing market. Relatively low wages and the lack of opportunity for job mobility created a situation whereby some middle-class blacks lacked a stable and reliable income. Black homeowners in Smithfield who lost their homes were few when compared to those who remained homeowners in the first three decades of the twentieth century.

Blacks and whites not only shared in the abstractions of what owning one's home meant but also shared in the more tangible aspect of homeownership—building construction. A flurry of new home construction occurred during the turn of the century. By 1902, the blocks in South Smithfield under examination reveal that a significant amount of building took place very early on. The absence of building regulations and codes allowed for a diversity in the style and quality of construction. Not until 1901 did Birmingham adopt a building ordinance whereby the Office of Inspector of Buildings was created "to provide rules for the construction of buildings; to provide for fire escapes, flues, location of stables, and regulations within the fire limits; to provide punishment for the violation of the same."[71] But as a village within Graymont, Smithfield still lay beyond the jurisdiction of Birmingham. Graymont had its own set of standards. The earliest homes in Smithfield were constructed without the imposition of codes that would have increased the cost and altered the design.[72] As properties were developed, they lacked the uniformity that became prevalent in the post World War II suburbs. Contractors' decisions whether to build in a certain area were dictated by various factors, including the lay of the land, the availability of materials, and the financial feasibility of construction. Smithfield was a new development, and any investment in the area either as a speculator, builder, or resident entailed a certain amount of risk. For many, the risk appeared modest. There were many opportunities for builders to turn a profit in the real estate market. In the late 1890s onward, the demand for housing created a residential construction boom. According to Sidney Smyer, Jr., president of the Birmingham Realty Company, building companies or small-scale contractors would build houses that all looked similar and then arrange financing. They would "buy a mortgage at a discount; then sell it to aspiring homeowners." Some commercial businesses such as the Wood-Dickerson Wood Lumber Company and the Enterprise Lumber and Manufacturing Company of Birmingham did this as did Phineas and George McAllister and T. C. Windham.[73]

Several clues can be used to unravel the mystery of who the builders were.[74] Deed and mortgage records occasionally reveal the identity of a builder. In 1899, the Enterprise Lumber Company held a mortgage of $320 on K. Edwards's property on Ella Avenue. For $150 Joseph Smith deeded to Edwards this property in 1898. The lumber company held the mortgage to cover the cost of building on the undeveloped property. As the property changed hands over the years and as land values increased, the new owners improved the structures, and by 1919 this same property was assessed at $940.[75] The Birmingham Building and Improvement Company was another firm that built some homes in Smithfield. It advertised in *Hot Shots:* "If you own a lot we will build you a house on plans to suit upon terms equal to paying rent. If you do not own a lot we will furnish one and build on plans to suit on terms about equal to paying rent, after a small payment is made. No one can afford to pay rent to others where such opportunities are offered."[76] The firm granted Joseph and Adele Barker a mortgage for $1,250 on two lots they owned at 515 Ella Avenue.[77] Other information offers additional insight and supports Smyer's assertion. The Smithfield Land Company often contracted a company to develop properties before interested parties could purchase it. In 1888, it hired the Birmingham Tool and Implement Works to build several homes in the area. A few lumber companies, such as the Enterprise Lumber and Manufacturing Company of Birmingham and Wood-Dickerson Lumber, did the same. And the Birmingham Realty Company sought "Home Seekers" who "can buy their lots and have [a] house built according to their own plans on easy monthly payments." All of these companies assumed the dual roles of builder and financier.[78]

Not only were midsized companies involved in the development of housing in Smithfield but also independent contractors, who found ample opportunity because the large-scale builders and community developers had not yet taken control of the housing market. Phineas E. McAllister and his brother, George, were among Smithfield's white landlords and independent builders. The McAllisters were born in Michigan and came to the Birmingham area where they participated in the real estate boom. The brothers remained active in Smithfield's real estate market throughout the early decades of the twentieth century, and they played a significant role in the development of the suburb. Early on, they bought large tracts of land directly from the Smithfield Land Company and from individuals, black and white, who had bought up property and then sold it quickly in pursuit of realizing a quick profit. The brothers parlayed their large property holdings into a profitable business, and they maximized their profits when they divided their lots. The McAllisters purchased property, developed lots that they then leased or sold, and operated a personal lending service. They jointly owned much of their property until the end of the 1890s, at which time they began divesting. In 1905, William Nabors, a black grocer, purchased his home at 724 Martha Avenue from George McAllister.[79] By 1908, the tax department assessed the brothers' combined Smithfield property at $9,900.00.[80] Although building permits were not available for this study, tax and mortgage documentation provides sufficient information to conclude that the McAllisters were significant players in Smithfield's housing market, as investors and as builders. They sustained an interest in the area as long as they reaped sufficient return on their investment. During Smithfield's development, George and Phineas lived next door to each other on 326 and 330 North Fourth Avenue, where they had several black neighbors. The brothers lived with their families in this area until they moved at about the same time as other white families sought residence elsewhere in Jefferson County. Other resident builders more than likely also constructed some of the homes in their own neighborhoods. Phillip Rietta, an Italian immigrant who came to the United States in 1882, lived in South Smithfield. In 1903 he owned a total of nine undeveloped lots in North Smithfield, in addition to the home he lived in on Eighth Avenue. The 1900 Census identifies his occupation as a merchant; however he was involved in construction and probably built the homes on the vacant lots he owned. Rietta invested in Smithfield's real estate market and further advanced his financial position when he personally developed the property.[81]

At least one Smithfield resident and likely several more found an alternative way of becoming homeowners without the involvement of local builders. A new trend took hold in the early twentieth century with the growing popularity of mail-order catalogs. Aladdin Homes, Sears Roebuck, and Montgomery Ward moved beyond selling household products to marketing entire houses. The prefabricated houses—factory-built homes manufactured in sections and assembled by a carpenter—first made their appearance in the 1880s; their appeal did not take hold until the 1920s. Both the mail-order houses and lumber companies promoted the concept and unique features of factory-built homes. For a modest price, they offered consumers a range of choices that allowed owners to express their personal taste. Dr. D. E. Bradford recalled that his parents "purchased a prefabricated house from Sears

Roebuck," that was constructed by a local contractor. "It was a two-story wooden frame house that had a living room, dining room, kitchen, sun parlor, plus four bedrooms and a bathroom." The Birmingham *Reporter* informed its readers of their unique purchase: "The house is one of the 'ready cut' and of its style, modern convenience and artistic interior decorations is considered one of the most beautiful homes in the city." The Bradford's home was complemented with the addition of a piano and a fairly extensive library of books.[82]

Black-owned companies also built Smithfield homes. Notible B. Smith, a Smithfield resident, was a notary public and the general manager of Metropolitan Homes. He advertised that he would "buy land, and build to suit your taste, [with] easy monthly installments." Elsewhere he advertised: "Wanted—To build 100 houses for people who own lots." Several other African American contractors and Smithfield residents also were involved in developing the area. Among them were native South Carolinians C. L. Goodson and L. S. Gaillard; also A. F. Jackson, R. E. Pharroah, and the Windham brothers.

Local historians have resurrected the legacy of Thomas C. Windham, who now stands out in Birmingham as the most successful African American contractor. The Windham Brothers firm has a secure place in history as a well-respected black-owned and black-managed Birmingham construction firm. Thomas C. and his brother Benjamin L. were native Louisianans who worked as partners to create a venerable business that was responsible for building numerous Smithfield homes and several noteworthy buildings in Birmingham, including Smithfield's Trinity Baptist Church, the seven-story Birmingham Light and Power Company, circa 1926–27, and the historic Sixteenth Street Baptist Church. The Windhams became business partners in 1897 when Benjamin joined Thomas in his construction enterprise in Birmingham. They quickly earned enviable reputations as stalwart businessmen. Benjamin Windham had numerous business interests, most notably the Booker T. Washington Life Insurance Company, which he founded and directed. He also served as State Temple Treasurer of the Mosaics of America of Alabama; he was a high ranking member of the Knights of Pythias; and he held the last degree of Masonry. For many years, he served as a clerk and deacon at the Sixth Avenue Baptist Church. Although Thomas was active as a layleader in the Sixteenth Street Baptist Church and had fraternal affiliations, he focused his energies on creating a credible construction business.[83]

T. C. Windham was the driving force behind the success of the construction company.[84] In 1912, he built the company's home office at

726 Eighth Avenue North, which stands today as the oldest remaining commercial building in Smithfield. Windham's business interests took him to Chicago, Detroit, Indianapolis, and Nashville, where he had branch offices.[85] He constructed buildings and homes throughout the South, including R. B. Hudson's two-story home in Selma, which was described as "one of the best and most substantial Negro homes in the state." Windham also built Richard H. and Henry Allen Boyd's $600,000 National Baptist Publishing House in Nashville and two buildings for Guadalupe College in Seguin, Texas. T. C., like his brother, pursued diverse interests. He sat on the board of directors of the Prudential Savings Bank, and he founded the Acme Finance Corporation of Birmingham in the late 1920s.[86] T. C. Windham's legacy continues. One resident recalled that "everyone here knew his standing. He was the more renowned brother who had his own chauffeur." Sam Finocchio added that Windham was an arrogant man whose company "moved houses, entire houses, to another location." He also built his magnificent residence known as "The Mansion," which was located along Eighth Avenue in a block of real estate that he owned and developed. Photographs and tax records reveal that it was a graceful home adorned with a marble foyer and stained-glass windows. A piano sat in the parlor, several ornate chandeliers hung from the beamed ceilings, and a car sat in the driveway. Despite Windham's flurry of early success, he encountered financial difficulties in 1915. In his letter to Emmett J. Scott, Booker T. Washington's personal secretary, he revealed that "our company has met with many reverses of fortune in the last year and it has been quite a struggle for us to stem the tide, and I am not sure we are yet on the safe side."[87] Nevertheless, Windham Construction pulled itself up from this downturn and continued constructing homes in Smithfield into the 1920s. Windham was one of the most successful African Americans in Birmingham. His longtime residency in Smithfield contributed to the neighborhood's standing, and it gave residents a sense of pride.

Incremental building was a relatively common phenomenon during the early twentieth century among many Americans who aspired to homeownership. Some families purchased a home and then improved upon the structure before they moved in. Seretha Jackson remembers that her frame house was previously only three rooms—a living room, bedroom, and kitchen—and a partial bathroom. "We remodeled it before we moved in and then later remodeled again."[88] The Jacksons hired a contractor to build the additions to their house. Incremental building allowed families to build a home as the need arose at a reduced financial expense primarily through the avoidance of meeting building code requirements and through sweat equity. In Mobile as in Smithfield, incremental self-building offered the possibility of home-ownership and with it a strong sense of personal accomplishment and pride. Henry Aaron, the outstanding left fielder, recalled his child-hood home:

> I was eight when we moved to Toulminville in 1942. They were tearing down an old house close to where we lived in Down The Bay, so we grabbed up the lumber and Mama spent her days pulling out nails. Daddy bought two overgrown lots at $55 apiece and paid a couple of carpenters $100 to build us six rooms, which was twice as many as we were accustomed to. When the walls and roof were up, we moved in, and that was it—no rent or mortgage, it was ours. We were a proud family, because the way we saw it, the only people who owned their own homes were rich folks and Aarons. After the house was built, we just kept patch-ing it up and putting on new layers—shingles, felt, brick, what-ever we could get. When I made some money in baseball, we added a back room, and my parents still live there.[89]

T. C. Windham worked in close alliance with Wallace A. Rayfield, Birmingham's first African American architect. Rayfield was born in Macon, Georgia, in 1874 and in his adolescence moved to Washing-ton D.C., where his aunt raised him. He attended Howard Univer-sity and continued his studies in architecture at the Pratt Institute in Brooklyn, New York. Upon graduation in 1899, Rayfield worked for a brief time at the A. B. Mullett and Company Architects in Washing-ton and then accepted an invitation from Booker T. Washington to teach in the Architectural Drawing Division at Tuskegee Institute. Rayfield left Tuskegee in 1907, after eight years of service, and moved to Birmingham. He did not teach school again until 1919-1920, when he taught at Industrial High School for a salary of $1,200. In 1908, Rayfield designed, financed, and built his own residence in Tittusville, which lies southwest of Smithfield. Rayfield began his business in 1908, and in that year, his letterhead reveals that he had branch offices in Atlanta, Macon, Augusta, Savannah, Montgomery, Talladega, and Mobile. He rapidly won contracts to design the Six-teenth Street Baptist Church; the older Sixth Avenue Baptist Church before it was razed to make way for the University of Alabama at Bir-mingham buildings; St. Paul's Episcopal Church in Batesville, Arkan-

Arthur H. Parker's home at 620 Mortimer (Fifth) Street. Rayfield designed the home c. 1909. (Jefferson County, Ala., Board of Equalization Appraisal Files, Catalog #22.35.3.11.18, Department of Archives and Manuscripts, Birmingham Public Library, Ala.)

sas; and Chicago's Ebenezer Baptist Church. Rayfield also designed local commercial properties, such as the O. K. French Cleaners building, the Dunbar Hotel, the Harriet Strong Undertaking Company, the Thomas School, and Tuggle Institute.[90] His business connections were reinforced through his position as secretary in Birmingham's branch of the National Negro Business League.[91] Rayfield's impact as an architect of stature persists to the present time, for several of the buildings and homes he designed remain standing.

Several African American residents of Smithfield commissioned Rayfield to design their homes, including Arthur H. Parker and E. A. Brown. Their Dutch gambled roof cottages were built adjacent to each other circa 1909. Over time, they added their own personal touch to the home's interiors. Brown accumulated an impressive library while the Parkers enhanced the home's appearance when they purchased a piano. Although technically their homes were single-family dwellings, they, like many other Smithfield residents, shared their living space

Edward A. Brown's home at 624 Mortimer (Fifth) Street. Rayfield designed the home c. 1909. (Jefferson County, Ala., Board of Equalization Appraisal Files, Catalog #22.35.33.11.19, Department of Archives and Manuscripts, Birmingham Public Library, Ala.)

with relatives and boarders.[92] Rayfield also designed Grand Chancellor Richard Blount's "classically styled residence with monumental portico."[93] Arthur McKimmon Brown, E. A. Brown's brother, commissioned Rayfield to design his new home and hired black builders to execute the plans that detailed an outstanding nine-room, two-story home at 319 Fourth Terrace North (formerly Martha Avenue). The house today serves as the home for the A. M. Brown Community Center for Arts and Crafts. Brown was one of the first African American doctors in Birmingham. He had established a solid professional reputation that enabled him to develop other business and philanthropic interests. He was instrumental in establishing the Children's Home Hospital, which was for several years the only hospital that would employ black doctors. During the early twentieth century as the Black Business District was evolving into a bustling commercial area, A. M. Brown helped to establish and served as president of People's Drug Company.[94] R. E. Pharrow's impressive home sat nearby Brown's home on Fourth Terrace, North. Pharrow was a Georgia-born black contractor who migrated to Birmingham to participate in the city's real estate boom. He built his home—a two-story modified classic-style frame bungalow—but he barely if ever occupied it; he and his family moved to Atlanta shortly after its completion in 1908. The Pharrow Contracting Company became a force in Atlanta's and the South's real estate development. His company built the Mernwood Building in Birmingham and several notable properties in Atlanta, including the First Congregational Church and the Odd Fellows Building and Auditorium complex. Pharrow probably built several homes in Smithfield as well as in Savannah and a bank building in Washington, D.C.[95] Dr. A. M. Brown and B. L. and T. C. Windham all lived in grand homes. Often they built on multiple lots and built vertically as well as horizontally. There were few homes that commanded the presence and envy that these grand residences did. The homes served as more than a private space for the nuclear family. They became showpieces and meeting places, where family members and friends would sometimes congregate for special occasions. These residents and their respective homes enhanced the desirability of Smithfield for many African Americans, including those who sought membership in the black middle class.

These more elaborate and costly homes were by no means the typical housing style in South Smithfield. Most housing was basic; many homes were single shotgun houses, with a scattering of double shotguns.[96] Alma Anderson Dickerson, a longtime resident of Smithfield, remembers that her "family lived everywhere in Birmingham in shotgun houses."[97] Several homeowners could afford only small homes, most of which were frame constructions of the shotgun style. Lula Tankersley owned a one-room frame house at 508 Martha Avenue in 1923. James Byrd, a mail carrier and Mason and treasurer at his church, and his wife Frances, owned a one-story three-room frame house on a John Street lot that had been subdivided several times. In 1921, their home was assessed at $600, which was consistent with other tax assessments of three-room frame houses at the time. Other families could afford larger homes: W. W. Greene, also a mail carrier and Knights of Pythias officer, lived in a single-story four-room frame house in 1921, and Fletcher A. Bailey, a minister, owned a five-room frame house. Hattie and her husband Dr. David Upshaw also owned a five-room frame house, which was assessed at $750 in 1915. They were longtime owners, having purchased the property for $500 from the Estate of Joseph Smith in 1906.[98]

As Smithfield property increased in value, lots became smaller and the houses less spacious. Several fire insurance and property maps drawn in the early twentieth century reveal a certain uniformity among many houses of the era, particularly in the materials used to construct the homes. The overwhelming majority of homes and commercial business buildings were of frame construction and were single-story dwellings. Frame construction was the quickest and cheapest way to build, but the dwellings tended to be poorly constructed and required constant maintenance. Failure to maintain the dwellings resulted in rapid deterioration. Nevertheless, many Smithfield residents had arrived from the rural regions of Alabama, and before arriving in Birmingham, they may have lived in housing similar to that described in Charles Johnson's *Growing Up in the Black Belt*. Most renters and owners in Smithfield lived in modest housing, but it was most probably superior to their rural shelters.[99]

There were very few brick homes, and the ones that existed were clustered in a group of two or three. The Trinity Baptist Church was constructed of brick in the heart of South Smithfield during the first decade of the twentieth century. T. C. Windham had built it during a time when he was also building a solid reputation for himself. In 1909, the Graymont School for black students was also a brick building. George and Phineas McAllister owned and probably constructed several of the brick homes on Martha Avenue. Some frame homes were of hollow concrete or cement block construction that provided for a more solid foundation. Both Arthur Parker and Edward Brown's houses were built in this manner, which served the occupants well during their long residency in the area.[100]

Perhaps none sought a private life away from public view more than the suburb's well-positioned black residents. Staying at home or socializing among those who shared an elevated status enabled them not only to eliminate the possibility of social class mixing but also to protect them from insults of whites. Visiting at each other's homes was an important aspect of family life, and blacks used visits to "reaffirm the bonds between relatives and friends."[101] Like the *Norfolk Journal and Guide* and race papers elsewhere, Birmingham's *Reporter* and the *Truth* offered insights into the visiting patterns of its residents. Weekly accounts revealed who went where, why, and for how long. The documentation of the patterns reveals the intricacies of social networks and the persistence of family and friendship ties, as well as the central role of the home.[102]

Through their carefully crafted network, the middle-class people secured their position of privilege. Ellen Tarry recalled: "Anybody who was anybody knew the others." It was "the old boys club. We had to keep the grapevine going."[103] Visiting among Birmingham's residents exhibited patterns whereby individuals and families developed a network with others who shared their socioeconomic status, even if they lived in different parts of the city. Birthday parties, informal gatherings of dinner followed by fun and games, and other casual get-togethers took place in the home. There they congregated with friends and family who were part of their inner circle. "Mrs. F. H. Cloud entertained a few friends at their home on south Twenty-seventh street, Thursday night, when she surprised her husband on the occasion of his birthday. Whist was the pleasant pastime, and the first prize was won by Mrs. W. E. Lacy. . . . [O]ther guests were [well-positioned Smithfield residents] Dr. and Mrs. A. M. Brown, Mr. and Mrs. Leroy and Herbert Gaillard, Mr. and Mrs. Andrew Sims." Friends often gathered for annual celebrations that strengthened friendship ties. Older elite blacks attended picnics, parties, and so forth with the younger men who were emerging as leaders in the early part of the twentieth century. In 1920, Bob Tarry, "one of Birmingham's oldest barbers and who is well known by both white and colored celebrated his 52nd birthday with a stag party at his home."[104] When E. A. Bradford, a local funeral director, invited a few friends to join him in a smoker, he "outdid his usual hospitality . . . with a seven-course dinner." Day trips or picnics outside of Birmingham often reflected a similar cast of characters.[105] Young singles followed in their parents' footsteps when they gathered together for class-specific functions at home and in larger facilities. The *Birmingham Reporter* described one such function at the Eureka Club: "The elite of the younger social set outstripped all of the past events of the season in grandeur and attire, and the style that the delicacies were served in while the orchestra played its sweet strains of music was an innovation in Birmingham society."[106]

More than any other class of African Americans, some of the more affluent members of the middle class had greater resources to travel beyond the Birmingham District to ensure the continuation of important ties with family and friends who had moved away. The newspapers tended to document the movement of the city's black middle class, just as white publications followed the movement of prominent white citizens. Three types of visitation patterns that emerged demonstrate the importance of these social networks and again the importance of the home. Whether for business travel, purely social reasons, or familial obligation, the home was where visitors convened.[107] The brief newspaper notices revealed the complexities of relationships and the maintenance of ties long after individuals had moved elsewhere. Those who moved away often returned for a visit with family members in their home. Such visits helped individuals maintain contact with kin and friends alike. A change in environment provided new life experiences for those venturing beyond the boundaries of Alabama, and upon their return, they served as a source of information.[108]

Records of visits by out-of-town guests who stayed in the homes of some of Smithfield's and Enon Ridge's most elite residents highlight the intricate nature of social networks. In the early 1900s, Birmingham had the Fraternal Hotel and the New Washington Hotel, which operated sporadically and advertised itself as the "only exclusive Negro Hotel in Alabama." Yet visitors preferred to stay in private homes, which were more economical and personally gratifying. The Tarrys opened their home to visiting guests who were among an elite class of blacks: Minnie Cox was a longtime friend of the Tarrys, and when she visited Birmingham, "she generally makes his house her home."[109] While Booker T. Washington visited the city, he was the guest of U. G. Mason and his wife.[110] And when the wife of F. A. Mena, the "distinguished officer of the Nicaraguan government," visited Birmingham she was the guest of Mrs. R. A. Blount. Frequently the host would throw a reception for the visitors. When Birmingham's affluent blacks visited other cities, the favor was reciprocated, and they were often the guests of African Americans who shared their status.[111] When Antoinette Brown visited Atlanta, she was the guest of Ada Crogman, who was the daughter of W. H. Crogman, president of Clark College. Sometimes visits extended throughout the summer months, when Birmingham residents temporarily migrated north to spend time with friends and families. And when family members moved away for economic or social reasons and then returned for a visit, they usually stayed with family: "Mrs. Rosa Diffay Washington of Chicago is spending this week with her sister, Mrs. Charles Mabry on 5th Ave." This example not only illustrates the elasticity of family ties but also shows that members of Birmingham's elite black community intermarried and thus reinforced the strength of the network.[112]

Smithfield took on a life of its own as external forces reinforced

racial separation. Home life and personal relationships were important to African Americans, as they were to other Americans. As racial
tensions among black and whites increased, blacks looked to their
home life for security and personal fulfillment. Collectively, middle-
class and working-class African Americans perceived an opportunity
in Smithfield where they could establish stability through residency,
participate in community building, and strengthen ties with peers. It
offered the chance to live among others who shared life experiences
and fundamental values and a place to work cooperatively toward
shaping their own space.[113] It was a place they could call their own,
whether they were renters or homeowners.

Many Smithfield residents, and particularly homeowners, demonstrated a persistence of tenancy and a commitment to the improvement of the area. When essential services were lacking, it was a small
number of the middle-class homeowners who mobilized residents into
neighborhood associations. Although lots were in high demand and
contractors were building homes apace, basic improvements took
longer to reach the district. Residents who demanded modest changes
to the neighborhood were often frustrated by the inaction of Graymont officials. When streets were paved and curbed and sidewalks
were laid, African Americans often found their streets beyond those
identified to receive those improvements.[114] In 1909, Ordinance No.
184 clearly stated where the improvements were to be made: South
and west of the blocks dense with black families.[115] Other times,
change came more quickly. After the turn of the century, city health
officials began emphasizing the need for improved sanitation to control typhoid and other menacing diseases. Not until after 1916, did
the city enact regulations on realtors to connect black housing to sewers. Yet, Smithfield property owners were targets of an earlier city
campaign to arrest the sanitation problem. In 1910 city officials imposed liens on Smithfield properties to ensure payment "for the cost
of providing and installing and connecting a water closet and water
pipe line." The city was not immune from what plagued the suburbs. In 1918 the city charged Smithfield residents accordingly: F. R.
Kennedy was charged $170 at 8 percent interest for the procedure
while Shepard Hollins paid $160 with interest for this work.[116]

Smithfield residents also strived to enhance the safety of their streets
when they petitioned for financial assistance to build a bridge over the
Elyton Canal on John Street. Around 1920, Smithfield residents
joined together and organized the Smithfield Improvement League.
League members met at their various local churches, where they dis-

cussed issues that affected the entire neighborhood. In 1921, they organized a coalition to present the City Commission with a complaint
about the unpaved streets and the inadequate drainage, street lights,
and fire hydrants. Their concern with sanitation and disease prompted
them to initiate a neighborhood clean-up campaign that coincided
with the citywide crusade.[117] In ensuing years, blacks continued to assert greater control over their home environment. In 1930, Nellie
Brown, as a member of the Traffic Committee of the Smithfield Improvement League, reported that they were trying to secure traffic
lights to protect their children at the intersection of Joseph Street and
Sixth Avenue where the Graymont School was located, and for Eighth
Avenue and John Street, at the Industrial School corner.[118] The city
finally graded several streets where blacks owned and rented homes,
including Third Avenue and Fifth Street for the placement of the Atlanta, Birmingham & Atlantic Railroad tracks. African Americans,
however, were less influential in directing the placement of railroad
tracks that had an immediate impact on their community: Tenants
were forced to move out as the railroad company razed their homes
or moved the homes elsewhere.[119] Residents were reminded that their
efforts to manipulate their environment had limitations; a broader
agenda dictated a process that did not consider their best interests.

Smithfield residents who were committed to building race institutions in the area commenced work early. Churches were community
institutions, and their presence in Smithfield encouraged cohesion
among many residents. Among the first black churches in the area
were the Seventh Day Adventist Church on Walker Street, St. Joseph
Baptist on the corner of Ninth Avenue and Mortimer Street, and the
Trinity Baptist Church on John Street. Discontented members from
the Broad Street Baptist Church that began in 1878 as the Spring
Street Baptist Church founded Trinity Baptist in 1902.[120] The church
members worked diligently to beautify the building, and even nonmembers took pride in the improvements. The *Voice of the People* reported that "the people of Smithfield are proud to see the progress of
work on Trinity Baptist church." Trinity's membership grew rapidly
as new members flocked to the church. Rev. W. L. Boyd had served as
pastor of the large congregation since his arrival in Birmingham in
1914. By 1928, he conducted services in the $45,000 church building.
Boyd lived at 418 Eighth Avenue, just a short distance from Trinity
Baptist, and his presence in Smithfield as pastor and homeowner enabled him to keep abreast of local matters.[121] Rev. Robert Durr, the
Royal Counselor and pastor of the Independent Methodist Church on

301 Emma Avenue at Charles Street was a high-profile local leader who engaged in outreach programs that were well received by the broader community.[122]

As the community began to take shape, middle-class residents exercised some choice of residency as they clustered themselves on separate blocks. They managed to practice at least some spatial separation on selected streets. Space did not allow for them to put much distance between themselves and those who lived in the shotgun housing and alley dwellings, yet some black homeowners in the area kept themselves separate from other blacks who were different. E. A. Brown and A. H. Parker were next door neighbors while A. M. Brown and R. E. Pharrow also lived nearby each other. Dr. Bradford remembered that "there were mostly professionals on my street—a doctor, dentist, barber, Pullman porter and a mail carrier." One resident recalled that the alley residents kept more to themselves: "We knew nothing about them." Residents and professionals alike often considered alley dwellers as a separate class, "the bottom of society."[123] Yet, the alley housing was sprinkled throughout Smithfield and forced residents to share transportation, patronize some of the same grocery stores, and share the larger space called Smithfield. Although they did not socialize with each other, they clearly had at least incidental contact.[124]

All Smithfield residents moved beyond their community boundaries when their needs could not be met at home. They too required diversions away from the home sphere. As African Americans sorted themselves into class-specific activities, they found forms of recreation that suited their particular interests and needs where they rarely encountered others who were not like them. Some blacks, particularly working-class blacks, preferred to patronize business establishments where they could drink, play cards, shoot pool, or dance. Others preferred to participate in what they considered character building activities: attending cultural performances and engaging in intellectual discussions. Whichever forms of recreation appealed to them, many found their choices limited by the introduction of new barriers to maintain and reinforce racial separation. Ellen Tarry remembered the beautiful city park, known then as West End Park and now as Kelly Ingram Park: "Although we had to walk through this park to reach the business district, we were not permitted to sit on any of the benches, or lie on the grass or drink water from the fountains on scorching hot days. We could not even get close enough to the flowers to get a good smell."[125]

The paucity of public recreational space moved black entrepreneurs to create some opportunities for African Americans searching for diversions away from their home environment. In 1907, a small elite corps of African Americans, including Richard Blount and Auguste Benning, recognized the need for their own green space and organized a company to build the new "Climax" park located three and a half miles from Birmingham. It promised to be "An ideal place for family outings and special picnic parties, day or night." The possibility of their own park drew considerable optimism and excitement. The fanfare may have been premature since there is no evidence that the park was ever built.[126] Sometime around 1916, African Americans could claim a fifty-five-acre playground known as Dozier's Park, located on the North Ensley car line near Thrash Station. Under M. C. Dozier's direction, the Colored Playground Association made improvements to the property.[127] In 1919, Dozier's Park provided the venue for a gathering of more than two thousand blacks to hear a program sponsored by their Playground Movement. They exercised their right to assemble, and the meeting went undisturbed. It is noteworthy that a large public gathering did not agitate a hostile reaction from whites. The park's location, in an area psychologically remote from the city, may have helped to divert attention away from the mass meeting.[128]

In 1928, the same year that a group of African American citizens organized a permanent Playground Association, a black entrepreneur opened a grand amusement park. It was the first of its kind for Birmingham's black community. Tuxedo Park had a roller coaster and merry-go-round, a swimming pool, which was lighted at night for evening swims, and other sorts of amusements. It advertised that it had "the newest and most expensive dance music equipment available. No other park in the South is so equipped." It lured patrons with the following offer: "You have never heard real dance music until you come to Tuxedo Park and attend one of our Free Radio Dances." The park was well maintained, and according to one account, "the supervision is better than that provided in most Negro municipal parks in the South." Fourth of July celebrations were held at Tuxedo Park, where guests swam, danced, and played. An advertisement for the annual event optimistically stated that fifteen thousand guests were expected to attend the festivities. The park drew patrons predominantly from the working class; however members of the middle class also used the public facility, albeit at different times.[129] Beyond the grandeur of Tuxedo Park, sprinkled around the district were smaller playgrounds for black children. Under the direction of the Park and Recreation Board of Birmingham, the ten public play centers were well attended by children and adults alike.[130] During the late 1920s, African American women coordinated their efforts to organize Camp Margaret Murray Washington, which provided an alternative form of recreation. Although the camp served young women, middle-class blacks took advantage of the facilities and convened there with regularity.

Blacks were drawn out of their home environment to support their Black Barons baseball team. Baseball was emerging as America's number one sport during the turn of the century, and blacks and whites shared in the excitement of the game as they supported their own teams. In 1910, Rickwood Park, a concrete and steel baseball park, was built in Birmingham's West End for the white Barons baseball team. When the white team was on the road, the Black Barons rented the field, but they were barred from using the locker rooms. Fans of both colors shared the stands, albeit in segregated sections. This arrangement persisted until the Birmingham Baseball Association made improvements at Rickwood Park, which included a grandstand for blacks. Fans flocked to the games to enjoy the thrill of seeing black players exhibit their athletic prowess. Bob Tarry was well connected with the owners and players, and his daughter Ellen recalled that when he went to Rickwood Park he sat "behind third base and talk[ed] to the players who came over to speak with him during the warm-up period." She remembered that attending the games with her father "were wonderful times" and that "Papa was the Birmingham Barons' number-one rooter." Baseball was one of the few events that drew together African Americans from different classes as thousands of fans attended the games religiously. The Black Barons had a special significance for Birmingham's black residents, for they all derived pride and a sense of worth from watching and supporting the team.[131]

Whites and blacks enjoyed the diversion of movies as a popular form of entertainment after the turn of the century. Although segregated seating provided whites with greater choice of venues, blacks were not completely excluded from sharing in the pleasure. The Lyric, which was a legitimate live theater that guaranteed blacks "courteous treatment," the Bijou, and the Majestic all offered segregated seating. The owners of the Jefferson Theatre allowed blacks to rent space for their own fund-raising productions. The theaters and movie houses appear to have operated successfully with little conflict between the races in the segregated venues, although interclass conflict did occur among African American patrons.[132] The showing of D. W. Griffith's film *The Birth of a Nation* in 1915 prompted protests from blacks across the nation who were familiar with the movie's stereotypical and degrading portrayal of African Americans during Reconstruction. Their protest coincided with a vigorous crusade against the film by the National Association for the Advancement of Colored People (NAACP). Birmingham fell in with the tradition of the antebellum cities when its white citizens enthusiastically praised the movie and the *Birmingham Ledger* acknowledged "Griffith's wonderful genius depicted in great film."[133] By the 1920s, blacks in Birmingham could patronize white-owned theaters that catered specifically to blacks. The Frolic and the Champion theaters were located in the BBD as was the New Queen, which offered vaudeville. African Americans congregated at the theaters and watched such race films as *Steamboat Days* with Bessie Smith in the starring role. The Tuxedo Theatre located in Ensley offered both moving pictures and "refined vaudville [*sic*]." These theaters played a special role for blacks who looked for alternate forms of entertainment where they could relax and escape from the drudgery of daily life.[134]

African Americans complemented their home life when they attended events that held entertainment value. As whites erected centers of recreation that either excluded or discriminated against blacks, African Americans built some of their own. They created parallel facilities that were perhaps lacking in sophistication or amenities but yet served the community's interests and needs. They refused to be held back during a time when recreational facilities for whites were also lacking because of disinterest and the absence of commitment.[135] Birmingham's black community created recreational facilities for themselves with little assistance from the city's coffers. When they pooled their resources, they were empowered to build venues where they could exercise greater control. Rather than subjecting themselves to discriminatory treatment in facilities that catered primarily to whites, black entrepreneurs attempted to provide space where African Americans could be free from prejudicial treatment. Yet, when the classes intersected in public places, conflicts sometimes surfaced. No blacks expressed outrage more than vocal members of the middle class, who sought to separate themselves from those who were not yet "uplifted." Their fear of being associated with the masses forced them to spend much of their leisure time at home, where they could insulate themselves. The home sphere was central to the lives of Smithfield middle-class residents who nurtured ties to their neighborhood through homeownership, extended residency, community participation, and interpersonal relationships. When they did venture beyond the neighborhood, they chose forms of recreation where they could surround themselves with other elite African Americans. Consequently, they spent a considerable amount of time, whether at home or in the broader community, in a carefully crafted environment.

4

Leadership, the Black Elite, and the Business Community

Birmingham's emergence as an industrial center in the late nineteenth century stimulated the influx of a migrant population. Employment opportunities spurred the dynamic growth that altered the racial composition of the city and Jefferson County. As whites sought to maintain the status quo of Anglo-Saxon dominance, local African Americans felt the sting of racism. Birmingham's blacks, like blacks across the nation, were developing strategies to dismantle the inequities and to cope with the environment of prejudice. Individuals with leadership qualities came to the fore and assumed the responsibility of informing and mobilizing their local communities.

African American leaders emerged and adopted a diverse array of strategies to improve conditions. Despite their distinct styles, leaders often shared a goal of racial progress. R. C. O. Benjamin, a native of St. Kitts in the British West Indies, was the firebrand editor of Birmingham's *Negro American*. Having migrated to Birmingham in 1886 from the North as a seasoned newspaperman, Benjamin brazenly editorialized about the need for change: "We want to see the volcanic fires of Southern prejudice and intolerance burst forth with sudden fury. We want the world to know just how matters stand with us of the South. It will cause the floods of indignation at such injustice and barbarity, to rise and swell, after that the deluge."[1] He was forced out of Birmingham when his aggressive manner provoked "the violence of some white roughs."[2]

In contrast to Benjamin's caustic style, William Pettiford's more cautious and deliberate manner enabled him to elicit change gradually without incident. His moderate approach was revealed in an address he delivered to promote the creation of a black-owned bank: "[The Alabama Penny Savings Bank] will develop the spirit of unity and cooperation, it will stimulate individual and corporate enterprise, it will inculcate the habits of economy, industry and thrift, safeguard our property, command respect for our race, and prove an excellent avenue of safe and profitable investment on the part of its stockholders."[3] Pettiford's preeminence as leader of the city's black middle class persisted until his death. Benjamin's leadership, in contrast, was short-lived when his political directives angered hostile whites who threatened him. Each leader's influence extended beyond the communities in which they lived. Although Benjamin's protest style of leadership prevented him from exercising lasting influence, he nonetheless invoked an awareness among at least some African Americans. Pettiford's more accommodating manner, conversely, enabled him to enjoy longevity as an African American leader in the South.[4]

Benjamin and Pettiford's roles as local leaders differed from that of Booker T. Washington's as a national leader. In 1895, Washington's ambiguous speech at the Atlanta Exposition elevated him to the status of a race leader. His emphasis on economic independence and away from social equality won him the support of the dominant elements of the New South. Although he by no means represented all blacks and ultimately alienated an elite faction headed by W. E. B. Du Bois, Washington wielded more influence than any other African American. His accommodationist strategy enabled him to win the support of white philanthropists who financed Tuskegee Institute located one hundred miles southeast of Birmingham. The proximity of Washington's home base to Birmingham had an impact on the development of African American leadership in the city.

Washington recognized that local figures were better equipped to lead their own communities. In an effort to assert modest influence in Birmingham, he engineered close relationships with several Birmingham leaders who implemented his strategies and inspired support for his philosophy of economic independence. Revs. W. R. Pettiford and T. W. Walker were among those who had strong ties to Washington, although they occasionally deviated from his accommodationist approach.[5] Other black business leaders demonstrated their support when they established a local branch of Washington's National Negro Business League and when several merchants and professionals participated in the organization's national meetings. A. G. Gaston was a young man when he attended one of Washington's appearances in Birmingham and was personally inspired by him. Gaston read Washington's autobiography *Up From Slavery* with regularity and adopted Washington's philosophy as his own. Gaston named his firm the Booker T. Washington Insurance Company and successfully engineered a modest business empire in the Magic City.[6] Washington, however, was not beyond reproach. E. A. Brown supported Washington and his National Negro Business League, but he was not reluctant to take issue with him personally when it was warranted. And several leaders publicly challenged Washington when his involvement in Birmingham affairs was resented and rejected.[7]

As Birmingham's black population expanded, individuals established a hierarchy whereby some individuals rose to leadership positions. William Pettiford mastered his role as race leader among middle-class African Americans when he adopted a strategy that gained him credence with members of both black and white communities. He, like Washington, mastered the formidable task of being the link to the white power structure while he maintained the finely tuned balance between the black and white communities. The white power elite accepted his accommodationist philosophy because he tended to work within the existing political system to effect change. Pettiford recognized the value of white support and shared the following account with members of the National Negro Business League: "There are in Birmingham nine banks operated by white persons who have been friendly to our business from the start, and today are better friends than ever before."[8] Pettiford assumed a different posture when he challenged the 1901 constitutional convention with a petition when no blacks were invited to participate. He and other Birmingham ministers formed the Colored Convention to discuss the conditions in which blacks lived and how to improve their future prospects. The convention issued a protest resolution against lynching in the state and issued a complaint against the Alabama Railway Commission for their Jim Crow policy on the railroads. These examples illustrate both Pettiford's influence and involvement beyond local boundaries and also his ability to carry the torch of leadership in both the accommodationist and the protest camps. There is no evidence to suggest that Pettiford was threatened when he issued such challenges.[9]

Others who aspired to leadership positions were not able to establish solid relationships with blacks and whites who held positions of influence. P. Colfax Rameau was one individual who sought recognition but failed to find the balance required to elicit support. Early biographical information about Rameau is scant and unreliable. He was born in Mobile, and according to Rameau himself, he held a Ph.D. (which is doubtful). He arrived in Birmingham some time during the 1910s and developed a carefully crafted persona that is difficult to unravel. Ellen Tarry remembers him as a well-educated, urbane, well-spoken man who was always well dressed with an endless supply of money. "He was accepted in professional circles and attended our churches on occasion even though he bragged about being a non-believer. . . . He was a card."[10] Rameau managed to earn the respect, for a time, of a few influential white businessmen.[11] Although Rameau did have contact with the professional class, he was not a board direc-tor, trustee, or officer in any of the numerous organizations and busi-nesses that blacks established in Birmingham, nor were his public ap-pearances or involvements featured in any of the papers other than the time he spoke at a Colored Community Chest fund-raising event. He, nonetheless, carefully crafted a reputation as a race leader among some whites. Under the auspices of the District-Wide Racial Confer-ence, Welfare Industrial Educational Meetings, and the Negro Indus-trial Fraternal Directory, Rameau appealed to Robert Jemison, Jr., and Donald Comer. Jemison, during correspondence with an associate, referred to Rameau as a "race leader." They contributed modest amounts to support his efforts at racial uplift and improved race rela-tions. However, Rameau clearly was either plagued by an inflated self-perception, or he hoodwinked Jemison and others into supporting his efforts. His letters reveal claims that were probably false: "I do not think that I need any introduction to any of the leaders of this Greater City or State, as practically every leader know [*sic*] me and my polity in teaching my people relative to the South and its industrial economic future." Although Rameau achieved some recognition as a race leader among a few prominent whites, others were less convinced of his self-proclaimed status. He failed to nurture any significant rela-tionships with prominent African American leaders although he re-ceived modest support from some black workers who read his *Work-man's Chronicle*. Whether Rameau wielded any significant influence among Birmingham's blacks is unknown, but there is no evidence to substantiate his claims that he was well positioned among Alabama's race leaders.[12]

Confidential correspondence between Carson Adams, a prominent white attorney, and James L. Davidson, secretary of the Alabama Mining Institute, illustrates that Rameau did not curry favor with other whites. The letter reveals that Adams had had "considerable dealing with a number of leaders among the negroes" in Birmingham during fund-raising campaigns for war, welfare, and civic work. Based on inquiries of some of these individuals, Adams had concluded that Rameau lacked any credibility and was, in fact, out of touch with any blacks of notable repute. Adams also expressed suspicion of U. G. Mason, physician and civic activist, whom he characterized as a disturbing factor among local negroes because he "points out to them the advantage they would enjoy by living North." Furthermore, Adams accused Mason of inciting resentment and unrest among blacks who he believed were entitled to a "high school comparable in all respects to the John Herbert Phillips High School."[13] Adams also accused Mason and other Knights of Pythias officers of fraudulent activities. Although Mason had earned a solid reputation among numerous African Americans, Adams perceived him as a threat. Adams suggested that William (W. B.) Driver, the district manager of the Union Mutual Insurance Company, was "the most dependable one of the local negro leaders." Driver and the company benefited from blacks remaining in the South, and he counseled his policy holders to remain in Birmingham "where the white people are friends." Driver also had the respect of members of the black community. He exhibited a civic consciousness in a variety ways. In response to the absence of downtown public restrooms for black women, Driver offered rooms free of charge where his Union Mutual Insurance Company was located. Yet, Driver, like all leaders, did not have support from all blacks. In 1920, the *Voice of the People* had denounced Driver's leadership skills and his role as chairman of the Republican Club: "This publication has never shared in the opinion that Driver was or is the type of leader in Jefferson County to carry the colored man to success-substantial and permanent success."[14] Although black leaders needed to develop an alliance with whites to be able to effect significant changes for members of their race, they also needed to achieve credibility and forge an alliance among their own.

Ministers were community leaders, particularly those with large congregations. Both Revs. Pettiford and Walker served their respective churches while they began careers as entrepreneurs. Their arrival in Birmingham in the early 1880s marked the beginning of a business community that grew significantly during the early twentieth century. Rev. T. W. Walker exhibited exceptional ambition as an entrepreneur among an emerging corps of businessmen. Walker was born into slavery in Coosa County, Alabama, on September 5, 1852. After Reconstruction, he moved to Montgomery County where he became a Baptist and served as Sunday School Superintendent in 1879. In 1881 Walker moved to Birmingham and joined the Sixteenth Street Baptist Church, where in 1884 he was ordained and licensed by Revs. W. R. Pettiford and J. R. Capers. Walker accepted the pastorate at one of the largest churches in Birmingham—Sixth Avenue Baptist Church—

and established a strong following. As minister there, his appeal drew larger audiences than there was room. His charisma continued to draw large crowds when he left Sixth Avenue Baptist and accepted a post at Shiloh Baptist Church, where audiences filled the sanctuary and crammed the halls to hear his sermons.[15] "He knew how to line up the average Negro and he knew how to speak and preach to the average Negro."[16] Walker, like Pettiford and numerous other pastors in Birmingham, was a strong advocate of thrift, race pride, and racial solidarity. From 1890 to 1896 he was moderator of the Mt. Pilgrim Baptist Association and a founder of Birmingham Baptist College, and for one year he served as moderator of the Jefferson County Association. For a brief period he was also president of the New Era Convention of Alabama.[17]

Walker moved within the religious sphere and beyond it as he developed and pursued entrepreneurial interests. In 1894, he organized the Afro-American Benevolent Association, a company that initiated conventional insurance enterprises in the lower South, particularly in Alabama and Georgia. In 1903, he worked as an undertaker, alongside P. Woolen and C. N. Garland, whose enterprise was located in the BBD; and he owned the Great Colored Dry Goods Store. In 1904, the *Truth* highlighted Walker's acute business sense and declared, "Another test of [Walker's] business ability, is that he is actuarally [*sic*] chewing what few men dare bite off, 'A Colored Drygoods Store', which is being successfully operated under his supervission [*sic*]."[18] And fifteen years later, on the eve of Walker's departure from Birmingham and his migration to the North, the *Voice of the People* paid tribute to his business contributions: "He succeeded in building several business institutions that meant everything in the life of any a Negro boy and Negro girl who are today doing business of some kind. He never ceased not only to talk Negro business enterprise, but to pull for them and to join in with every dollar he could raise, to assist in the effort."[19]

In 1899, Walker attempted to take advantage of the burgeoning industrialization of Birmingham when he founded the Birmingham Grate Coal Mining Company to engage in "the mining of coal, the manufacturing of coke and the quarrying of stone of all kind and descriptions." Pettiford was the company's general manager, and Booker T. Washington held an interest in the company. In 1899, the *Birmingham People's Weekly Tribune*, a local white newspaper, recognized the promise of the company in reviving Helena and the vicinity by offer-

Rev. Thomas W. Walker, c. 1900 (Birmingfind Collection, Catalog
#829.1.1.63, Department of Archives and Manuscripts, Birmingham Public
Library, Ala.)

ing employment to at least one hundred men.[20] But by 1900, Washington made a personal appeal to bail out the financially troubled company. Walker was also involved in the Woodlawn Cemetery Company,
a drug store, a livery stable, a newspaper, and a brick manufacturing firm. In 1909, Walker founded the Afro-American Land, Improvement and Investment Company to develop real estate and participate
in all activities involved with land development and home building.

He moved into civic affairs and was elected to the Board of Trustees of the Alabama Colored Orphans and Old Folks Home. Clearly, Walker attempted to create a well-rounded empire, which served himself and the community in the tradition of W. W. Browne.[21]

Before the twentieth century, other entrepreneurs played key roles in developing a business tradition among African Americans. In 1899, W. E. B. Du Bois detailed the presence of black businesses in several southern cities; Birmingham's total surpassed that of any other urban center in Alabama, most notably the antebellum cities of Montgomery and Mobile.[22] At the 1903 Hampton Negro Conference, Pettiford proudly reported on the progress of black-owned businesses in Birmingham: "We have there a large number of grocery stores, a few drug stores, undertaking establishments, and mutual aid associations doing a tremendous business, and many other business interests, including the bank with which I am connected."[23] Businesses opened to serve the growing African American population.

Pettiford perceived business as one of the essential keys to creating a stable and strong community. His commitment to the self-help philosophy based on economic foundations is highlighted in an address entitled, "The Importance of Business to the Negro" where he stated that "No substantial progress can come to any race unless the race is developed in a very large degree along business lines. . . . The substantial progress of an individual, a race, or a nation is measured by its ability to rise from the position of earning wages to that of profitably directing its own business."[24] At first, growth of black businesses was slow. The *Birmingham Weekly Pilot,* one of the city's earliest race papers, urged the creation of businesses: "Why not organize a stock company and buy up land and build houses thereon, rent and sell them? A brick yard company would be a paying enterprise. The colored men of this city could buy and operate a coal mine."[25] The shortage of black-owned businesses was a recurring theme, and the black press continued to castigate capable entrepreneurs for their apathy. Thirty-four years later, the *Weekly Voice* asked, "Negro business men of Birmingham where are you? Are you cowardly slackers? Why don't you get together, pull yourselves out of the mire and do business with a big B?"[26] And in 1920, the *Voice of the People* went a step further: "The Negro complains of being Jim-Crowed at the theatre, and in the street cars and at the soda fountain, and even at the white banks and what not. But who prevents him from the establishment and operation and maintenance of Negro business enterprises?" The editor admonished black leaders for not accepting responsibility when the "Birmingham white man has more than done his part for the Negro business man."[27]

As African Americans flocked to the city and created an ever-expanding consumer market, businesses continued to open in different parts of the city and surrounding area. Numerous small service-oriented businesses opened around the Terminal Station between Twenty-Fourth and Twenty-Sixth Streets and Fourth and Fifth Avenues. There large numbers of travelers patronized the black-owned businesses of shoe blacks, blacksmiths, and soda-stand operators among others. With the large concentration of blacks in the Southside, numerous businesses opened there. One familiar landmark was the Union Pharmacy that Dr. D. L. Johnston, "The Wizard of the Southside," ran for many years.[28] Others were located downtown, in the city's Central Business District. As the number of black businesses increased, they were forced out of the CBD and relocated in what became the BBD around Fourth Avenue and Eighteenth Street. A unique feature of Birmingham's BBD was that it was not located within a black residential area. Rather its development adjacent to the CBD required African Americans to travel some distance to patronize black businesses. Among the earliest enterprises to settle there were barber and beauty shops, a drug store, restaurants, saloons, undertaking establishments, and the Alabama Penny Savings and Loan Company.

This pattern of relocation as well as the type of black businesses that emerged was repeated throughout the entire South, as African Americans were denied access to prime downtown real estate. Black entrepreneurs created a parallel community that relied solely on the patronage of black residents: segregation provided them with a captive clientele. As the BBD began to attract pedestrian traffic, some men and fewer women tried their hand at retail trade.[29] But they were faced with stiff competition from white retailers. Blacks had significant cumulative buying power, a fact that was acknowledged by astute entrepreneurs. In 1928, when blacks constituted 38 percent of Birmingham's population, they were credited with 12 percent of the purchases, spending over $16,000.00.[30] Seretha Jackson recalled that although African Americans could not work as sales help and could not try on clothes they were interested in purchasing, white retailers encouraged them to shop at their downtown department stores. "Your money was good anywhere."[31]

Black entrepreneurs recognized the benefits of a self-imposed segregated economy, and they worked to stimulate loyalty and solidarity among African Americans. Pettiford articulated this philosophy at a meeting of black business leaders: "The colored wage-earner must be prevailed upon to spend his earnings so that a portion of the same may be retained by his own people."[32] Emphasis on economic segregation in no way undermined Pettiford's commitment to achieving civic equality, which included the right to vote and patronize public facilities. Rather, he recognized that economic advancement was a more realistic and attainable goal because it was within their control, whereas civic equality depended upon white approval. Fifteen years later, J. T. Harrison of the Atlanta Insurance Company repeated Pettiford's urgings when he advised an audience of ministers to teach their congregants the importance of patronizing black-owned businesses.[33] Other editors followed suit. African American entrepreneurs felt the sting of prejudice when black customers supported white businesses. Bob Reed was forced to close his movie theater when black customers failed to support his business. Reed did not fault his white competitors, whom he noted "did all any man could do to assist me in every way they could." Rather, he laid the blame on African American consumers: "I just failed to get the patronage, couldn't meet the bills, had to close up. I have lost more than $2,000 in an effort to give my people a high class amusement business." J. O. Diffay's business relied on black patrons, and he probably feared a similar fate: "Soon Negroes will refuse to patronize their own barber shops, restaurants, shoe shops, doctors, drug stores, bootblacks and all other kinds of business that our people try to conduct. We must stop the old way of knocking each other, talking about what the white folks will do for you and let each other succeed."[34] These businessmen recognized the connection they had to the working class. In articulating this dependency and the value of a self-segregated economy, black entrepreneurs hoped to engender an economic nationalism among African Americans. Strict segregation ordinances and the passage of *Plessy vs. Ferguson* created a symbiotic relationship between Birmingham's black population and the black business community.

As the area was evolving into a viable BBD, the black-owned buildings were the physical anchors. The Alabama Penny Savings Bank building, the Pythian Temple building, and the (U. G.) Mason building all carried both emotional and practical significance. These structures were multifunctional. Not only did they provide blacks with symbols of their achievements and abilities, but the structures also became offices to numerous businesses and provided meeting space. The three-story brick Mason building housed the Prudential Bank and

People's Drug Store and provided office space for William B. Driver, district manager of the Union Mutual Aid Association. Space in the building was also rented to local newspapers, including the *Baptist Leader,* the *Reporter, Sparks,* and the *Free Speech,* and the building had a meeting hall for professional and private affairs. It became a social center when few other facilities beyond the church were available to African Americans. It served as a social center for the local Colored Soldiers' Organization at "the War Camp Community Club Rooms" during an event that included speeches and entertainment offered by the Tabernacle Baptist Church Quartette and other local talent.[35] In 1914, when the Alabama Penny Savings Bank building relocated to the corner of Eighteenth Street and Fourth Avenue, it further "stabilize[d] black businesses in this section of the CBD," which had become the BBD.[36] Space in the bank building was also rented for meetings of local organizations, including the Colored Citizens League, and to many black businesses and professionals whose practices were located on the upper floors. The *Messenger* and the *Voice of the People* had offices there, as did W. A. Rayfield & Company, Windham Brothers Construction Company, and E. A. Brown. In 1924, the black Masons erected the seven-story Masonic Temple building at the corner of Fourth Avenue and Seventeenth Street, to where many black professionals relocated their offices.[37] Flanking the bank buildings were Goodgame's Cafe and the Dixieland Cafe, "The Colored People's Best and Most Up-to-Date Cafe"; Mabry Bros. Tailors and Gents' Furnishers; and Diffay's Barber Shop and Bath House. Nearby were poolhalls and saloons that catered to African Americans. Although some of the businesses were short-lived, they were quickly replaced with new ventures that kept the BBD a vital and vibrant commercial area that drew black residents from all corners of the Birmingham District. The business initiative that Birmingham's African American entrepreneurs exhibited earned praise from Montgomery, a city that had its own black business tradition. The *Colored Alabamian* was moved to declare that "when it comes to 'Business Push' and co-operation in business . . . Birmingham stands in the lead of all the others."[38]

Insurance companies and banks acted as anchor institutions that linked together the black business community. Neither one operated in a vacuum; their success depended on a cooperative relationship.[39] One of the most prominent leaders in insurance, C. C. Spaulding of North Carolina Mutual Insurance, recognized the interdependent link between banks and insurance companies and the necessary role they played in the community: "Negro insurance companies and Negro banks represent the outstanding achievements of Negroes in this country in the field of finance. Disrupt them and you strike Negro effort in the field of economics a staggering blow, the reaction from which will be felt in every phase of Negro life."[40] African Americans could not organize a bank without a source of income beyond the small deposits of their wage-earning customers. The early financial institutions were often created to serve as depositories for black fraternal insurance orders, which offered a healthy deposit to the bank's coffers and secured the bank's financial position. Once having achieved that, black banks loaned money to the orders and to individuals and generated activity within the African American community.[41] The anchor institutions were the foundations of the cyclical phenomenon of black capital.

The BBD was not only a business center but like its white counterpart it also provided numerous auxiliary functions for African Americans. It operated as a social, cultural and economic center, much like the CBD for white patrons. Even when African Americans didn't have money to buy goods from black businesses or when they chose not to patronize race-owned stores, people gravitated to the BBD where they congregated with others who shared their culture. There the streets took on a life of their own as African Americans crowded the sidewalks. And it was there that throngs of people crowded the district to catch a glimpse of African Americans expressing their freedom as parades passed through the BBD.[42] Ellen Tarry remembered the parades fondly: "I always loved a parade—especially if the parade was part of a civic or patriotic celebration."[43] In 1920, black organizers staged a "mammoth parade" marking the beginning of the State Fair. The procession commenced at Fourteenth Street and Fourth Avenue and proceeded east along Fourth Avenue to Eighteenth Street down to First Avenue, east to Nineteenth Street north to Third Avenue, and on to the fairgrounds. In traveling through the streets of the city and through the heart of the BBD, the marchers helped to define a sense of community, to foster unity, and to draw together dispersed members of the black community to enjoy the camaraderie of a cultural event.[44] Public displays such as these allowed African Americans to assemble in a common space that they identified as their own, and it provided many spectators with pride and dignity.

Casual social interaction often occurred in the BBD where a vibrant street life and engaging environment prevailed. The local pharmacy offers an illustration of one of several companies that played dual roles; it operated as more than a dispensary for prescriptions and medications. As W. E. B. Du Bois noted in his survey of black businesses in the South, "[D]rugstores are especially popular in the South for the social feature of the soda fountain and for their business partnership with sick-benefit societies."[45] I. B. Kigh's People's Drug Store offered not only medical-related services but also acted as a social venue for those visiting the BBD. The rear of the store was fashioned with a long mahogany bar and stools where patrons could purchase refreshments. Kigh, like many other small business owners, extended credit to customers who were unable to pay their bills. As community institutions, the businesses played as important a role, though a different one, than the church and other social organizations. Although the businesses did not create large fortunes or employ large numbers of African Americans, the black businesses served an important community function just by being there. They represented what blacks could and did achieve, they offered inspiration and pride for members of the black community, and they offered public space where African Americans could congregate.[46]

William Pettiford's pivotal contribution to the creation of the BBD and his role as a race leader for middle-class blacks requires closer examination. He was a pioneer in Birmingham, who most likely fashioned himself after William Washington Browne. Although Browne's most significant impact was in Richmond, Virginia, he had first established a reputation for himself in Alabama.[47] William Reuben Pettiford had been exposed to W. W. Browne and his empire-building activities when Pettiford arrived in Marion, Alabama, from Roxbury, North Carolina, in search for employment in railway construction. Pettiford had taken a somewhat circuitous route from his birthplace in Granville County, North Carolina. During those years he had engaged in a self-study program and had worked as a pastor. Once in Alabama, Pettiford held a variety of positions, including a teaching job at Selma University, a black Baptist institution. There, he engaged in missionary work and fund-raising. His visibility in the Colored Baptist State Convention and his success as a financial agent at Selma University propelled him into a leadership position at Birmingham's Sixteenth Street Baptist Church in 1883.[48] Alabama's black leaders had urged him to accept the post because they felt he could provide the necessary guidance to the city's rapidly growing black population.

At the time of Pettiford's arrival, blacks were scattered residentially throughout the city, were employed in diverse occupations but primarily in the heavy industries, and were affiliated with various religious institutions. The Sixteenth Street Baptist Church (then known as the First Baptist Church) in the early 1880s had 150 congregants who convened in a downtown storeroom. The church was known as the "people's church" and served as the meeting place for many community functions. Pettiford capably eliminated the church's $500 debt in less than one year and stimulated the growth of his congregation with his strong leadership skills. In 1887 he was elected president of the Colored Baptist State Convention of Alabama at its 20th session and remained in that position through 1901. Locally he was also achieving prominence. He founded the city's first missionary society at the Sixteenth Street Baptist Church and by 1887 was operating four missions. He served as president of the Ministerial Association in Birmingham, and as his influence spread, his congregation swelled to 425 members by 1887. Pettiford, however, had interests that extended beyond his assigned responsibilities as a pastor, although he had proved himself a progressive and accomplished clergyman.[49] He demonstrated his business acumen when he accumulated proceeds from the church's building fund and erected a new church. The value of the property increased exponentially, in concert with the surge in property values in Birmingham overall. In 1908, Wallace A. Rayfield designed, and Thomas C. Windham began to build, a grander edifice for the Sixteenth Street Baptist Church. The building was completed in 1911, and it stood as testament to the abilities and achievements of Birmingham's blacks.[50]

Pettiford laid the groundwork for community building at the church. In the late 1880s, Pettiford founded the Representative Council as an umbrella organization to coordinate separate but related functions that served Birmingham's African Americans. The Council was composed of three major departments—missionary, educational, and business—that addressed a broad range of needs and offered an array of services. Delegates from Sunday schools, social clubs, conventions, societies and lodges, and business organizations promoted and taught the self-help philosophy. About the same time as Pettiford founded the Representative Council, he and R. C. O. Benjamin, among others, founded the Robert Brown Elliott School of Technology. Although the plan failed to materialize and the dream of such a specialized school for blacks was not realized, it is noteworthy that Pettiford and Benjamin worked cooperatively toward a common goal. Their divergent strategies did not overshadow their ultimate goal—racial progress.[51] In 1903, Pettiford organized a committee with other prominent blacks and whites from Birmingham and influential blacks

Rev. William R. Pettiford, c. 1900 (Birmingfind Collection, Catalog #829.1.1.61, Department of Archives and Manuscripts, Birmingham Public Library, Ala.)

from elsewhere in Alabama when he was seeking state funding for a reformatory for African American boys. His efforts failed to win sufficient support for the facility.[52] Frustration did not lead to inaction. Rather, the corps continued their pursuit for a reformatory. Early in the decade, a Juvenile Court Association was organized, composed of one woman from each of thirty black churches, to take charge of black delinquents. In 1907, the women raised enough money to buy land near Montgomery where they erected a building and started a school that became Mt. Meigs Reformatory.[53]

William Pettiford received more attention than any other black entrepreneur in Birmingham. Under Pettiford's direction, the Alabama Penny Savings and Loan Company (from this point forward to be called Alabama Penny Savings Bank) realized early success and earned the trust of African Americans who were initially reluctant to support it.[54] Pettiford and his colleagues worked relentlessly to promote economic independence, and the campaign served the bank well as interest was aroused both within Birmingham and beyond.

Pettiford's initiative to create a black bank in 1890 occurred when few cities could boast such an institution. The primary stimulus to founding the bank may have come from African Americans themselves, who Pettiford saw frittering away what little money they had. He recalled how he was struck with the idea while riding an electric railway through a Birmingham suburb where many blacks worked: "There were a number of these people on the car who had just been paid their weekly wage. I had not gone far when I was shocked by seeing a woman among the crowd on the car drinking whiskey. . . . [T]he thought came to me that there should be some sort of business which would take care of the money of that class of people." He assumed the responsibility of educating a different class of people on the importance of thrift.[55] One other integral factor created a sense of urgency in founding a black bank. That came in the person of Rev. William Washington Browne. Browne's familiarity with Alabama and Birmingham during his tenure in the state revealed a promising environment in which to establish a bank. When he moved to open a branch of the True Reformers Bank in Birmingham, the local black business elite established one of their own.[56]

These men had a strong commitment to the success of the bank. At the 1906 National Negro Business League's (NNBL) meeting, Pettiford reported that "A number of our men, stockholders, as well as those on the Board of Directors, were so determined to push their business to a successful issue, that they were ready to stand by the bank with everything they had, including the raising of money on their homes and private property, had it been necessary." The Alabama Penny Savings Bank was created in 1890, when a capital stock of $25,000 in shares was issued at $25 apiece and a building was leased for $30 per month.[57] As individuals purchased company shares, the bank accrued additional resources: Burton H. Hudson, Sr., whom the *Truth* declared was "known by every leading citizen of Birmingham, white or colored," was the largest shareholder with well over 300 shares. Pettiford and T. W. Walker held 130 and 17 shares respectively. Others involved in the bank's founding were Peter F. Clarke, the bank's first vice-president, N. B. Smith, A. H. Parker, Joseph O. Diffay, and J. C. Barker, all of whom lived in Smithfield and had collateral business interests in Birmingham.[58] Through their business affiliations and their presence on unrelated committees that had nothing to do with the bank, they exerted considerable influence within their community. Without exception, these men were interested in the broader community, and their involvement in the bank elevated their status and influence.[59]

Birmingham as a postbellum city was in its infancy. Its migrant population was beginning to sort itself out. Pettiford's arrival in the city was at a propitious time, when the black community was still relatively small and an elite unit of African Americans was beginning to take shape. The fact that there was not a black aristocracy in place as in antebellum southern cities, allowed individuals with unique skills and ambition to create a leadership class. Pettiford's ministerial position secured him a leadership role among more prominent community members who were vying for a position in the emerging elite class of African Americans. When he sought support in the creation of a bank, these were the people he called on—aggressive men who were ambitious, hardworking, articulate, and who were interested in the collective welfare of African Americans.[60] Pettiford's leadership enabled the bank to succeed in spite of internal dissension among the directors. Pettiford recalled a time "when the stockholders' meeting was not held in absolute harmony and union . . . when we found it difficult to get all to decide upon various points or methods of conducting the business." Yet, they overcame their differences and developed unity among "a strong and forceful set of businessmen in whom the stockholders have complete confidence."[61]

The Penny Savings Bank opened its doors on October 15, 1890, after a brief financial setback.[62] The first day's deposits amounted to $55, and on the second day, Pettiford, as president, made the first loan—$20 for thirty days at 50 cents interest. Business grew briskly as blacks and even a few whites gained confidence in the enterprise. The Alabama Penny Savings Bank's reputation earned additional respect when it weathered the 1893 Panic, an economic crisis that caused the failure of several white banks. In 1895, by a special act, the Alabama state legislature incorporated the bank with a capital stock of $25,000 and the privilege of increasing it to $100,000.[63]

During the bank's first decade, Pettiford engineered numerous lucrative real estate transactions. In 1896, bank officials bought a $6,500 building, and as Birmingham's real estate values soared, sold the building for $20,000 one year later. In 1905, a Birmingham fire destroyed the bank and other buildings located nearby. The loss was estimated at $25,000, which was partially covered by insurance. In 1913, the bank built its own home on the edge of the BBD. The bank

Interior of the Alabama Penny Savings Bank, c. 1900. Peter F. Clarke is third from the left. (Birmingfind Collection, Catalog #829.1.1.21, Department of Archives and Manuscripts, Birmingham Public Library, Ala.)

building, which was designed and built by W. A. Rayfield and T. C. Windham, became another symbol of black pride and sophistication for Birmingham's African American community. This building was testament to Pettiford's deep commitment to the philosophy of self-help: built by blacks and built for blacks. It also stood as a commitment to a self-segregated economy, where blacks engineered the creation of an economic force whose success depended on the integrity of its officers and a pledge of loyalty from the masses.[64]

The Alabama Penny Savings Bank set a fine example for other businessmen to establish similar organizations in Birmingham and elsewhere. In the early 1900s, several local businessmen joined forces and founded a number of financial institutions including two other banks. The Peoples Investment and Banking Company opened its doors in 1906, with Rev. William L. Lauderdale acting as president, and in 1911, the Prudential Savings Bank commenced business, with U. G. Mason, a physician, as president.[65] The Penny Savings Bank achieved greater success than the other two, and its longevity is testament to the respect and trust it earned from black depositors and a few whites.[66] On July 15, 1902, the deposits were $78,124.21; on July 15, 1903, the deposits totaled $100,948.96; and by July 15, 1907, they amounted to $215,455.26. In 1909 the bank claimed $75,000 worth of real estate holdings on which was earned "a nice rental." The bank paid 4 percent interest on savings accounts and offered shares in the bank for $5 each; by 1913 it had resources totaling $540,955.63.[67]

Pettiford was frequently on hand to boast of his success in changing the ways of lower- and working-class blacks. He told of how he reformed the behavior of a washerwoman's husband who had frittered away their money. Pettiford's lessons in thrift moved the husband to save enough money to buy "a home on the instalment [sic] plan."[68] Pettiford's account not only illustrated his pride in teaching the value of thrift but also his belief that black culture, not racism, was responsible for the lack of capital. He, like other middle-class blacks, blamed lower-class blacks themselves for their situation; he did not accept that blacks were inferior to whites. Pettiford was teaching middle-class values for the benefit of the entire community: "[Our bank is] reaching out and touching a class of people that has not been . ... reached by other banks, of changing the wasteful expenditure of their money ... to use it profitable for themselves and the good of the community."[69] He revealed his disdain for the masses and further underlined the class differences within the city's black community when, in 1910, he proudly declared that "Over and beyond the howling mob and the criminal element of our own race, we are making great and substantial progress, and this fact should engender new faith and hope in our future."[70]

The bank under Pettiford's direction promoted homeownership through carefully engineered real estate transactions. The Board of Directors agreed to spend half of the money invested in the company to purchase real estate in large quantities, which they then subdivided and sold in small packages to encourage homeownership and to produce additional profit. Strategies to engage blacks and some whites in the acquisition of property and homes sparked a flurry of activity as revealed in deed and mortgage records.[71] Pettiford used prudence in conducting business among African Americans, since he recognized that they did not have the earning power or a credit rating that could secure them a mortgage with most other banks in the city. To remedy this problem, the bank offered unconventional conditions on loans — very small down payments and small monthly payments with interest between 6 and 8 percent due over long periods of time. Although the strategy was somewhat risky, Pettiford was engaging in self-help at a profit. He was committed to improving the standard of living among blacks and enhancing their social conditions and self-esteem. A. G. Gaston recalled how in the early 1910s, the Alabama Penny Savings

Bank helped him: "After I had discussed my plans for buying a home with Mr. B. H. Hudson, the cashier, he sold me a lot for $200 and arranged for me to make payments on it through the bank. Each time I sent in a deposit, I made out a check payable to Mr. Hudson for my property."[72] Pettiford's homeownership program achieved rapid success.

Pettiford's involvement in creating a black-owned bank extended beyond the boundaries of Birmingham; he was instrumental in initiating a more far-reaching banking system. He opened branches located in Selma, Anniston, and Montgomery. The Selma and Anniston branches opened in 1909 and cost an outlay of $18,000. Selma's first day of deposits amounted to $2,012.45. And the Montgomery branch opened in 1910.[73] When the Alabama state legislature impeded any further extension of branches, Pettiford's dream of a nationwide banking system was quelled. Nonetheless, his success at building financial institutions had an impact beyond state borders. As the *Reformer* reported in 1908, Pettiford "started the ball to rolling" in Atlanta for the organization of the first Negro bank in the state.[74]

Pettiford rose to prominence in the NNBL and frequently spoke at their annual meetings. From there, his influence radiated across the country and reinforced his status in Birmingham.[75] He had nurtured a close relationship with Washington prior to the founding of the NNBL. As Alabamians their paths had crossed prior to Washington's rise to national prominence. In 1894, Washington recommended Pettiford's appointment as an Assistant Commissioner for the Atlanta Exposition in 1895. And, in 1901, Washington recommended Pettiford for the position of U.S. Revenue Collector from Alabama.[76] The bond was strengthened when Pettiford assumed leadership roles in the early NNBL meetings, where local Birmingham businessmen joined him to participate in the annual proceedings. T. W. Walker spoke at an early meeting, and in 1905, Pettiford, U. G. Mason, and J. O. Diffay represented Birmingham business when the NNBL held its meeting in New York City.[77] They returned home prepared to organize local NNBL branches and to share their experience with others.[78] The *Truth* noted their presence at the event and declared that "A sense of pride awakens the appreciation of the citizens of Birmingham in having such an able representation of Negro thrift."[79] Pettiford further expanded his role as a business leader when he helped to found the National Negro Bankers' Association, "to foster and encourage the establishment of banks among our people and to look after the interests and welfare of those already organized." It operated as an umbrella organization that promoted the creation of black-owned banks as "the means of gathering up the millions that are now wasted by our people as well as to teach the act of savings."[80] Pettiford also was director of the National Economic League, was president of the Negro American Publishing Company, which published the *Negro American Journal,* and had interests in other diverse business ventures.

By the time of Pettiford's death in 1914, the Alabama Penny Savings Bank was the largest and strongest black-owned bank in the United States, with a capitalization of $100,000 and an annual business exceeding $500,000. Glowing tributes appeared in both white and black papers when Pettiford died on September 21, 1914. The *Birmingham News* declared that Pettiford was "pre-eminent among his people. . . . He was quiet and unspoiled by his success in the business world and was cordially esteemed by his white acquaintances. Would that Birmingham had a hundred Pettifords."[81] The *Nashville Globe* honored Pettiford when it ran the following obituary that was carried in a Birmingham paper: "White and black united today in paying tribute to the memory of Dr. W. R. Pettiford, noted preacher, sociologist and financier . . . more than 3,000 people crowd[ed] into the spacious church he once pastored." It continued: "Telegrams poured in from all portions of the country from leading men in all walks of life including Booker T. Washington. . . . Representatives of the Birmingham Negro Business League, the Civic and Educational League, the white banks, and the interdenominational ministers' alliance took part on the program, and all the Negro business houses closed their doors two hours during the funeral."[82]

Although the bank's financial status may have been weak prior to Pettiford's death, publicly it gave the appearance of strength. The officers attempted to enhance its financial position when they merged the Alabama Penny Savings Bank with the Prudential Savings Bank. Upon learning of the merger, Booker T. Washington wired a message to U. G. Mason, president of the Prudential Bank: "Am very much pleased to learn of the amalgamation of the Alabama Penny and the Prudential Savings banks. The consolidation of these two splendid institutions will strengthen the resources of our people in the State of Alabama and will in every way increase the progress of our people along business lines and in other fundamental directions."[83] The Penny-Prudential sought to attract new business with advertisements that promised 4 percent interest on all savings accounts. It also reached out to the community when in 1915 the bank initiated a school savings department whereby students were encouraged to learn the value of thrift. The manager of the program remarked that he had "never seen children more enthusiastic over any thing. . . . [C]hildren of all ages . . . considered it an honor to be a depositor in the Alabama Penny–Prudential Savings Bank."[84]

The facade of "business as usual" hid any signs of fiscal problems. Nevertheless, the die had been cast, and the Penny-Prudential closed its doors on December 23, 1915. The branches were given no warning and their officers were as surprised as were the depositors. George E. Newstell, president of the Montgomery branch, declared that "he had no intimation that the affairs of the parent bank at Birmingham were in bad straits. As far as our branch was concerned we were in good financial circumstances, there being enough available assets to cover the deposits."[85] Acting president J. O. Diffay issued a statement that the bank's closing would create regret not among blacks but among whites who also took pride in the bank as an example of "negro achievement."[86] Just weeks later, Diffay tried to lay to rest the rumors that had led to a run on the bank. The African Methodist Episcopal Zion Church, one of the bank's very good accounts, had, like the small depositors, withdrawn its money. The loss of the Church's $15,000 pushed the bank over the brink.[87] By 1916, in an effort to encourage the bank's reorganization, Diffay addressed a meeting of shareholders and offered additional reasons for the bank's closure: "The branch banks, which seemed to be a very good investment during times of prosperity, during the panic and depression proved to be a very disastrous burden. . . . [C]ustomers who were poor and many of them out of employment, many times could not pay their interest much less the principal." Diffay, nonetheless, tried to offer hope and optimism: "Let us be willing to sacrifice as a people and as a race and let us leave here tonight with a grim determination that we will come back, come what will or may."[88]

It is difficult to unravel the mystery surrounding the closure of the Alabama Penny Savings Bank.[89] The unavailability of official bank records makes it impossible to state definitively what happened. A variety of sources have offered their interpretation of the turn of events: When B. H. Hudson's son, who was employed as a teller, fell short in his accounts and a run on the bank started, it could not be halted. A former official offered a different explanation: when the Alabama Penny Savings Bank ran into financial difficulties, the Steiner Brothers Bank, which was the financial agent for both the Alabama Penny Savings Bank and William Berney's First National Bank, opted to bail out only the white-owned First National Bank, which also was in the midst of a crisis.[90] Without help from the Steiner Brothers Bank, the Alabama Penny Savings Bank was forced to liquidate and sell its $150,000 building to the Knights of Pythias for $70,000. N. B. Young, Sr., an officer with the Alabama Penny Savings Bank, claimed that the officer froze the bank's assets primarily because of the long-time loans to churches, the merger with the financially unsound Prudential Savings Bank, the too rapid expansion of branches (which were probably poorly managed), and the death of William Pettiford. Although these explanations may hold some truth, the last variable was the crucial one. William Pettiford was much more than "Birmingham's Napoleon of Finance." He had nurtured a unique relationship with the white power structure, and his successors may not have been able to maintain such a finely tuned connection that took years to develop. As early as 1894, Pettiford had been meeting with local white leaders to change public sentiment toward blacks. He stated in a letter to Booker T. Washington that he was "trying to get civil and political rights for blacks."[91] Pettiford had established a cooperative relationship with many influential whites who assisted him in gaining benefits for blacks. Whatever the reasons for the bank's demise, one can conclude after examining the available data that nothing untoward took place. As the *Crisis* reported in February, 1916, "The Alabama Penny Prudential [*sic*] Savings Bank, at Birmingham, the safest and soundest colored bank in the United States, is closed. . . . There is no hint of dishonesty and the bank may resume." It never did.[92]

No bankruptcy records exist. Although the officers and directors asserted confidently that "the depositors will ultimately be paid in full," there is no evidence to support or refute this statement other than to declare that in all likelihood the small depositors lost their life savings. Some oral histories offer insight into the pain suffered by depositors. Ellen Tarry recalled that her father deposited money in the Alabama Penny Savings Bank. Mr. Green, one of his associates, tried to dissuade Tarry from depositing money there, and her mother "knew there was going to be a run on the bank. . . . It was the most tragic thing. There were all the old people out there crying. They wanted their money." It was, indeed, a tragic event because Pettiford had worked hard to earn the trust of Birmingham's African Americans, and once he achieved that goal, many families improved their lifestyles through applying Booker T. Washington's philosophy. Some fared better. A. G. Gaston recognized his good fortune for having invested his money in property instead of depositing his savings in the Penny Savings Bank: "[M]any people in the Birmingham area lost their entire life savings. I only lost $15.00, the last payment on my lot."[93] Shortly after the doors closed, the Steiner Brothers Bank and other local banks assumed the mortgages that were held by the Alabama Penny Savings Bank. Most small wage earners lost their savings and consequently lost their confidence in black banks. Women and children were among the disappointed who had joined the Christmas clubs, the funds of which were to have been paid out one day before and on the day of the bank's closing. In 1926, after years of legal wrangling, A. E. Jackson, superintendent of banks, acting by and through his liquidating agents, Al C. Garber and Peter F. Clarke, reached a settlement. They paid depositors, who had not stipulated for interest, and other creditors entitled to a dividend, $2^3/_4$ percent in the Alabama Penny Savings Bank liquidation. The dividend was paid at Mabry Brothers Dry Goods Store in the BBD.[94]

Some evidence suggests that a group of entrepreneurs rallied to fill the gap left by the Penny Savings Bank. In 1916 Dr. M. H. Freeman Jr. and N. B. Smith, among others, entertained the idea of establishing a new bank. According to a report by the *Birmingham Ledger,* the "Bank will be located near Fourth Avenue and Eighteenth Street. More than 200 have agreed to take stock, among them some of the wealthiest negroes of the city and county."[95] It is doubtful whether this venture went beyond this early stage. In 1920 and well into the following year, another attempt was made to start a bank. The *Reporter* shared its enthusiasm and optimism with its readers when it pronounced: "Let us have a bank. Let us have it quick. Every church congregation where the subject has been presented as well as fraternal orders in their regular meeting voted unanimously to have it. The people want a bank. Let the men who can whip the plans together, and let us have a Bank."[96] The *Voice of the People* expressed its confidence in local African Americans when it declared that "The Negro bank will not make Negroes great, but the great Birmingham Negro must make a great Negro Bank."[97] Despite the promise of a newly organized bank, the officers were unable to actualize their ideas. In 1927, T. C. Windham and others founded the Acme Finance Corporation. It was intended to serve as a financial institution that would circulate money from the black community through "channels to aid and strengthen struggling Negro enterprises." Despite the company's initial phenomenal growth, Windham's company did not have much time before the Great Depression struck and devastated even the most solid businesses.[98]

As African Americans struggled to reorganize another financial institution, some white-owned banks took the initiative to entice black depositors. The Traders National Bank actively pursued new depositors: "This bank endeavors to give prompt and courteous attention to the business of colored patrons." It had a history of conducting a Christmas Savings Department "exclusively for colored people," and the officers attempted to build on its history of positive race relations. When blacks had no other choice but to deposit their savings with white-owned banks, they also patronized the Bank of Ensley and its branch, the Bank of Wylam. But these banks, too, succumbed to the depression, and in 1930 they both closed their doors. Not until 1957, when A. G. Gaston started his Citizens Federal Savings and Loan Association did the city's African Americans have a black bank in which they could place their savings.[99]

Black banks were not the only institutions that spurred the growth of black business. Insurance companies also played a pivotal role in the creation and perpetuation of Birmingham's BBD.[100] African Americans patronized black insurers because they preferred to conduct business with members of their own race and because they were required to pay lower premiums than the white insurers charged them. Also, the large northern insurance companies limited the amount of insurance that their southern agents were permitted to sell to blacks.[101] When blacks established their own fraternal insurance and benevolent associations, they appealed to the small wage earners who were looking for burial services and sick and death benefits. As notable and respected businessmen entered the field, insurance companies gained respect.[102]

In Birmingham, T. W. Walker organized the Afro-American Benevolent Association in 1894. After he observed the injustices directed at blacks by the Southern Mutual Aid Association, which was the only company of its kind doing health and accident business in Alabama, he founded a company that offered blacks a viable alternative. Almost from its inception, Walker ran the benevolent association as an industrial insurance company. It changed its name to the Union Central Relief Association, and in 1901, the legislature of Alabama granted it a special charter under the name of the Union Central Relief Association. Premiums ranged from 5 cents per week with a $10 death benefit and a $1 per week sick benefit to a premium of 40 cents per week with an $80 death benefit and an $8 per week sick benefit. By 1916, the Union Central Relief Association had twelve thousand members.[103] In 1898, Walker's company established offices across Alabama, and it opened a branch in Atlanta in the same year under the name Union Mutual Association to circumvent charter restrictions. It was the first black-owned health and accident insurance company operating in Georgia at this time. Despite efforts at presenting a solid image through advertisements in local and state newspapers, Walker's company was experiencing internal troubles. In 1915, the venerable Atlanta Life Insurance Company took over its assets and reinsured its policy holders. This move increased the prestige of Atlanta Life, and it secured the status of policies held by Birmingham residents. Atlanta Life saw the value of conducting business in Birmingham and kept abreast of local business activities through local agents.[104]

Several African American entrepreneurs with other business interests moved into the lucrative insurance industry. B. L. Windham and John Common, among others, founded the Booker T. Washington Life Insurance Company, which received its charter in 1921. The *Birmingham Times Plaindealer* proudly reported that the new company was a credit to all blacks for the services it offered and for the employment opportunities it created for "talented young men and women of the race." Furthermore, it congratulated "the caliber of men who have cast their lot with influence and money to make the company a success."[105] Four months later, the paper reported that the company's growth was proceeding well and would reach its $1,000,000 goal by the year's end, with new policies that were secured in Birmingham and in other parts of the state. In 1925, with B. L. Windham serving as president, the Booker T. Washington Life Insurance Company purchased two local white-owned insurance companies: a mutual benefit organization and the First National Mutual Aid Insurance Company, which was owned and controlled by whites but operated to insure the lives of African Americans. It was securing a foothold in the local market and gaining a reputation beyond the city limits.[106]

In 1930, the Booker T. Washington Life Insurance Company merged with Atlanta Life Insurance Company—the same company that had consolidated with Walker's Union Mutual fifteen years earlier. Although it was an aggressive profit-seeking company it was also community oriented. Atlanta Life was one of the oldest and strongest institutions owned and controlled by African Americans. It had earned a solid reputation under the guiding hand of Alonzo Herndon, who had engineered its aggressive program of growth through acquisitions and mergers. Although Herndon's death in 1927 preceded the merger, his strategies were adopted by his successors. Atlanta Life quelled the threat of the Birmingham-based company when the companies agreed to consolidate their businesses. In 1930, the merger was finalized and the Booker T. Washington Life Insurance Company was the fifteenth company to join the Atlanta Life family. Although the merger could have damaged the morale of local policy holders, leaders urged them to support the decision. Oscar Adams reasoned that consolidation was a positive move toward building a stronger business community: "It is imperative that such combines be made in order to give strength and safety to business projects that find it hard to compete with the opposition in their fields."[107]

Other out-of-state insurance companies also opened branch offices in Birmingham. The Durham-based North Carolina Mutual Life Insurance Company aggressively pursued new accounts and employed creative strategies to generate more businesses there. In 1930, in a business dominated by men, the North Carolina Mutual organized a contest in which only women could participate. The company conducted a school for several weeks prior to the campaign where participants were instructed on the principles and practices of insurance. Women enthusiastically grasped the significance of the opportunity, and their performance exhibited their abilities. "Under the influence of the drive, the district produced more than $114,000 in industrial business." Although they were not hired on as permanent employees, the company awarded the top two winners cars, while others received cash prizes. North Carolina Mutual's ninety-day campaign not only benefited the company but also demonstrated that women were valuable resources in the business community.[108] Mississippi Beneficial Life Insurance Company also opened offices in Birmingham. In 1919, Joseph E. Walker, a "leading business talent of the race," and Minnie Cox, the former postmaster of Indianola, saw the potential for growth in the Magic City. There was a considerable amount of excitement about the arrival of a new insurance company with a paid-up capital stock of $100,000 and more than $4,000,000 in business. Despite its promise, it failed to remain in Birmingham when white-owned Southern Life of Nashville purchased the troubled company in 1924. Mississippi Life, the oldest black-owned legal reserve firm in America, had suddenly passed into white hands. A furor erupted in Memphis (Mississippi Life's headquarters) and throughout black America. the *Reporter* declared that the transaction closely resembled a "race funeral" and proceeded to lash out against the dishonest officers within black organizations including Birmingham's "three failed banks, a number of insurance companies and fraternal orders."[109] Mississippi Life's twenty-five Birmingham employees risked unemployment and "turned in their books[,] and the clerks and janitor of the building turned in their resignations also and walked out." Van L. Burnett, the manager who was largely responsible for the rapid growth of the company in the Birmingham District, called the white buy out "a race outrage and a scandal." The Mississippi Life employees' collective boycott of the company illustrates their racial solidarity, their commitment to race institutions, and their pride. It was difficult for African American white-collar workers to secure suitable employment in Birmingham, as in other southern cities; they primarily relied on black-owned businesses for positions. Yet, the insurance agents and other employees at Mississippi Life's branch office in Birmingham and elsewhere would not betray their heritage.[110]

Although not part of the above-stated evolutionary process, black undertakers were often involved in the insurance business: they ensured a proper burial and performed the burial service. A brief profile of Charles M. Harris, Sr., offers an illustration of the evolution of a burial company into a fully licensed insurance company. Harris was born in Mobile in 1871 and was raised in Montgomery. In 1899, he and his family moved to Birmingham, where he founded Charles Morgan Harris Undertaking Company, the first of its kind to serve blacks in the city. Harris and his sister, Hattie Davenport, shared ownership in the business when in 1904 Hattie bought a half interest in the company. Harris purchased his first caskets with a loan from the Alabama Penny Savings Bank. With Birmingham's mass migration of African Americans seeking employment and the reluctance of some white burial companies to handle black corpses, Harris built a successful business. Following the success of this venture, "Boss" Harris (as he was affectionately known) started the Protective Burial Association, which evolved into the Protective Industrial Life Insurance Company. The small monthly fees paid to the company ensured a family a respectable burial for themselves and their loved ones.[111] Numerous African American entrepreneurs entered the field. By 1927, there were approximately three thousand black funeral directors in the U.S., and the *Colored Embalmer,* a trade journal, was published by an African American. Although there were several black undertaking firms in Birmingham, including the E. A. Bradford Undertaking Company, Smith and Gaston Funeral Services, and C. M. Harris' business, in 1930 white-owned companies were "burying more colored people in the Birmingham district than are buried by colored funeral directors. . . . One of these [white] societies took in more than all the colored burial societies."[112] To prevent the eventual takeover of the black undertaking businesses, the Alabama Funeral Directors Association met in Birmingham to discuss strategies.[113] Although most companies eventually closed, the venerable Davenport and Harris Funeral Home adopted effective management techniques that enabled it to serve the black community throughout the 1900s.

Birmingham had several African American newspapers that also served as anchor institutions of the black community. The *Reporter, Truth,* and *Wide-Awake,* as well as other race papers, disseminated information to their readers. Although the newspapers' circulation was limited, those who read the papers often passed on information to others. A communication grapevine wove its way around the neighborhoods, where residents learned about the important social and political issues on the local and national levels. The papers created a group consciousness and enhanced the readers connection to the national culture.[114]

In 1902 nationwide, there were approximately 156 newspapers and magazines devoted to the interests of African Americans; 95 of these were published in the South. Eleven newspapers appeared in Birmingham between 1880 and 1890, and several others appeared between the late 1890s and the early 1900s, including the *Wide-Awake,* the *Blade,* the *Truth,* and *Hot Shots.* Although most of the editors were from the business or professional class, an occasional editor and publisher deviated from this pattern.[115] The tenor of the papers reflected the editors' political views and, in some cases, their courage. R. C. O. Benjamin, who founded the *Negro American* in 1886 unabashedly criticized Alabama's political system. He claimed that the law, as administered in the city police court, was "a farce, a travesty upon justice, [and] a disgrace to our Christian civilization. We contend only for constitutional rights and civil privileges." Rev. T. W. Coffee, who migrated from Memphis, also proved to be a caustic editor who fearlessly moved to defend the rights of blacks.[116] Editorial style gave each paper a unique appeal that dictated the demographics of a paper's readers. Birmingham's diverse African American community had a broad range of publications, white and black, from which to choose. Although race papers presented its news and features with the black reader in mind, whereas the white press presented news chiefly with the white reader in mind and rarely mentioned blacks, more black households demonstrated a preference for the *Birmingham News* followed by the *Birmingham Post.* When the *Truth* and *Reporter* reader demographics were compared, the results revealed that professional households preferred the *Reporter,* whereas skilled households showed no preference, and common and semiskilled workers exhibited a taste for the *Truth*.[117]

After the passage of the new state constitution, black newspapers in Birmingham adopted a less militant voice. The political environment had turned increasingly hostile to African Americans, and the toned-down editorial tenor reflected the change. Despite their reluctance to comment on other political issues, the publishers of newspapers like the *Truth* and the *Voice of the People* took a strong stand on equal rights and disfranchisement. Oscar W. Adams's *Reporter* mastered an editorial approach that stirred its readers and ensured the paper's success. The *Reporter* was one of the most highly regarded papers of the South during the first three decades of the twentieth century. Adams became one of the city's preeminent race leaders through his visibility as editor and civic activist. He was a member of Scott's Chapel A. M. E. Zion Church where he served for thirty years as the Sunday School Superintendent, and in 1921 he was elected a delegate to the Ecumenical Conference in London, England. He also held official positions with various fraternal organizations including the Masons, Knights of Pythias, and the Mosaic Templars. A. G. Gaston recalled that Adams "was a leader of considerable influence throughout the state as an officer in the Knights of Pythias."[118] Adams was raised in Mobile, where he received his early education. He completed his studies at the A&M College at Normal, Alabama, and then moved on to Birmingham in 1906. At a desk in the Great Southern Life Insurance Company he began publishing the weekly *Reporter*. Adams gradually built a respectable reputation for his paper and with persistence capably created a venerable black institution.[119] Although he did not reach the majority of black residents, he appealed to an audience large enough to support his paper from 1906 to 1934. The *Reporter* carried items of local and national significance, and editorials and advertisements that promoted black business, homeownership and black enfranchisement.[120] In contrast to the admonitions of U. G. Mason and others who encouraged African Americans to move to the North, in 1919 Adams addressed an audience of Detroit blacks on the advantages of living in Birmingham and the South: "My people are accustomed to plenty of air and freedom and the natural comfort of life. I am proud of the South. I am there with 80 percent of our people. . . . [W]hen you decide to come home, the doors are open."[121] Black papers also promoted their own importance as social organs in the community: "The Negro newspaper serves as a beacon light guiding the race to a safe harbor."[122] Adams's influence reached beyond Birmingham.

Although historians do not consider the *Reporter* militant, it did publicize racial violence and documented race problems throughout Alabama. Adams wielded considerable influence as a social and civic activist who devoted time and energy to the betterment of his race. In 1918, Adams was president of the Colored Citizen's League, which was founded in 1916 to improve the city's racial climate. In early 1919, the League combined forces with the Interdenominational Ministerial Alliance to protest the showing of *The Birth of a Nation*. Their objection went unheeded, and the film enjoyed a renewed run.[123] Later that same year, the League evolved into the Birmingham branch of the National Association for the Advancement of Colored People (NAACP). Initially Adams and others expressed reluctance to support an outside agency; they ultimately rallied behind the organization albeit briefly. He was also chairman of the Four-Minute Men Negro Organization of Birmingham, a World War I creation designed to win fair employment for returning war veterans; better educational facilities for black war orphans; improved city services; and black suffrage.[124] Adams rallied support from the black business class, from black women, and from ministers, as well as from influential whites who worked in the interest of improved African American institutions and "a more friendly relation between the races."[125] He also won the respect of white Birmingham when his patriotic address on the United States' entrance into World War I mirrored the white establishment's views. The *Birmingham News* saw fit to reprint Adams' speech in its entirety.[126]

Generally, the black press served to energize the race, impart middle-class values, and create a sense of pride and solidarity. The *Weekly Pilot*, one of the city's earliest race newspapers, urged the budding community to take advantage of business opportunities. And when individuals succeeded in their pursuits, the papers were the first to highlight their achievements. The *Blade's* account of the success of the Alabama Penny Savings Bank offers an example of how the editor praised black success: "[The] Alabama Penny Savings Bank owns such property as its own bank building; a 3 story stone and brick building on 18th [worth approximately] $51,000 and such others as Drug Stores and Industrial Insurance Cos, Dry Goods Businesses." Many of the race papers featured profiles of well-known community members "who could serve as inspirational figures for the less fortunate."[127]

James Arthur Coar was held up as an example of a capable individual who worked his way up from an office boy at the Tennessee Coal, Iron and Railroad Company at Ensley to his position as manager of transportation for the company. The *Reporter* held him in high esteem and declared him "a natural leader and organizer." The paper attributed Coar's success to his middle-class behavior, which included punctuality, obedience, and commitment to hard work.[128] The papers provided a vehicle through which to promote self-help and racial uplift. Beyond that, some editors expounded on the importance of appropriate behavior and working within the structure of the established system. Newspapers helped to bind the larger community together, and because the editors handled the external relations of the group, they achieved a visibility often absent for neighborhood leaders.[129] The African American press in Alabama made a significant contribution to black community life and in the twentieth century offered local leaders a "powerful forum for promoting their opinions and publicizing their solutions to race problems." The newspapers offered a variety of services, from informing the public of local affairs to educating them about national crises. Above all else, "the newspapers served as town criers, announcing events of special importance to Negroes, thus strengthening belief in the presence of a separate black world within the larger urban society."[130]

The triumvirate of anchor institutions—black-owned banks, insurance companies, and newspapers—promoted the black community. They provided economic and social services to African Americans who were working toward developing an identity for themselves apart from the one assigned to them by whites. Their own institutions gave them a sense of pride and stood as testament to their abilities and aspirations.[131] And from the board of directors and trustees of these institutions, arose the most elite and visible members of Birmingham's black community. Through their affiliation in these businesses and in the local and state chapters of the NNBL, leaders like Pettiford, Walker, and Adams exerted their influence on business and race matters. Local Birmingham business leaders also served as officers for the Alabama State Business League, which suggests that African Americans who lived beyond Birmingham and Jefferson County recognized the accomplishments and influence of the Birmingham elite. The officers often urged local businessmen to attend the League's meetings to foster cooperation.[132]

Cooperation among business leaders was essential for the growth of a BBD in light of the political climate during the late nineteenth and early twentieth centuries. The factions that developed among some of Birmingham's elite blacks who jockeyed for leadership roles prevented them from creating a cooperative organization such as a merchant's association by 1930.[133] Yet their wrangling did not impede their willingness to achieve a shared goal—the creation of their own business community. Without the cooperation and ambition of numerous African American leaders, entrepreneurs, and residents, the BBD would not have expanded and thrived as it did. Their commitment to creating a separate district for themselves ensured its survival and growth. Their efforts to maintain a viable business district that catered to African Americans were realized with the creation and assistance of the anchor institutions, the modest help of some white businessmen, the support of black patrons, and the adoption of prudent business practices. When competing businesses opened, they served segments of the city's diverse black population. Birmingham's three black-owned banks—the Alabama Penny Savings Bank, the Prudential Savings Bank, and the Peoples Investment and Banking Company—each attempted to carve out a niche and serve a specific segment of the black consumer market. This strategy enabled the banks to reach out to a large number of African Americans who helped to stimulate the separate black economy in Birmingham that business leaders created. "It was this group that was especially instrumental in the burgeoning of the philosophy of racial solidarity, self-help and the group economy, the rationalization of the economic advantages to be found in segregation and discrimination."[134]

Birmingham's black business leaders often lacked formal training in business practices, yet they exhibited the ability to address the needs of the community through economic means. Through trial and error, black businesses emerged and maintained themselves in spite of the obstacles. Frequently, entrepreneurs employed strategies that were contrary to accepted practices. Community building was their goal, and if the community was served through mismanagement, then that strategy was adopted.[135]

Birmingham's African Americans enjoyed a vibrant BBD during the early twentieth century. As middle-class blacks created the businesses that provided the foundation for the area, members from the working and lower classes generated sufficient support for the district's survival. Despite their differences, these diverse groups recognized the significance of the BBD. African Americans created a world for themselves in the BBD, a place of economic and social activity. It served many of their practical and emotional needs. As blacks opened businesses and constructed buildings, many African Americans felt a sense of pride at the tangible evidence of their abilities and achievements. They knew that the business district belonged to them and was a place of comfort and familiarity.

5

Institution Building

The Creation of Schools and Their Significance in the Community

The black leadership in Birmingham recognized the importance of creating institutions beyond the successful businesses in the Black Business District. They knew that strong foundations were essential in building a solid and well-developed community. Education was a key factor in laying the groundwork for future growth. To ensure that their children would reap the benefits that education offered, African Americans pooled their energies to establish schools. They faced an uphill battle living in the South, especially in Alabama, where education was not a priority for the state government. All the state's children failed to receive adequate training, but none more so than African American youngsters. The many whites in the South found it particularly troublesome to educate blacks without altering a social order that defined the region's distinctive character. As historian Dewey Grantham noted, "no segment of [the elaborate caste system and the institutionalization of the Negro's inferior position] was fraught with more uncertainty or more unforeseen implications than the education of black children."[1]

Many African Americans took the initiative to educate themselves and their children. Booker T. Washington was among the strongest and most visible supporters of industrial education as the key to promoting the concept of self-help and creating group solidarity. Financial assistance from such northern philanthropic foundations as the American Missionary Association (AMA), the John F. Slater Fund, and the Peabody Fund, as well as money raised by black benevolent societies and individuals, ensured the continuation of black education in Alabama. Unfortunately, the support and funds fell far short of meeting the overwhelming demand for education. Public education, though anathema to the majority of Alabamians, was the solution.[2]

A state level approach misses important African American achievements at the local level.[3] If one looks at the more densely populated cities, it becomes clear how different the black urban experience in education was when compared to the education offered to many children living in rural areas. Overall, urban reformers had the greatest impact in urban centers where children fared much better than their rural counterparts. Not only were the school terms longer, but the quality of education was superior in cities and towns, and residents displayed a higher literacy rate. Some urban blacks had the opportunity to attend the AMA's graded schools—Emerson Institute in Mobile and its Swayne School in Montgomery.[4]

When improvements in education for African American children were made in Birmingham, it was the black community under the guidance of strong leadership that forged ahead in pursuit of reform. Although they were compelled to settle for meager improvements compared to their white counterparts, their stamina, integrity, and forthrightness were primarily responsible for whatever progress they made. The evidence presented in this chapter supports Patricia Graham's contention that "Credit for the accomplishment [of declining illiteracy rates among blacks by 1910] belongs primarily to southern blacks, who managed to educate themselves with minimal help from their white neighbors and only a little more assistance from northern philanthropic groups. Mostly [they] did it themselves."[5]

As a New South city, Birmingham struggled to define itself. City leaders recognized that to maximize the possibilities for growth, they needed to reconcile the question of race relations. Birmingham's economy revolved around the coal, iron, and steel industries, where a highly segregated work force reflected the social order of Birmingham society. White workers who sought to maintain their preferred status in the work force were among those opposed to black public education. An uneducated and illiterate African American worker posed far less threat to white workers and the established hierarchy than did an educated black. But industrialists held a different view: they recognized that education would provide them with a more efficient and stable work force.[6]

African Americans pushed passionately for education as a means to uplift their race. They sought to build schools of their own where they could exercise control over the environment and instill pride and confidence in students during their formative years. In Birmingham, the first record of the black community's attempt to secure a school was in 1876, two years after the establishment of a free white school. In that year, Alfred Jackson and other African Americans not only petitioned "for the establishment of a Free Colored School for colored people in this city," but they also sought the fair distribution of school funds "as prescribed by law."[7] One year later, the Board of Aldermen recognized the Free Colored School and elected Julia Scott as principal for the academic year. African Americans furnished a building (most likely a private home) in which to conduct classes, while the state agreed to pay the teacher's salary. Throughout the early 1880s, Burton Hudson, George Turner, and H. C. Crawford agitated for a building for the Free Colored School: "There is not a foot of ground, nor a schoolhouse in this city for the education of the colored children; we have begun a struggle to raise the money to buy a lot and build a schoolhouse thereon." When a fund-raising event failed to raise sufficient funds from the black community, they used the progressive rhetoric as a strategy to secure a building: "Feeling as we do that there is no other way of bringing our people up to the desired standard of education, intelligence, and morality but to build schoolhouses and educate them, we therefore present a most urgent appeal to the white citizens for aid to buy a schoolhouse in our city. If you want us to make better citizens, then help to educate us!"[8]

Although their appeal failed to bring the much-needed schoolhouse at that time, it yielded additional public financial assistance. In 1882, the Mayor appointed a special committee to select a suitable lot for a Free Colored School. The board appropriated $250 per month for the building and an additional $20 a month for black school teachers' salaries. When African Americans from the Southside and the west side also appealed for monies for schoolhouses in their districts, the Board acquiesced. By June 1883 the city had one black principal and three black teachers on its payroll, and by 1884, 318 black students were enrolled in their schools.[9] The efforts of blacks to create a satisfactory education for their children did not stop there. African Americans initiated their own schools beyond the public eye and without public funds when they established grade schools and kindergartens in some of their churches. Both the Shiloh Baptist and the St. John AME were among the churches that operated schools.[10] In addition to the church-founded schools was the Tuggle Institute, which received financial support from four black fraternal organizations and from several white individuals. African Americans pursued improved conditions and their continuous agitation often brought modest results. Whenever public aid was not forthcoming, they turned inward and appealed to members of the community to volunteer their services and raise money to operate their own schools. Blacks were making inroads in education, but at a slower pace than their white counterparts.[11]

Mayor Alexander O. Lane recognized the need to improve public education in Birmingham when he recruited John Herbert Phillips to fill the position of school superintendent. Phillips, a native Kentuckian who arrived in Birmingham from Ohio, drew a "shower of protests on the part of many of the old-timers who protested against Yankeeizing the schools by bringing a superintendent from the other side of the Mason and Dixon line."[12] Phillips initiated his aggressive campaign for improved public education when he overhauled the entire system and created a more efficient and centralized organization. In doing so, Phillips placed black schools under the authority of the city and his office.

When African Americans sought to improve local conditions, they found an ally in a member of the "independent" Board of Education.[13] Samuel Ullman, a Jewish merchant, was appointed to serve as a member of the first Board of Education for the city of Birmingham. He played a critical role in the advancement of education in the city, and he particularly benefited the black community. Ullman was elected as vice-president of the Board and chairman of a special committee to review teacher salaries, and then in 1893, he assumed the presidency.[14] Ullman's campaign to elevate the standards of education in Birmingham included a mixture of academic and industrial education for both black and white students, with greater emphasis on manual training in the black schools. In 1899, Ullman argued for additional industrial training in the black school and suggested that the board should offer a curriculum "to improve the possibilities of our colored children, recognizing that . . . nearly all our domestic help are colored, and as such are in daily contact with our children; hence the duty of raising their moral stand [is] indicated as much as their educational standard."[15] Ullman and Phillips's paternalism moved them to improve black education within defined parameters. Not only would black children benefit from a better education but also mainstream society, that is, white Birmingham, would reap the rewards. The combination of academic and manual training for black students won greater support among resistant whites than would have a purely academic curriculum.[16] This agenda persisted well into the twentieth century.[17] As Board president, Ullman kept abreast of most matters concerning the operations of these schools; overall, he worked toward improving the standards of education offered in Birmingham's public schools.[18]

The first school for African American children that was established during Phillips's administration was the Fifteenth Street Colored School, founded at the initiation of Burton Hudson. The school was housed in a six-room schoolhouse and was renamed Slater School in 1888, with B. W. Arnett as acting principal. By 1887, there were two additional black schools: the Lane School building, named for the mayor and built in 1886, with Frank S. Hazle as principal, and the East End School with J. L. H. Watkins as acting principal. At first, none of these schools had more than six grades. In 1890, the Lane School had six grades, the Slater School had four, and the East End School, which conducted classes at the Methodist Church, had only two grades. The black schools were governed by their own set of black trustees and charged tuition (as did the white schools).[19] Black school buildings were poorly constructed with insufficient heating and inadequate books, desks, and lighting. Overcrowding was particularly grim. In 1889, the student-teacher ratios ran as high as fifty-three to one at Slater School and seventy-four to one at Lane School; at East End School, one teacher tried "to manage, not to teach, 125 pupils." In 1905, Superintendent Phillips reported that he remedied the problem at the Slater School when he converted the room used for the Washington Library into a classroom; at the other schools he moved to assign an extra teacher to assist the regular teachers to temporarily relieve some of the congestion and overcrowding. The problem persisted. In 1907, the Board responded to the conditions at the Cameron School when it agreed to rent for $10 a month the basement of an African American church.[20]

Local appropriations for black education rose dramatically in the late 1880s and early 1890s; however, during the mid to late 1890s, educational cutbacks were essential as the economy suffered a downturn.[21] Despite opposition from some whites who demanded that no white tax money be used to support black schools, taxes from whites continued to pay the largest portion of black school salaries, since African Americans owned disproportionately little property.[22] Overall, black and white schools were unable to establish a firm foundation until 1916, when the state finally approved an amendment that earmarked city and county taxes for educational purposes.[23]

By the early 1890s, some improvements appeared in black school facilities. The Cameron School was housed in the old (white) Henley school building, which had since relocated to an eight-room school structure. In 1891, the costly $5,000 nine-room building was erected for the East End School, at which time it was renamed the Thomas School. When this building burned down in 1894, no replacement school was available for children living in the eastern part of the city until 1898 when the school reopened in the basement of St. John's Methodist Episcopal Church. The church basement proved to be an inadequate facility that flooded with every rainstorm. In 1900, African Americans agitated for construction of a new Thomas School, but it was not until 1902 that Samuel Ullman reported to the Board of Education that the conditions at Thomas School "require immediate attention." The following year, J. M. Mason, the health inspector, reported that the Thomas School quarters were "utterly unfit for school purposes and should be abandoned." He was particularly concerned with the high incidence of tuberculosis among African Americans and determined that the conditions that surrounded the students at the Thomas School were "the very things which are most conducive to its development." Although tuberculosis could reach into the white community, change came slowly.[24]

African American leaders continued to press for improved facilities. In 1904, B. H. Hudson and Drs. Ulysses G. Mason and U. G. Goin were appointed to a Negro Advisory Board that reported to the Board of Education. In 1905, Drs. Mason and Arthur M. Brown and attorney Edward A. Brown, among others, again pushed for construction of a new school building. Chiefly, these spokesmen were Smithfield residents who represented the larger black community. These leaders were not only addressing their children's eroding facilities but also working to correct the much larger problem that plagued all of Birmingham's black children. A victory would have symbolic significance. As Carl Harris noted, "Black leaders looked upon the inadequacy of black school buildings and upon the great difficulty of obtaining new buildings as crucial bottlenecks holding back the progress of black education." These leaders recognized that the environment played a significant role in the effectiveness of teachers and the responsiveness of students. Those who struggled for improvements achieved sporadic and incremental rewards that reinforced their efforts. Although they were not achieving equality with their white counterparts, blacks were accomplishing some of their goals. It was an uphill battle, but they were gaining ground.[25]

Phillips responded to their agitation for new school buildings, but he was hampered by the difficulty in selecting appropriate sites for black schools. The placement of black schools proved to be a thorny problem for Phillips as racial separation dictated the decision. He noted that "the Board has been thwarted in its purposes by objections to the locations selected. The rapid changes in the residence, as well as in the business districts of the city, keep the negro population of the city constantly shifting, and real estate and other interests are keenly expectant regarding land values and vigilant regarding such factors as may affect these values."[26] Finally, Phillips recommended that a permanent and substantial brick structure replace the buildings used for black schools. Phillips had the support of Mayor George Ward, who worked toward securing improvements for black education.[27]

No decent school building for Smithfield's African American children was available until 1908, yet for a long time in the Graymont area, white children had suitable facilities. In 1908, Graymont's city aldermen considered a new building for the "colored high school" and identified W. A. Rayfield as the architect. Three months later, the board accepted four general bids from contractors—two from white-owned companies (Garlington and Caperton) and two from black contractors (Windham Brothers and Goodson and Canttrell). Revised lower bids were submitted one week later, and the board selected the lowest bid from yet another white bidder—R. M. Alexander. The site for the new school was purchased for $2,000 and was located on the southeast corner of Ella Avenue and Joseph Street; construction was completed in 1909. In contrast, in 1908, a new site was also purchased for Graymont School for white children at a cost of $12,500. Although Smithfield provided more desirable living conditions and the possibility of homeownership for African Americans, they faced obstacles to securing some essential services.[28]

When Graymont was annexed into the Birmingham city limits, African American children from Smithfield became part of the larger Birmingham black population that suffered discrimination in education. By June 1910, a report on the status of Birmingham public schools revealed the discrepancy in funding. (See table 1.)

In addition to working to ameliorate the school buildings, Phillips initiated a program to provide more equitable salary schedules for African American teachers. Prior to 1883, the Board of Aldermen decreed that no black teacher should be paid more than $20 per month, far below the base salary of $35 per month for white teachers. Phillips established a formal salary schedule, and he raised the minimum black salary to the previous minimum salary for whites. Black teachers lost ground when their salaries, but not white teachers' salaries, were pushed down during an economic downturn. This move again widened the gap between white and black teachers' salaries.

Discriminatory salary schedules maintained a significant distance between the salary of black and white teachers. In 1903, the salary schedules reveal the discrepancy: The principal of the white high

Table 1. Annual Report of the Birmingham Public Schools, for the year ending June 30, 1910

Expenditures		Average Membership	
Whites	$220,598.69	Whites	10,879
Blacks	35,467.96	Blacks	4,646
		Total	15,525
Number of Schools		**Average Daily Attendance**	
Whites	35	Whites	10,080
Blacks	20	Blacks	3,982
Number of Teachers		**Length of Term**	
Whites	393	Whites	178 days
Blacks	101	Blacks	178 days
Actual enrollment		**Average Annual Salaries**	
Whites	13,870	Whites	$448.01
Blacks	6,390	Blacks	299.88
		Total Value of School Property	
		Whites	$1,374,002.87
		Blacks	81,680.51

Source: Cited in *The Common School and the Negro American,* Atlanta University Publication 16 (Atlanta: Atlanta University Press, 1911), 70.

school earned $137.50 a month, whereas Arthur H. Parker, the principal of the black high school earned $65 a month. The female principal of a white grade school earned a monthly salary of $110 (59 percent more than a black male principal). When the Board of Education determined salary schedules of teachers and principals and other educators, it moved to reinforce the discrepancy in salaries. Point nine of a resolution introduced on June 13, 1904, stated that "the above schedule of salaries shall not apply to *principals and teachers of negro schools.*"[29] African Americans were well aware of the discriminatory practices of Birmingham's Board of Education. Their school buildings and equipment stood as tangible evidence of the perceived superiority of white children and their future place in society. Yet, these signs of racism did not discourage blacks. Even their modest gains inspired them to push for more. Their commitment to education thrust them into engineering a movement for a black high school.

In the South, only urban centers offered high school education to white or black students. Almost all of the southern rural communities with large African American populations and more than half of the major southern cities failed to offer black youth a secondary education.[30] In 1900, there were 8,395 black students in public high schools, and in 1910, the number rose to 12,636.[31] The shortage of black high schools was particularly acute in the South, where in 1910, half of all black high students studied at private schools financed primarily by blacks.[32] When it was finally decided that white children needed an advanced education, local and state governments moved to supply them with a secondary institution. Some cities in the South had acquiesced to black campaigns for a secondary school. In the case of Birmingham, several key players, black and white, worked together to make this a reality. Their interest in establishing a secondary school for African American children was a direct challenge to the overt discrimination of Birmingham's educational system that had earlier offered only white students a high school education, grades eight through eleven.[33]

William Pettiford and Hattie Hudson launched a campaign for a black high school.[34] Pettiford had been instrumental in founding both the short-lived Robert Brown Elliott School of Technology in 1887 and Lauderdale College in 1905.[35] Together, Pettiford and Hudson formed an alliance with whites who helped them to achieve their goal. Unfortunately, they had to proceed without the support of Superintendent Phillips, who had established a *white* high school as early as 1883. Clearly blacks needed a commitment from more sympathetic whites to achieve their goal. This they found in the persona of Samuel Ullman. As president of the school board, he had shown his support when he pushed for improvements in black school buildings and proposed night-school classes for blacks in 1885. In June 1900, when a cadre of black citizens called a meeting to request a secondary school for African Americans, Ullman "encouraged the movement."[36] Members of the Board, who were also city boosters, recognized the advantages connected with improving the city's schools and carefully considered the benefits of a black high school.[37] Nevertheless, many whites continued to oppose black education of any kind, and particularly when it was provided at the expense of white taxpayers: "We disfranchise the negro as a negro, yet we EDUCATE the negro as a negro on the disfranchised white illiterate's tax money. Maybe this is 'the white man's burden.' "[38] Despite opposition, the unique coalition of business interests carried sufficient influence to gain support for the movement. The need for a stabilized work force supplemented with the assurance to Superintendent Phillips that the students' tuition would cover the school's operating costs, moved the notion of a black high school into a reality.[39] It was a remarkable feat, considering the pervading sentiment against the very concept of black high school education. To further emphasize the significance of the victory is the fact that Montgomery, the capital of the state, did not have a public senior high school for African Americans in 1930. In the same year, over 50 percent of all black students enrolled in the tenth, eleventh, and twelfth grades of public schools in Alabama attended Industrial High School.[40]

Ullman had taken a courageous step when he supported higher education for African American students, but he paid a price for this unpopular stand. The opposition of key white political leaders was obvious when members of the Board of Aldermen, a board on which Ullman served from 1895 to 1897, refused to reelect him to the Board of Education in 1900. They were punishing him for his progressive views. According to the *Age-Herald*, his expulsion was unexpected and irresponsible given Ullman's "rare devotion, enthusiasm, and unselfishness." Although he was reinstated to the Board in 1902 and served through 1904, he no longer exercised the same influence. African Americans became uncomfortably aware of this fact when, in 1905, they petitioned for better facilities for their school and were told that their request was "ill-advised and insulting."[41]

At the same time that the Constitution of 1901 disfranchised African Americans, whites in Birmingham built Industrial High School in response to black requests. Such relative success in black secondary education was not universal.[42] Many southern cities denied their black residents an education beyond the elementary level. Appreciating the significance of their victory, members of Birmingham's black community and the teachers and students cooperated in transforming the school into a unique community institution. Industrial High began offering classes in one room on the second floor of the Cameron School building, at Eighth Avenue, South and Fourteenth Street.[43] The fees for attending the high school were set at a monthly rate of $1.50 for residents of Birmingham and $2.50 for nonresidents. Eighteen students enrolled for the first term of the school's operation. The enthusiasm around the school's commencement drew many locals to attend the opening day ceremonies. Reverends Pettiford and Wilhite and Mrs. Hattie Hudson, among others, "pledged their full support to the program in any manner needed." The Board chose A. H. Parker to direct the school after he had achieved a notable reputation during his tenure as teacher at Cameron School. His salary of $47.50 per month that he received as a teacher in the grade school remained the same when he assumed his new position.[44]

Arthur Harold Parker was the key player in transforming Industrial High School into a community institution. A brief biography provides a better understanding of his character and his goals.[45] Parker was born on May 7, 1870, in Springfield, Ohio. His biography claims that his paternal grandfather was a white man, about whom he knew little. His father was born a slave in Decatur, Alabama, and took the name of Parker from his master. His mother was born a slave in Virginia and was freed upon emancipation. Parker's father escaped to Canada on the Underground Railway and then returned to the United States when the Civil War ended. He settled in Springfield, where he became a barber and owned a shop. The younger Parker was raised in Springfield and attended a separate elementary school, where all his teachers were black. It was not until he attended an integrated high school that he was first exposed to the race question. "I did not know then what had gone out of my life to make it so different. I remember well that I did not care for the high school as I did for the elementary school. Gradually, I came to understand." Throughout the school year, Parker worked at his father's barbershop and learned the trade. Despite plans to attend law school, circumstances forced him to move south to Nashville and then on to Atlanta, where he worked as a barber. In 1887, Parker arrived in Birmingham to join extended family members. Parker continued his barbering until an opportunity to change careers allowed him to move into teaching. Education became his life's mission.[46]

Superintendent Phillips appointed Parker, who had completed a teacher's examination, to work at the Slater School in 1888. As Parker acknowledges in his autobiography, he was enamored with the prestige awarded African American teachers. Teaching was one of the few white-collar professions open to African Americans at this time, and Birmingham offered more opportunities for those with teaching aspirations than did other southern cities. In 1905, after several years of teaching, Parker was elected to the presidency of the [Black] State Teachers Association (STA), an organization that grew out of a meeting of sixty teachers of black schools in Selma in 1882.[47] He also studied to become a principal, with ambitions to enhance his career opportunities. These ambitions were realized when Superintendent Phillips appointed him the principal of Cameron School in 1892. This solidified his position as a credible educator, which would lead to greater fruition in 1900. However, due to a personal crisis, Parker resigned from the educational field to accept a position with the Internal Revenue Service. He was soon lured back to education by another attractive offer—the principalship at the new Industrial High School, which was named in honor of the industrial tradition of Birmingham.[48]

Industrial High School's beginnings were modest. Parker taught the first class in one room; the second year J. R. Coffey was appointed to teach the first year high school class, while Parker moved on to teach the second year class. In the third year, Orlean D. Kennedy was transferred from Slater School to teach the female students sewing, cooking, and assembly singing. In time, additional faculty members were hired as student enrollment rapidly increased. Word spread quickly and by year's end, forty-five students were enrolled at a tuition of $1.50 per month. The student population increased exponentially over the years, drawing its membership from different black neighborhoods within and outside Birmingham. The good streetcar network enabled children who lived far from Industrial High School to attend the school; other students walked long distances to save the five-cent fare. Distance did not deter them from taking advantage of the opportunity to receive high school instruction.

A cross-section of pupils were represented in the student body who lived in such diverse areas as Woodlawn, South Birmingham, and the more affluent neighborhoods of Smithfield and Enon Ridge. How well these students from such diverse backgrounds mixed can only be inferred from various interviews conducted. Several elite families "looked down upon Industrial High," and they chose not to send their children because "they had the feeling that the teachers and the students were not getting a good instruction. They had the feeling that the mingling of students of all walks of life was not really to their advantage." Consequently, some children attended such private school as St. Mark's Academy and Episcopal School or Miles College, as well as the preparatory department of Alabama's Talladega College or Mississippi's Rust College. "Any place other than Industrial High. Others, who had no alternative than Industrial High went along with the program and remained because they were proud to know there was a high school there."[49] Ellen Tarry remembered that "many parents felt that our local high school did not measure up and that their children would be handicapped by attendance there. So, most of the conversation at our house was related to the choice of a school for me to attend the next year."[50] These recollections reveal that Industrial High School was not for everyone. Families secured additional prestige based on where they sent their children to school; for some of the more elite families in Birmingham, Industrial High School failed to meet their standards or expectations. They linked education with the quest for respectability and proper behavior, and they sought institutions that would teach their children more than what Industrial offered. Middle class blacks put a premium on education and sent their kids to schools where they could also learn to become middle class citizens and perpetuate the business and professional class that they belonged to.[51] Those middle-class students who did attend remember the divisions within the student body. One former student recalled that "since it was the only black high school, black children from everywhere in the city attended classes there. And they came from all different social classes. Kids from East Birmingham were different." He didn't know why they were different, just that they were. And, that was reason enough not to interact.[52] Class distinctions separated numerous students who elected to attend elsewhere, whereas differences among Industrial students moved them to sort themselves out along class lines.[53]

Yet the mass of Birmingham's African Americans strongly supported Industrial High School. This is reflected both in the overwhelming response of the black community to the school's commencement activities and in the growth of the student body. In 1904, fifteen students graduated; in 1905, eleven students graduated; in 1910, there were nineteen graduates; and by 1920, there was a total of seventy-two graduating students.[54] At the end of the third year, the work of the school was noted and acclaimed not only by the parents of the school and the members of the Board of Education, but by other civic minded persons who were interested in the progress of Birmingham. In 1903, the larger white community was informed of the school's success when the *Birmingham News* praised Industrial High's progress: "It is easy to see that this school is doing a great work for the Negro and for the community." Blacks who learned of this account were likely proud, since rarely did the white papers portray blacks in a positive manner.[55]

The first graduation exercises were held on June 4, 1904, at the end of the school's fourth year of operation. It was a monumental event for many African Americans. Parker recalled that "Practically every Negro family in Birmingham was represented at the Sixteenth Street Baptist Church Friday Night. The High School commencement is a feature in Negro life. . . . [T]hese are events the colored people look forward to in Birmingham during the whole school year as the one thing worth while."[56] The ceremony included musical performances, inspirational speeches, and the awarding of diplomas. The subsequent six graduation ceremonies were held at the Shiloh Baptist Church.[57]

Nearing the end of the first decade of its founding, the increasing demand for instruction forced Industrial to expand its facilities into the Sixth Avenue Baptist Church. In 1910, the Board of Education rented an old three-story frame building on the north side, commonly known as Lane's Auditorium, for the high school. Progress in teaching was made despite the largely inadequate new facility. "Housed in an unattractive, old, ramshackle building with unspeakable surroundings, as far as comfort and equipment for school purposes is concerned, this work goes on progressing, assisting hundreds of young Negro men and women, reaching into the family life, making better citizens of them and fitting each for this problem peculiar to themselves."[58] Only four years later, the city inspector condemned the structure and Industrial High School moved again. The Congregational Church at Seventh Avenue and Fifteenth Street provided a temporary home until a more suitable location was made available at the former schoolhouse of the United Presbyterian School. The new facilities for 325 students included the small church and a seven-room house. The church had four big classes and the house offered three classrooms, a kitchen, and a sewing room. The manual training class used the coal house. Shortly after classes began, Superintendent Phillips and Mayor George Ward secured the next lot that contained fourteen small cottages.[59] By 1920, the rapid expansion of the student population warranted a new building, long overdue. In 1918, the *Reporter* complained that the school "is being conducted in a row of shanties on Eighth Avenue." Negotiations for a new facility began in 1920 for the block in Smithfield where the present school is located.[60]

Black leaders who were pushing for change in the public school system relied on the cooperation of city officials. During World War I, the black community acquired leverage when officials worried about the stability and loyalty of the African American workers, many of whom were migrating north in pursuit of better paying industrial jobs. After the death of Superintendent Phillips in 1921, Charles B. Glenn assumed the position of superintendent and continued his predecessor's policies. Under Glenn's direction, in 1922 the school board built new concrete and brick buildings for blacks, but the buildings remained significantly inferior to white school facilities. Carl Harris noted that despite African American advancements in education, their advancement kept them behind the better-funded education of white students.[61] Nonetheless, the teachers and students maintained an enthusiasm for teaching and learning that was the key to the school's success.

A. H. Parker was strongly influenced by the doctrine of Booker T. Washington, and this was readily acknowledged by Parker, who called Washington his "patron saint." Parker was keenly aware of Washington's philosophy, particularly because Tuskegee was located nearby and acted as a role model for many black schools in the South. In addition to the classical high school curriculum of academic courses Industrial High School offered, Parker promoted the concept of industrial education. He was "firmly convinced that our boys and girls should be taught in the schools how to do thoroughly and well the everyday duties that they find right around them."[62] The struggle to obtain a secondary school was wrought with difficulties, and much of the controversy centered around the curriculum. Parker recognized that to limit outside interference, it was necessary to maintain a core of industrial courses at the school. He, too, was cognizant of the value of an academic education; Louise McCauley recalled that "Dr. Parker took great interest in vocations, and he had an equal interest in the academics as in vocations."[63] Many former students found only praise for Parker and the curriculum he espoused: "I think the [industrial] training had inherent value. There a student was introduced to sewing, cooking, band, and beauty club. Being able to get an overview. Getting an avocation and not necessarily a vocation. Something they could pick up on money when they were in school. It helped to make better homemakers."[64]

Like his role model, Booker T. Washington, Parker was faulted for providing students with an industrial education that would secure their place as second-class citizens and impede progress of the race.[65] When Parker added laundry and cooking courses to the curriculum, some African Americans accused him of trying to make servants out of the children. Ellen Tarry remembered that Birmingham parents became increasingly irritated and frustrated with Parker and Industrial High School when friends who had migrated north "wrote back and told how their children of high school age had to be 'put back' to lower grades in the schools of other cities because they had had no Latin or French and found it impossible to keep up with their classes in mathematics."[66] Yet, Parker stood firm in offering practical training as a way to fit the students into the community. He promoted a well-balanced education to create better citizens—the same goal asserted by many white social reformers.[67] He recognized that only certain types of occupations were open to African Americans, and he believed that it was foolish to equip them with an education that would not secure a job for them. In 1925, a statistical analysis was tabulated that revealed how Industrial High School's students fared in society after graduation. Since its inception until 1925, there was a total of 993 graduates. Fifteen were college graduates; 166 were teachers; 298 were housekeepers; 20 were in the professions; 198 were engaged in various business enterprises; 20 were nurses; 157 were still active students; and 1 was convicted by a court of law.[68]

In the first year of its operation, Parker established a woodworking shop; in the second year, he introduced sewing, and then continued in this vein when he expanded the program to include a variety of "household arts."[69] The *Birmingham News* fully supported industrial teachings; it declared that "Excellent Work Which is Being Done by the Negro High School," and described the results of a practical education. The Birmingham School Board continued to encourage a curriculum that emphasized practical teaching in the 1930s. Reporting on the progress of Industrial High School, the Board stated that the school was providing its students with a combined curriculum that would prepare them for "the work of life." The Board's report probably tried to appease some white citizens who continued to oppose an academic education for black students: "A visit to these schools during their daily operation should convince one that the negro youths of our city are actually getting a type of education which will help them to become intelligent, law-abiding, cooperative, and useful members of our community."[70] Among the academic subjects offered were mathematics, geometry, and history—including history of the negro race. During the Progressive era, the emphasis on race pride was accompanied by an expressed interest in race history.[71] In light of the strong resistance to higher education for black students, it is noteworthy that the faculty was able to manipulate the curriculum. To further reinforce feelings of race pride and self-esteem the school also began their performances and assemblies by singing the "Negro National Anthem."[72] Morale among the student body was evident in the manner in which students conducted themselves within the school boundaries and within the larger Birmingham community.

In addition to academic and manual training, Parker also encouraged the development of extracurricular activities that stimulated school spirit and attracted city-wide respect and adulation. As students participated in the construction and maintenance of the school buildings, Parker noted that "there was being built into the fiber of

Industrial High School Band, c. 1920 (Birmingfind Collection, Catalog #829.1.1.10, Department of Archives and Manuscripts, Birmingham Public Library, Ala.)

the spirit of the school a strength and purpose that made it irresistible. The school popularity grew apace." In 1903, the strong music tradition was established when Orlean Kennedy presented a school musical. Former students fondly recall the emphasis that was placed on the music program under the directorship of Miss Kennedy and later John "Fess" Whatley, and proudly reminisced about the successful musicians who had graduated from Industrial High School. "A lot of black musicians came out of that school. They went on up East, [where they made a name for themselves]."[73] Through music, Industrial High School reached out to the broader community.[74] Fess Whatley organized the school band in 1917, and borrowed instruments from members of the community. Within four months, the band had played its first concert. From this first public performance grew the Sunday afternoon outdoor concerts that welcomed interested listeners from the Birmingham area. In 1918, these informal performances evolved into the popular "Community Sing." African Americans took personal pride in the accomplishments of Industrial High School's music program and the Sunday public performances. The *Reporter* kept the community abreast of the concerts and reported on the impact of the open-air free performances given on campus: They are "an innovation that is elevating, inspiring, educative, entertaining. The crowds . . . attest to the popularity of this new feature. It shows too that our people really appreciate a community sing of their own, where they do not have to be 'jim-crowed.' " The school's theatrical performances, concerts, and other entertainment maintained their popularity throughout the decades. When the minstrel at the school was late in starting it was due to the crowds of peoples trying to find a place to sit. In addition to those who settled with standing room only, "there were actually hundreds more who did not get in."[75] The concerts became increasingly popular, and frequently the band performed at the Jefferson Theatre, where a few seats were reserved for whites and the remainder of the hall was filled with black patrons.[76] The quality and style of the performances were unique to the city's African American community, and African Americans flocked to these performances not only to share in the pride of the occasion but also to experience a cultural event that was purely secular. Except for the few middle-class families who might have attended similar events elsewhere, working-class blacks in Birmingham had little opportunity to experience cultural activities that were "non-religious and non-commercial."[77]

The commencement ceremonies at the annual graduations had become so powerful a source of pride for the black community that in 1919 the event was held at the Jefferson Theatre to accommodate the warm reception. The keynote speaker during this particular graduation was Dr. Robert Moton, president of Tuskegee Institute. He praised "the spirit of service; of the appreciation of the dignity of labor, the spirit of being a blessing to the community, the spirit of cooperation, the spirit of racial good will and helpfulness." He recognized that Industrial High School was a community institution that extended its influence far beyond the boundaries of its site, which grew to cover a city block in Smithfield. The school's reputation had also transcended Birmingham's city limits: State and federal representatives recognized Industrial School "doing one of the most interesting pieces of educational work in the state," emphasizing the manual training courses and recommending that other black high schools adopt a similar program of industrial work.[78]

Dr. Parker had high expectations of the teachers employed at Industrial High School. The vast majority of teachers were single women who had limited opportunities in other professions. They embraced teaching and channeled their energies into neighborhood

Industrial High School Graduating Class, 1920. A. H. Parker is seated at the far right. (Birmingfind Collection, Catalog #108.5.1.4, Department of Archives and Manuscripts, Birmingham Public Library, Ala.)

schools during a time when schools operated as one of the frontiers of racial group consciousness.[79] Parker inculcated the teachers with his own enthusiastic dedication to the students and the school: "Wherever you are at work and however small may be your pay, give to that work every ounce of soul-service that you possess."[80] Collectively the teachers recalled that he was a tough taskmaster. "We were workaholics. Dr. Parker really made you work."[81] He urged them to take their job as role models beyond the confines of the school and into the community. The teachers became middle-class role models who touched their students during their formative years. While in their home environment, teachers were expected to maintain a middle-class posture that reflected their status and their commitment to helping uplift the race. Marvine Bradford explained what she perceived to be the overbearing responsibilities attached to teachers as role models: "Teachers had to live by different standards. Horrible as it was. . . . [y]ou had to have a different attitude toward life in general in order to survive if you were a teacher."[82] Concerned black citizens even issued petitions intended to dictate appropriate behavior for teachers. In 1894, five African American ministers, representing a large contingent of middle-class blacks, presented a resolution to the Board of Education. They protested against the "shameful and sinful amusement" of dancing and requested that the school board "insist that the teachers of our children refrain from the evil while they are teaching our schools."[83] The status conferred upon teachers may have been a high price to pay for some who resented having their lives controlled by outside forces.

Clearly, parents recognized the value of teachers and fully accepted them as members of the community. Since many teachers boarded with families, they had direct and frequent contact with parents and their children who attended the school. Having a visible presence in households placed the teachers in a unique and demanding situation; their behavior was always visible for praise and for criticism. Parker recognized the prestige and responsibility of the teaching profession, and he demanded that the teachers strive to earn that honor. Industrial High School was considered by teachers to be the most desirable school at which to teach. One former teacher recalled that "it was a real honor to be a faculty member there. Most teachers wanted to teach there. If you weren't there, you weren't anywhere." These sentiments were shared by many African Americans. Even those who did not have children attending Industrial High School held it in high esteem.[84]

Parker and other African American leaders were keenly aware that Industrial High was an experiment and that it had to meet expectations to ensure its financial support. Its success was measured by the effectiveness and competence of its administration, the student body enrollment, the incidence of placing graduates in jobs, and by how the white community perceived Industrial High School. Parker transformed the school into more than a learning center. He and the teachers created a separate and independent community institution that offered a much-needed source of pride. The school transcended its original purpose in a variety of ways. From its inception, Industrial High became an institution that built strong familial bonds among teachers and students. Parker recalled that he "lived very close to this first class[,] for I wanted it to set the spirit, discipline and tone of classes to follow. We worked and played together. We made gardens, had quilting bees, hikes and parties all as one big family."[85] To foster camaraderie and a sense of self-worth among male students, the school held what was called "HI Y Week" to familiarize them with the HI Y Club and recruit new members. In 1929, the week highlighted such inspirational speeches as "Awake, Opportunity Has Arrived"; and P. D. Davis's closing address entitled "Citizenship" encouraged the young men to find a direction for themselves and also help the community to reduce the problem of crime committed by young black men.[86] This pattern of fostering a family feeling and operating as a community institution was permanently adopted and expanded as the school activities extended beyond its grounds and penetrated Birmingham's black communities. In 1911, Industrial High School reached out to the community when it offered to adults a broad range of night-school classes. Industrial was one of several schools that aggressively worked to erase the problem of illiteracy in Birmingham.[87]

The school reinforced its visibility in the community through outreach activities that enhanced the status of the school. Female students were sent from the nursing class to care for the sick and elderly living in private homes. During the 1918 influenza epidemic, Industrial High School was converted into a temporary hospital for ailing blacks. Some of the school's faculty and students offered care, and fifteen nursing students served at Camp McClellan in nearby Anniston to attend to infirm soldiers during World War I. Other students were involved in catering and serving at private parties and dinners, and the printing facility printed tickets, programs, invitations, and so forth for society functions. The students drew accolades from the *Birmingham News* when a Thanksgiving offering was taken in all the Birmingham public schools. Industrial High School students raised per capita $1.23, whereas the white students from the "Central High School" raised a per capita contribution of $.37. "It is a matter for profound humiliation for the white people of this community—not merely that they have been outdone in humanity and charity by the Negroes, but that out of their abundantly greater resources they have given so grudgingly." The *News* continued to berate the white community when it acknowledged the vast discrepancy in wealth between whites and blacks. "Why is it that these Negro children, coming out of shanties and hovels, out of miserable poverty for the most part, have outdone the whites?" The *Reporter* quickly reprinted this editorial "to give a wider expression among our people far and near to the compliment of the *News* of the efforts of colored children in their Thanksgiving offering."[88]

Industrial High filled an enormous void in the education and lives of African Americans. Black teachers and principals carried a responsibility larger and more important than teaching academic or industrial subjects. They were providing a protective environment for children at the same time that they were teaching students important

lessons in self-esteem and race pride. Parker recognized this enormous responsibility, which probably contributed to his reputation as
a tough taskmaster. He held one of the most important roles in the
African American community, yet he did not operate independently.
Parker was required to report to Phillips, the white superintendent
who represented not only the head of education in Birmingham but
also represented the dominant white society. As Hylan Lewis noted,
the black principal finds himself in "a strategic role with respect to
both the white and Negro communities."[89] Parker achieved a balance
that earned him respect from many blacks and some whites, a respect
that enabled him to achieve important academic goals. He assumed a
leadership role that paralleled the work of ministers, other educators
and some businessmen.[90] He was elevated to the status of a godlike
being, who was revered by many African Americans. He was so ex-
alted that one former student was moved to declare that "if saints
were beatified here on earth, I would recommend Dr. Parker."[91] The
Reporter declared Parker the "dean of education," for the "wonderful
work he has done throughout the great number of years the city has
seen fit to have him at the head of its colored High School."[92]

It would be folly to elevate the school and its principal to a status
that was appreciated by all of Birmingham's black residents. Although
all the official written records, including white and black newspapers,
praise the principal, the teachers, and the school, some people leveled
harsh criticisms of the curriculum (as noted earlier) and of Parker's
choice of light-skinned teachers who conducted themselves in a manner that denoted superiority; but rarely were these dissenting voices
heard.[93] As Robin Kelley noted, their hidden transcript lies "mainly
in slums, bars, shacks, barber shops, jokes, songs, toasts, and other
spaces or forms of black working-class expression."[94] Their stories are
told through inference and through private conversations. Other
families recognized the value of a secondary education and were eager
to send their children to Industrial High, but circumstances may have
interrupted their children's education. Families too poor to take advantage of what a high school offered were often focused on a basic
human instinct—survival. Children old enough to work played an essential role in a family living on a shoestring. Their ability to supplement a meager income often made the difference between putting
food on the table, paying the rent, or buying a pair of shoes. Education may have been a luxury for families living on the edge. Children's
work and schooling choices were part of a family's adaptive strategy
to maximize family welfare, and depending on the children's age,

their economic contributions took precedence over their education. As Zane Miller noted, "By 1920, 90 percent of the children of grade-school age of both races attended school. But blacks still found it difficult to secure access to high schools."[95]

The early twentieth century was hardly a time in American history when blacks were receiving a fair share of public allotments. Birmingham adopted patterns similar to other states in the region while it was creating a social order that suited its unique needs as an industrial city that relied heavily on semi- and unskilled labor. Yet, with perseverance and carefully planned strategies, the black leaders developed an alliance with white philanthropists, merchants, and industrialists that enabled them to achieve a remarkable feat. Industrial High School, renamed A. H. Parker High School in 1939, created an aura about itself that persists to the present time. As the new school building in 1924 was located in Smithfield, the residents won the presence of the quintessential black institution of Birmingham. Residents, former students and former teachers proudly state that it was the largest black high school in the world.[96] Their praise is unending and their willingness to share their experiences is a testament to the impact Industrial High School had on their lives. One former student sees the school in this way: "I think it made the blacks say, 'Look here, look what we have. Look what our boys and girls can do.'"[97]

Industrial High School was the first black *public* secondary school in Alabama, but there were private schools that offered a high school education. African Americans had shown their abilities at the higher level in private schools in the late nineteenth century. Before 1920, southern black secondary education was available primarily through private institutions; the southern revolution in public secondary educational opportunities had bypassed black children.[98] Christian education was important to African Americans to protect their freedom and uplift themselves, and the private schools in Birmingham all had a strong religious component included in their curriculums. The first private school in the metropolitan area of Birmingham to offer a higher education to black students was St. Mark's Academy, which was founded in 1892 by the Protestant Episcopal Diocese of Alabama. Rev. Charles Brooks, a black clergyman from Baltimore, Maryland, was the church rector and principal, and two white teachers from the North instructed the school's first students. The American Church Institute for Negroes and the Episcopal Board of Missions provided the necessary funding for the school, supplemented by the tuition fees. In 1899, high school grades were added, and in the following years, the school issued its first high school diploma. By 1914, St. Mark's had earned a presence among many of the city's elite families: enrollment had reached 171 elementary and 21 secondary students, and the school could boast a brick school building valued at $15,000. As noted earlier, St. Mark's offered a viable alternative for children from elite families who were unimpressed with Industrial's program and could afford to send their children to a private school. St. Mark's developed a strong relationship with Tuskegee Institute. Although the two schools did not share the same philosophy of education, several graduates from St. Mark's attended Tuskegee to continue their studies in the trades and in agriculture.[99] The North Alabama Conference of the Colored Methodist Episcopal Church also founded its own high school in the Birmingham area. Miles College evolved out of a high school established in Booker City in 1902 and a high school founded in 1898 in Thomasville, Alabama. The two schools merged, and Miles College opened in Birmingham in 1907.[100] Most of the students were enrolled in elementary grades, a small number in the secondary department, and a few in college.[101] The Negro Baptists of Jefferson County established the Birmingham Baptist College in 1913. Despite its name during the 1920s, it offered mostly high school–level academic courses. The school primarily served an adult population interested in the ministry, religious work, or teaching. Daniel Payne College moved from Selma to Birmingham in 1927. The AME Church of Alabama supported the school, which consisted of a junior college and a theology school. By 1930 it was in full operation.[102]

Although these privately funded schools were outside of the public forum, they did not operate in a vacuum. The teachers and principals were members of the local black community, and they kept abreast of community issues and events. They were acutely aware of the city dynamics, and they too worked to instill race pride and self-esteem in their students, who represented a more elite population who could afford the cost of private-school instruction. Together, the privately and publicly funded schools shared goals but employed somewhat different strategies in achieving them.

Birmingham's growth as an industrial center created an environment in which change was essential to ensure the city's appeal to both southern and northern investors. Alabama legislators did not realize how important public education was, but a coalition of progressive Birmingham boosters were more prescient. As they joined forces with African American activists, they built schools, developed curriculums, and raised teachers' salaries—but they never provided equitable services for black children or faculty members. Without frequent petitions and verbal challenges from black leaders, black children would have suffered more dramatic discrepancies in their education than they did. The leaders, along with the cooperation of Samuel Ullman and Superintendent Phillips, created a public education system for African American children generally superior to that in rural Alabama. Although Birmingham's black community struggled unsuccessfully for equality in education, they pushed forward and refused to be deterred by the southern brand of racism that was engaged in its own conflict with progressive reformers. By 1930, glaring inequities in black education continued. Yet strides were made, and African Americans were cognizant of this fact. P. D. Davis, during his dedication speech to the New East Thomas City School, characterized the progress as phenomenal.[103] In building a separate learning environment for their children, African Americans were empowered to create a setting that featured the positive and unique aspects of black life. The schools, perhaps none more so than Industrial High School, served as pillars in a segregated environment.

6

Men Seeking an Identity

Involvement in Churches, Clubs, and Civic Associations

African Americans who lived in and around Birmingham at the beginning of the twentieth century diligently worked to create a better life for themselves. They sought to construct an environment that satisfied their personal and emotional needs and one that provided them with concrete improvements that benefited the black community in the context of a racially hostile setting. The stratified nature of Birmingham's African American community reflected similar tendencies in the city's white community. African Americans' interest in creating their own institutions was not a response to the barriers they would have encountered had they tried to penetrate the ranks of the white middle class. Rather their actions reveal how they separated themselves into class-segregated activities that reflected their status in black Birmingham, raised their race consciousness, and insulated them from intrusion by the black masses. Members of the black middle class restricted membership in their organizations and clubs, just as their white counterparts did. And the black and white middle class also exhibited similar levels of organizational activism.[1] They enhanced their status when they joined a particular church, fraternal order, or civic organization. Even their choice of residence could bestow additional prestige on them. Each affiliation brought them something different, but nonetheless valuable.

During the Progressive era, white reformers who worked to uplift the nation from the ravages of rapid urbanization, promoted the idea of increased racial separation.[2] African Americans, however, had their own ideas of how to improve their situation. They identified three fundamental goals—social reform, race consciousness, and personal fulfillment. The organizations and clubs they established addressed these goals to varying degrees. Frequently the functions overlapped, and a single association allowed members to simultaneously realize all three goals.[3] Although African American men and women worked toward common goals, each group had its own particular agenda that set the sexes apart. Many social and civic associations were gender specific, as men and women sought different avenues through which to realize their goals.[4]

Middle-class black males in Birmingham sought political expression and power through a variety of associations. The regular meetings at clubs, churches, and other organizations "served to retain mass involvement in politics while transplanting political discussions to specialized places where working class and middle class, male and female were often set apart from each other."[5] The church was the oldest and most powerful political forum for African Americans. Although it was not the singular choice for political expression, it played a unique role in the black community and offered African American males in particular a plethora of leadership opportunities.

African Americans in Birmingham had always had control over their own churches. The city's postbellum roots allowed them to create and direct their own churches without white interference. The church served as an agency for group cohesion, solidarity, and racial uplift, and it strengthened its influence in this arena by adopting a secular character that assumed a diverse array of functions.[6] The church offered security, reassurance, and a promise for salvation in the afterlife, and it symbolized freedom for the race. It played key roles in leadership-building, education, social control, economic development, recreation, and so forth, which all contributed toward the advancement of the race. The black church was a solid race institution that became the focal point of African American community life.[7]

Individuals from all classes who were active in the church's programs realized personal growth and achieved a level of social status that they were denied in the mainstream society. For those who held official positions in the city's more elite churches, their status within the church often mirrored or enhanced their status in the broader black community.[8] Their affiliations with specific churches became public each Sunday as African Americans strolled to Sunday church services. Ellen Tarry recalled, "I can remember Sundays. Sunday was like a parade—people from the Hill and Smithfield [going to church]."[9] People from all classes dressed in their Sunday finest, took pride in their appearance and used the opportunity to show themselves off to anyone who would notice. The middle class chose a manner of dress and deportment that reinforced the distinctiveness of the elite class in their own minds if not in the minds of the broader black community or in the minds of white society.[10] And they chose their church as carefully as they chose their residence, their clubs, and their friends. When selecting a church, individuals considered a minister's personality and education, for a pastor's reputation and his style of worship affected the demographics of a church's congregation. Potential members also evaluated the congregation's level of education, their socioeconomic status, their residence, their behavior, and their lifestyle. All these factors contributed to a church's congregation, development and appeal and its place in the larger black community. The members' station in life influenced the role they played in the church, their expectations of the church, and the type of "charity" and missionary work they practiced.[11]

Several denominations formed churches in Birmingham to meet the diverse needs of the city's growing population. By 1900, the Baptist church served the largest number of Birmingham residents, but Presbyterians, Episcopalians, Roman Catholics, African Methodists, Colored Methodists and Congregationalists also had their own churches.[12] In 1930, there were 131 Baptist churches compared to 28 AME churches and 21 Holiness churches.[13] The Baptist churches under the guidance of such leaders as the Reverends John Goodgame, William Pettiford, and Thomas Walker achieved respect and appealed to the broadest number of African Americans.[14]

A church derived status from its membership rolls. No one church in Birmingham won the support of the city's black elite. Rather, its membership was scattered about the city just as the churches were. The Baptist churches that could boast a large number of middle-class members included Sixth Avenue Baptist (originally named Second Colored Baptist Church) and Sixteenth Street Baptist. The Methodist churches that had at least a core of elite members included Metropolitan AME Zion, St. Paul's Methodist Episcopal, Thirgood CME, St. John AME, and Scott's Chapel AME. They stand out as churches that were led by formally educated pastors who received support from professionally employed layleaders.[15] The First Congregational's elite membership ranked among the highest of all the city's churches, followed by St. Mark's Episcopal, founded in 1891 and Miller Memorial Presbyterian. St. Mark's Episcopal Church and Miller Memorial Presbyterian attracted more middle-class members because they practiced more staid services.[16]

In 1882, several Congregationalists under the direction of Burton and Hattie Hudson organized First Congregational Church. B. H. Hudson like several other early members was a graduate of Talladega College, which proved to be an important connection. It became known as the "education church" because of the large numbers of teachers and principals among its members. From its modest beginnings in a storefront at Seventeenth Street and Second Avenue North, with AMA money First Congregational erected a small building at Third Avenue and Twenty-Sixth Street North. Although it had a limited membership of approximately two hundred, the vast majority of its members belonged to the black professional class.[17] The reserved style of worship mobilized a congregation that was largely well educated, refined, and cultured. Despite the reputation of First Congregational as an elite church, the members themselves were not self-absorbed. They organized activities that served the broader community. As noted in the previous chapter, members of the First Congregational provided a temporary home for Industrial High School until it could find a permanent location. This is particularly significant because, although they helped Industrial High School, many members of the church were Talladega College graduates, and they elected to send their children to Talladega or to some other private school where they could receive a purely academic education.

The Baptist churches vied for recognition and aggressively recruited new members who held elevated positions in the community. The Sixteenth Street Baptist was *the* black church in Birmingham during the early twentieth century. It had about a thousand members in 1900, many of whom were established leaders beyond their Smithfield and Enon Ridge neighborhoods: James O. Diffay, Thomas C. Windham, Charles T. Mabry, Arthur H. Parker (until he moved to First Congregational), Peter F. Clarke, and Dr. Ulysses G. Mason were all layleaders who realized personal satisfaction as they contributed to the church's status and growth.[18] Over time they served on the board of trustees and held positions as deacons, treasurers, and officers. All these titles enhanced their status within the church as they asserted their influence in important matters and increased their visibility among other congregants. They were Baptists who exhibited a particular reservedness that was uncharacteristic of many other Baptist churches. Numerous Smithfield residents who were respected in their local community were also practicing Baptists who participated in both local and state affairs. Rev. F. R. Kennedy had presided over a church in Anniston before arriving in Birmingham. In 1895, he was a member of the Board of Incorporators of the Colored Missionary Baptists Convention of Alabama when it held its annual meeting in Anniston and he conducted devotional exercises during their 1898 annual session in Tuscaloosa.[19] He increased his visibility and enhanced his credibility through his participation in these sessions, but he never achieved the status of William Pettiford. T. W. Walker, an effective and charismatic orator, drew hundreds of parishioners to the Sixth Avenue Baptist Church, where the devoted crowds swelled from the pews and aisles into the streets. In 1891, Walker left the Sixth Avenue Baptist Church in response to some disgruntled members who disapproved of his arrogant manner and theatrical style of worship. After briefly serving at a Brighton church, Walker established the Shiloh Baptist Church with six members. Within four years, the membership had increased to more than two thousand members, and a second larger building was erected for $40,000.[20] Although Shiloh was a working-class church, Walker elicited almost unprecedented recognition from the broader black community as he received respect for both his abilities as a pastor and his success as a business leader. He was often requested to speak at political and social functions: In 1905, he preached the commencement sermon at the Tuggle Institute, and in the following year, he gave a sermon in Atlanta.[21] In contrast to Walker's flamboyant style, Reverends Fountain G. Ragland and Eugene C. Lawrence capably directed the First Congregational Church through its formative years. They were formally educated, and they conducted reserved services that appealed to professional blacks; working-class blacks preferred the more emotional services of Walker or the highly charged services of Rev. A. D. Dunlap of the Church of the Living God.[22]

In their unparalleled study of the black church, Mays and Nicholson concluded that "nothing can compare with this ownership and control except ownership of the home and possibly control of the Negro Lodge."[23] The church was always the first black-owned community building and one of the only ones that African Americans completely controlled.[24] The church building itself held considerable social significance; it was a source of pride and symbolized the material progress of the black community. Pastors who had connections to influential whites had the greatest success in winning financial assistance for a new church building. When William Pettiford sought funds for a new building after the city condemned the older Sixteenth Street building, he approached the Steiner Brothers Bank. Although Rev. Charles Fisher was pastor of Sixteenth Street Baptist at the time, he needed Pettiford to orchestrate the deal. In 1909, the Sixteenth Street Baptist Church and Mamie Steiner entered into a mortgage agreement, whereby Mamie Steiner loaned the church $15,000 of the $62,000 needed for construction of the building located on the northern boundary of the Black Business District.[25] In 1905 the Shiloh Baptist Church under Walker's leadership, spent $45,000 to build a sanctuary and basement. In 1926, when members of the Shiloh Baptist decided to build a new building, they chose to erect a building on land not yet purchased. Before construction began, the church satisfied an earlier debt with the Steiner Brothers Bank.[26] Before turning to the outside community for financial assistance, board members first appealed to the congregants for aid. Although women are credited with being the moving force behind most of the church fund-raising campaigns, B. L. Windham, as head of the Faithful Workers' Club, was declared "the greatest layman church financier of the city."[27] Under the capable guidance of Rev. John Goodgame, who had strong connections to the white community, Sixth Avenue achieved greatness.[28] During the 1920s, Goodgame declared that membership at Sixth Avenue had reached 4,500. Unlike either Walker or Pettiford, who were accomplished businessmen, Goodgame was a pastor who devoted his energy to building church membership, nurturing ties with the white power elite, promoting self-help and black business, and reaching out to the broader African American community. He capably managed the church's finances and built grand edifices that included a Sunday-School annex that cost $30,000.[29] Numerous ministers in Birmingham aggressively campaigned for financial support from not only their church members but also from nonmembers, both black and white. Whatever strategy they adopted to raise funds seemed to work; churches continued to purchase lots and construct buildings.[30]

The churches with the most solid foundations engaged in a variety of outreach programs that were designed to provide personal fulfillment for its members; to improve the social conditions within the broader community; and to furnish a site where African Americans could assemble without interference.[31] Such local race newspapers as the *Reporter*, the *Truth*, and the *Voice of the People* sporadically covered the diverse social, cultural, and religious programs at the various churches in and around Birmingham. Coverage tended to focus on the social and professional activities of the African American community's more distinguished members.[32] The *Reporter* covered cultural events and commented on their social value: "Great concert held at 16th St. Baptist. The Williams Singers came to Birmingham. . . . [T]he program was rather in advance of our people, and a few more demonstrations of this kind would certainly be of benefit to the community and to the colored race particularly."[33] The *Truth*'s front-page coverage of a wedding at the Sixteenth Street Baptist revealed the church's elite status and the size of a growing "better class" of African Americans, and it provided insight into the vastness of the building itself: "Miss Mabel Harris weds Mr. R. M. Neely, Jr. Over 700 of Birmingham's society attended at 16th St. Baptist."[34]

The large and centrally located church buildings became the sites for highly emotional meetings that centered around moral issues that often, although not always, underlined class differences within the community. St. Paul's became the focus of a highly charged evening when a mass meeting convened to discuss alcohol use and its broader ramifications. Nearly a thousand people, predominantly women, heard Revs. Pettiford, McGill, and Walker speak out against alcohol abuse. They issued a petition to the city authorities protesting against the sale of alcohol to women or to children who were sent to purchase it.[35] And Rev. John Goodgame was not alone when he expelled some of his Sixth Avenue Baptist Church members for gambling, drunkenness, and immoral behavior. However distasteful these activities were to some groups whose members were champions of the temperance movement, drinking, gambling, and dancing were legitimate forms of entertainment that primarily working-class blacks and whites enjoyed. The strong interest in these activities supported the numerous saloons and pool halls that were located in both the black and white business districts.[36] Movies and live theater had also become popular forms of entertainment for all Americans during this time. But live theater also caused grief for some pastors. Sixteenth Street's Rev. C. L. Fisher spoke out against theater as "Satan's Reception Room," where audiences were seduced with unsavory and immoral images.[37]

Politically charged events drew enthusiastic listeners to the church. In 1928, during an Emancipation Day Celebration, Rev. Frank Alstork of the Metropolitan AME Zion Church used the occasion to challenge the unfair treatment African Americans received in light of the sacrifices they made during the nation's wars.[38] Occasionally, such notable speakers as W. E. B. Du Bois, Booker T. Washington, and Marcus Garvey appeared at a handful of churches where they espoused their diverse philosophies to a cross-section of Birmingham's black communities. When unprecedented numbers came to hear Washington speak at Walker's Shiloh Baptist Church during a National Baptist convention, a stampede occurred that resulted in several deaths. The church building also served as a politically democratic venue where laypeople expressed their grievances and staged their own protests. In 1895, numerous blacks convened at the Shiloh Baptist Church to protest the police shooting of a young black girl who was caught stealing coal from a coal car.[39]

Churches also joined forces to challenge racism. The Interdenominational Ministerial Alliance organized to address serious problems that plagued the black community. The more formal structure, with headquarters at the Pythian Temple Building, challenged the prevailing Jim Crow laws.[40] The alliance condemned the Birmingham Railway, Light and Power Company for its "practices with colored people." Specifically, they opposed the mistreatment of black women and the inadequate supply of seating that resulted in blacks standing when white seating remained vacant: "Some of your conductors are gentlemen and treat the Negro passengers as they should be treated, while others are cruel and almost inhuman. Our people spend their money freely on your cars, and we feel that we ought to receive better treatment."[41] Rev. R. H. Keller organized the Union Conference of the White and Colored Ministers of Birmingham to open the lines of communication between the races, while other black pastors strongly supported the Interchurch World Movement.[42] In 1920, 173 black delegates attended the conference in Birmingham, and a special session was held on the last day of the conference at Sixteenth Street Baptist Church. The black clergymen demonstrated a more cooperative and sincere commitment than did their white counterparts, and they agreed that "the movement would be helpful in promoting better race relations and in combating prejudice, injustice, and lynching."[43]

Essentially, the African American churches shared a common goal—racial uplift—and they worked independently and cooperatively toward achieving it. Sixth Avenue and Shiloh Baptist, among many other smaller churches, hosted social functions while the First Congregational Church provided the venue for numerous highbrow social functions and political rallies.[44] They all promoted programs that benefited various aspects of the community in one way or another. The Young Men's Christian Working Circle of the Shiloh Baptist Church held regular meetings and sought to assist their younger members to develop a strong moral character. In the mid-1920s the Mt. Pilgrim Baptist Association had instituted a Baptist Young Peoples Union. Under the leadership of P. D. Davis, the organization worked to coordinate the activities of BPYU workers and youth from its ninety churches for "training fellowship and spiritual renewal." The AME church had a similar association called the Allen Christian Endeavor Society. A Junior Church movement was also popular in the 1920s when young adults assumed the roles of church elders once every few weeks. Taken together, these youth-oriented programs not only offered opportunities to inculcate doctrine teaching but also provided leadership training and recreation time, albeit in a religious setting.[45] The Sixteenth Street Baptist organized the first African American missionary society in Birmingham, and other churches such as the First Congregational, followed suit. The cooperative events were designed to foster unity within and across denominations and to reach out to the broader community. The Sixteenth Street Baptist often held its monthly meetings at the Shiloh Baptist and urged its members and other churches' congregations to attend. In 1918, the Sixteenth Street Baptist and the Colored Methodist Church engaged in a Sunday School contest held at Sixteenth Street Baptist. The competition was staged to raise funds for community services.[46] These programs also provided a forum in which church members could develop leadership skills and exhibit their elevated position to members of other churches.

Whereas the multifunctional character of the black churches met most of the needs of its members, sometimes individuals looked elsewhere for fulfillment. The fraternal and benevolent orders often filled the gaps. Although such organizations were often targeted for usurping the influence of the church and duplicating its role in the community, they more often complemented the church's varied roles. Winfield Henri Mixon, the presiding elder of the African Methodist Episcopal Church in Birmingham in 1887, 1897, and 1920, recognized how these organizations worked in concert with the church's function: "We believe in the church first; masonry second."[47] The church had multiple dimensions including social, economic, political, and educational; but whether the orders duplicated the services offered through the churches seems somewhat immaterial since the African American community overall sorely needed a vast range of community services and avenues for personal expression.

On April 25, 1930, the *Birmingham Truth* posed the question, "Is Fraternalism Dying?" The author not only dismissed the possibility of the decline of fraternalism but also offered a detailed and enthusiastic reminder of the central role that fraternal orders played in the growth and development of the black community in Birmingham. The following quote reveals the intrinsic value of these organizations: "Most of us who have risen to any heights socially, economically, politically have done so on the back of Fraternal Organizations and, morally, educationally and spiritually the fraternal organizations have made large contributions."[48] The period between 1880 and 1890 was called the "Golden Age of Fraternity." Such secular organizations as the True Reformers, the Prince Hall Masons, and the Knights of Pythias proliferated among urban blacks.[49] Before the turn of the century, fraternal orders and mutual aid societies had already established a strong presence in counties throughout Alabama as African Americans recognized the importance of these organizations that "gave a special flavor and unity to Negro urban life."[50]

Although E. Franklin Frazier disparagingly called the black fraternal orders a "world of make-believe," and Gunnar Myrdal renounced them as "pathological," their contributions cannot be overlooked.[51] Organizations that were purely social or had a strong social element provided blacks with a forum where they could elicit status and prestige. African Americans suffered the psychological effects associated with slavery, and they were continually subjected to discrimination and segregation as Jim Crow laws reinforced racial separation. Through the creation of their own institutions and fraternal orders, African Americans empowered themselves and gained a sense of belonging.[52]

The multiple and overlapping functions of these organizations spurred their growth and enhanced their appeal to whites and African Americans. Although they belonged to segregated organizations with the same or similar names, the members shared an enthusiasm for creating secret associations. Birmingham's black organizations, such as the Tri-State Order of Beneficiaries and the Union Central Relief Association, provided financial support to members, including sick and death benefits, and aid to the poor and to families whose members were ill or who were unemployed. The weekly dues that varied from five, ten, and twenty-five cents a week and from ten cents to a dollar a month returned members many times their original value in services and peace of mind.[53] Some sought to enhance and protect their status through their affiliation with different orders, whereas others joined for utilitarian reasons and maintained a low profile. Ellen Tarry recalled: "My father belonged to the Knights of Pythias so he could be assured of an appropriate burial."[54] These organizations also provided members with a forum to espouse and perpetuate middle-class behaviors and values and ergo functioned as agents of social control. Furthermore, there was the opportunity to develop fictive kinship ties within the group. The social benefits derived from membership in fraternal orders extended into business circles, as individuals networked professionally and expanded their alliances beyond the local environment. Although several of the orders had women's auxiliaries, the lodges within the orders were gender specific. What emerged were lodges created by African Americans who further separated themselves along gender lines: their affiliation within these orders cemented ties through gender solidarity and racial segregation.[55]

Fraternal orders and benevolent societies, like the church, provided individuals with opportunities for personal and political expression within the framework of the orders' hierarchies.[56] From the information available, it appears that the leading lodge members were often high profile church officials whose employment reflected an elevated status in the black community. While the working class comprised the bulk of the membership in most orders, elite African Americans rose to the top of the secret society hierarchy.[57] The Mosaic Templars boasted that "there are several lodges here at Birmingham headed by some of the best members of the race." Similarly, the Knights of Pythias attracted "some of the best business and professional men of the race. . . . Most of them hold distinct and honorable positions in their communities, as well as being highly respected by the organization of which they are a part."[58]

The opportunity for membership in several orders was open to many middle-class African Americans who exercised this right freely. Oscar Adams held memberships in the Masons, Knights of Pythias, Odd Fellows, Mosaic Templars, and other similar organizations, whereas Charles M. Harris, Sr., was a member of the Masons, the Knights of Pythias, and the Elks, among others. Although complete rosters for the different organizations were inaccessible for this study, from the available information it appears that the more prominent members of the black community served as officers in the local lodges. Smithfield residents also rose to prominence in the lodges, including E. A. Brown, who offered his legal expertise and was acting attorney for the Knights of Pythias, and I. B. Kigh, who served as chairman of Lodge 23, and, of course, R. A. Blount. Smithfield residents, including Charles T. Mabry, were also well represented in the Masons' Triune Lodge. Official titles held prestige for the officers within the order, and they enjoyed recognition from the broader African American community through newspaper accounts of the lodges' activities.[59]

Primus D. Davis's affiliations in the church and in several fraternal orders reflected the broad range of opportunities and connections an individual could achieve through membership in multiple organizations. In 1899, upon arriving in Birmingham from Montgomery County, Davis started at Harris Brothers Grocery at $1.50 per week. By 1907, he incorporated the Peoples' Grocery Company, but the nationwide panic forced him to declare bankruptcy. The reputation he had earned among his creditors enabled him to reopen his enterprise after a brief lapse. As financial secretary and deacon at the Sixteenth Street Baptist Church, Davis established a relationship with Rev. C. L. Fisher. Together they and Peter Clarke started the Peoples' Grocery Company located in the heart of the BBD. Davis held the position of secretary at Windham Brothers Construction Company, where he enhanced his connections with elite African Americans. His final and most lucrative foray in the business sector was as a real estate broker. His involvement in social and fraternal affairs were numerous: he was an active member and master of a Masonic lodge for more than twenty years; he was an Elk, a member of the Knights of Pythias, and a Mosaic Templar. Davis was president of the Mt. Pilgrim BYPU Convention comprising the local and Jefferson County societies. His lifelong membership in the National Negro Business League propelled him to found the Birmingham Civic and Commercial Association. He was a member of the Baptist Laymen's Movement, Secretary of the Board of Trustees of Birmingham Baptist College, a member of the Board of Trustees of Tuggle Institute, and a member of the Board of Trustees of the Alabama Association for the Colored Blind. He donated generously to religious and educational institutions. For a time he also served as Chairman of the Colored Division of the Community Chest for Birmingham. During World War I, he was secretary to the Colored Division of the Speakers' Bureau of the Four Minute Men of Alabama and received a certificate of honor from President Woodrow Wilson.[60] He was a successful black businessman in Birmingham whose diverse interests and activities provided him with the means to develop a valuable network of relationships among the city's African American elite circles. Davis wrote for the *Birmingham Truth* and used his weekly column, "Current Gleanings," to comment on race-related affairs. In 1929, as the nation's economy continued its downward spiral, he was one of many elite blacks who recognized the responsibility of the leadership class and urged social and economic cooperation among African Americans: "The individual 'on top' who deserves to remain 'up' is the fellow who is willing to reach down and lend a helping hand to his less fortunate brother. . . . Here is a great opportunity for our fraternal organizations, our religious units and educational institutions."[61]

It is useful at this point to take a closer look at specific fraternal orders which drew members of Birmingham's black community into the organizational fold. Like their white counterparts, who founded such secret societies as the Knights of Pythias, the Oddfellows, and the Masons, local blacks demonstrated an interest in their parallel but separate orders. The large national African American orders such as the Masons, "one of the bulwarks of the black middle class" and the Odd Fellows (both founded during antebellum times) and the Knights of Pythias, and the Elks (post Civil War organizations) were not merely replicas of the white orders; rather they were organizations that developed a character which reflected the distinct needs of the community they served.[62]

In 1869, Alabama Free Masonry had its beginnings in Mobile, when the Grand Lodge of Ohio chartered Hiram Lodge in Mobile and seven other subordinate lodges elsewhere in the state. The Alabama Masons experienced remarkable growth at the turn of the century: by 1902, there were 104 lodges statewide with a total of 1,800 members. They collectively owned $90,000.00 worth of real estate and other property, and the cash and securities owned by the Grand and Subordinate Lodges totaled $50,000.[63] One of Birmingham's earliest African American Masonic lodges met in 1883. By 1887, other Masonic lodges had been established, including the Mt. Ebron Lodge, No. 18, whose members and officers included John Tuggle and A. A. Sensabaugh.[64] Birmingham became the focus of major decision-making processes and the center of social and political functions of the Free Masons in Alabama. Like the white Masons, the Prince Hall Masons were the accepted elite of the fraternal world.[65]

America has long been identified as a "nation of joiners," and African Americans shared this character trait. Choices abounded for individuals searching for affiliation in one or several fraternal orders.[66] The Knights of Pythias attracted legions of blacks and experienced rapid growth in Alabama and specifically in Birmingham during the early part of the twentieth century. W. T. Jones founded the Excelsior Lodge No. 1 at Birmingham in December 1887, with John L. Tuggle as the first Chancellor Commander. Local residents founded other Knights of Pythias lodges in and around the city. The Iron City Lodge No. 3 was founded in the same year and P. W. Williamson, a Smithfield resident, held the highest official position. Tuggle, with the assistance of other members, aggressively led the order through a rapid and successful expansion throughout Alabama.[67] When in 1888 the Knights organized the Grand Lodge in Birmingham and Tuggle was appointed Grand Chancellor, the city was earmarked as the center of Pythian activity in Alabama. Tuggle served in that capacity until 1901 when Richard A. Blount replaced him as Grand Chancellor, a position he held for over thirty years. Under Blount's direction, the order experienced marked growth. The Knights, like the Masons, tried to attract a "better class" of men who exhibited middle-class lifestyles. In 1905, the *Truth,* the official organ of the Knights of Pythias, reported that I. B. Kigh had gathered together a convention of "brilliant young men of good character and standing."[68]

During the early 1900s, the Order had weathered internal strife that threatened to blow apart the state organization. Blount's leadership had held the Alabama Pythians together, but a more divisive internal conflict that transpired in the mid-1920s required outside legal intervention to settle matters.[69] By the late 1920s, the Knights was rife with problems and the conflicts became increasingly ugly as Oscar Adams and others brought charges of graft and theft against the Order and specifically against Blount, E. A. Brown, U. G. Mason, and I. B. Kigh. Adams took legal action and filed suit that found its way to the Supreme Court of Alabama. The factions within the order underline the presence of variance among the city's elite class of African Americans. They were not always united, and their differences came to the fore when they had the opportunity to express themselves in a politicized environment.[70] Like the Knights of Pythias, the Elk lodges were targets of some biting criticisms and internal dissension. Nationally, the Elks were suffering an internal crisis. In an address to a packed house in Birmingham, W. W. Greene, Grand Esteemed Loyal Knight of the Grand Lodge, articulated his pride in the lodges and the realities of external accusations. He urged members to abandon their petty accusations and to move toward cooperation so that "the highest possible standard is established."[71]

The local lodges maintained their independence from national problems, and they continued to recruit new members and proceed with their fraternal activities. Unlike the internal problems that continually troubled the orders, conflicts between the different fraternal orders were avoided because of the overlapping memberships. Members differentiated one order from the other and carefully selected the specific lodge they chose to join. The overlapping memberships might illustrate enhanced status derived from multiple affiliations rather than membership based on the different services each order provided its members.[72] The Improved Benevolent and Protective Order of Elks of the World competed for members in the Birmingham District, but because the national order was founded much later than the other prominent organizations, it entered a very competitive market. Yet it could boast among its members many middle-class citizens and leaders of Birmingham's black community, including Drs. A. M. Brown and L. U. Goins, and, too, the Elks reached into the ranks of the masses unlike no other order. The Jones Valley Lodge, No. 14, was the preeminent lodge among African American Elks in Birmingham and in the state. By 1919, the lodge had about six hundred members and was the second largest of the Elk lodges in the U.S., just behind a lodge in Philadelphia. Its Executive Committee members were W. B. Driver, P. D. Davis, B. L. Windham, R. A. Blount, C. M. Harris, and P. F. Clarke. Other prominent entrepreneurs were among members of the Committee on Business Propositions, including T. C. Windham, I. B. Kigh, Sr., and J. T. Harrison; and W. A. Rayfield and E. A. Brown, among others, were on the Committee on Race Relations.[73]

To rise within the ranks required a proven record of service and ability. Robert Mabry was selected as secretary to the Endowment Department of the Knights of Pythias state office. Mabry, a renowned tailor, lived in Smithfield. His success as an artisan enabled him to become a proprietor when he branched out into establishing a retail trade. In 1917, the *Weekly Voice* highlighted Mabry's achievements when it noted that "he has built up a successful business of his own in Birmingham. . . . In the gent's furnishing business and haberdashery . . . he has done well and has a large trade, a big following and does business in a business like way."[74] His middle-class status could rival that of most other elite blacks in Smithfield. The *Weekly Voice* ran a subjective profile detailing his entrepreneurial acumen, his integrity, and his commitment to the organization. According to the article, "No better man could be selected for this important post than Bob Mabry."[75]

Fraternal leaders did not rest on their laurels while they proudly enjoyed their lofty titles. They were expected to recruit new members, oversee the finances, and, furthermore, to attend to the duties outlined in their constitutions. All fraternal organizations shared the vision of racial uplift through cooperation. Although the orders distinguished themselves from one another, their constitutions and stated objectives sounded strikingly similar: Uplifting the fallen, burying the dead, caring for the widows and orphans and placing man upon a platform of social equality. When James Byrd, a fraternal member died, his "brothers" drew together and collected a "small token of esteem and sympathy" for his spouse. They had developed strong ties with Byrd and followed through on their commitment as Knights.[76]

Membership in a fraternal lodge offered individuals a retreat from the marginality they experienced in the broader community. The

Knights of Pythias, c. 1912 (Birmingfind Collection, Catalog #829.1.1.32, Department of Archives and Manuscripts, Birmingham Public Library, Ala.)

middle-class members who had achieved relative success in their occupations and enjoyed some respect within the African American community sought a forum in which they could reconcile the dissonance they experienced. Their annual elections provided opportunities for members to vote.[77] By exercising this privilege, the members exacted a certain amount of self-esteem as they engaged in an activity they were restricted from in the broader society. The ritualistic character and rigid codes of behavior reinforced the secretive and elitist nature of the group and "heighten[ed] the sense of being among a select group of influentials." The Knights of Pythias, the Odd Fellows, the Masons, and the Elks all used similar regalia, paraphernalia, rituals, and passwords as did their white counterparts. Members could proudly adorn themselves in elaborate uniforms and could share a handshake or password that was unknown to outsiders. These rituals reinforced their self-esteem and strengthened their sense of moral unity. All the orders considered a breach of duty an offense which they dealt with promptly and judiciously.[78]

The orders were not political bodies that exercised influence in the mainstream community, yet they espoused a conservatism that reflected their members' middle-class position. The officers often acted as politicians when they vied for elected office and took a public stance on controversial matters. Through these statements, they asserted their authority and influence to members and nonmembers alike and sought to represent the moral character of black Birmingham. When labor unions began appealing to African Americans and invited their participation, many black laborers joined with the hope of improving their working conditions. In 1908, Henry C. Binford, then Grand Master, threatened black Masons who supported the unions: "If any Mason is killed while affiliating with the labor unions his heirs will not be entitled to benefits from the endowment department of the grand lodge of Alabama Masons. I consider every Mason in the Birmingham district connected with these unions fighting the laws of the state a murderer."[79]

The orders espoused the importance of and worked toward racial uplift. P. D. Davis, as State Secretary of the Masons, often traveled about the region seeking to unite and strengthen the branches scattered throughout Alabama. When he delivered the St. John's Day address to a large Masonic audience, Davis highlighted the community-oriented spirit of the Order. Furthermore, he urged the audience to take personal responsibility for their uplift when he called for "better and more well ordered homes and improved [home] environments as essential elements to character building and moral growth."[80]

When an Order was in trouble, members demonstrated a cooperative spirit that was an integral part of the organizations' objectives. In 1917, when the Masonic order was carrying a debt of nearly $1,000,000, members rallied together and pulled the Order out of its financial crisis. Early on, they also demonstrated their commitment to other members when they established educational scholarships. The Masons' emphasis on responsibility to one another and to the community was internalized by its members who needed the Order as much as the Order needed them. The Knights of Pythias shared a similar commitment: In 1929, when a flood ravaged southeastern Alabama where many members lost their homes, Grand Chancellor Blount issued the following proclamation: "I am calling upon each and every member of the Order and every lodge to send a donation of whatever you may have to give . . . to aid the flood sufferers and members of the Order. If there ever was a time to show your loyalty and demonstrate to the world your obligation, it is now."[81] The lodges complied. Members also initiated programs to improve benefits for themselves: In 1907, the Pythians entertained the idea of establishing their own bonding company rather than paying their fees to a white organization: "We think it would be policy to have the Supreme Lodge to organize such a branch of business keeping all of our moneys possible in the body." In 1908, the members of the Uniform Department, Knights of Pythias, held a meeting to perfect plans to organize an Endowment Department or Pension Department for the members of their branch.[82] The Elks engaged in community-oriented activities: all the local lodges combined their efforts and provided a turkey dinner for the Alabama Colored Orphans and Old Folks Home. They also enjoyed and hosted both private and public social events. The *Reporter* was moved to declare that "No other organization in the city has provided more entertainment this year, wholesome and cultural, than the Elks." And they responded to the cries of an alarmed black community which was afraid of losing its community center. When it learned that the federal government would no longer fund the Center of the War Camp Community Service, which blacks used for recreational and social activities, the Elks assumed the responsibility of keeping the center open.[83] The Elks, and specifically Jones Valley Lodge, was actively pursuing a higher and more positive profile in Birmingham. At the turn of the century, several fraternal organizations demonstrated their commitment to the broader community when they helped establish the Tuggle Institute and financially sustain the Alabama Colored Orphans and Old Folks Home.[84]

Although the orders had gained considerable recognition among themselves, they sometimes encountered hostilities from members of the white orders who resented the black organizations. The white and black Masonic Orders operated as separate entities; however, confrontations occurred that challenged the credibility of the black order. In 1921, Aaron Jackson, a black Mason was publicly harassed. He wrote a letter to the *Birmingham Reporter* recounting the incident: "Saturday, May 21st, the Southern Railroad Detective drew a pistol on me, made me pull of [*sic*] my Shrine pin, told me don't let him see me with it on again, do [*sic*] it will be trouble."[85] Jackson urged the August Grand Lodge not to meet in Selma at the appointed time because of the hostile atmosphere. The black Masons had established a reputable Order in Alabama and in Birmingham, but a few white Masons felt threatened by their presence. The black Elks faced similar confrontations and challenges from members of the white order. Harry Pace, who held an official position in the national organization, concluded in 1907 that "[not] only are Negro Elks unsafe anywhere in the country, but it means that Odd Fellows, Pythians and others will, in one way or another feel the force of the blow. The fight is not against the Elks alone, but is the beginning of a fight against all negro organizations."[86] None of the orders bowed to the threats; they would have been hard pressed to abandon the orders that they had worked so hard to build and which gave them personal satisfaction.

In the earlier years before the African American orders built meeting places, they met in rooms rented over a black-owned store or in a black business building, such as the Alabama Penny Savings Building. Eventually, most of the larger Orders owned their own buildings that were built by members of their race. The lodges typically met at a hall built specifically for the Order, and if an organization did not have sufficient funds to erect its own meeting place, it often shared space with another lodge. Both the Knights of Pythias Hall and the Grand United Order of Odd Fellows Hall were located at 1524 1-2 2nd Avenue. In 1917, the 32nd Grand Session of the Grand Lodge of Knights and Ladies of Honor met at the Knights of Pythias Hall, and the Supreme Club of the same order met at the Masonic Temple in 1929. The following year, the National Grand Lodge of the Mosaic Templars also met at the Masonic Temple Hall, and it met at the Sixth Avenue Baptist Church, where one of its officers, Rev. John Goodgame, was the pastor. Eventually, the Knights of Pythias, the Masons, and the Odd Fellows all had their own buildings as did the Order of Elks, whose meeting place was built by T. C. Windham at a cost of $68,000.[87] They could maintain their codes of secrecy when the organizations and members controlled their environment, and they could enhance their status within the broader black community when they met in their privately owned quarters. These buildings had symbolic significance as a measure of race progress and African Americans delighted in the fact that they owned and controlled these properties. "There are scarcely any cities of note and in which there are not some stately brick buildings which have been built by these various fraternities and whose constructors were negroes. These signs of progress are worthy of note."[88] The grand lodges not only recognized and promoted property ownership, specifically homeownership among their individual members, but the lodges themselves also acknowledged the value of investing in real estate, and their sizable property holdings bear witness to this fact. By 1928, Masons owned real and personal property in the U.S. valued at $3,000,000. On the state level, in 1911 the Knights of Pythias owned property worth $75,000.00; by 1917 the Order had achieved sufficient financial stability to purchase the Alabama Penny–Prudential Building for $75,000. In 1930, the Order was worth in excess of $500,000 in property and cash.[89]

An estimate of membership in the larger national orders reveals that in the early 1920s the black Elks, eventually the largest African American order, had 70,000 members; the Masons had approximately 9,000 lodges with 150,000 members; and the Knights of Pythias had 250,000 members. The Odd Fellows surpassed these orders with 304,000 members. W. E. B. Du Bois in 1899 had declared the Odd Fellows "the most powerful and flourishing secret order" among blacks.[90] On the local level, lodges achieved a remarkable rate of growth during the early twentieth century. The ranks of the Alabama Masons swelled during the first part of the twentieth century; by 1920, it proudly declared a state membership totaling more than 18,000.[91] The Knights of Pythias also experienced unprecedented growth: from 1906 to 1909, 270 lodges had a combined membership of 11,000. By 1913, the order had suffered a decline in membership of 1,400, and by 1915 the membership stood at 6,950 although the number of lodges had increased to 298. Despite the decrease in the Knights of Pythians in Alabama, in 1917 in the Birmingham District alone there were thirty-five lodges with about 3,000 members. Perhaps Blount's residency in Smithfield may have won local support thereby reinforcing the strength of Pythians in the district.[92] In contrast to the visibility of the other orders, in 1923 there were only three Elk lodges in the state.[93] The hard numbers reveal the appeal and allure that fraternal orders had for African Americans. Members found like-minded men who shared their values and their goals, and the lodge provided an environment in which they could assert their political aspirations and engage in community uplift, while they secured a status for themselves.[94]

Blacks from all classes found no greater comfort than when they were among their own. Although the fraternal orders strengthened the bonds of brotherhood, the orders did not meet all the social needs of their members. They looked to the more informal clubs for greater personal satisfaction. And, for those elite individuals who were not interested in formal group associations and their ritualistic character, the less-structured clubs offered a more suitable and relaxed setting. Although the men's purely social activities were less frequently documented by the race papers, they nonetheless were important.[95] Smithfield residents and their Enon Ridge neighbors participated in such clubs to satisfy their personal needs. Although women in the area had more of these social clubs than their male counterparts, the men did congregate in less structured get-togethers that complemented their affiliation in fraternal orders. The largely social component of these clubs should in no way suggest a trivial character. To the contrary, these clubs carried a significance perhaps unmatched by any other type of organization. They reveal a deeper level of intimacy among participants. How and with whom someone shares their leisure time away from an structured environment reveals who, in fact, are close friends. The clubs tended to have a rather limited membership composed of men of similar status who often shared fraternal memberships. In that sense, the clubs that originated in Smithfield were exclusive and elitist. But this club phenomenon was in no way unique to Smithfield; blacks living elsewhere in Birmingham also established clubs that operated to fulfill their own specific needs.

Club activity of the most distinguished black families was recorded in the *Reporter* and the *Truth*. According to Drake and Cayton's study of the African American community in Chicago, "middle-class social-club world thrives on publicity." It appears that the professional class in Smithfield also prized the mention of their names. Alumni of Booker T. Washington's institute founded the Tuskegee Club, which functioned as a literary and social organization. Meetings were held in the members' homes, where they would conduct "business" and engage in purely social activities. Members were not immune from the realities of Jim Crow, and they addressed pressing issues periodically. In 1919, at the Diffay's home in Smithfield, president Charles Mabry presided over a meeting that addressed the need for a more permanent home for the club with a rest and waiting room for "our ladies while downtown shopping." Each of the attending twenty-eight members pledged from $5 to $25 to make their first payment on the home. Peer pressure undoubtedly moved all those in attendance to make a donation. The evening concluded on a lighter note when one of the members gave an impromptu musical performance.[96] Younger men from more prominent families had their own brand of social club. The Iroquois Club was one of the first social clubs among African American males in Birmingham. It was established before 1898 and persisted well into the 1920s. The members gave a Xmas Hoo-Ray at the Elk's Rest in 1919; it was considered the big social function of the season and it included the college set and numerous out-of-town guests.[97] Other men's clubs included the Coterie Club, Strollers' Club, and the Creepers' Club. Birmingham historian Martha Bigelow concluded that these black men's clubs did not have as great an influence nor were they the arbitrators of "high" society as were the white men's organizations. Yet it is almost impossible and without merit to compare the influence of black and white social organizations and the impact they had on their members. Within the context of the black community, membership in these social clubs played a role that was essential to individuals who were restricted from participating in mainstream society. Affiliations in these class-specific clubs provided members with an opportunity to entertain and socialize in a relaxed environment apart from the critical eye of other African Americans and that of the dominant social structure.[98]

The abundance of fraternal and purely social clubs among African American males in no way suggests that these individuals ignored their responsibility to the broader black community. In fact, as noted earlier, middle-class men were the most influential figures in matters concerning business, education, and the church. In addition, they established other organizations designed to remove obstacles that impeded their own mobility and hampered the progress of the race. Enthusiasm for enfranchisement was rekindled among many African Americans when returning war veterans expected to exercise their right to vote.[99] Returning black war veterans were unable to secure their status as voters, nor could other black men and women who met the constitutional requirements register to vote. In 1918 black males organized the Colored Citizens' League. The League, which was originally suggested by the *Reporter* and endorsed by the *Birmingham News*, stood for law and order, advocated the rights of African Americans, and sought to make "better citizens than ever before . . . that if buying homes, paying taxes, building race enterprises would mean anything we would go our limit."[100] Its numerous committees were composed of influential black men; a membership list reads like a Who's Who of African American leaders in Birmingham. Among the businessmen were Robert Mabry, J. O. Diffay, and Oscar Adams, who served as president of the League; Revs. T. W. Walker and John W. Goodgame were only two of the many pastors involved, A. H. Parker and Drs. A. M. Brown and L. U. Goin were just a few of the many professionals who sat on the different committees. Many of Smithfield's most outstanding residents contributed to the vitality of the organization. These members were joined by "men from all walks of life . . . the laborers, miners, carpenters, bootblacks, artesans [*sic*], cooks, chambermaids, hairdressers, barbers and grocers."[101]

The League evolved into the Birmingham branch of the NAACP. In its first year, it drew strong support, boasting nearly a thousand members, both men and women. Male leadership in the local branch reflected the pattern of most southern branches and of the other African American civic organizations in Birmingham. In its initial stages, some supporters wanted a democratic organization, and they tried to delegate responsibility to the "workers and toilers, miners, carpenters, bricklayers, washwomen, hairdressers and workers in general as well as the ministers of the gospel and the few physicians and other professional men." But businessmen and professionals came to dominate it, and other professionals, government employees, active clubwomen, and domestic servants filled out the roster.[102]

The NAACP achieved its greatest visibility during its first two years when it worked to build public awareness and support.[103] However, African Americans failed to exhibit a commitment to the NAACP, an apathy uncharacteristic of many middle-class blacks who had demonstrated their commitment to improving black life in Birmingham. A few members of the NAACP were committed to the organization, such as E. W. Howell, the editor of the *Voice of the People*, and Oscar Adams, who blamed the self-serving black middle class for the organization's decline and powerlessness.[104] Unlike the national NAACP, the local branch failed to take direct action against the racism and discrimination that penetrated most aspects of Birmingham's society.[105] Even the reality of their political powerlessness did not move them to use the local NAACP to organize challenges. Not even the returning twenty thousand World War I black veterans could exercise their rights as citizens.[106] The NAACP also adopted a low profile for fear of alienating any sympathetic whites. Both the black middle-class and the black masses rejected the Birmingham branch of the NAACP and opted to secure some reform measures through more familiar and perhaps safer avenues. The NAACP's middle-class leaders tended to be self-serving, when they focused on black business concerns rather than on the general welfare of African Americans living in Birmingham.[107]

The Birmingham Business and Professional Men's Booster Club under the direction of Dr. M. H. Freeman, Jr., worked more effectively to improve societal conditions for the black community and specifically for black youth.[108] Another group that focused its attention on young African Americans was the Young Men's Christian Association (YMCA), which was initiated in Birmingham by Dr. D. L. Johnston in 1916. Through its emphasis on moral improvement and Christian uplift, it reached a class of the population that the church did not.[109] Young men who loitered on the streets and spent time in the pool halls were a concern to members of the black community. They sought to teach them middle-class values that would ensure their uplift and in turn would help the entire race. There was also the Industrial YMCA Welfare Workers of the Birmingham District that drew members from the various plants and factories in the area. During the well-attended meetings, black officials and local guest speakers addressed issues that were directly relevant to African American workers—economic and industrial conditions of blacks and religious and moral topics. The local branches used a more personal approach whereby teachers offered school lessons and recreational activities to young men who needed instruction and direction.[110] By 1928, there were 78 city and 140 student associations serving African American men and boys throughout the U.S. composed of black members, administered by black and inter-racial governing committees, and served by black officers who were YMCA employees.[111]

Another avenue through which African Americans organized to improve social conditions and generally to help uplift the race were the professional organizations. Southern doctors especially felt the effects of segregation when they were denied membership in the American Medical Association and thus were not allowed to practice in white hospitals.[112] Except for a brief time when Birmingham's black doctors operated a hospital at the Alabama Colored Orphans and Old Folks Home, African Americans did not have a facility of their own. Unlike blacks in Louisville who had their own Red Cross Hospital in 1899 and blacks in Durham who had their own Lincoln Hospital in 1901, Birmingham's African Americans were served in the segregated wards of Hillman and St. Vincent's hospitals.[113] The city's African American physicians combined forces when they organized their own medical union to educate the public on proper health care, to administer health services, and "for the betterment of race uplift."[114]

As noted in earlier chapters, physicians and other professionals were also leaders in business and civic affairs that took them beyond their fields of expertise. Dr. U. G. Mason, a Birmingham native and graduate of Meharry Medical College, was one of several medical practitioners who directed the pursuit of various reforms. Although he had numerous business interests beyond his medical practice that kept him busy, he recognized the need for a community facility that would encourage literacy and race pride among African Americans. He played a central role in securing a library for Birmingham's African American residents. After the Washington Library disappeared from the Slater School to make room for additional classrooms, blacks managed with a small inadequate facility for several years. When in 1903 a new public library opened on the fourth floor of City Hall, African Americans could not patronize it or any of the other suburban branches. On October 1, 1909, the free public library opened that

coincided with the Board of Education's deletion of the formal pro-
scription against blacks from the library rules.[115] Yet, the tradition of
excluding African Americans persisted and they were not permitted to
patronize any library building. In 1913, Dr. U. G. Mason took a leadership role when he appealed to the Carnegie Corporation, a foundation that had donated funds to build Birmingham's three branch libraries.[116] During 1917 and 1918 blacks, especially school principals,
petitioned for a branch of the public library, and Mason again appealed to Andrew Carnegie: "At present, the Colored people of this
city are not permitted to use the libraries—not even the ones donated
by you."[117] Although Carnegie did not respond, the city's Library
Board finally released over $3,200 held in a trust fund. (Black schools
had raised this money through entertainment.) The Board used a portion of the money to rent a former storeroom in the BBD to house the
segregated branch and authorized a $50 per month salary for the li-
brarian. The money also bought approximately two thousand books
covering a wide range of subjects, and the librarian subscribed to numerous magazines and periodicals, several of which were published by
and for African Americans.[118] When the library opened on October 9,
1918, African Americans celebrated their victory of securing a publicly funded facility.[119] U. G. Mason led the successful campaign that
resulted in the creation of a community institution where African
Americans could learn about their history and celebrate their heritage
during such annual observances as National Negro History Week.
Mason had moved beyond serving his own needs and those of his elite
cohorts when he worked toward establishing a public library that
served the best interest of all African Americans.[120]

This chapter demonstrated how African American males created a
separate infrastructure that served a variety of purposes. The church
played a unique role for black men who needed a place for self-expression. It gave them that and more—it gave those who aspired to positions of leadership a place where they could develop their skills and
assert their individual talents. The church offered the possibility for
political expression in the election of ecclesiastical office and in the
formulation of church policies. Many men who rose to prominence in
the church parlayed their status to the fraternal orders where they also
assumed leadership positions. The lodges where fraternal brothers met
brought together like-minded individuals who were seeking an identity and an affiliation that could set them apart from other blacks. The
regalia and rituals reinforced their sense of belonging and their sense
of separateness, and the collegiality they developed strengthened their

Mattie Herd, first librarian at Booker T. Washington Library,
1918 (Birmingfind Collection, Catalog #108.5.1.1, Department
of Archives and Manuscripts, Birmingham Public Library, Ala.)

ties within and beyond the order. Casual socializing at informal gatherings reinforced these ties. However introspective these men may have been while involved in their individual pursuits, they were not self-absorbed. They looked beyond their cloistered world, through their involvement in the church and in professional and civic organizations, and they used their affiliations to initiate movements for racial uplift. By creating their own world, many African American men maintained their racial identity while aspiring and actively pursuing goals that would satisfy their needs. In 1928, Robert Moton optimistically concluded after assessing the organized black effort for racial progress. "He is assuming an ever-increasing share of the responsibility for his own progress. At no time has the outlook for the Negro in America been as promising as it is today."[121] It is true that strides were made during the late nineteenth and early twentieth century, but men alone could not cover the entire playing field. They in no way could achieve all that they did without the involvement and commitment of African American women.

7

Women Seeking an Identity

Improving the Social and
Political Environment

Many outspoken African American women came to the fore during the late nineteenth century, including Sojourner Truth, Mary Church Terrell, Fannie Barrier Williams, and Anna J. Cooper. Cooper's urgings to women to "explore worlds outside the traditional realm of home and family" did not undermine the belief that the home played a central role in the progress of the race.[1] Black women recognized that the home was a source of strength and emphasized it as the starting point for racial uplift. The home was the foundation upon which African American women—mothers, wives, daughters who were also activists, and educators—built an infrastructure of organizations and institutions. Yet for some women, their place was not at home. Rather, there was a place for them in civic organizations and clubs where they could devote their time to social work. All these women, whether in the home or in the broader community, made a difference.[2]

Nellie Brown was an inspiration and a role model for many African American women in Birmingham during the early twentieth century. She served as president of the City Federation of Colored Women's Clubs, was an officer in the Southeastern and National Federation of Colored Women's Clubs and president of the State Federation of the Colored Women's Clubs, a black organization that founded the Margaret Murray Washington Home for Delinquent Girls outside of the Birmingham District. She was an active member of the Sixteenth Street Baptist Church where she participated in fund-raising events. She donated her time to such local organizations as the black branch of the Young Women's Christian Association (YWCA), where she served on the Board of Directors. Brown, along with William Driver, headed the building committee of Tuggle Institute when the school burned, and for a time she served as general chair of the black division of the Community Chest. She was also an active member in the Inter-racial Commission and donated her services to the Colored Orphans and Old Folks Home. Brown demonstrated her concern and commitment to her neighborhood when she participated in the Smithfield Community Improvement League, an organization that addressed the quality of life in the area. Nellie Brown's contributions to the African American community were recognized in 1927 when the Jones Valley Booster Club of Birmingham awarded her its annual loving cup for community service. The presentation took place at Industrial High School, where a record crowd witnessed the ceremony that paid tribute to the "woman who for years has been a familiar figure in the homes for the poor and the unfortunate, whose shoulder has even been under the wheel that has helped lift [the] fallen humanity and whose voice has often been heard as she plead for aid and for justice for the underprivileged of her group."[3]

Beyond her civic duties, Nellie Brown attended to her own personal needs as an African American woman in the South. She built a network of friends and acquaintances that provided distraction from the realities of the city life that discriminated against her. She was a member of such women's clubs as the Semper Fidelis and Sinovodad Clubs, and she attended informal gatherings where she and her colleagues socialized in gender-segregated and class-specific activities and couple-oriented functions. Brown did not take for granted her station in life as the wife of Dr. Arthur M. Brown, one of the few African American physicians in Birmingham. Rather, she recognized her privileged position among the most elite black families and strengthened her place through her various social and civic club affiliations. Her membership in both the purely social clubs and the civic organizations placed her among the most widely respected women in Birmingham during a time when women were struggling to gain a place not only among African American men but also among white women.

In 1910, when the Census enumerator came to the Brown household at 519 Fifth Avenue and inquired about the occupations of the household members, either Arthur or Nellie Brown responded that she was not employed in any trade or profession. Although this response is technically accurate, it is also misleading. Anyone casually perusing the manuscript census would conclude that Georgia-born Nellie Brown stayed at home caring for her children, while her spouse financially supported the family. This would be an incomplete picture. Nellie Brown was as busy as any employed person who held a full-time position, but her work did not earn her any wages. She was the primary caretaker of the children, and she was engaged in time-consuming volunteer organizations that focused on the improvement of social, political, and economic conditions among African Americans residing in Birmingham.[4]

Although Nellie Brown did not publicize her personal struggle—being black and being a woman—she undoubtedly was motivated by this duality.[5] Anna Julia Cooper, a former slave, feminist, and educator, recognized that African American women held a distinct position in society. In *A Voice from the South,* Cooper wrote that "The colored woman of to-day occupies, one may say, a unique position in this country. She is confronted by both a woman question and a race problem, and is as yet an unknown or an unacknowledged factor in both."[6] Black women became increasingly conscious of their place on the sidelines when the white women's suffrage movement excluded them from their organization and the black males' quest for voting rights also overlooked them. They recognized the need to unite forces to overcome the stigmas attached to being both black and female. The Progressive era was a time when women were asserting their independence while traditional family values continued to dominate the landscape—a woman's place was in the home. Nevertheless, relatively few African American women could afford to stay at home and look after the children. Their financial contributions to the household were tantamount to the survival of the family and the home. Nellie Brown's socioeconomic status freed her from such fiscal responsibilities that burdened black women and allowed her to dedicate herself to racial and gender uplift.[7] She assumed the important and demanding roles of mother and wife inside the home, and she applied her knowledge and skills outside the home where she worked for improvements that would uplift the race. Racial solidarity motivated her to improve the community while her special identity as a black woman moved her a step further. In response to the sexism operating within her race, she committed herself to improving the status of women.[8]

African American women drew together in the late nineteenth century as conditions worsened. The abandonment they felt propelled them to organize clubs and associations where they could assume positions of leadership and where they could direct action that would correct problems specific to black women. Poor women also organized associations to take care of their immediate and future needs. A few pennies each month and attendance at weekly meetings provided them with personal interaction and security that otherwise would have been missed. Women's groups in Mobile, Montgomery, and Birmingham, as well as most other large southern cities, had societies dedicated to a wide array of charitable, recreational, cultural, and re-

ligious purposes. Without the women's dedication and resourcefulness, many communities would have been without orphanages, old
age homes, schools, and recreational centers.[9]

The grassroots organizations that women created on the local level
moved them toward taking collective action nationally. In 1896, their
combined efforts culminated in the founding of the National Association of Colored Women (NACW). Under the motto "Lifting as We
Climb," the elite members of the NACW concentrated their efforts on
uplifting the lower classes through instruction on home improvement
and on proper deportment and the development of respectable morals
and attitudes.[10] The clubwomen who were among the better-posi-
tioned black women in the U.S. wanted to be recognized for their
achievements and standing and worked to create middle-class citizens
out of members of the lower classes. Some of the more privileged and
educated women assumed an elitist posture when they characterized
their role in uplifting the masses as an encumbrance.[11] Some black
men rallied to the women's side, including editors of race papers who
decried the allegations about their daughters, sisters, wives, and mothers. The *Birmingham Truth* defended local black women when it
stated: "The Negro women are uplifted. Go where you will from the
highest to the lowest you will find they compare more than favorable
with any other women of any other race." When they realized that
a concerted effort would effect more substantial results, they organized.[12]

Local organizations began joining the NACW. The better educated
and more elite women organized clubs in urban centers, where it was
easier for women to assemble for meetings and where greater resources existed. In Montgomery, the Sojourner Truth Club was organized by a group of women who established a free reading room
and library. In Birmingham, women organized another branch of the
Sojourner Truth Club, which had Hattie Hudson and Mrs. William
Pettiford among its members. This branch, with funds collected from
its members, renovated the living room of the Colored Orphans and
Old Folks Home. It also hosted parties in honor of such nationally
known women as Minnie Cox of Indianola and Madame C. J. Walker.
Between 1899 and 1901, black women in Alabama established seven
other NACW-affiliated clubs, including those in Eufaula, Greensboro,
Mount Meigs, Tuskegee, and Selma. The NACW's influence complemented the forces already at work in the local communities. To gain a
greater understanding of these women and their development as social
reformers, it is useful to examine their roles and involvement in a va-

riety of local institutions and organizations that raised their consciousness, elevated their self-esteem, and moved them to reach out to the broader community.

African American women who delivered social reforms to the black community drew from their experiences in the church. In the nineteenth century, the church "was the most influential force for collective self-help and self-determination in the black community."[13] It was also the organizational base for the women's benevolent activities and served as the training ground for developing leadership skills.[14] Although some of these activities were often narrow in scope and were short-lived, they did provide women with the structure through which they "became informed about current issues and skilled in fund-raising, accomplishing limited projects, and conducting meetings."[15]

Black women in Birmingham were innovators who brought their church traditions with them from other locales and combined their efforts to create something personally satisfying and utilitarian. They not only constituted the majority of the membership of a church, often approximating a two-to-one ratio, but they did "more of the church work."[16] Various women's groups emerged in the Baptist churches during the late nineteenth century as they took the initiative to establish their own self-help programs.[17] Although males held the power and authority in the Baptist church, women made a place for themselves. They often established and served as instructors of the educational and vocational training programs, they were principal organizers of fund-raising activities, they developed "race-conscious self-help" initiatives, and they were hosts, choir members, and ushers.[18]

Selma University (Alabama Baptist University), which was founded and funded by black Baptists under the direction of Edward Brawley, served as the training ground for many African American women who assumed leadership positions in secular church work in Birmingham.[19] This exposure to other female activists in the church enabled women to create a collective consciousness.[20] Women from Birmingham and elsewhere who attended these inspirational and educational meetings, returned home to share their newly found knowledge. They created a separate space for themselves where they could develop self-help programs and reach out to the community. Often, middle-class women were at the helm. Since 1873, the Mt. Pilgrim Association had comprised the Baptist churches of Birmingham and Jefferson County; then in 1883, the women branched out under the direction of Mrs.

William Pettiford to form the Mt. Pilgrim Women's Missionary Association.[21] Through this organization women exposed themselves to new experiences, as members from different neighborhoods and from different classes worked together. The Shiloh Baptist Church hosted numerous gatherings where elite women addressed attentive audiences about newsworthy topics, including "The Negro Woman of Today and the Place She Must Fill in the Outside World and In the Home."[22] The Home Mission work conducted by the various church denominations placed importance on the role of the wife and/or mother as "caretaker of the home, urgo [*sic*] the caretaker of the race."[23] The religious and the secular women's organizations often had similar agendas, because many women participated in both. Dinah Smith Jordan's experiences in Birmingham mirror lives of other women who were drawn to the city to improve themselves and to reach out to others. In 1883, she moved from Blount County to Birmingham, where she encountered William Pettiford. He had ambitious dreams for the city and the means to implement them through the help of some dynamic women, including her. Jordan became a missionary with the Woman's Missionary Society and devoted her time to visiting the sick and the homes of nonchurchgoing individuals and holding fireside schools for neighborhood children.[24] Her personal commitment to nonmembers illustrates her efforts at attempting to uplift people through the gospel of religion. Many other Baptist women frequently organized fundraising activities to help their churches meet their mortgage payments and to assist congregants who were ailing or unemployed. The Pastor's Aid Committee of the Shiloh Baptist church relied on the efforts of a "small number of loyal women [who] in their quiet way" collected provisions for the church's pastor.[25] Smithfield activists Margery Gaillard and Nellie Brown also organized fund-raising bazaars at the Sixteenth Street Baptist Church.[26]

Baptist women were not alone in their commitment to racial uplift. Although black Methodist women were primarily involved in the maintenance of such Methodist schools as Miles College, they also did missionary work and supported local institutions, such as when the Woman's Home Missionary Society of St. Paul's Methodist Episcopal Church cared for an inmate in the Colored Orphans and Old Folks Home. St. Mark's Episcopal and the First Congregational were among the numerous churches whose female members held bazaars to raise funds to help the church and the indigent. Birmingham's black church women also organized a Juvenile Court Association in the early twentieth century, which took charge of black delinquents. Composed of one woman from each of thirty African American churches, the association in 1907 raised $2,000 and bought twenty-five acres of land near Montgomery. There they built an industrial school that evolved into what became Mt. Meigs Reformatory.[27] The Woman's Missionary Society of the First Congregational Church also became active during World War I. They contributed to the war effort in a variety of ways and sponsored big fund-raising rallies at their church.[28]

On a lighter side, the members of the different missionary societies also sponsored cultural events. The Woman's Missionary Society of the First Congregational Church sponsored Henry Etbride, a vocalist from Chicago. They also held teas, receptions, fashion shows, debates, and cultural events. Sometimes the First Congregational's elite members socialized in the more spacious homes of congregants: In 1920, Mrs. A. H. Parker and Mrs. R. M. Neely gave a benefit entertainment and fund-raiser for the First Congregational Church at the Neely home. In doing so, they were assured a larger turnout because the homes were often closer than the church building to the residences of many members. The agendas covered both business and social activities. Once the business affairs were completed, socializing began over dinner followed by fun and games.[29]

Although African American women attained a remarkable level of achievement through the church affiliations, they were not allowed to hold high official positions in the church hierarchy of most denominations. In response, numerous women searched beyond the church for opportunities to fulfill their personal goals.[30] Many joined voluntary and beneficial societies as a means to address their immediate and future needs, whereas others sought membership in fraternal orders or devoted their time to civic associations. In contrast to the overwhelming presence of elite African American males in the Birmingham branches of fraternal orders, the wives of these elite men tended to avoid the women's orders. Could it be that black women from a more elevated socioeconomic status removed themselves from more democratic organizations and activities that attracted women from a diverse array of backgrounds? Although the information is sketchy, it appears that, with few exceptions, there existed a rather sharp delineation of fraternal membership among women from different socioeconomic classes. The Courts of Calanthe, the Eastern Stars, and the Mysterious Ten were orders that attracted women, some of whom belonged to the middle class, searching for an opportunity to assert their independence from men and for a place to realize their personal and political goals. Carrie Tuggle set an example for her daughter

Mamie, who also became very active in these organizations. She was the Endowment Secretary of the Courts of Calanthe, Grand Secretary of the Knights and Ladies of Honor of the World, and Secretary of the Rising Sons and Daughters of Protection. Carrie Tuggle created the latter organization solely for the purpose of supporting Tuggle Institute, and it and the Knights and Ladies of Honor were housed there. Although Mamie enhanced her position in society when she married Oscar Adams in 1910, she did not have the company of some of the city's most elite African American women.[31] There is no evidence that Nellie Brown, Ethel Parker, or Hattie Hudson ever joined the orders. Their interests and affiliations lay in organizations and clubs where their elite positions could be protected. Their absence from the fraternal orders is revealing as a reminder of the social stratification that was in place within Birmingham's black community, just as it was among the city's white population.

Women who joined orders tended to engage in gender-segregated activities. Nevertheless, there were exceptions. The Knights and Ladies of Honor of America exemplified an order that had gender-integrated membership and encouraged cooperation among men and women. According to the *Truth*, "The Knights and Ladies of Honor [was] the leading secret organization in and around her vicinity."[32] Charlotte L. Proctor, who was a Birmingham resident and the Grand Protector of Knights and Ladies of Honor, was described as "a thorough going race woman who has done much for Negro women of Alabama. . . . [She] is also a leader in other social and fraternal organizations."[33] The Pride of Birmingham was one of the orders' more popular lodges that engaged in community work.

The Courts of Calanthe, the female auxiliary of the Knights of Pythias, experienced rapid growth from its inception in the 1880s. The leading Knights moved toward establishing a women's branch when they recognized that "if the wives of the men in charge would take an interest in the Order it would build both branches up and both would grow together."[34] The Courts, like its male counterpart, practiced an exclusionary membership policy which kept the order free from a lower class of women. The members were involved in community work and were proud of their achievements. In 1909, the Courts of Calanthe held their fifteenth anniversary commemoration at the Shiloh Baptist Church in Birmingham. It was an extravagant affair where members celebrated their longevity as an organization and their accomplishments as a civic-minded order. They also shared their celebration with the larger community as they paraded through the streets of the Southside. The Grand Officers carriages were "lined up in front of the armory of the uniform department and the procession was formed. . . . The march went south on 14th St. to Ave. F, then up Ave. F until 18th St. was reached, north on Ave. G to the church." The *Truth* reported that although the Shiloh Church was the largest black church in Birmingham, it "clearly demonstrated that there was not a church large enough to accommodate this fast growing order, but after filling all conceivable space on the first floor, leaving the several companies and the band on the outside."[35] The order's male officers were present and strikingly visible at the event. Clearly the women's auxiliary did not operate as a completely autonomous body.

Carrie L. Tuggle, an Alabama native and resident of Birmingham, had advanced her position in the Courts of Calanthe. In 1901, eight years after her Grand Court was established, she defeated her male opponent and was elected Grand Worthy Counsellor. When she assumed her office, the *Truth* remarked that "the Order took new life it seems."[36] Tuggle emerged from her poor beginnings and became one of Birmingham's race leaders. She was born of slave parents at Eufaula, Alabama, and in 1884 migrated to Birmingham in search of employment. While working as a domestic, Tuggle received an education and married John Tuggle. She then moved into doing welfare work. In 1903, Tuggle followed the doctrine of the Courts of Calanthe and founded Tuggle Institute, a school and home primarily for poor black children and juveniles located in Enon Ridge. It became a fixture in the black community and was called "one of the most effective and beneficial institutions of the South."[37] During its earliest years, the Trustee Board of Tuggle was composed of women from the Independent Order of Calanthe and the Knights and Ladies of Honor of Alabama who banded together and sustained the Institute through its infancy. Their commitment to the orphanage exemplified the racial solidarity that existed during a time when public monies were primarily allotted to white facilities. Numerous African Americans donated their time to the Institute and took pride in its success. William Lauderdale frequently visited Tuggle Institute and gave his support. Annually they celebrated Founders Day when the school's achievements were recognized, and throughout the year and at commencement ceremonies, tributes were paid by Rev. T. W. Walker and others.[38]

Carrie Tuggle aggressively sought the support of the white community and "spent most of her time visiting these people, soliciting funds for the school."[39] With the help of two local judges, four black fraternal organizations, and Louis Pizitz, a local merchant, Carrie Tuggle established the institute. Brother James A. Bryan, Mrs. C. P. Orr, Mrs. A. B. Loveman, Mrs. James Bowron, and Mrs. Louis Pizitz were among other white supporters who devoted time and money to Tuggle Institute.[40] Under Carrie Tuggle's direction, the facility with its makeshift wooden building expanded and developed a comprehensive education program: It offered academic and industrial training as well as nursing, music instruction, and various scholarly activities that promoted character building. In 1908 when the school outgrew its quarters, W. A. Rayfield was hired to design a new building. The school had become a race institution that embodied racial solidarity as it imparted middle-class values to its young charges. The community was recruited to support the venture. "Come and be in the meeting and here [*sic*] for your self and help to arrange for your building your self for the benefit of your children. We will expect every sister who is interested in education to be present[;] come we need your prayers, your songs, your money."[41]

Students received academic and industrial training and religious instruction in the new complex, which included a one-and-a-half-story building and a two-story frame building with dormitories and classrooms. They also received lessons in race pride and self-esteem through classroom instruction and from books held in the Institute's small library, books such as those written by Booker T. Washington and other contemporary African American leaders.[42] In September 1919, progress was temporarily halted when a fire killed two orphans and destroyed both buildings, valued at $35,000. Dedicated workers immediately took action to raise funds to rebuild the school. Over one hundred students were housed by residents nearby and continued to be educated in temporary quarters until construction was completed.[43] In December 1919, the Tuggle Institute staged a Thanksgiving rally and raised $1,785.00. The *Reporter* declared: "The movement to rebuild the Tuggle School is powerfully appealing and good men and good women, both white and colored, have heard the cry of these children." Louis Pizitz raised his donation to the institute from $500 to $2,000. He was one of several white "friends" who declared the Tuggle Institute "a great benefit to both the white and colored races of Birmingham." By the following year, the facility had received an endorsement from the Alabama Federation of Women's Clubs (white): "We must all recognize that a community is one whether it is part black or white, and when we care for the thorough training of the colored people we not only help them but safeguard our own."[44] White organization women were among the school's supporters who recognized that Tuggle Institute was raising young children to become model citizens.

Carrie Tuggle's strong leadership and organizational skills made the school a noted institution in Birmingham and in the South. She was a tough taskmaster who expected complete obedience and respect from the children. A. G. Gaston's mother placed her son at Tuggle Institute to receive a solid education in a well-controlled environment. Gaston fondly remembered his experience there: "New vistas opened for me at Tuggle." He also recalled how he was inspired by Carrie Tuggle's business acumen: "When classes and homework were finished, Granny [his affectionate name for Tuggle] let me go around with her to various fraternal and church meetings, where members often gave her donations for the school. As I watched her skillfully budget this sometimes meager fund to keep the children entrusted to her care well-fed, warm and comfortable throughout the year, I decided that the secret to attaining my goal of a pretty home for Mama and me would depend upon the number of nickels, dimes and pennies I could save—not on dollars, for dollars were awfully hard to come by."[45] Gaston placed Carrie Tuggle in the company of his mother and grandmother as the women who had taught him well. He went on to become the most successful African American entrepreneur in Birmingham in the twentieth century.

When Carrie Tuggle died in 1924 the Birmingham *News* eulogized her as the "female Booker T. Washington."[46] Although her goal was not to elevate her own status in the community, the school stood as testament to her legacy. The complex she had built consisted of a large school building, two two-story buildings, one one-story building, three dormitories, and an infirmary. The hospital, which received the "lion's share of support from the fraternal organizations," passed the experimental stages and received state recognition after having met the requirements of the Board of Nurse Examiners.[47] Fannie Cosby Blevins capably assumed the presidency of the school after Tuggle's death and assumed the title of Grand Worthy Counsellor of the Courts of Calanthe. She successfully increased the support of the Order of Calanthe, the Rising Sons and Daughters of Protection, and the Knights and Ladies of Honor of the World—which was the first organization to donate money when Carrie Tuggle founded the school. By 1928, Blevins had cleared the school of its $30,000 debt with a campaign initiated at a Founders Day celebration in 1928. The

Knights of Pythias and Courts of Calanthe rallied their support, and individuals gave generously. Fannie Blevins remained president of Tuggle Institute until her death on March 28, 1930.[48] Tuggle Institute closed in 1933 when it faced "insurmountable difficulties" and when "some of its functions had been made unnecessary with the rise of public secondary schools for Blacks."[49]

The significance of Tuggle Institute is threefold: First, it was a community institution that was founded by African American women who were committed to serving a sector of the black population. They were reformers who banded together during a time when the public coffers were reluctant to support most facilities, especially a black facility. Second, this "better class" of African American women effectively earned respect and subsequently won the support of a "better class" of white women who devoted time and energy to the cause. As black and white women worked cooperatively, they moved into unfamiliar territory. Although their agendas may have differed, their common goal—to uplift the children and subsequently the race—brought them together. In addition, its third significance is that the Tuggle Institute was financially supported throughout its history by fraternal organizations. Those who have charged that black fraternal orders did nothing more than serve male egos and accomplish little in comparison to what their members set out to achieve are mistaken. The Knights of Pythias, the Mysterious Ten, and the Knights and Ladies of Honor of the World, as well as Carrie Tuggle's own Daughters of the Rising Sun demonstrated their financial support and loyalty to Tuggle Institute over the decades.[50] They all shared the views of President Blevins when she stated, "This great institution is making good citizens of those who, if allowed to grow up in ignorance might become a menace instead of a blessing to our civilization."[51] Tuggle Institute was one of Birmingham's several race institutions that taught middle-class values to individuals. In doing so, its agenda mirrored that of its original organizers: to encourage behaviors and lifestyles that would contribute to the uplift of the race.

The Tuggle Institute is an early example of black women's involvement and dedication in organizing a program designed to uplift the race in Birmingham. Tuggle "got lots of support. She was raising that money and it all went for the school. She didn't have nothing when she died. She gave every bit she had to that school."[52] Carrie Tuggle's success came at a time when many women failed in their attempts to create reform programs because of the absence of financial resources. As historian Dorothy Salem noted: "The black women with solid support in the white community or in well-organized black institutions such as the church, fraternal groups, or schools produced more long-lived services."[53] Carrie Tuggle had both. Nevertheless, it was not the only effort at institution-building as a vehicle for social betterment. As the decade progressed, women assumed new responsibilities and created new civic associations in Birmingham and elsewhere in Alabama.[54]

With the rise in interest in juvenile reform during the Progressive era, southern clubwomen organized and built some facilities. The Southern Federation of Colored Women was affiliated with the National Association of Colored Women (NACW) and through its urgings, the Alabama federation founded the Mt. Meigs Reformatory for Juvenile Negro Law-Breakers.[55] In 1911, when it became a state-run institution, the women did not relinquish their influence. They kept a close watch on the reformatory and ensured that the children received fair treatment. The movement to establish a similar type of reform school for girls was initiated in 1903, when Julia Tutwiler, a white reformer, offered land to build the facility. In the same year, the ASFCWC raised the issue at their fifth annual meeting in Tuscaloosa, and support was forthcoming. Nevertheless, implementing the proposal was a long and involved affair. By 1919, the federation women had organized a building committee to begin the erection of the Girls' Rescue Home. Thereafter, the federation moved on track, and the Mt. Meigs Rescue Home for Girls was ready to serve the community.[56]

In Birmingham, local federation members made strides in bringing and maintaining municipal welfare reforms. Membership in the local clubs mirrored the elite nature of clubwomen at the national level.[57] Education and care for the sick, the young, and the elderly were high-priority issues. In 1900, William Pettiford's Representative Council in association with various women's clubs established both the Children's Hospital and the Colored Orphans and Old Folks Home. The City Federation served the needy through their work at the Home.[58] The Home frequently found itself in financial trouble, but even more so when Pettiford's Penny Savings and the Jefferson County Banks failed. This crisis moved members of the board of directors of the Home to publicly appeal for white financial support.[59] Although they relied on some outside assistance from black ministers, secret societies, individuals from both the black and white community, and from a white advisory board, the Federation of Colored Women's Clubs maintained control of the facility.

In 1919, when the passage of the Nineteenth Amendment guaranteed women the right to vote, local women organized Negro Suffrage Leagues designed to offer information and education about citizenship and registration. Mrs. R. A. Blount was president of the black women's Suffrage League. In cooperation with the NAACP, the League sponsored many of the well-attended meetings that were held at various local churches on a rotating basis. Topics of lessons illustrate the nature of the programs: "Statistics of Colored Men in Politics of Alabama Since Emancipation" and "How to Become a Citizen" and "The Work of the N.A.A.C.P." The Birmingham NAACP ran a Citizenship School at the Sixteenth Street Baptist Church, where women were taught how to prepare for registration and how to mark a ballot.[60] Although black women in Alabama had supported woman suffrage before their white counterparts, their exclusion from voting renewed their interest and mobilized them.[61] White women were also organizing their own associations, significantly later than when black women had first done so.

On September 4, 1920, Alabama women celebrated the ratification of the Nineteenth Amendment with a Victory Parade in Birmingham.[62] African American women shared in the euphoria and demonstrated their excitement by organizing voter registration campaigns and marching to the county court house to register. In Jefferson County in October 1920, 23,000 women exercised their right to vote. The total number of African American voters in the county was 454, at least 100 of whom were the leading black women from the community who had fulfilled the qualifications necessary to exercise the franchise. Carrie Tuggle was the first African American woman to register in Jefferson County. Others were faced with obstacles strikingly similar to their male counterparts who had been stymied in their attempts to register. Prior to Tuggle's registration, some of the best women who played a major part in the development of the community, "among them mothers, teachers, stenographers and welfare workers," had been denied the right to vote and were disappointed that "none of the fine fair minded people of Birmingham have deigned to offer a protest." To register, local black women needed the endorsement of Dr. M. H. Freeman or Carrie Tuggle, individuals who were deemed respectable by whites in power. Furthermore, they had to wait until after 6 P.M., at which time there was only one registrar to handle the long lines of eager black citizens. The *Voice of the People* concluded, "The truth is, the white man knows that he intends for the white women to have full and free access to the ballot, and that the colored women must abide in matter of suffrage the hard luck that has all along marked the way of the colored man."[63] Nevertheless, there were white supporters of limited black enfranchisement who dared to express their views publicly. J. Melancon wrote a letter to the *Birmingham News* on September 8, 1920, that closed with the following question: "Will not Alabama grasp the honor of being the first State with a sufficient number of unselfish, broadminded white leaders to inaugurate a movement looking to the gradual enfranchisement of the Negro?"[64] Mrs. Oscar Reinhart, missionary from the white Methodist Church, showed her support when she traveled about the city urging black women to register.[65] The celebratory Victory Parade that proceeded on September 1920 was intended solely for white women (the state was not about to register black women), and white women in Alabama could not see beyond themselves. Some middle-class black women exercised their voting rights whereas others remained outside the fold. Only some carried sufficient status to transcend the racial boundaries. Having been excluded from the political process, these women, along with the county's other African American women, continued their struggle for suffrage.[66]

Elite African Americans were moved to demonstrate their opposition to their disfranchisement during the "Indiana Little Affair." In 1926, Indiana Little, a Birmingham school teacher, led a thousand black women and a few men before the board of registrars and demanded their right to vote as "American Citizens." Little was arrested and charged with vagrancy, of being too boisterous, and of misconduct. She was released on $300 bond. The members of the board of registrars maintained their position and succeeded in avoiding registering even one of these demonstrators. Shortly thereafter, when twenty-five hundred black veterans (who through the temporary plan of the constitution were granted voting rights) were also denied their right to register in Jefferson County, most African Americans were forced to face the reality of their powerlessness.[67]

The City Federation not only worked toward securing the vote, but members also worked with other civic organizations to elicit reforms.[68] African American women from the federation and from other associations were drawn to the YWCA because it too sought to improve the quality of the home sphere through the personal development of young women.[69] They struggled to organize a local branch without outside support, and they responded to this sexism and racism by staging their own campaigns to attract attention and to draw financial support. Discrimination had not discouraged them from organizing their own YWCA; rather it motivated them to take control.[70]

Birmingham was without a black YWCA until African American women united and secured enough financial resources to organize a branch. Although the first black YWCA branch was chartered in Dayton, Ohio as early as 1893, southern branches were slow to organize. Southern branches expanded in response to World War I, when black women entered YWCA work on a large scale.[71] In Birmingham, black organization women recognized the need for an agency to assist young girls who were coming into the city to work. Some who had arrived were unable to find a job and were without the necessary network to assist them. They were among the population targeted for reform when middle-class women sought to instruct individuals on deportment and lifestyle. By 1917, local women had formed a YWCA but desperately needed additional funding. Their campaigns brought support from both whites and blacks. Tennessee Coal, Iron and Railway Company, Louis Pizitz, and Drennen and Company were among the white donors, and such women's clubs as the local Semper Fidelis and the Phillis Wheatley Club of Marion also gave money. Several black churches, including Birmingham's Sixth Avenue Baptist, Shiloh Baptist, and AME Zion, and ministers of Pratt City, Ensley and Bessemer, also showed their support through donations.[72] Nevertheless, funding continued to be a problem. In 1919, Pauline Bray, president of the local black YWCA, issued an appeal for stronger support: "For about four years a few women in this city have been struggling to maintain a Y.W.C.A. . . . It is a grave reflection upon the colored citizens of this city with all their intelligence and means that they do not support a well ordered Y.W.C.A."[73] The women's diligence paid off as new programs were offered through the local branch. In only one decade, the branch had outgrown its temporary facility on Eighteenth Street North in the BBD. They organized a building-fund campaign and raised $1,558 in 1928. The new site was a large stately home located at 1609 Seventh Avenue, on which they affixed a prominent sign: "Branch of YWCA Colored All Ladies Welcome." The Federated Clubs pledged their support as all women recognized that their best interests were served through this organization.[74]

As the national YWCA was in a state of conflict, the United States entered World War I. Black men and women joined forces in the war effort in response to the country's rallying cry for support. Numerous young African Americans from Birmingham who joined the service shared W. E. B. Du Bois's sentiments that out of victory for the Allies would rise "an American Negro with the right to vote and the right to work and the right to live without insult."[75] They eagerly sought to serve their country with the hopes of eliciting a policy of greater democracy at home.[76]

On the home front, African Americans coordinated their talents organizing drives to sell War Bonds. The Four Minute Men, comprised of black entrepreneurs, often made public appearances appealing to African Americans. The *Reporter* carried strong messages to its readers to support the war effort through the purchase of Liberty Bonds, Baby Bonds, and Thrift Stamps, and through membership in the local Red Cross.[77] Working within a segregated framework, black women waged a quiet struggle for more effective wartime organization. They achieved some success in aiding African American soldiers and their families; raising money through Liberty Loans, War Savings Stamps, and United War Work campaigns; and improving the social conditions of their communities. But they found that their patriotic efforts were not always well received. The local (white) Red Cross denied them permission to do canteen work at the railroad station, "because they would not permit the colored women to wear the canteen uniform."[78] In response, in 1917 the women organized their own Booker T. Washington Auxiliary of the Red Cross. It was an independent organization that had the support of various businesses including the *Birmingham News* and the *Reporter.* It proudly staged a parade with fourteen marching bands, which were considered some "of the most attractive features of the occasion, and the work of the colored women and the colored people generally is being favorably commented upon by both white and colored leaders."[79] As they rose above their disappointment over their exclusion from official participation in the more important aspect of the war effort, they anxiously mobilized to demonstrate their patriotism. One of the most pressing issues for Americans was food rationing. Early in 1918, prominent women organized a course at the Hoover Kitchen, where they offered demonstrations on how to stay within wartime guidelines for meals.[80] Black women had a long history of successfully practicing conservation just to survive, and their skills were easily applied to the national concern. Alice Nelson recognized their efforts when she described the Jefferson County Woman's Committee as "more thriving, active and alert than any that I have come across anywhere thus far—I mean so far as its work among the colored women is concerned."[81] Other black women also applied their talents as fund-raisers to war work when they participated in several initiatives, including five Liberty Loan drives, six Red Cross campaigns, and other programs. It was not unusual for black teachers to encourage their students to raise funds for the war effort as a sign of their patriotism: Orlean Kennedy organized a fund-raising campaign with primarily Industrial High School's female students, who raised a record $4,000 from Baby Bond sales.[82] Members of the community at many levels—men and women, boys and girls, professionals and laborers—had pulled together to demonstrate their allegiance.

African American women used the war effort to improve social conditions in their community, and as they gained acceptance for their patriotism, they maintained their momentum and pushed for social welfare improvements after the armistice.[83] Pauline Bray Fletcher applied the skills she developed in the YWCA and the war effort to other programs designed specifically for young women. She established the Girls Service League, named after a New York organization founded by Miss Elizabeth W. Martin of Birmingham. After a visit to New York in 1924, Fletcher adopted the name and started a drive to establish a recreation camp in Birmingham. She presented her plan to the local nurses' association of which she was president, to organize something like the Campfire Girls. The *Truth, Reporter, Eagle, Banner, Baptist Leader,* and *News* all gave space to advertise the new project and put the proposition to the people. In 1926, the organizers chose a site for the camp located twenty-two miles from Birmingham on 57 ½ acres of land near Shades Valley school for black children and renamed it Camp Margaret Murray Washington.[84]

Camp Margaret Murray Washington became a community project, as scores of individuals and organizations donated their time and money. Distinguished men supported the women's efforts: Drs. Arthur M. Brown and W. E. Lacy donated headquarters with desk space and a phone, and T. C. Windham led a campaign to raise interest. He, with the assistance of the principals and teachers of Birmingham public schools, constructed a large building named the Rosa Windham hut, after his daughter. Boys from Industrial High School helped to dig the foundation and, once the construction was completed, painted the building. Initially, the camp had three huts valued at $1,700 on twenty acres wired in for an orchard and a truck garden. The wire was contributed "by a Jewish friend." Other friends donated money or a day's work, and some firms donated necessary materials: The Tennessee Coal, Iron and Railroad Company provided financial support for any necessary sanitary improvements. The camp opened on July 22, 1926, under the direction of Pauline Fletcher. By November 1927 the organization was incorporated, with Edward A. Brown in charge of legal services. In that same year, Fletcher found it necessary to solicit funds to keep the camp in operation when the Community Chest budget for the facility fell short.

Members from Birmingham's black community not only helped get the camp started but also used the facilities. Girls from the Tuggle Institute and from TCI villages enjoyed lengthy stays swimming, hiking, embroidering, and many other recreational activities. Smaller parties composed of Birmingham residents spent briefer stays relaxing, and church groups celebrated their annual picnics at the campgrounds. The facility's success drew hundreds of requests from girls looking to spend their vacation there, but it could not accommodate them all. Clearly the camp was fulfilling the needs of not only young girls but also of the greater Birmingham black communities. Women were responsible for the camp from its inception to its full operation. They asserted their skills and earned the trust and commitment of both the white and black citizens.[85]

Civic reform in Birmingham often evolved out of race- and gender-segregated efforts; yet when African American men and women combined forces, they realized significant gains. The Colored Division of the Community Chest was one such organization that enabled blacks to see the benefits of mixed-gender cooperation. The Community Chest was founded in 1923 to correct Birmingham's incompetence in the welfare arena.[86] Blacks were not represented on the homogeneous thirty-member board of the Community Chest; however they were not completely outside the fold. In an effort to show their support, and with the hope of receiving increased allotments, blacks created a Colored Division.[87] Under Nellie Brown's leadership, the organization initiated fund-raising activities at churches, theaters, industrial plants, and elsewhere to rally support. Diverse segments of the African American community demonstrated their commitment, and the campaign was declared a success.[88]

Despite the rhetoric of the members of the white Community Chest, who declared that "the Chest knows no barriers or creed or color," the truth was that African Americans were a low priority. In early 1928, the black YWCA received $2,200 while the white YWCA received $20,559.21 from the Community Chest coffers. Later that year, the black Children's Home Hospital received $300 while the Chest donated $3,494.63 to the white Children's Hospital.[89] The effects of the Great Depression delivered a particularly harsh blow to Birmingham, and some of its effects can be seen from the sizable Community Chest disbursements of $34,282.48 in the first quarter of 1930. In June, the Chest distributed additional funds, this time totaling \$33,822.40 to forty agencies. Blacks again felt the sting of discrimination when the chest's disbursements favored white organizations.[90] Undeterred by their exclusion, black businesses, individuals, and social clubs rallied and demonstrated a healthy response to appeals from the Colored Chest.[91] These donations were distributed among several black social service facilities, including the Alabama Association for the Colored Blind, the (colored) YWCA and the Carrie Tuggle Orphanage.[92] Unfortunately, African American agencies fell far short of assisting their needy, and the Chest barely made a dent in the depression's impact on the hardest hit.[93]

Many African American women who demonstrated a commitment to community affairs often found themselves lacking in personal fulfillment. They, like their white counterparts, looked to social clubs for personal development. As women were reaching out through their affiliations with community-oriented projects, they were also looking inward. They wrestled with their dual identity as black women and sought solutions to their own personal conflicts. Membership in social clubs helped them to reconcile their place in society. The prevalence of these clubs among middle-class women and the creation of additional clubs among younger elites "mirrored the growing stratification of [Birmingham's] black community" during the early twentieth century.[94] These women separated themselves from the very people they wanted to help. Ellen Tarry recalled that she was pleased to be a member of a club that included several young professional women who dedicated themselves to the "task of eradicating some of the cultural lacks in our community." When she tried to recruit two young women to join the club, her pleasure turned to displeasure "when the club informed us that we could not invite either of the women—because they were 'different,' not 'our kind,' 'not in our social circle.' "[95] The members blackballed young women who they felt threatened the homogeneity of their group. They knew that their membership in an elite junior auxiliary group conferred on them a prestigious position that they were unwilling to jeopardize.

Despite the stratified nature of their clubs, middle-class women were congratulated for their community spirit as their club activity not only served members' needs but also reached out to the broader community. Polly Prattermuch, the *Reporter*'s society columnist, declared that black women in Birmingham had organized "about 40 clubs, with a total membership of 2,000. . . . [T]he force and influence of the Women's Clubs of Birmingham has helped humanity in many and far reaching ways. The Civic Consciousness of the club woman has been awakened."[96] Women's social clubs had two distinct dimensions, serious and social. The social side filled personal needs while the more serious facet directed its efforts toward providing some kind of service to broader concerns. Although the majority of the club meetings focused on cultural expression and social interaction, it was important for members to "earn a reputation for an interest in civic problems and racial advancement."[97] Clubwomen, whether in East Birmingham, Pratt City, or Smithfield, engaged in small-scale demonstrations and lectures in their homes to improve themselves, and they often participated in some kind of intellectual discussion. Their social activities were highly publicized in the *Truth* and *Reporter,* and their status depended on others' awareness of their weekly or monthly goings-on. Furthermore, the newspapers' accounts also lent credence to the belief that middle-class people were socially active.[98] Smithfield-based club activities were particularly well documented because the members were among the most elite married women in Birmingham's black society. During one meeting, a member of the Semper Fidelis led a discussion of "Roosevelt and the Negro"; another meeting at Nellie Brown's home was set aside as a "Booker T. Washington evening."[99] The Cosmos Circle, the Twentieth Century Club, the Semper Fidelis, the Francis Harper League of Smithfield, and one simply named the Smithfield Social Club are examples of clubs that attracted affluent women in the community. Their status was tied to their social networks, and they derived an elevated place in society through their associations with other elite club members. The interconnectedness of their affiliations expanded their network of relationships while it simultaneously fulfilled their personal goals.

Although the weekly reports on the society page reveal the simplicity of the organizations and their self-absorbed social functions, a closer look suggests that these clubs were more than petty pursuits to elevate one's status. Clearly, the clubs achieved that goal, but they also worked to mobilize women who participated in raising funds for charity and who sponsored notable guest speakers. Under the auspices of the Semper Fidelis Club, Mary Church Terrell, a moving force in and the first president of the NACW, lectured at the First Baptist Church to a "cultured audience" of approximately one thousand Republicans.[100] She was more than a spokesperson for women: she had become an agitator for the betterment of the race. Birmingham's clubwomen recognized the importance of her work and organized a lecture to share her ideas with interested members of the community. The Sojourner Truth Club was an official club of the NACW as early as 1900. It too drew well-heeled women into its fold; the *Truth* referred to it as "a leading ladies' club in Birmingham."[101] This club, like other ladies' clubs in the city, had pet charities. It was one of several clubs that assumed the responsibility of renovating a room in the Colored Orphans and Old Folks Home.[102] Through fund-raising, the members helped the home maintain its facilities when public funding was inadequate. In 1903 members hosted a social in honor of Minnie Cox, the former postmaster of Indianola. Minnie Cox and her husband were leading citizens of the black community of Mississippi and were well known among many blacks in the South and elsewhere. Madam C. J. Walker also honored the club by her presence at one of their meetings. Minnie Cox and C. J. Walker were well-known and accomplished women in their own right. They offered inspiration as role models for women everywhere. And, their connection to and public appearances sponsored by the Sojourner Truths, added to the club's prestige.[103] The Sinovodad Club could also boast an elite membership of women, many of whom were residents of Smithfield and Enon Ridge. Their meetings were similar in content to other women's clubs, and they often hosted gatherings that members from other clubs attended. On one occasion, the theme of the meeting was "progress," and visiting members from the Climbers Club (composed of single women) and from the Inter Se Club gave a presentation on "The Machine Age, a Blessing or Blight to Mankind?" These women were aware of their contributions to uplifting the race, and they congratulated themselves with such papers entitled "Women Who Are Winning Success Among Us."[104] Clubwomen shared an interest in women's issues and set aside meetings to discuss, among other concerns, suffrage as it "affects Negro women," and "problems pertaining to the home."[105] As health problems persisted among black families, it was clubwomen in Birmingham who organized additional tuberculosis clinics and hired a few nurses from the Anti-Tuberculosis Association who conducted home visits.[106] They also sponsored health campaigns and worked for improved sanitation conditions. Clubwomen were in touch with the problems that ravaged their community, and they took collective action to remedy the situation.[107]

All elite African Americans were keenly aware of how other black Birmingham residents trivialized their club work. When they were given a chance to demonstrate the more serious nature of their associations, they rose to the occasion. In 1899, when Birmingham boosters moved to organize a state fair at Smith Park, African Americans were granted permission to organize a separate Negro Department.

The Climbers, Pre-World War I (Birmingfind Collection, Catalog #108.5.1.2, Department of Archives and Manuscripts, Birmingham Public Library, Ala.)

Management of the Negro Department recognized this as an opportunity to exhibit their skills and achievements and worked diligently to overcome their subordinate status on the fair's program. Male organizers urged clubwomen to become involved "so that people will see that clubs are not formed especially for the social life, but that there is something deeper in them."[108] They also staged such community events as an "old fashion BBQ at Tuxedo Park" to demonstrate their connection to and extend fellowship to the black masses.[109]

African American women who gained recognition for their success in their gender-specific and gender-mixed organizations were energized by their successes. They recognized the difference they made through their organization work, and they continued to offer their assistance to those in need. Their work was a vital facet of community building and uplifting the race—Tuggle Institute, the Colored Orphans and Old Folks Home, the Camp Margaret Murray Washington, Industrial High School, and other community institutions were created through the determination and commitment of black women. Although black women from all classes worked to uplift the downtrodden, the middle-class women held leadership positions in the organizations discussed in this chapter. They not only founded the local branches of the YWCA and the City Federation but they also were the moving forces behind many of the more broadly based social programs that received attention in the city's race papers. With a somewhat "patronizing, missionary attitude," they reached out to those who needed guidance and practical assistance.[110] The middle-class women assumed that as role models they could teach by example and secure a more favorable place for the entire race. Like their white female counterparts, these women mobilized in their separate sphere. Whether they were wives or mothers, daughters or sisters, the outreach activities of these black middle-class women benefited both the community and themselves.

Conclusion

Ralph Ellison in his *Shadow and Act* recognized how white America had dismissed not only the contributions of African Americans but also the very fact that they had often acted of their own accord independent of what white America was doing. In the preceding pages, I have attempted to illustrate that blacks in Birmingham did exactly that: they contemplated the environment and actively shaped the world around them. Their lives unfolded against the backdrop of mainstream society, from where prejudice and discrimination emanated. But their actions were not always in response to those directives; rather, blacks evaluated what needed to be done based on their own community's needs and took the necessary steps to effect change. A strategy of self-segregation served them well as gains were realized in a variety of arenas including business, education, and civic reform.

Birmingham was a New South city that offered opportunities for people—black and white—to improve their station in life. As they settled in their new environment, they found a place for themselves in the social fabric of the city that had strong southern traditions. A hierarchy emerged that reflected both socioeconomic and racial distinctions. Within the black and white communities, individuals separated themselves along class lines. In doing so, affluent whites reinforced their position in the broader society while elite African Americans created a separate world for themselves within the black community. A brief article that appeared in the *Southern Workman* in 1899 entitled "Negro Class Distinctions" concluded that this separation into classes was "inevitable."[1] As we have seen, the black middle class was composed of businessmen and professionals and their families who joined forces to create the economic elite *and* the social elite of black Birmingham. Although they could not completely isolate themselves from the black masses, middle-class African Americans attempted to segregate themselves along class lines. Residential ordinances undermined any aspirations they may have had to create a class-specific neighborhood, yet it was within their homes, social clubs, fraternal orders, and churches that they most effectively achieved separation from other African Americans. Furthermore, through their combined memberships in these organizations, they were able to perpetuate and protect a tightly knit black middle-class community.[2]

These class divisions within the larger black community were responsible for some conflict among African Americans. Many members of the middle class believed that it was their duty to perform as role models for the downtrodden and that the crude behavior displayed by members of the lower classes was responsible for the race's problems, including Jim Crow legislation. They believed that racial uplift would not only help those in need of assistance but also help the entire race. However, those outside the middle class often resented their interference, mocked their pretenses, and rejected their help. By creating a separate world for themselves, the "better class" of blacks reinforced the differences among African Americans. Even within the middle class conflicts surfaced. Oscar Adams often took issue with other elite leaders. The fact that he filed suit against members of the Knights of Pythias and that he charged the officers of the city's three black banks with fraud suggested deep factions within the elite class itself. Clearly racism was not the only problem in the black community.

Despite these class differences, professionals and entrepreneurs who comprised the "better class" of blacks, recognized the value of maintaining workable relationships with those not like them. Businessmen particularly depended on the black masses to patronize their businesses and thus had to maintain good relations while simultaneously socially insulating themselves. Since for most black elites, their only source of income was from other blacks, total separation was anathema to business success. African American entrepreneurs who faced competition from white businesses espoused the rhetoric of economic nationalism to encourage race loyalty among blacks. To do so required the establishment of a cordial relationship between lower-class and middle-class blacks.

Booker T. Washington played an influential role among Birmingham's blacks and most notably among upwardly mobile African Americans. They shared his philosophy of self-help, economic independence and racial solidarity. Evidence of his influence abounds. Washington had nurtured close relationships with some of the city's most eminent blacks including William Pettiford, Thomas Walker, Ulysses Mason, Thomas Windham, and Edward Brown. Their correspondence with Washington and some of their appearance at NNBL meetings reveal their support. Many showed their allegiance when they named their organizations and businesses after him: Both B. L. Windham and A. G. Gaston chose to name their enterprises the Booker T. Washington Insurance Company. Women called their branch of the Red Cross the Booker T. Washington Auxiliary, and other clubwomen devoted entire evenings to discuss his work. Editorials that appeared in the *Voice of the People,* the *Reporter,* and other race papers, frequently endorsed Washington's philosophy of self-help and racial solidarity. Washington's influence reached beyond Birmingham's middle class: when he spoke at a local church, a stampede ensued that resulted in numerous deaths. Birmingham lay in close proximity to Washington's headquarters at Tuskegee. His impact was inevitable, and he rallied considerable support from the Magic City's African American population.

Although membership in the middle class did not necessarily determine one's involvement in community building, it did tend to figure into who assumed leadership positions. Oscar Adams created the Colored Citizen's League to improve the city's race relations, whereas Pauline Bray Fletcher focused her energies on uplifting young women. The necessity of essential services was apparent to all, and a cooperative spirit was elicited among those who participated in creating agencies designed to uplift the needy. Without the political power to affect legislation, individuals formed neighborhood associations to alter their immediate environments, and others established civic organizations that had a broader range. Elite African Americans tended to spearhead the civic organizations that had high visibility and enjoyed greater longevity.[3] Typically, the organizers were longtime residents of Birmingham who had achieved a degree of success in business or in a professional career and who had exhibited a level of stability in residency relative to other African Americans. They did not create the civic organizations and social agencies merely to serve as avenues for ego gratification. Rather, they sought "to do good for the city's black population and to do well for themselves individually as a class."[4] They may have elicited a measure of personal fulfillment through their involvement, but the evidence suggests that they had further-reaching goals. They engaged in self-help agencies to serve the needy, to uplift the race, and to undercut charges of black inferiority; that is, they were interested in the collective welfare of African Americans. As stable residents in Birmingham, they acquired some recognition in their own neighborhood and among some other blacks through their community involvement, but a few also achieved a level of credibility among some whites.

Paternalism played a significant role in the creation and maintenance of some African American institutions, for several black middle-class leaders entered into nuanced relationships with a few influential whites. Although their initiatives were maintained through strong support from members of the black community, white help was welcomed, encouraged, and necessary. But help from outside the black community did not come without its own set of expectations. Whites who reaped financial rewards and who recognized the benefit racial uplift had on the entire community, assisted African Americans in realizing important goals. Individuals like Carrie Tuggle, who were committed to self-help and racial uplift, created institutions with the financial support of black fraternal orders. Yet, the scarcity of resources in the African American community limited how much blacks could do for themselves. Without the financial assistance and influence of some whites, blacks would have faced greater difficulty than they did in sustaining some very important community institutions. The more prominent members of the middle class, many of whom lived and owned homes in Smithfield, had nurtured relationships with some reform-minded whites. Rev. Henry M. Edmonds, Samuel Ullman, and Louis Pizitz worked diligently to help uplift blacks when the city was not forthcoming. Edmonds, pastor of the Independent Presbyterian Church and for a time president of the CIC, with the help of white charity worker Mrs. C. P. Orr, supported blacks who organized and directed the Negro Kindergarten and Day Nursery. Without Rev. William Pettiford's initiative, Samuel Ullman's commitment, and John H. Phillips' influence, Industrial High School would never have been founded in 1900, at a time when few other southern cities provided blacks with their own high school. And when Tuggle Institute suffered a devastating fire, Louis Pizitz gave a generous donation that helped to rebuild the facility. Over the decades, he had extended his philanthropy to African Americans in a variety of ways.[5] Tuggle Institute and Industrial High School were among the facilities that taught middle-class virtues and worked toward creating "better citizens" and thus gained acceptance and support from white reformers. Many black homeowners would have remained renters if not for individual members of the Steiner family and the Steiner Brothers Bank, which guaranteed mortgages not only to aspiring black homeowners but also to such venerable institutions as the Shiloh Baptist and Sixteenth Street Baptist churches. The Bank extended the possibility of homeownership for many when it assumed numerous mortgages held by the Alabama Penny Savings Bank when it filed for bankruptcy. And blacks recognized the value of their white allies in personal as well as business affairs: "We are grateful to those hundreds of white patrons both as readers and as advertisers, who have so constantly been our supporters and who have all along given us so much encouragement."[6]

In an American society where whites held the power, African Americans recognized that they could not achieve many of their goals without assistance. Yet they accepted this assistance at a price. Rarely did black middle-class leaders speak out against racial injustices. Pettiford and others issued petitions and Tuggle railed against disfranchisement in the *Truth,* but few engaged in civil disobedience to elicit change. Rather they focused on self-help, racial solidarity, and economic independence. T. W. Walker's challenge against Jim Crow streetcars was one of the few times that a high-profile leader acted in protest. Despite Mayor George Ward's recognition of the inadequate accommodations for African Americans, the city moved aggressively toward implementing Jim Crow more comprehensively.[7] When U. G. Mason agitated for a high school comparable to that for white students and when he encouraged blacks to move North, whites rejected him as a credible race leader. Black middle-class leaders recognized that they were hamstrung in the political arena by these relationships and worked within the defined boundaries. Yet they pushed for and realized essential improvements in areas that did not threaten the status quo.

The fact that some whites aided African Americans does not suggest that whites sought reforms that would bring the races closer together. They morally and financially supported the creation of parallel black facilities that reinforced the separate black economy while a small number also worked toward developing interracial coalitions via the Commission on Interracial Cooperation. But their commitment did not take the next step—to alter the system.[8] The reformers did not breach the subject of racial equality or integration. African Americans received little support when they agitated for enfranchisement. Rather, such ordeals as the Indiana Little Affair were reminders of the limits of white support. It appears that the local branch of the NAACP received no white support; its agenda of social equality was too radical for even the most committed liberals in Birmingham. Interracial alliances were just beginning to take shape during these early decades.[9]

African Americans recognized the limitations of their sometime allies, who almost summarily remained silent on black disfranchisement and increased segregation. Yet blacks did not expend excessive energy trying to win their civic rights back. Rather, the vast majority of blacks looked inward where they had significantly more control over their environment. Through cooperative and tireless efforts, blacks organized associations and local leagues that focused on improving the black experience. Neighborhood associations provided the vehicle through which disfranchised blacks exercised some influence. Members issued petitions to local politicians demanding paved streets, transportation services, lights, and improved sanitation. Their home environment provided them with the greatest personal gratification, and they sought to assert control over it. Through self-directed initiatives, middle-class blacks assumed responsibility for themselves and demonstrated racial solidarity as they worked toward creating their own institutions and improving their community. In doing so, they derived pride in the accomplishments and hope for the future.

Notes

INTRODUCTION

1. Earl Lewis coined the term "home sphere," which he used to illustrate "the intersection between the household and the community." This is a very useful term when analyzing the dynamics of community building. Earl Lewis, *In Their Own Interests: Race, Class, and Power in Twentieth-Century Norfolk, Virginia* (Berkeley: University of California Press, 1991), 5–6.

2. The term "black middle class" is not intended to suggest the same meaning as "white middle class." Rather than focusing on income as the determining variable, the term "middle class" here suggests an internalization of middle-class values and behaviors. The population under examination is largely the people who historians have called the "new elite"—business persons who support the idea of racial solidarity, self-help, and a segregated economy. The term "new elite" is inapplicable in this study because Birmingham, a New South city, did not have an antebellum black social elite who found themselves replaced by an emerging black elite who derived status from their business orientation. Earl Lewis refers to this group as an "entrepreneurial middle class" in his *In Their Own Interests* (38), whereas numerous other historians refer to this group as the middle class.

3. Seretha Jackson, interview by the author, Birmingham, Ala., May 11, 1994. Ellen Tarry, interview by the author, Smithfield Public Library, May 10, 1994. Ellen Tarry enjoyed a relatively privileged childhood in Birmingham "by virtue of her family's gentility, respectability, and good education." As a young woman, Ellen Tarry moved to New York to pursue a writing career. While there, she became involved with members of the literary set who clustered around the Harlem Renaissance writers. The Tarry family lived in Enon Ridge, a very small and elite black neighborhood located north of Smithfield. Enon Ridge residents shared membership in the same churches, clubs, and organizations as did Smithfield's middle-class residents. Consequently, they shared status within the small but growing African American middle class. Gerda Lerner, ed., *Black Women in White America: A Documentary History* (New York: Vintage Books, 1973), 296. In fact, Enon Ridge was "the only highlands about Birmingham where colored people have entire possession." *Birmingham Truth*, August 3, 1907.

4. Roots of black nationalism can be found in David Walker's *Appeal*

to the Colored Citizen of the World (1829) as well as in Henry Highland Garnet's and Martin Delaney's respective writings during the early to mid-nineteenth century. See Sterling Stuckey, *The Ideological Origins of Black Nationalism* (Boston: Beacon Press, 1972), and his *Slave Culture: Nationalist Theory and the Foundations of Black America* (New York: Oxford University Press, 1987). August Meier, *Negro Thought in America, 1880–1915* (Ann Arbor: University of Michigan Press, 1963), 106, 156.

5. Meier, *Negro Thought in America*, 156.

6. Ibid., 106.

7. In 1919, Dr. William Saunder's play *Maniac* was performed to raise funds for the Tuggle Institute. *Birmingham Reporter,* November 15, 1919; *Birmingham Wide-Awake,* September 22, 1906; *Birmingham Weekly Voice,* May 26, 1917; Ellen Tarry, *The Third Door: The Autobiography of an American Negro Woman* (New York: D. McKay Co., 1955; reprint, Tuscaloosa: University of Alabama Press, 1992), 75. For further discussion on class relations in the black community, see Elsa Barkley Brown and Gregg D. Kimball's "Mapping the Terrain of Black Richmond," *Journal of Urban History* 21 (March 1995): 296–346. Historians have long struggled with the concept of class and how to unravel its mystery when studying African Americans. Accounts about the black middle class abound. Among the more helpful publications are William A. Muraskin's *Middle-Class Blacks in a White Society: Prince Hall Freemasonry in America* (Berkeley: University of California Press, 1975) and August Meier's, "Negro Class Structure and Ideology in the Age of Booker T. Washington," *Phylon* 23 (Fall 1962): 258–66. See also Loretta J. Williams, *Black Freemasonry and Middle-Class Realities* (Columbia: University of Missouri Press, 1980); Charles Pete T. Banner-Haley, *To Do Good and To Do Well: Middle-Class Blacks and the Depression, Philadelphia, 1929–1941* (New York: Garland Publishing, 1993), and his *The Fruits of Integration: Black Middle-Class Ideology and Culture, 1960–1990* (Jackson: University Press of Mississippi, 1994). Among the numerous useful studies of class in the black community are John Dollard's *Caste and Class in a Southern Town* (New Haven: Yale University Press, 1937); Meier's *Negro Thought in America;* and David M. Katzman's *Before the Ghetto: Black Detroit in the Nineteenth Century* (Urbana: University of Illinois Press, 1973), especially chapter 5 entitled "Class." Also useful is E. Franklin Frazier's controversial *Black Bourgeoisie: The Rise of the New Middle Class in the United States* (New York: Free Press, 1957). Leon Litwack's most recent *Trouble in Mind: Black Southerners in the Age of Jim Crow* (New York: Alfred A. Knopf, 1998) offers insight into the working and lower classes within the black community.

8. As James Horton noted, "It will not be possible to comprehend the meaning of class structure among blacks until we establish some method for evaluating occupations and their relation to status in the black community. Clearly the traditional approaches to class based on occupation must be modified to have meaning for the limited job opportunities traditionally open to blacks." James Oliver Horton, "Comment," in *The State of Afro-American History: Past, Present, and Future,* edited by Darlene Clark Hine (Baton Rouge: Louisiana State University Press, 1986), 133.

9. August Meier, "Vogue of Industrial Education," *Mid-West Journal* 7 (Fall 1955): 246.

10. Mary Lethert Wingerd explained that "The cultural lure of paternalism for managers was always inextricably linked to economic self-interest," and this was the case among Birmingham's industrialists. "Rethinking Paternalism: Power and Parochialism in a Southern Mill Village," *Journal of American History* 83 (December 1996): 884.

CHAPTER 1. THE BIRTH OF A COMMUNITY

1. Ethel Armes, "The Spirit of the Founders," *Survey* 27 (January 6, 1912): 1461. There were several agencies for social betterment, including the Children's Aid Society and the privately funded Colored Old Folks Home established by W. R. Pettiford in 1899, but the services fell far short of the needs.

2. The poor air quality moved the city officials to introduce in 1917, a strict air pollution ordinance that restricted the emission of black smoke from trains and factories to a short designated period each day. Blaine A. Brownell, "Birmingham, Alabama, New South City in the 1920s," *Journal of Southern History* 38 (February 1972): 32.

3. Kenneth Jackson states that "historically, city fathers tended to be concerned with the rate of growth and with the relative standing of their community and rival cities." Kenneth Jackson, *Crabgrass Frontier: The Suburbanization of the United States* (New York: Oxford University Press, 1985), 138.

4. Money from Cincinnati and Louisville helped build Birmingham, and in the postwar era, Richmond also nurtured Alabama and Birmingham's industrial growth. W. David Lewis, *Sloss Furnaces and the Rise of the Birmingham District: An Industrial Epic* (Tuscaloosa: University of Alabama Press, 1995), xiv, 3, 88.

5. For a more detailed account of why the two camps reacted differently to the arrival of U.S. Steel, see ibid., 293–95.

6. Birmingham's northern competitors in Cleveland, Buffalo, and Pittsburgh had long overcome the problem of producing steel, caused by the iron content of the area's iron ore. They were mass producing steel, at the expense of iron. John N. Ingham, *Making Iron and Steel: Independent Mills in Pittsburgh, 1820–1920* (Columbus: Ohio State Press, 1991), 77. Gavin Wright notes that although U.S. Steel did not suppress the growth of Birmingham, it did not put Birmingham at the center of its corporate attention. Wright suggests that, in effect, U.S. Steel purchased a rival solely to slow its growth. *Old South, New South: Revolutions in the Southern Economy Since the Civil War* (New York: Basic Books, 1986), 14, 168.

7. Carl V. Harris, *Political Power in Birmingham, 1871–1921* (Knoxville: University of Tennessee Press, 1977), 22. Smithfield will be discussed at length in the following chapters and Avondale is briefly described in Graham Romeyn Taylor's "Birmingham's Civic Front," *Survey* 27 (January 6, 1912): 1464–84.

8. Charles E. Connerly, in his article "One Great City: Birmingham's Struggle for Greatness Through Suburban Annexation and Consolidation, 1890 to the Present" (paper presented at the ACSP-AESOP Joint International Congress, Oxford, July 1991), cites four factors to explain Birmingham's slow growth relative to the county's: a large initial suburban population, a large number of industries located outside Birmingham, industries controlled by outside capital, and a large number of blacks in Birmingham. He asserts that these factors had a significant impact on Birmingham's efforts to expand its political boundaries. In contrast to Birmingham's population in 1880 of 3,800, the county's population amounted to 23,272.

9. U.S. Bureau of the Census, *Ninth United States Census: 1870—Population*, vols. 1, 2 (Washington, D.C.: Government Printing Office, 1870); *Tenth United States Census: 1880*, 340; *Eleventh United States Census: 1890*, 402; and *Twelfth United States Census: 1900*, vol. 1, p. 573.

10. It has been stated by numerous sources that loan sharking was virtually an epidemic during these early decades of Birmingham's history. Conversation with Charles Crim, January 1993.

11. In 1870, only 1 percent of the white population in Birmingham was foreign born, but the number increased to 25 percent by 1890. Most immigrants were employed in the industrial labor force, while others established restaurant and grocery businesses. Carl V. Harris, *Political Power*, 35; Paul B. Worthman, "Black Workers and Labor Unions in Birmingham, Alabama, 1897–1904," *Labor History* 10 (Summer 1969): 378.

12. Brownell, "Birmingham, Alabama," 30.

13. Wife of Alfred N. Hawkins, a well-known businessman and a partner in the firm of Cheek and Hawkins in Birmingham, as cited in Lucille Griffith's *Alabama: A Documentary History to 1900* (University, Ala.: University of Alabama Press, 1968), 608.

14. U.S. Bureau of the Census, *Ninth United States Census: 1870—Population*, vols. 1, 2; *Twelfth United States Census: 1900—Population*, vol. 1, p. 573; *Thirteenth United States Census: 1910—Population*, 177–78; *Fourteenth United States Census: 1920—Population*, vol. 2., p. 49. See also Zane L. Miller, "Urban Blacks in the South, 1865–1920: An Analysis of Some Quantitative Data on Richmond, Savannah, New Orleans, Louisville, and Birmingham," in *The New Urban History: Quantitative Explorations by American Historians*, edited by Leo F. Schnore (Princeton, N.J.: Princeton University Press, 1975), 188.

15. Worthman, "Black Workers and Labor Unions," 379.

16. John A. Fitch, "The Human Side of Large Outputs: Steel and Steel Workers in Six American States: IV, The Birmingham District," *The Survey* (January 6, 1912), 1527–28. Blacks were overrepresented in unskilled backbreaking work because of the absence of occupational opportunity and because white furnace employees were a rarity in Birmingham.

17. Tarry, *The Third Door*, 3.

18. Beyond the fact that black businesses lacked the capital to compete for commercial space in the CBD, the downtown property owners refused to renew the leases, and those blacks who owned the property were forced to sell and relocate their businesses elsewhere. Furthermore, the city stopped issuing

operating licenses to blacks unless they agreed to locate their businesses away from the heart of what became the white business district. Franklin D. Wilson, "The Ecology of a Black Business District: Sociological and Historical Analysis," Institute for Research on Poverty Discussion Papers, University of Wisconsin, Madison, November 1975, 6, 12, 15.

19. Carl V. Harris, *Political Power,* 58, 282; John Sparks, "American Negro Reaction to Disfranchisement, 1901–1904" (master's thesis, Samford University, 1973), 86–92; Malcolm Cook McMillan, *Constitutional Development in Alabama, 1798–1901: A Study in Politics, the Negro, and Sectionalism* (1955; reprint, Spartanburg, S.C.: Reprint Co., 1978), 356; Horace Mann Bond, *Negro Education in Alabama: A Study in Cotton and Steel* (Washington, D.C.: Associated Publishers, 1939; reprint, Tuscaloosa: University of Alabama Press, 1994), 168–70. Responses to their expected disfranchisement moved blacks to adopt somewhat different strategies when appealing for a reconsideration—from the somewhat conciliatory petition signed by Booker T. Washington, William Pettiford, and William Councill, among others to another petition that threatened to withdraw their much needed labor from the state through the formation of the Afro-American Exodus Union at Camp Hill, Alabama. Blacks were not alone in their efforts to organize mass black exodus from the state, albeit for other reasons. In 1894, four Birmingham white men organized the International Migration Society and then reorganized under the name Liberia Colonization Society. William Ivy Hair, *Carnival of Fury: Robert Charles and the New Orleans Race Riot of 1900* (Baton Rouge: Louisiana State University Press, 1976), 103. See Sheldon Hackney, *Populism to Progressivism in Alabama* (Princeton, N.J.: Princeton University Press, 1969), chap. 12, for a well-documented account of both the racial sentiments of the dominating convention forces and the attempts of blacks to gain recognition.

20. *Montgomery Advertiser,* June 1, 1905; *Mobile Weekly Press,* June 6, 1914, as cited in Joseph M. Brittain, "Negro Suffrage and Politics in Alabama Since 1870" (Ph.D. diss., Indiana University, 1958), 168.

21. These organizations coincided with James H. Hayes's founding of the National Negro Suffrage League, which had a "decidedly radical tone." Meier, *Negro Thought in America,* 174.

22. Brittain, "Negro Suffrage," 173; *Huntsville Journal,* November 21, 1901; David Alan Harris, "Racists and Reformers: A Study of Progressivism in Alabama, 1896–1911" (Ph.D. diss., University of North Carolina, Chapel Hill, 1967), 182, 236–37; and Jimmie Frank Gross, "Alabama Politics and the Negro, 1874–1901" (Ph.D. diss., University of Georgia, 1969), 275.

23. Carl V. Harris, "Stability and Change in Discrimination Against Black Public Schools: Birmingham, Alabama, 1871–1931," *Journal of Southern History* 51 (August 1985): 385.

24. In 1887, Florida enacted its first Jim Crow law, which set a precedent for other states to follow. Mississippi followed in 1888, Texas in 1889, Louisiana in 1890, and Arkansas, Kentucky, and Georgia joined Alabama in 1891. Dewey Grantham, *Southern Progressivism* (Knoxville: University of Tennessee Press, 1983), 124–25; C. Vann Woodward, *The Strange Career of Jim Crow,* 2nd rev. edition (New York: Oxford University Press, 1966); C. Vann

Woodward, *Origins of the New South, 1877–1913* (Baton Rouge: Louisiana State University Press, 1951), 212.

25. Alabama, *House Journal,* 1890, p. 370; as cited in Hackney, *Populism to Progressivism,* 45–46; *Huntsville Gazette,* February 14, 1891.

26. Howard N. Rabinowitz, *Race Relations in the Urban South, 1865–1890* (Urbana: University of Illinois Press, 1980), 127. In 1887 and 1889, the new Interstate Commerce Commission ruled that trains crossing the state line had to provide one passenger equal accommodations to another for the same price, "but they are not compelled to permit a passenger to take any car or any seat that may please his fancy." The "equality of accommodations" must be "real and not delusive." The mixed message left the allocation of seating to the discretion of the conductor or the white passengers. One railroad in Alabama, which undoubtedly had numerous black patrons, avoided the costly suits engendered by the "first-class ticket conflict" by running its own separate and identical car for blacks as early as 1882. Edward L. Ayers, *The Promise of the New South: Life After Reconstruction* (New York: Oxford University Press, 1992), 141–43.

27. *Anniston Union-Leader,* August 23, 1900, and *Anniston Baptist Leader,* September 13, 1900; *Birmingham Age-Herald,* January 7, 16, 1902, as cited in Hackney, *Populism to Progressivism,* 182. In 1890, Georgia and Louisiana passed Jim Crow railroad car laws whereby blacks were provided with significantly inferior accommodations. By 1908, most southern states had passed Jim Crow railway laws and streetcar segregation laws. Meier, *Negro Thought in America,* 72, 162; Rogers et al., *Alabama: The History of a Deep South State* (Tuscaloosa: University of Alabama Press, 1994), 447.

28. As Earl Lewis has indicated, blacks carefully selected the Jim Crow laws they challenged while quietly accepting others. See *In Their Own Interests,* 23.

29. Between 1898 and 1894 citizens of Augusta, Atlanta, Columbia, New Orleans, Mobile, and Houston boycotted the streetcars. In Houston, Austin, Nashville, and Savannah, blacks organized their own short-lived transportation companies. Between 1900 and 1906, blacks staged a series of boycotts against Jim Crow streetcars in at least twenty-five southern cities. Grantham, *Southern Progressivism,* 243; Meier, *Negro Thought in America,* 175; August Meier and Elliot Rudwick, "The Boycott Movement Against Jim Crow Streetcars in the South, 1900–1906," *Journal of American History* 55 (March 1969): 756–75; quotation from the *Birmingham Wide-Awake,* July 20, 1905.

30. B. F. Riley, *The White Man's Burden* (Chicago: Regan House, 1910; reprint, New York: Negro Universities Press, 1969), 205–7.

31. *Birmingham Wide-Awake,* March 10, 1906.

32. *Birmingham Truth,* September 24, 1906.

33. Quotations are from the *Birmingham Ledger,* November 11, 1906. Early on, Birmingham's streetcars were segregated by custom and by rules practiced by the private utility corporation rather than by ordinance. Carl V. Harris, *Political Power,* 182.

34. *Birmingham Reporter,* February 21, 1914.

35. *Birmingham Reporter,* March 30, 1918.

36. The installation of moveable partitions on the Birmingham Railway,

Light and Power Company's cars was part of a larger concession made by the company to ensure it's dominance as Birmingham's major mode of transportation. When a city commissioner played the race card to undermine the competitive jitney operations, the railway company's position was secured. See Blaine Brownell, "The Notorious Jitney and the Urban Transportation Crisis in Birmingham in the 1920's," *Alabama Review* 25 (April 1972): 110–11, 115.

37. *Montgomery Advertiser,* January 25, 1923; March 13, 14, 21, 1923; April 13, 1923; *Birmingham Reporter,* March 17, 1923; *Dallas Express,* March 24, 1923; *Birmingham News,* March 13, 1923. *New Era,* May 1924, as cited in Brownell, "Birmingham, Alabama," 30; Woodward, *The Strange Career of Jim Crow,* 116; Ordinance to Amend Section 6002 of the Code of the City of Birmingham of 1930, Section 6002: Separation of Races in Street Cars and Motor Busses.

38. *Birmingham Reporter,* January 12, 1918; *Savannah Tribune,* August 26, 1921.

39. *Birmingham Weekly Pilot,* June 7, 1884.

40. *Birmingham Age-Herald,* October 1907.

41. A letter from J. A. Whitted to the *Birmingham News,* in George Ward Scrapbook, March 15, 1913–January 10, 1915, Southern History Collection, Department of Archives and Manuscripts, Birmingham Public Library, Birmingham, Ala. In 1912, civic boosters had organized the Birmingham Zoological Garden Society to build a small zoo. Carl V. Harris, *Political Power,* 165.

42. *Birmingham Reporter,* n.d., George Ward Scrapbook. Although the zoo was established without the support of city funds, it did use taxes to maintain the facility. Carl V. Harris, *Political Power,* 166.

43. Unidentified newspaper.

44. *Birmingham Ledger,* n.d.

45. Although the timing was never good for blacks to win support for most of their demands, their timing in requesting a park was particularly bad during the Avondale Park controversy. In 1916, Birmingham was in the midst of a fiscal crisis and the city was cutting back its social services. The limited supervised recreation program for whites fell victim to its cuts. When the program was reinstated in 1919 it received only half of its original appropriations. Carl V. Harris, *Political Power,* 166.

46. *Record of Incorporation,* Jefferson County, 1887, A492; *Birmingham City Directory,* 1887, 1900, 1901, 1916, and 1930.

47. *Birmingham Reporter,* July 26, 1919.

48. Blacks had witnessed and experienced the consequences of southern Democrats' influence in Washington during Wilson's administration. Wilson had expanded segregation practices at the federal level when he implemented the separation of government workers and he had denied federal appointments to blacks. Furthermore, a flood of Jim Crow bills was introduced in the Sixty-third Congress (1913–15). These developments sent a clear message to African Americans. Grantham, *Southern Progressivism,* 362; *Birmingham Reporter,* January 18, 25, 1919. For examples of Birmingham's determination to maintain Jim Crow throughout subsequent decades, see Robin D. G. Kelley,

Race Rebels: Culture, Politics, and the Black Working Class (New York: Free Press, 1994).

49. Burton had difficulty locating a chairman of the local branch because of the city's tense race relations. By 1928, James Dillard chaired the local committee, and Dr. Henry Edmonds, William Driver, Rev. John W. Goodgame, and Dr. U. G. Mason were among its members. The quotation is from James Burton to W. W. Alexander, June 21, 1926, Robert Moton Papers, Tuskegee University, Tuskegee, Ala. *Birmingham Truth,* October 5, 1928. By 1931, Robert Jemison, Jr., and C. B. Glenn, superintendent of city schools, had joined the CIC. Robin D. G. Kelley, *Hammer and Hoe: Alabama Communists during the Great Depression* (Chapel Hill: University of North Carolina Press, 1990), 262 (n. 13).

50. Not all blacks were employed as unskilled laborers. Ore mining, like coal mining, was considered a skilled job, and blacks dominated iron ore mining. Blacks were also employed as pick miners, a skilled position in coal mining, and they practically monopolized all the unskilled coal mining jobs. Henry M. McKiven, Jr., *Iron and Steel: Class, Race, and Community in Birmingham, Alabama, 1875–1920* (Chapel Hill: University of North Carolina Press, 1995), 47; Daniel Letwin, "Interracial Unionism, Gender, and 'Social Equality' in the Alabama Coalfields, 1878–1908," *Journal of Southern History* 61 (August 1995): 523 (n. 7).

51. McKiven, *Iron and Steel,* 30.

52. McKiven challenges Paul Worthman's earlier thesis that race relations within the iron and steel industries was characterized by class struggles, not racial hostility. McKiven, *Iron and Steel,* specifically pp. 1–3; Worthman, "Black Workers and Labor Unions," 375–407. See also Letwin, "Interracial Unionism," 519–54, especially p. 538, for quote, and his "Race, Class, and Industrialization in the New South: Black and White Coal Miners in the Birmingham District of Alabama, 1878–1897" (Ph.D. diss., Yale University, 1991).

53. Robert J. Norrell, "Caste in Steel: Jim Crow Careers in Birmingham, Alabama," *Journal of American History* 73 (December 1986): 671.

54. Sterling D. Spero and Abram L. Harris, *The Black Worker: The Negro and the Labor Movement* (1931; reprint, New York: Atheneum Press, 1968), 168.

55. The unions had limited success in Birmingham's industries as employers hired black strikebreakers and fought long battles to operate and create an open-shop city, both before and after World War I. State governors were sympathetic to the industrialists' plight and frequently intervened during the numerous strikes that plagued industry. The UMWA in Alabama was temporarily crushed after World War I because of state violence and race baiting. In 1919 and 1920 when Birmingham coal miners, 75 percent of whom were black, struck for higher wages, their efforts and the UMWA were crushed by Tennessee Coal, Iron and Railroad Company (TCI). Biracial unionism ended with this defeat and would not reemerge until the 1930s. Kelley, *Hammer and Hoe,* 5; Carl V. Harris, *Political Power,* 222–23.

56. Rameau received money from coal operators and other industrialists. He discouraged black workers from affiliating with the American Federa-

tion of Labor through his *Workman's Chronicle* and his *Southern Industrial-Fraternal Review,* which circulated among black secret societies. McGill, editor of *Hot Shots,* also used his paper to communicate the industrialists' message as did Robert Durr through his *Weekly Review.*

57. The quotation is from Marlene Hunt Rikard, "An Experiment in Welfare Capitalism: The Health Care Services of the Tennessee Coal, Iron and Railroad Company" (Ph.D. diss., University of Alabama, 1983). Many ministers were reluctant to take a stand on organizing, although their reticence was probably magnified by Rameau, who criticized their inaction while he was trying to recruit members into his brotherhood. At least one of those preachers declared that "the only mission of the Church of Jesus came to establish is to save souls." According to an editorial in the *Workman's Chronicle,* they avoided involvement in "a crusade for the moral, economic and industrial uplift of the Negro man and woman in the coal fields." *Birmingham Workman's Chronicle,* January 12, 1918; Letwin, "Interracial Unionism," 535; Worthman, "Black Workers and Labor Unions," 386–87. For information on Washington's opposition to black involvement in labor unions, see August Meier and Elliott Rudwick, "Attitudes of Negro Leaders Toward the American Labor Movement from the Civil War to World War I," in *The Negro and the American Labor Movement,* edited by Julius Jacobson (Garden City, N.Y.: Anchor Books, 1968), 39–41, and Louis R. Harlan, *Booker T. Washington: The Making of a Black Leader, 1856–1901* (London: Oxford University Press, 1972), 90–91.

58. As Henry McKiven concluded: "With the exception of a brief period during World War I when union membership increased, organized labor in Birmingham remained only a shell of what it had been at the height of its strength in the nineteenth century." McKiven, *Iron and Steel,* 170.

59. See Carl V. Harris, "Reforms in Government Control of Negroes in Birmingham, Alabama, 1890–1920," *Journal of Southern History* 38 (November 1972), especially 586–87, for management's use of convict labor to undermine unionism.

60. It was also a system of social control. "Guided by a white determination to return the Negro to 'his place,' the problems of crime, tax relief, internal development, and control of the labor force all intersected in the convict-lease system." Alabama *House Journal* (1896–97), 28, as cited in David Alan Harris, "Racists and Reformers," 66; William Cohen, "Negro Involuntary Servitude in the South, 1865–1940: A Preliminary Analysis," *Journal of Southern History* 42 (February 1976): 56.

61. For Parke's reaction to and denouncement of Sloss Furnace's mining operation in Coalburg, which was run with convict labor, see W. David Lewis, *Sloss Furnaces,* 212–13. See also Albert Burton Moore, *History of Alabama* (Tuscaloosa: Alabama Book Store, 1951), 814–15. Some reforms were implemented by the turn of the century, but the system continued to flourish, and the state's income from convict leasing was increasingly profitable. Jack Leonard Lerner, "A Monument to Shame: The Convict Lease System in Alabama" (master's thesis, Samford University, 1969), 160–61; Thomas McAdory Owen, *History of Alabama and Dictionary of Alabama Biography,* vol. 3 (1921; reprint, Spartanburg, S.C.: Reprint Co., 1978), 901; Marlene

Hunt Rikard, "A Case Study on Welfare Capitalism and Industrial Communities: The Tennessee Coal, Iron and Railroad Company of Birmingham, Alabama, 1907–1950," paper presented at the Conference on Steel and Coal Communities in Comparative Perspective, 1900–1990: United States and Germany, Pittsburgh, April 20–22, 1990, p. 63.

62. For street work to proceed on schedule, the city imposed more aggressive vagrancy laws to ensure an adequate supply of convict workers. Carl V. Harris, "Reforms in Government Control," 583. Jane Zimmerman, "The Penal Reform Movement in the South During the Progressive Era, 1890–1917," *Journal of Southern History* 17 (November 1951): 468–69.

63. The fee system was directly tied into convict leasing: officers arrested large numbers of black laborers, who were then charged and put to work on the city streets and in the mines. Fees were paid to law enforcement officers according to the number of legal notices they served and the number of court cases and arrests they made. Officers' dependency on these fees in lieu of salaries motivated them to aggressively pursue the loosely defined "law breakers."

64. *Birmingham News,* December 23, 1895, as cited in Martha Mitchell Bigelow, "Birmingham's Carnival of Crime," *Alabama Review* 3 (April 1950): 127.

65. *Birmingham Reporter,* September 28, 1919.

66. *Birmingham Age-Herald,* September 30, 1919.

67. According to one account, black women were being taken from their washtubs and charged with vagrancy. Although black women may have been taken from their yards while doing laundry, a more probable scenario is that black domestics and those engaged in doing the laundry of white families were arrested while traveling to and from their employers' homes. In Richmond, a white newspaper urged the city to adopt a vagrancy law to rid the streets of black women traveling on the street after dark. Yet, the long hours that domestics worked inevitably forced them to be out during the evenings. See Brown and Kimball, "Mapping the Terrain," 323.

68. *Birmingham Voice of the People,* November 30, 1918, February 15 and April 5, 1919.

69. Carl V. Harris, "Reforms in Government Control," 596–97.

70. It was a powerful political weapon that enjoyed popularity among Democrats in Alabama during the 1870 election. Thereafter it fell out of favor for various reasons, it disbanded, and by 1871, the same year as Birmingham's birth, it was almost dead in Alabama. Rogers et al., *Alabama,* 251–52. In 1883, a black man who had been jailed on a rape charge was taken out and lynched. The mayor called out the militia in response to rumors of a black protest riot. Another lynching occurred in the city; this time a white man was the victim. Particularly during the economic roller coaster of the 1890s, when labor unrest was frequent, lynchings and racial disturbances occurred in the surrounding mining camps. Bigelow, "Birmingham's Carnival of Crime," 128–29.

71. The only larger southern cities that effectively resisted a well-established KKK order were Louisville and New Orleans. See Kenneth T. Jackson, *The Ku Klux Klan in the City, 1915–1930* (New York: Oxford University Press, 1967), 86–87, 245.

72. Flynt, *Alabama*, 430–31.

73. Jackson, *The Ku Klux Klan*, 82.

74. William R. Snell, "Masked Men in the Magic City: Activities of the Revised Klan in Birmingham, 1916–1940," *Alabama Historical Quarterly* (Fall and Winter 1972), 211, 212; Jackson, *The Ku Klux Klan in the City,* 82, 83.

75. Before this wave of vigilante lawlessness, the editor of the *Voice of the People* had naïvely expressed his confidence in the Klan: "Long live the Ku Klux Klan, and may its tribe increase, if by and through such there shall be less violators of the law, and hence better communities in which we may live. Let colored men join . . . for there is no such thing as bettering the community for one, without bettering the community for all." *Birmingham Voice of the People,* November 13, 1920; *Birmingham Reporter,* May 19, 1923.

76. The Bar's efforts to pass an ordinance to achieve this goal was unanimously struck down, as were the efforts of a committee of twenty-five citizens who joined in a campaign to rid the city of lawless individuals. *Montgomery Advertiser,* September 4, 8, 1922, and Atlanta *Constitution,* September 15, 1922. In the same session, an ordinance was passed to make it a misdemeanor to lure a person from home for unlawful purposes. This achieved little since individuals continued to forcefully remove residents from their homes to terrorize them. In the following year, Montgomery adopted an ordinance prohibiting KKK demonstrations. *Montgomery Advertiser,* May 3, June 2 and 7, 1922, and August 2, 1923; *Birmingham Age-Herald,* May 31, June 2, 3, 6, 7, 12, and 14, 1922; *Birmingham Reporter,* June 2, 10, 1922.

77. Walter B. Weare, *Black Business in the New South: A Social History of the North Carolina Mutual Life Insurance Company.* (Urbana: University of Illinois Press, 1973), 153.

78. *Birmingham Age-Herald,* July 2, 5, 6, August 5, 6, 7, 1927, as cited in Snell, "Masked Men in the Magic City," 223.

79. De Priest was raised in Alabama, and in 1899 he moved to Chicago where he pursued a political career. The Mosaic's session would have brought to Birmingham about 6,000 delegates and visitors. *Birmingham Truth,* June 27, 1930. Twenty-three years earlier, an attack was leveled directly at a fraternal officer. When W. L. Houston, Grand Master of Negro Odd Fellows, was visiting from Washington, D.C., he was summarily removed from the Jefferson Theatre, arrested, and jailed. *Birmingham Truth,* August 10, 1907.

80. *Birmingham Truth,* April 20, June 15, 1928.

CHAPTER 2. SMITHFIELD: THE SUBURB

1. Interview with anonymous speaker.

2. *Birmingham Silent Eye,* October 28, 1905.

3. *Birmingham News,* July 19, 1907.

4. *Graymont City Minutes,* July 30, 1907–September 22, 1908, pp. 99–100.

5. In 1907, citizens of Smithfield were still wrestling with the issue of incorporation. If the village was incorporated, it would achieve the political designation "town," and the residents would be granted a vote on whether to

be included in Greater Birmingham. *Birmingham Age-Herald,* 1907; *Birmingham Ledger,* July 18, 1902; Robert S. Newbill, "A Study of the Growth of the City of Birmingham's Corporate Boundaries from 1871 to the Present," unpublished manuscript, April 1980, 17.

6. Ordinance 14, August 3, 1905, resolution regarding sanitary conditions, Birmingham Real Estate Association Minute Book, Department of Archives and Manuscripts, Birmingham Public Library, Birmingham, Ala.

7. *General Laws (and Joint Resolutions) of the Legislature of Alabama,* Special Session 1909 held in Montgomery (Brown Printing Co, 1909), p. 419. The advocates of "Greater Birmingham" managed to get the bill passed when they agreed to leave the property of the Tennessee Coal, Iron and Railroad Company outside the new boundaries. Hackney, *Populism to Progressivism,* 311.

8. Paul Worthman, "Working Class Mobility in Birmingham, Alabama, 1880–1914," in *Anonymous Americans: Explorations in Nineteenth Century Social History,* edited by Tamara K. Hareven (Englewood Cliffs, N.J.: Prentice-Hall, 1971), 200–201.

9. Brownell identified a more integrated pattern. He also found that blacks settled into the "city's 'vacant spaces'—areas of undeveloped land bypassed for more pleasant sites by industry and white neighborhoods." Brownell, "Birmingham, Alabama," 28.

10. John P. Radford, "Race, Residence, and Ideology: Charleston, South Carolina, in the Mid-Nineteenth century," *Journal of Historical Geography* 2, no. 4 (October 1976): 330.

11. Horace C. Wilkerson, *Brief and Argument for the Appellants in the United States Court of Appeals,* 5th Circuit No. 13518, *City of Birmingham et al. vs. Monk et al.,* 8, and *General City Code of Birmingham, Alabama* (1947), 636–59, as cited in Leavy W. Oliver, "Zoning Ordinances in Relation to Segregated Negro Housing in Birmingham, Alabama (master's thesis, Department of Government, Indiana State University, 1951), 13.

12. Oliver, "Zoning Ordinances," 9–10.

13. Pastors from First Congregational, Sixteenth Street Baptist, and St. John AME churches among others lead the protest. Wilson Fallin, Jr., "A Shelter in the Storm: The African American Church in Birmingham, 1815–1963" (Ph.D. diss., University of Alabama, 1995), 160.

14. *Birmingham News,* June 15, 1926. Charles S. Johnson and Herman H. Long noted in *People vs. Property* (Nashville, Fisk University Press, 1947), 8, that such laws provoked further racial antagonism: They dwell on the fears of white property owners, and they demoralize blacks.

15. Although the housing shortage was of crisis proportions, it appears that the annexation movement was motivated more by the promise of increased tax dollars than by an interest in correcting the housing situation. In 1889, Birmingham officials made a step toward expanding the city's tax base when they successfully annexed a large tract of land that "brought in approximately 15,000 new citizens and a minimum of 5 million dollars in taxable property." Newbill, "A Study of the Growth," 13. This is a well-researched and thorough analysis of Birmingham's annexation campaign. See

also Jere C. King, Jr., "The Formation of Greater Birmingham" (master's thesis, University of Alabama, 1936), for another account of the process.

16. Cited in Ruth Beaumont Reuse, *Molton, Allen & Williams: The First One Hundred Years* (Birmingham: Birmingham Publishing Co., 1988), 4.

17. These areas lay adjacent to the railroads and industries. As John Kellogg noted, generally black urban clusters were located near railroads or city dumps, or they were adjacent to cemeteries, on land with a very steep slope, or in any area near the city's edge. John Kellogg, "Negro Urban Clusters in the Postbellum South," *Geographical Review* 7 (July 1977): 311.

18. W. M. McGrath, "Conservation of Health," *Survey* 27 (January 6, 1912): 1510, 1512.

19. Skilled white workers received the best housing, whereas unskilled blacks and whites lived in dwellings that tended to be small, cramped, and lacking in sanitation. Although these conditions for African Americans were common, some companies took a different approach. Marlene Rikard's description of TCI's welfare practices, which were introduced to stabilize the work force, offered a contrasting perspective on company housing. TCI provided modernized company villages with improved living conditions and extensive health and welfare programs to all its workers in a racially segregated environment. Both black and white laborers were the beneficiaries. Rikard described a rather utopian scenario: "Other company-provided facilities in the villages included clubhouses, fraternal halls, churches, community bathhouses, basketball courts, swimming pools, playgrounds, tennis courts, a large stadium for pageants and athletic events, and numerous ball fields." Rikard, "A Case Study on Welfare Capitalism," 14.

20. Tarry, *The Third Door*, 3–4.

21. Avondale and Kingston were other early developments.

22. Carl V. Harris, *Political Power*, 21–22.

23. John Smith's last will and testament reveals that he had distributed to his children a considerable amount of his holdings prior to his death. His wife, Sally Riley, predeceased him. A copy of the last will and testament appears in Mittie Owen McDavid, *John Smith, Esquire, His Ancestors and His Descendants: A Story of the Pioneers* (Birmingham, Ala.: Birmingham Publishing Co., 1948), 56–58.

24. John Witherspoon DuBose, *Jefferson County and Birmingham Alabama, Historical and Biographical* (Birmingham: Caldwell Printing Works, 1887), 378–80; Owen, *History of Alabama and Dictionary*, 1859–60.

25. From Sarah E. Nabors's memoirs written in 1903, as quoted in the *Birmingham Post-Herald*, October 4, 1978.

26. Unidentified family history, Smith family file, Southern History Collection, Department of Archives and Manuscripts, Birmingham Public Library, Birmingham, Ala.

27. "Smith Family," unpublished manuscript, no author, no date, Department of Archives and Manuscripts, Birmingham Public Library, Birmingham, Ala.; "Dr. Joseph Riley Smith," unpublished transcript compiled by and in the possession of Henley Jordan Smith.

28. Legend has it that Smith's strong-willed character touched many lives.

The following tale provides an illustration of his indomitable spirit: The Alabama and Chattanooga was the first railroad built through the Jones Valley in about 1870. Joseph Smith and his neighbors blocked the building of the South and North Alabama railroad through their lands. Consequently, the two railroads intersected in the new town of Birmingham, rather than in the intended location of Center Street in Elyton. McDavid, *John Smith, Esquire,* 124–25; Mittie Owen McDavid, "The Smith Family of Smithfield," Birmingham, October 1944, unpublished transcript, Hill-Ferguson Collection, Tutwiler Collection of Southern History and Literature, Department of Archives and Manuscripts, Birmingham Public Library, Birmingham, Ala.

29. *1850 Agricultural and Manufacturing Census Records,* Dale—Marengo, Schedule—Agricultural, microfiche, Auburn University, Ala.; 1860 Alabama, Dekalb—Morgan, Agricultural; *Alabama Schedules,* 1860, Slave Population, Augauga—Madison Counties, microfiche, Auburn University, Ala.; *1860 Census—Population Schedule* (Free Inhabitants in Greene Precinct), P. O.—Elyton, Ala., Jeff.—Lawrence, microfiche, Auburn University, Ala.; *1880 Agricultural and Manufacturing Census Records,* Ala., Jeff.—Limestone, Agricultural, microfiche, Auburn University, Ala.

30. Unidentified document in the possession of Henley Jordan Smith, Jr.

31. *Tax Return List—Real and Personal Property,* 1904, Tax Assessor's Office, Jefferson County Court House, Birmingham, Ala.

32. The continuity of this forty-acre plot was destroyed about 1905 when the Tidewater carline condemned a right-of-way through it, along what is known as Fifth Avenue (formerly Graymont Avenue). Birmingham—Neighborhood—Smithfield, Clipping File, Tutwiler Collection of Southern History and Literature, Department of Archives and Manuscripts, Birmingham Public Library, Birmingham, Ala. The Birmingham Trust & Savings Company, the trustee, held Smith Park in trust for several years while it loaned money on vacant lots to construct business buildings in what was to become a new commercial district. When the last of these debts was paid off, the amount was divided among the heirs. McDavid, *John Smith, Esquire,* 131; "Smithfield: An Historic Birmingham Neighborhood" (Birmingham Historical Society, 1986), copy found in the Hill-Ferguson Collection, Department of Archives and Manuscripts, Birmingham Public Library, Birmingham, Ala.; *Birmingham News,* March 13, 1927; and *Weekly Iron Age,* August 8, 1885.

33. *Weekly Iron Age,* August 8, 1885.

34. Ibid. In 1883, William Berney had founded the National Bank of Birmingham with a capitalization of $50,000. It went through several name changes until it ceased operations before the turn of the century. *Birmingham City Directory,* 1883–1905.

35. Marcus B. Long prepared the original map on January 5, 1887. It is held in the Probate Court Record Room, Jefferson County Court House, Birmingham, Ala.

36. McDavid, *John Smith, Esquire,* 124.

37. Ibid., 126; *Birmingham Ledger,* January 21, 1903; Hill-Ferguson Collection, June 13, 1952; *Birmingham Post-Herald,* May 4, 1950.

38. The investors were J. V. Richards, B. W. Taber, A. O. Lane, B. W.

Moore, J. P. Mudd, F. D. Nabors, J. L. Watkins, Reavis J. Terry, and C. W. Ware. The declaration stated that the general purpose of the company "shall be the sale and purchase of lands and the improvement of the same and the laying out of street, avenues, and alley and grading. . . . [It will] have the power to borrow and loan money, to issue bonds, stocks, and secure the same by mortgage or other security and to do all things else in connection with said business authorized by the laws of Alabama." This company engaged in several direct transactions with Joseph R. Smith. By 1889, the company decreed to issue additional stock to raise sufficient monies to clear its debt with Joseph Smith. *Record of Incorporation,* Jefferson County, A481, filed in office for record on November 30, 1886; DuBose *Jefferson County and Birmingham,* 262; *Direct Index to Deeds and Mortgages, Deed Record,* Probate Court Record Room, Jefferson County Court House, Birmingham, Ala. (hereafter cited as *Deed Record*), vol. 78, p. 47, documents the details of the exchange of property between Smith and the Land Company. On September 22, 1888, Smith released all the mortgages he held against the property he had sold to the Smithfield Land Company.

39. Ethel Armes, *The Story of Coal and Iron in Alabama* (1910; reprint, New York: Arno Press, 1973), 356. Ordinance No. 35, *Graymont City Minutes,* August 27, 1907, 88. Location was a key factor in the success of Smithfield. As Henry Taylor noted: "Residential location determined the type and quality of housing one might occupy, the employment opportunities and the public and private facilities accessible to the resident, and the overall physical, economic, political, and social setting in which urban residents lived and raised their families." Henry L. Taylor, "Spatial Organization and the Residential Experience: Black Cincinnati in 1850," *Social Science History* 10, no. 1 (Spring 1986): 45.

40. United States Department of the Interior, National Park Service, *National Register of Historic Places,* Inventory—Nomination Form, Smithfield Historic District, Department of Archives and Manuscripts, Birmingham Public Library, Birmingham, Ala.

41. Birmingham—Neighborhood—Smithfield, Clipping File. Smithers Avenue was the broad dividing line between North and South Smithfield. Tax records reveal that an official distinction was made between the property lying north and south of Smithers Avenue.

42. One year earlier, Joseph Smith, along with Henry F. DeBardeleben and others, incorporated the second horse railway known as the Birmingham and Pratt Mines. It was capitalized at $100,000 and divided into 2,000 shares at $50 each. It merged with the Birmingham Street Railway Company to form the Birmingham Union Railway, which in 1890 was absorbed by the Birmingham Railway and Electric Company. Alvin W. Hudson and Harold E. Cox, *Street Railways of Birmingham* (Forty Fort, Pa.: Harold E. Cox, 1976), 11–12.

43. Ibid., 14. In 1907, the Birmingham Railway, Light and Power Company agreed to place stations at John Street on the North Ensley line and at Owenton station on the Owenton line. Also, the company added additional cars and "earlier morning cars and later cars in the evenings and better the

services on all the lines running through the City of Graymont." *Graymont City Minutes*, July 30, 1907–September 22, 1908, 99–100.

44. The agreement allowed for the "[construction of] a sanitary sewer through the City of Graymont," which would then connect to individual properties. The sewer connected with the "trunk line of sewer known as the Valley Creek Trunk Sewer, constructed by Jefferson County." Ordinance No. 81, p. 243, provided for the regulation of the maintenance of dry closets in Graymont. Adopted May 16, 1908.

45. Other neighborhoods were more clearly defined racially, as the city circumscribed where the vast numbers of new black migrants could and could not live.

46. U.S. Bureau of the Census, *Twelfth United States Census: 1900—Population; Thirteenth United States Census: 1910—Population;* and *Fourteenth United States Census: 1920—Population.*

47. Historians and sociologists have identified six major factors in determining why people migrate to and within cities: "background characteristics; life cycle factors; employment opportunities, family connection, or other attractive features elsewhere; bonds to residence and neighborhood; space considerations; and housing structure." Economic opportunity played the largest role in drawing migrants to Birmingham. Howard P. Chudacoff, "A Reconsideration of Geographical Mobility in American Urban History," *Virginia Magazine of History and Biography* 102, no. 4 (October 1994): 504.

48. Glenn N. Sisk, "Social Aspects of the Alabama Black Belt, 1875–1917," *Mid-America* 37 (January 1955): 31–47.

49. Bond, *Negro Education in Alabama*, 236. In 1879, a law was passed that imposed a state tax on labor recruiters who drew blacks away from the Black Belt. As the labor pool continued to decline in the 1880s, the state legislature passed another law making it a criminal act to break a sharecropping contract after acceptance of advances. Despite these efforts to curtail movement of the rural black population, blacks continued to migrate. McKiven, *Iron and Steel*, 44.

50. Earl Lewis, in his study of Norfolk's black community, noted that as African Americans sought to improve their economic position they were empowered. "Expectations, Economic Opportunities, and Life in the Industrial Age: Black Migration to Norfolk, Virginia, 1910–1945," in *The Great Migration in Historical Perspective: New Dimensions of Race, Class, and Gender*, edited by Joe William Trotter, Jr. (Bloomington: Indiana University Press, 1991), 25.

51. Weymouth T. Jordan, *Ante-Bellum Alabama, Town and County* (1957; reprint, Tuscaloosa: University of Alabama Press, 1986), 22.

52. W. E. B. Du Bois, "The Negro in the Black Belt, A County Seat: Marion, Perry County, Alabama," *Bulletin of the Department of Labor*, no. 22 (May 1899): 411–13. See Jordan's *Ante-Bellum Alabama* for a more detailed account of the significance of Marion. See J. L. Chestnut, Jr., and Julia Cass's *Black in Selma, The Uncommon Life of J. L. Chestnut, Jr.* (New York: Farrar, Straus and Giroux, 1990) for a narrative about growing up in Selma after 1930. Also see William J. Edwards, *Twenty-Five Years in the Black Belt*

(1918; reprint, Westport, Conn.: Negro Universities Press, 1970) for an account of growing up in Snow Hill, Wilcox County. Edwards was born in 1869 and reared in the Black Belt, where he founded a Normal and Industrial Institute. For a detailed account of the AMA's impact, see Joe M. Richardson, *Christian Reconstruction: The American Missionary Association and Southern Blacks, 1861–1890* (Athens: University of Georgia Press, 1986).

53. James and Sally Curry were born into slavery in Perry County and elected to remain living there until their deaths. They purchased property after the Civil War and built a small house at 310 Polk, where they reared their children. "The Polk Street house would be the center of life for the Curry family for more than a hundred years." Andrew Billingsley, *Climbing Jacob's Ladder: The Enduring Legacy of African-American Families* (New York: Simon & Schuster, 1992), 313–19.

54. James Whitehead, interview by the author, Birmingham, Ala., January 11, 1993.

55. *Birmingham Truth*, December 13, 1929.

56. Tarry, *The Third Door*, 3. Other Smithfield residents came from Mississippi and exhibited a similar pattern of migration. S. M. Hutton and his wife Effie, a Mississippi native, lived on Mortimer Street. They had purchased their home from the Balls, who also migrated from Mississippi. Both the Davis and Cole families who boarded with the Huttons were Mississippians. As Mississippi natives, the families more than likely knew each other prior to their arrival in Birmingham and were probably friends or even appropriated family members. This eased the period of adjustment to a new environment as shared behavioral and cultural practices were carried with the migrants. U.S. Bureau of the Census, *Thirteenth United States Census: 1910—Population;* and *Fourteenth United States Census: 1920—Population.* When some Smithfield residents left to move north, they recreated their community elsewhere. One Birmingham paper reported that, "no less than a score of Negro families have gone in recent months to certain Chicago suburbs, notably Evanston,from one southern community." *Birmingham Weekly Voice*, January 13, 1917. Chudacoff, "Geographic Mobility in American Urban History," 509.

57. Reports of life in the North from relatives combined with encouragement from the *Chicago Defender* and enticements from northern labor recruiters, lured many workers away from Birmingham. Ellen Tarry remembered that her father claimed that "all the big companies had to do was send special trains down, back the coaches into Terminal Station, and say: 'All aboard for Detroit, Akron, Columbus, or Pittsburgh!' and Negroes would fill the cars." The laborers were often joined by members of the middle class: "It was not long before [the laborers] were followed by merchants and a small number of the professional people that we knew." Tarry, *The Third Door*, 24. In his study of African American coal miners in West Virginia, Joe Trotter noted that early in the twentieth century, professional agents were hired by West Virginia coal companies to recruit black coal miners from Birmingham. One such agent located his operations in the Jefferson County Bank Building. According to Trotter, several variables attracted Alabama's black coal workers to West Virginia, including higher wages and unrestricted voting. Trotter, *The Great Mi-*

gration in Historical Perspective, 52, 53. See also Peter Gottlieb, "Migration and Jobs: The New Black Workers in Pittsburgh, 1916–1930," *The Western Pennsylvania Historical Magazine* 61 (January 1978): 1–15 and his larger work *Making Their Own Way* for an analysis of migratory patterns during the Great Migration. Many of the southern rural migrants who arrived in Pittsburgh did, in fact, initially spend a period of time in Birmingham.

58. Worthman, "Black Workers and Labor Unions," 379–80.

59. As well as drawing migrants into the city, chain migration also played a role in migration out of the city. As James Grossman noted, "black southerners, like European immigrants and white southerners, established migration chains linking North and South by means of kin and community relationships." James R. Grossman, *Land of Hope: Chicago, Black Southerners, and the Great Migration* (Chicago: University of Chicago Press, 1989), 90–91. A few middle-class families in Birmingham, including the U. G. Mason family, visited the North before moving there permanently. Having sent their children to be educated in the North, families often helped their children with the early periods of adjustment in the new environment. Vacations spent with kin who settled elsewhere stimulated interest in northern cities, as did glowing accounts of northern conditions. E. W. Tankersley sent a letter to the *Birmingham Reporter* from his new home in Chicago boasting of his improved life with a $35-a-week job at International Harvester Co. and his leadership position in the Bethlehem AME Church. June 26, 1920.

60. Chudacoff, "Geographic Mobility in American Urban History," 509.

61. James Whitehead, interview.

62. Seretha Jackson, interview, May 11, 1994.

63. *Birmingham City Directory,* 1901.

64. United States Department of the Interior, National Park Service, *National Register of Historic Places,* Inventory—Nomination Form, Smithfield Historic District.

65. Kathleen Conzen noted that "A strong 'congregational instinct' on the part of an ethnic group or, on the other hand, a strong tendency on the part of society at large to segregate the group can lead group members to select residence on the basis of ethnicity rather than socioeconomic or family status." Kathleen Neils Conzen, "Patterns of Residence in Early Milwaukee," in *The New Urban History: Quantitative Explorations by American Historians,* edited by Leo F. Schnore (Princeton, N.J.,: Princeton University Press, 1975), 149. Earl Lewis emphasizes that "congregation was important because it symbolized an act of free will." Earl Lewis, *In Their Own Interests,* 91–92.

66. Whites took flight from cities across the nation when they perceived blacks threatening their neighborhoods. The *Birmingham Age-Herald* carried a Washington, D.C., report in which a white resident declared that "he bought a new home in the northwest section of the city a few years ago, paying therefore $7,500. Very soon, a negro family was domiciled the next door to me. I had to move. I can't sell my property for $4,000." *Birmingham Age-Herald,* December 30, 1915. Undoubtedly the white families who fled from Smithfield shared his concerns and chose to relocate to more homogeneous areas.

67. Seretha Jackson, interview, May 11, 1994.

CHAPTER 3. STEPS TOWARD BUILDING THE HOME SPHERE

1. This phenomenon is well documented in Sam Bass Warner, Jr.'s *Streetcar Suburbs: The Process of Growth in Boston, 1870–1900* (Cambridge, Mass.: Harvard University Press and MIT Press, 1962), 3

2. The discussion of homeownership in this chapter specifically examines the homes that were located in South Smithfield. The boundaries were Smithers Blvd. on the north, Ruth Avenue on the south, Walker Street on the east, and David Street on the west. Any further discussion of Smithfield refers to the entire area known as Joseph R. Smith's addition to Birmingham, which included streets and avenues running north of Smithers Blvd. to Emma Avenue.

3. As George Haynes noted, "The consciousness of kind in racial, family and friendly ties binds them closer to one another than to their white fellow-citizens." George Edmund Haynes, "Conditions Among Negroes in the Cities," *The Annals of the American Academy* 49 (September 1913): 109–12.

4. The sociological construct of community that best suits this study is one that emphasizes the idea of "shared activities, experiences, and values, common loyalties and perspectives, and human networks that give to an area a sense of continuity and persistence over time. Residents of a neighborhood are seen to share a special and somewhat unique destiny arising from their ecological position in the city, their ties of past and present, and their general orientations toward the area and to one another." Suzanne Keller, *The Urban Neighborhood: A Sociological Perspective* (New York: Random House, 1968), 91.

5. According to environmental psychologist Mary Jasnoski, a sense of community has an impact on happiness. It is determined by how long you have lived someplace, your satisfaction with the area, and how many neighbors you can identify by their first names. "These three things indicate the number of support systems you have available in your neighborhood, the number of social outlets you have, and how secure and safe you feel." *Toronto Star,* February 22, 1994.

6. Olivier Zunz, *The Changing Face of Inequality: Urbanization, Industrial Development, and Immigrant in Detroit, 1880–1920* (Chicago: University of Chicago Press, 1982), 176. John R. Logan and Glenna D. Spitze's article, "Family Neighbors," concurs with Zunz's conclusion: "Homeownership is widely considered to represent a concrete material interest in the community, leading to more involvement in local social networks." *American Journal of Sociology,* 100, no. 2 (September 1994): 451–76. See also Terry Blum and Paul W. Kingston, "Homeownership and Social Attachment," *Sociological Perspectives* 27 (1984): 159–180; Geraldine Pratt, "Housing Tenure and Social Cleavages in Urban Canada," *Annals of the Association of American Geographers* 76 (1986): 366–80; and Ray Forrest and Murie Alan, "Transformation through Tenure? The Early Purchasers of Council Houses, 1968–1973," *Journal of Social Policy* 20 (January 1991): 1–25.

7. Carla A. Hills, in addressing the American Bar Association in August 1975, articulated this concept. "The family who owns its own home, not only has an investment in a house, it has an incentive to take an active role in the

decisions which shape its neighborhood, its community, its schools, and churches. Because the family has a real investment in a structure, it also has an investment in its environment." Cited in Constance Perin, *Everything in Its Place: Social Order and Land Use in America* (Princeton: Princeton University Press, 1977), 78. E. Franklin Frazier stated that "Nothing showed so vividly as the progressive stabilization of Negro family life . . . of the community as the increase in home ownership." *The Negro Family in the United States* (Chicago: University of Chicago Press, 1966), 128–35. See also Edith Elmer Wood, *Recent Trends in American Housing* (New York: Macmillan, 1931); Charles S. Johnson, *Negro Housing*. Report of the Committee on Negro Housing, The President's Conference on Home Building and Home Ownership, Washington, D.C., 1932.

8. Walt Whitman declared that "A man is not a whole and complete man unless he *owns* a house and the ground it stands on." In Walt Whitman, *New York Dissected*, edited by Emory Holloway and Ralph Adimari (New York, 1936) as cited in David P. Handlin's *The American Home: Architecture and Society, 1815–1915* (Boston: Little, Brown, 1979), 69.

9. Various accounts of homeownership during the nineteenth and twentieth centuries reveal how homeownership was promoted during a time of social and geographic upheaval, and why the American public readily and wholeheartedly embraced the dream. John F. Bauman coined the phrase "cult of homeownership" to describe this phenomenon in "Housing the Urban Poor," *Journal of Urban History* 6 (February 1980): 212.

10. Robert Wiebe, *The Segmented Society* (New York: Oxford University Press, 1975); Clifford Edward Clark, Jr., *The American Family Home, 1800–1960* (Chapel Hill: University of North Carolina Press, 1986), 3–36; Jackson, *The Crabgrass Frontier*, 50.

11. Builders, land speculators and the lumber industry, all of whom promoted homeownership, clearly were motivated by self-serving purposes. Moral, urban, social, and structural reformers all espoused the value of owning one's own home, but their agenda did not match that of the dollar-minded entrepreneurs. The reformers' agenda was one of social control. Distressed over the housing conditions and particularly over the scarcity of decent housing, reformers perceived homeownership not only as a way to improve citizenship but also as a stabilizing force in an otherwise disorganized society. Several urban planners at this time, including Clarence A. Perry, promoted the concept that environmental intervention (that is, creating healthy neighborhoods) would result in enhanced citizenship and an improved social life. Howard Gillette, Jr., "The Evolution of Neighborhood Planning," *Journal of Urban History* 9 (August 1983): 424.

12. Criticism of personal property dates back to Friedrich Engels, who determined that homeownership was a means of impeding workers' mobility and freedom of movement. Workers who owned homes were viewed as weakening their job mobility and weakening their ability to strike because they could not afford to forego their wages. Friedrich Engels, *The Housing Question* (1874) as cited in Handlin, *The American Home*, 250–51. Authors Matthew Edel et al. see homeownership as a poor vehicle for social mobility and substantiated their argument by studying Stephen Thernstrom's sample at

a later time period. They noted that most families neither added to nor subtracted from possibilities for advancement through homeownership. Matthew Edel, Elliott D. Sclar, and Daniel Luria, *Shaky Palaces: Homeownership and Social Mobility in Boston's Suburbanization* (New York: Columbia University Press, 1984). Clark views homeownership as guaranteeing neither independence nor permanence due to the changing definition of standards and quality. These uncertainties create unsettling pressures that cause people to feel the need to improve their station in life by improving their living standards through purchasing a new home or rebuilding and remodeling their present home. Clifford Edward Clark, Jr., *The American Family Home.* For additional criticisms of homeownership see Gwendolyn Wright's *Building the Dream: A Social History of Housing in America* (New York: Pantheon Books, 1981). See also Daniel D. Luria, "Wealth, Capital, and Power: The Social Meaning of Home Ownership," *Journal of Interdisciplinary History* 7 (Autumn 1976): 261–82. Other opponents went so far as to charge that the widespread promotion of homeownership was irresponsible. John Dean argued that prospective homeowners needed to be educated on the various responsibilities associated with purchasing and owning a home. Rose M. Stein handily articulated these concerns when she warned, "Every prospective home buyer should be immunized with an anti-toxin against the blah-blah of own-your-own home campaigns." "More Homes or More Mortgages," *New Republic,* September 7, 1932, 90, as cited in John P. Dean, *Home Ownership: Is It Sound?* (New York: Harper & Brothers Publishers, 1945), 39.

13. Nationally African Americans were gaining a hold on homeownership. The percentage of black-owned homes across the nation increased from 18.7 percent of the total black population in 1890 to 23.9 in 1930; they realized a 79.3 percent increase in homeownership. In contrast, white families had realized a 94.8 percent increase in homeownership from 1900 to 1930. For the nation overall, 45 percent of all American families were homeowners. U.S. Bureau of the Census, *Negro Population, 1790–1915,* and *Negroes in the United States, 1920–1932.* These census figures were also used in Charles S. Johnson, *Negro Housing,* and Charles Louis Knight, *Negro Housing in Certain Virginia Cities,* Publications of the University of Virginia Phelps-Stokes Fellowship Papers No. 8 (Richmond: William Byrd Press, 1927), 109–12, to illustrate the growth of homeownership among blacks from 1890 to 1910. These figures refer to "all homes" owned by blacks, and thus the figures include both "farm homes," which are defined as "a home located on a farm," and other homes, which are located in urban settings. The South in 1910 had 89 percent of the country's black population and 88 percent of all the black-owned homes. Sixty-nine percent of the black urban population lived in this region, where they owned 82 percent of "other homes" owned by blacks. In the period 1900–1910, for the nation overall, the number of black-owned homes increased by 30.9 percent and the number of black homes "owned free and unencumbered" increased by 35.9 percent. Although these statistics include both "other homes" and "farm homes," homeownership increased more quickly in cities and towns than on farms. *Pittsburgh Courier,* August 6, 1932.

14. They encouraged women they visited to fill in a form that stated:

"I hereby solemnly pledge myself to buy a home within . . . years." The federation focused on the home as the central place in family life and earnestly sought to convert renters to homeowners. Addie Waits Hunton, "The Southern Federation of Colored Women," *Voice of the Negro* (December 1905): 852.

15. "Like It Ain't Never Passed: Remembering Life in Sloss Quarters, 1930s–1950s," Sloss Furnaces Association and the Oral History Project of the University of Alabama at Birmingham, April 12, 1985, 16.

16. McKiven, *Iron and Steel*, 60–61.

17. Paul Worthman concluded that "One of four black workers remaining in the city until 1909 owned some property (compared with 57 per cent of the white workers). By 1930, the rate increased to 34.1 percent and then declined to 25.7 percent during the depression. See his "Working Class Mobility in Birmingham," 187. See also *Fifteenth and Sixteenth Censuses, Real Property Inventory of 64 Cities* as cited in Dean, *Homeownership: Is It Sound?* 207.

18. Frederick Lewis Allen, "The Big Change in Suburbia," in *North American Suburbs: Politics, Diversity, and Change,* edited by John Kramer (Berkeley: The Glendessary Press, 1972), 63.

19. During the late nineteenth and early twentieth centuries, Smithfield's transportation was not reliable. The Birmingham Rail, Light and Power Company agreed to give the public of Graymont "better service on the Owentown Car Line . . . and better provisions for the separation of the races." *Graymont City Minutes,* August 20, 1907. It appears that Birmingham's public transportation served many residents of Smithfield who worked in the surrounding industries. Many who could not afford the trip had to walk the distance.

20. In a study of homeownership, one homeowner remarked, "Renters are nonpermanent, renters have different motivation in terms of maintaining their units, in terms of commitment to community, in terms of involvement in community." However, it is important to remember that if, in fact, renters do have different motivations, they may share the ultimate goal—to maintain a healthy and safe environment. Perin, *Everything in Its Place,* 38. See also Zunz, *The Changing Face of Inequality,* 185.

21. Renters had the flexibility and mobility to respond to employment opportunities and changing family circumstances. Renting prevented the loss of savings if and when a neighborhood deteriorated, and furthermore, the renters' finances were liquid. However, unstable employment could lead to missed rental payments that might result in an eviction notice. Their dependence on landlords to maintain the property left them vulnerable if the roof leaked or the pipes backed up. Unless a landlord exhibited good faith, renters' living quarters could deteriorate quite rapidly to the point of becoming uninhabitable.

22. Although this individual was not a Smithfield or Birmingham resident, his attitude was shared by many renters. Charles S. Johnson, *Negro Housing.* Report prepared for the Committee on Negro Housing. The President's Conference on Home Building and Home Ownership (Washington, D.C., 1932), 90.

23. Marvine Bradford, interview by the author, Birmingham, Ala., January 18, 1993.

24. Privacy also concerned this resident: "[The landlord] kept a key to my house and went in my house all the time when I wasn't there." Interview conducted with anonymous speaker in 1994.

25. *Birmingham Age-Herald,* December 9, 1886. The "Own Your Own Home" campaigns persisted well into the twentieth century. The *Birmingham News* urged real estate mogul Robert Jemison, Jr., to advertise in their "Real Estate" columns where home properties appear. The paper assured him that it would continue its campaign through the Christmas Season: "[The *News*] is making even greater effort right now to take advantage of the psychology of the moment and to impress the advantages of land and home ownership on its readers." Letter to Robert Jemison, Jr., from the *Birmingham News* dated December 19, 1923. Robert Jemison Jr., Papers.

26. *Hot Shots,* March 2, 1905.

27. *Birmingham Truth,* August 20, 1903.

28. *Birmingham Truth,* February 24, 1906.

29. The North Alabama Colored Land Company and the Colored Mutual Investment Association were short-lived organizations that recognized the importance of homeownership and also the opportunities offered in real estate investment. More than likely, they were undercapitalized. *Record of Incorporation,* F177, A492, and A326 and 378; *Birmingham City Directory,* 1887.

30. Robert Jemison became a very successful real estate developer who was responsible for the development of the prestigious suburb of Mountain Brook. Privately, Jemison supported the construction of homes to own *and* rent. He recognized that "the growth and prosperity of any city is not only dependent upon homeownership but also dependent upon landlords who are willing to provide houses and apartments for the class of citizenship that is not able, inclined, or ready to purchase a home." He was committed to participating in Birmingham's growth through property development. Without suitable rental housing, Jemison feared that Birmingham would "lose many good citizens who would locate in other cities." Confidential letter from Robert Jemison to *Birmingham News,* August 16, 1922, Robert Jemison Jr., Papers.

31. *Birmingham Truth,* March 16, 1907; May 21, August 20, 1903; *Birmingham Age-Herald,* December 9, 1886; *Hot Shots,* March 26, 1904, and November 7, 1898.

32. Collectively, the census figures from 1890 to 1930 reveal a notable increase in the percentage of homeownership among the black population nationally. Furthermore, the statistics reflect an overall increase of the African American urban population. It is important to note that "urban area" does not refer to urban centers per se. The majority of homes in the classification "other homes," were located in small villages and towns with populations of less than 2,500. Knight, *Negro Housing in Certain Virginia Cities,* 111; U.S. Bureau of the Census, *Negroes in the United States, 1920–1932,* "Population, Number of Owned Homes, and Number of Persons Per Home, by Color, for Cities and Other Urban Places Having 10,000 or More Inhabitants: 1930."

33. The availability of early tax records determined the sample size for the study.

34. The 1920s offered an increased choice of residency as the automobile granted personal mobility to approximately 25 percent of all Americans. Birmingham, like every other large American city, found its development affected by the presence of the automobile. During the 1920s, Birmingham and Jefferson County realized a sizable increase in privately owned vehicles. Early in the decade, there was about one vehicle for every 19.4 people; by 1930, there was close to one vehicle for every 6.6 persons. Brownell, "The Notorious Jitney," 105.

35. Sam Finocchio, interview by the author, South Smithfield, June 24, 1994; James L. Lowe, interview by the author, at Jazz Hall of Fame, May 25, 1994. Despite the rigidity of the 1915, 1919, and 1926 city ordinances concerning residential segregation, they did allow for property ownership by one race in areas designated for the other race; thus, the lucrative and often exploitative practice of white landlordism in the black community was protected. *Deed Record,* vol. 132, p. 112, and vol. 187, p. 637; *Direct Index to Deeds and Mortgages, Mortgage Record,* Probate Court Record Room, Jefferson County Court House, Birmingham, Ala. (hereafter cited at *Mortgage Record),* vol. 240, p. 236, and vol. 240, p. 237.

36. Charles Octavius Boothe, *Cyclopedia of the Colored Baptists of Alabama: Their Leaders and Their Work* (Birmingham: Alabama Publishing Co., 1895); *Birmingham City Directory,* 1902, 1911, and *Tax Return List—Real and Personal Property,* 1907, 1911, 1916.

37. *State-Herald,* November 17, 1895; *Tax Return List—Real and Personal Property,* 1914, 1916, and 1920.

38. Henderson also held shares in the Alabama Penny Savings and Loan Company. *Memphis City Directory,* 1904; *Mortgage Record,* vol. 269, p. 220; vol. 562, p. 4; and vol. 610, p. 130; *Deed Record,* vol. 605, p. 308.

39. *Birmingham Ledger,* February 24, 1903.

40. As Stephan Thernstrom noted, "The function of the mortgage was simple: it allowed [the laborer] to enter the class of property owners before he had accumulated enough savings to pay the full purchase price on a lot or house." Thernstrom found that laborers borrowed small sums for a relatively long term, at substantial interest, ranging from 7 to 10 percent. Although he studied working-class families in Newburyport, Massachusetts, his analysis applies universally to the function of mortgages. Stephan Thernstrom, *Poverty and Progress: Social Mobility in a Nineteenth Century City* (Cambridge: Harvard University Press, 1964), 120–21.

41. *Deed Record,* vol. 8, p. 15; U.S. Bureau of the Census, *Twelfth United States Census: 1900—Population;* Reuse, *Molton, Allen & Williams,* 6; *Labor Advocate,* July 11, 1891.

42. Morris's second year ended prematurely upon his resignation. When Birmingham suffered a financial crisis, Morris became a scapegoat of sorts and was accused of allying too closely with blacks to win the election. He was called the "Negro Leader of Birmingham." *Early Days in Birmingham* (Birmingham, 1937) and *Iron Age,* August 8, 1877, as cited in Martha Mitchell

Bigelow, "Birmingham: Biography of a City of the New South" (Ph.D. diss., University of Chicago, 1946).

43. Legend has it that many African Americans who engaged in business transactions directly with Smith, formerly had been his slaves. No records exist to substantiate whether this is true. *Joseph Riley Smith's Will*, Items of Receipts, Department of Archives and Manuscripts, Birmingham Public Library, Birmingham, Ala.

44. *Birmingham City Directory*, 1902, 1911, and *Tax Return List—Real and Personal Property*, 1907, 1911, 1916, and *Deed Record*, vol. 425, p. 437.

45. Black barbers in Birmingham achieved a coup when in 1901 they organized and secured a charter from the national union with the approval of the city's white barbers. Worthman, "Black Workers and Labor Unions," 391. U.S. Bureau of the Census, *Fourteenth United States Census: 1920—Population; Tax Return List—Real and Personal Property*, 1905–16; *Block Book Survey*, 1905–11 and 1916–19, Tax Assessor's Office, Jefferson County Court House, Birmingham, Ala.

46. *Record of Incorporation*, V220.

47. *Birmingham Wide-Awake*, October 27, 1906.

48. *Deed Record*, vol. 776, p. 562, vol. 718, p. 510; *Mortgage Record*, vol. 625, p. 71; and *Birmingham City Directory*, 1911.

49. Peabody Collection, Clipping File, Hampton University, Va. The date and publication is unclear—January 9, 190[?]. In a white paper, possibly the *Birmingham Age-Herald;* address delivered at the Sixth Annual Convention of the National Negro Business League, New York City, August 15, 17, and 18, 1905.

50. Pettiford also organized a real estate department within the bank. James Napier, a League official and Nashville banker, shared Pettiford's philosophy. He further asserted the importance of a well-organized local real estate business as "a great force in the working and building up of our people, making them frugal, and securing them money, lands, homes and withal respectability and standing as citizens." *Southern Workman* 31 (January 1902): 10–15. *Mortgage Record*, vols. 354, 426, and 584.

51. Its stated purpose read: "to buy, own, sell, rent, trade and improve real estate . . . to build houses, grade streets and to engage in general contracting and building business," and to loan money. *Record of Incorporation*, T53.

52. *Record of Incorporation*, A326, A378, and A389; *Birmingham City Directory*, 1905, 1911; the *Record of Incorporation* for the Great Southern Home Industrial Association and the Afro-American Benevolent Society held in the Probate Court Record Room, Jefferson County Court House, Birmingham, Ala.

53. *Birmingham Age-Herald*, December 31, 1915. The mortgage and deed records reveal that the standard rate of interest on mortgages for most white and black borrowers was 8 percent, although lower rates were sometimes granted. Mary Pickens borrowed $600 from W. R. Lisenbaum, a contractor, at 8 percent; while B. Mulholland, a widow, borrowed $1,000 from the Title Guarantee Loan and Trust Company, and she too paid 8 percent interest. Often a lower rate was offered on a larger debt. In 1926, Mamie Steiner, the

wife of Carl Steiner, loaned Anthony and Lula Turner $4,000 at 7 percent interest. In 1905, J. W. Minor, president of the Bessemer Fire Brick Company loaned to T. M. Edwards $7,500 at 6 percent interest. *Mortgage Record*, vols. 612, 616, and 503.

54. *Deed Record*, vol. 983, p. 305; *Tax Return List—Real and Personal Property*, 1920, 1923, and 1925; *Advance*, October 4, 1913; and *Birmingham Age-Herald*, January 1, 1916.

55. Although William McGill was a real estate broker and publisher of *Hot Shots*, his position in the community did not guarantee him ownership of his principal residence. *Hot Shots*, March 26, 1904; *Birmingham Reporter*, January 12, 1918; *Block Book Survey*, 1910–16 and 1923–30; *Lease Record*, vol. 895, p. 194; *Mortgage Record*, vol. 880, p. 54; *Chancery Court*, Case #7927, vol. 58A, p. 109, and *Birmingham City Directory*, 1924.

56. As T. J. Woofter noted, "To borrow money, even with friendly relations, is a test of character. Steady employment, prospects, character, and savings must be considered." *Negro Problems in Cities* (New York: Doubleday Doran, 1928), 143.

57. Although Granville was married to a clerk at TCI, she held ownership of the property and continued to do so when she remarried. *Mortgage Record*, vol. 373, p. 219; vol. 383, p. 157; vol. 528, p. 199; vol. 580, p. 590; vol. 689, p. 43.

58. Diffay had attempted to expand his Smithfield real estate holdings in 1908 when he submitted an offer for two lots at $1,000 each. His bid was rejected when the location was designated for a school for black children. Once construction was completed in 1909, the Graymont School began accepting students for instruction. *Birmingham Free Speech*, April 5, 1902; *Birmingham City Directory*, 1901, 1905. *Graymont City Minutes*, December 9, 1908, p. 51; and *Sanborn Fire Insurance Maps*, vol. 3, 1911, no. 361.

59. For a biography of Diffay, see J. H. Moorman and E. L. Barrett, eds., *Leaders of the Colored Race In Alabama* (Mobile, Ala.: News Publishing, 1928), 96. *Birmingham Truth*, October 1, 1903; U.S. Bureau of the Census, *Fourteenth United States Census: 1920—Population; Tax Return List—Real and Personal Property*, 1905–16; *Block Book Survey*, 1905–11 and 1916–19. Black newspapers of other cities also carried Diffay's ascendancy to the presidency of the bank: *Freeman*, January 30, 1915, and the *Montgomery Advertiser*, April 22, 1914.

60. Moorman and Barrett, *Leaders*, 96. Diffay's social position had enabled him to secure his son Fred a cashier's job at the Diffay barber shop and employment as an enumerator for the U.S. Census. U.S. Bureau of the Census, *Thirteenth United States Census: 1910—Population*; and *Fourteenth United States Census: 1920—Population*.

61. Several other middle-class families also invited single female teachers to board with them. Among them were the DeYampert, Blount, and Kennedy families. Sometimes a head of a family acted as the guardian of a boarder who relocated to the city without a network of support. Their parents may have prearranged their living arrangements to ensure their safety and well-being. U.S. Bureau of the Census, *Fourteenth Census of the United States: 1920—Population*.

62. In addition to the piano, the family personal property also included jewelry and household furnishings, and their ten-room frame home was assessed at $2,400. *Tax Return List—Real and Personal Property,* 1923.

63. Although Kennedy did not live in Smithfield, but rather in the city of Birmingham, her achievement is noteworthy. As a single woman her steady employment as an educator enabled her to establish sufficient credibility and savings to independently secure a mortgage and own a home. *Mortgage Record,* 719, p. 109, and vol. 356, p. 506. By 1922, the tax assessment on her home amounted to $1,260. Her prudent business sense also provided her with the means to afford a piano. *Tax Return List—Real and Personal Property,* 1923.

64. Carol Aronovici addresses the dangers of homeownership in *Housing the Masses* (New York: John Wiley & Sons, 1939), chap. 5. Even Edith Elmer Wood, an early and committed advocate of homeownership, recognized its potential liabilities. "A bad location, a poor house plan, shoddy materials and workmanship, an unscrupulous vendor or mortgage holder may spell ruin to a hard-working couple. They need—most home-buyers need—reliable, disinterested expert advice. Their interests should be guarded for their own sake, for their children's, and for society's." Wood, *Recent Trends.*

65. *Deed Record,* vol. 691, p. 326, and vol. 708, p. 121.

66. *Birmingham Age-Herald,* April 9, September 4, 1895.

67. U.S. Bureau of the Census, *Twelfth United States Census: 1900—Population;* and *Thirteenth United States Census: 1910—Population; Tax Return List—Real and Personal Property,* 1909, 1910, 1911, 1912, 1916, 1921; *Block Book Survey,* Roll #47, Alpha Start: J. M. Morgan, End: Walker City, 1st Add; *Block Book Survey,* Roll #37, 1916–19, Alpha: Queenstown—block 40 To: Waverly Terrace including South Smithfield.

68. C. E. Leonard held two mortgages for $350, one in 1900 and the other in 1904; J. C. McFee of St. Louis, Missouri, held a $309 mortgage in 1902; and in 1908 Mary J. Dobbins held a mortgage for $900 on DeYampert's one-story, five-room house and a two-story store. In 1934, Deyampert arranged a loan with the federal government's Home Owners' Loan Corporation (HOLC) for $4,962.43 at 5 percent interest. *Birmingham Free Speech,* May 24, 1902; U.S. Bureau of the Census, *Thirteenth United States Census: 1900—Population; Block Book Survey,* 1928; *Deed Record,* vol. 264, p. 58; *Mortgage Record,* vol. 274, p. 292; vol. 302, p. 128; vol. 310, pp. 319, 320; vol. 495, p. 96; vol. 650, p. 232.

69. *Birmingham Free Speech,* May 24, 1902; U.S. Bureau of the Census, *Thirteenth United States Census: 1900—Population;* and Birmingfind files, Department of Archives and Manuscripts, Birmingham Public Library, Birmingham, Ala.

70. Paul Finocchio, an Italian immigrant and peddler, also combined his business with his residence. He purchased his home at 504 Walker Street from Rossa and Myer Slaughter in 1919. For $5,250 Finocchio bought an existing grocery store, a two-room frame house, and a four-room frame house. By 1924, he had improved his holdings by building a barn and another shotgun house on the lot, and he added another room to his principal residence. *Deed Record,* vol. 983, p. 305; *Tax Return List—Real and Personal Property,* 1920,

1923, 1925; *Advance,* October 4, 1913, and *Birmingham Age-Herald,* January 1, 1916; *Deed Record,* 537; *Suits or Transactions with State of Alabama or Jefferson County,* vols. 54A and 55A.

71. *City Minutes of the Board of Alderman,* May 15, 1901.

72. Sometime after the turn of the century, Graymont required the use of building permits. A record for building permits was set in 1915. The *Birmingham Ledger* reported, "Residential construction and repairs swell total of certificates. Homes go up everywhere. Large amount of construction work. People were building homes to live in and homes to rent. Progress [is] everywhere in Greater Birmingham." *Birmingham Ledger,* December 24, 1915.

73. Sidney Smyer, Jr., interview by the author, at the Birmingham Realty Co. Building, January 1994.

74. The Birmingham City Hall fire of 1925 destroyed the building permits that would identify the builders.

75. *Deed Record,* vol. 226, p. 226; *Mortgage Record,* vol. 140, 199; *Block Book Survey,* Lot 14, Block 28, 1919.

76. *Hot Shots,* March 26, 1904; *Birmingham Free Speech,* December 13, 1902; *Birmingham Truth,* August 20, May 21, 1903.

77. *Mortgage Record,* vol. 356, p. 268.

78. *Deed Record,* vol. 105, p. 173; the quotation is from the *Birmingham Free Speech,* December 13, 1902.

79. Nabors converted shares he held in the Jefferson County Building and Loan Association to pay the $1,100 he owed McAllister. *Block Book Survey* 1905, 1906, 1907; *Deed Record,* vol. 401, p. 233, and vol. 377, p. 271.

80. The McAllisters also owned property located elsewhere in Jefferson County. *Tax Return List—Real and Personal Property,* 1909; U.S. Bureau of the Census, *Twelfth United States Census—1900; Birmingham City Directory,* 1901.

81. Rietta offered to lease the city of Graymont some ground and let the city build its own jail, or he would build the jail and lease it to the city. Although the city selected Joe Vincent to build the jail, Rietta was involved in the construction business. *Tax Return List—Real and Personal Property,* 1904; U.S. Bureau of the Census, *Twelfth United States Census: 1900—Population; Graymont City Minutes,* August 27, 1907, p. 100–101.

82. Clifford Edward Clark, Jr., *The American Family Home,* xiv and 181; Dr. D. E. Bradford, telephone interview with the author, May 2, 1994; *Birmingham Reporter,* November 27, 1920; *Tax Return List—Real and Personal Property,* 1929.

83. Benjamin L. Windham was a founding member of the Booker T. Washington Life Insurance Company in Birmingham in 1921. (This is not to be confused with A. G. Gaston's Booker T. Washington Insurance Company.) Moorman and Barrett, *Leaders,* 92. Windham was an astute businessman who invested his money wisely. In the early 1920s, B. L. Windham owned a car valued at $250 and in 1927, he and his wife Loretta held property assessed in excess of $14,000. *Tax Return List—Real and Personal Property,* 1923, 1928.

84. According to local chroniclers of black history, Kamau E. A. R. Afrika and his mother Ivory Dawson Walker, T. C. Windham was a slaveowner who

had substantial business interests in Arkansas before he arrived in Birmingham. If this were true, however, Windham would have been in his eighties when he founded Acme. Furthermore, according to the 1910 U.S. Census, T. C. Windham was born in 1882. Marjorie Longenecker White, "Images of Smithfield," *The Journal of the Birmingham Historical Society* 9 (December 1985).

85. United States Department of the Interior, National Park Service, *National Register of Historic Places,* Inventory—Nomination Form, Smithfield Historic District.

86. *Montgomery Colored Alabamian,* January 21, 1911. Windham had developed a business relationship with the Boyds of Nashville. When Windham built the Sixteenth Street Baptist Church, Richard Boyd made the designs in wood in his woodworking shop for the Church's pulpit. Wallace Rayfield to Emmett J. Scott, February 21, 1908, Booker T. Washington Papers, Library of Congress, Washington, D.C.; *Crisis* 35, no. 1 (January 1928); listed on letterhead of letter from U. G. Mason to Emmett J. Scott, September 9, 1910, box 70, no. 44, Booker T. Washington Papers.

87. Interview with an anonymous speaker in 1994. Sam Finocchio, interview by the author, South Smithfield, June 24, 1994, in his grocery store which still is located in South Smithfield. Finocchio also provides a check-cashing service for many of his black customers who he knows by name. August 5, 1915, Booker T. Washington Papers. Photograph of Windham's home is held in the Kamau Afrika Collection, Civil Rights Institute Archives, Birmingham, Ala. In 1926, T. C. Windam's tax assessment for developed and undeveloped property he owned in Smithfield, Sherman Heights and Ensley totaled more than $21,000. *Tax Return List—Real and Personal Property,* 1923, 1927. Elsewhere in the Birmingham District, African American builders constructed homes and churches. Rev. R. N. Hall developed Zion Park among other black settlements where he sold property to members of his church and to other interested parties. Moorman and Barrett, *Leaders,* 26.

88. Seretha Jackson, interview by the author, Smithfield, May 11, 1994.

89. Henry Aaron with Lonnie Wheeler, *I Had A Hammer: The Hank Aaron Story* (New York: HarperCollins, 1991), 8. The official records suggest that some African Americans built their own homes incrementally in light of their limited resources. Richard Harris asserts that building permits cannot be used to provide a reliable estimate of the prevalence of self-building because of the bias inherent in the permits. That is, those building their own homes would most likely bypass obtaining a permit to avoid drawing the attention of authorities who "might force them to spend more than they wished, and perhaps more than they could afford, in building their homes." He prefers to use tax assessment records. In doing so, Harris calculated a "self-built" threshold, "a level that is defined in terms of the market value below which speculative builders will not build because profit margins are too small or nonexistent. The only people who can build homes below this figure are owner-builders since they are, in effect, substituting sweat equity for wage labor. The implication is that any new dwelling with a market value below this threshold may be assumed to have been self-built." Although this may be accurate for some cities, as an industrial city, Birmingham's growth was based

on industries that built cheap company homes en masse to house unskilled, black laborers. Therefore, a system was in place whereby poorly constructed homes, particularly shotgun houses, could be slapped together with little cost to the builder. Smithfield most likely was not targeted as a prime location for *mass* building of cheaply built homes by speculative builders because of its absence of uniform housing types. Nonetheless, a large number of shotgun and some double-shotgun houses were constructed in Smithfield. Richard Harris, "Self-Building in the Urban Housing Market," *Economic Geography* 67 (January 1991): 4.

90. Charles A. Brown, "W. A. Rayfield: Pioneer Black Architect of Birmingham, Ala." (Birmingham: Gray Printing Co., n.d.); Letter from W. A. Rayfield to Emmett J. Scott, January 25, 1909, Booker T. Washington Papers. According to the content of the correspondence between Rayfield and Washington, they had a friendship that allowed Rayfield the latitude to request favors of Washington.

91. "Negro Business League of Greater Birmingham," Booker T. Washington Papers.

92. Brown's two brothers, who were dentists, and Anna Dudley, a schoolteacher, lived with Brown's family for a time. U.S. Bureau of the Census, *Thirteenth United States Census: 1910—Population; Tax Return List—Real and Personal Property,* 1926, 1927.

93. U.S. Department of the Interior and *Historic Sites of Jefferson County, Alabama,* prepared for the Jefferson County Historic Commission by Carolyn Green (Birmingham: Gray Printing Co., 1976; reprint, Birmingham: Loury Printing, 1985). Max Pizitz held a $3,000 mortgage on the property to help Blount finance construction of his home. *Mortgage Record,* vol. 781, p. 231. Besides his Smithfield home, Blount also owned other properties in North and South Smithfield, in East Irondale, and in Masonton. In 1923, the total assessed value of his property was $17,695. *Tax Return List—Real and Personal Property,* 1923.

94. *Birmingham City Directory,* 1901, 1902.

95. There is a discrepancy in the spelling of the family name: The tax records spelling of A. E. Pharoah is not the same as in the Census, where the contractor's name is spelled R. E. Pharrow. The latter appears to be correct. *Historic Sites of Jefferson County, Alabama;* Michael Leroy Porter, "Black Atlanta: An Interdisciplinary Study of Blacks on the East Side of Atlanta, 1890–1930" (Ph.D. diss., Emory University, 1974), 56–57.

96. Shotgun architecture, which is distinguished by its small one-story frame structure and absence of halls, is represented throughout the South in urban and rural settings. George Haynes remarked that shotgun housing was often constructed for a sizable profit. "Loose building regulation allow[ed] greedy landlords to profit by 'gun-barrel' shanties and cottages . . . and by small houses crowded upon the same lot, often facing front street, side street and the alley. Haynes, "Conditions," 111–12.

97. Alma Anderson Dickinson, interview by the author, Birmingham, Ala., February 1, 1993.

98. *Birmingham Weekly Voice,* August 11, 1917; *Tax Return List—Real and Personal Property,* 1916, 1921, 1923; *Birmingham City Directory,* 1920–

21; U.S. Bureau of the Census, *United States Thirteenth Census: 1910—Population;* and *Deed Record,* vol. 425, p. 437

99. *Baist's Property Atlas of the City of Birmingham and Suburbs, Alabama* (Philadelphia: G. W. Baist, 1902), and *Sanborn Fire Insurance Maps,* vol. 3, 1911, nos. 359, 361, 364, 365, and 366. See also Charles S. Johnson, *Growing Up in the Black Belt: Negro Youth in the Rural South* (1941; reprint, New York: Schocken Books, 1967), 55–58.

100. *Tax Return List—Real and Personal Property,* 1909, 1921; *Birmingham City Directory,* 1909, 1920–21; U.S. Bureau of the Census, *United States Thirteenth Census: 1910—Population.* Shortly after A. H. Parker's death in 1939, Anna, his widow, left the family home. She purchased and moved into a duplex that was located one block south on Fifth Street. *Board of Equalization Appraisal Files,* Department of Archives and Manuscripts, Birmingham Public Library, Birmingham, Ala.

101. Lewis concluded that "visiting became an integral part of the congregative character of urban living and the attempt by Afro-Americans to define their world." Earl Lewis, *In Their Own Interests,* 102. Women were burdened with tending to boarders and to attending to out-of-town visitors. Although they enjoyed having out-of-town visitors, having guests increased their workload.

102. Ibid., 109.

103. Ellen Tarry, interview by the author, Smithfield, May 10, 1994.

104. F. H. Cloud was a well-known black photographer in the city whose photographs document aspects of Birmingham's African American elite society. *Birmingham Reporter,* February 7, 1920.

105. *Birmingham Reporter,* January 10, 1920. Arthur M. Brown, E. A. Brown, and Robert Mabry were among the frequent participants in these social functions. *Birmingham Reporter,* May 25, 1918.

106. *Birmingham Reporter,* September 11, 1920, July 12, 1919.

107. Birmingham residents traveled to tend to an ailing relative or to attend a funeral, as did alley dwellers in Washington, but they also extensively traveled to reinforce ties. James Borchert, *Alley Life in Washington: Family, Community, Religion, and Folklife in the City, 1850–1970* (Urbana: University of Illinois Press, 1980), 84. Earl Lewis, *In Their Own Interests,* 103; *Birmingham Truth,* June 16, 1906, and May 24, 1919; *Birmingham Reporter,* February 16, 1918, October 11, 1919. Business travel more than likely included a social component, since businessmen probably stayed with friends, family, or associates.

108. Other times mothers accompanied their children who studied at northern schools. Sometimes families sent their children to study in the North and arranged for their children to stay with relatives. Gatewood found these variable patterns among numerous southern elite families. Willard B. Gatewood, *Aristocrats of Color: The Black Elite, 1880–1920* (Bloomington: Indiana University Press, 1990), 259. When a family migrated North, the male breadwinner sometimes remained behind in Birmingham if he was securely employed: U. G. Mason's family moved to Chicago while he kept his practice in Birmingham. Oftentimes, he would join his family temporarily. In August 1920, Dr. H. F. Harris left Birmingham for Buffalo, N.Y., where he joined his

family for a vacation. Younger unmarried men who were part of the society crowd also visited family members who had moved elsewhere. C. W. Hadnott left Birmingham for a three-week vacation, first to Chicago where he visited his sister and then to St. Louis to socialize with friends. *Birmingham Reporter,* February 7, August 14, November 6, 1920.

109. Bob Tarry's sister, Annie Moore, worked for Minnie Cox in Indianola. *Birmingham Ledger,* January 6, 1903.

110. *Birmingham Wide-Awake,* November 3, 1906.

111. Rarely did they visit a city where they did not have friends or associates. *Birmingham Wide-Awake,* February 16, 1907.

112. *Birmingham Reporter,* August 14, 29, 1920, February 16, 1918.

113. As Earl Lewis notes, as social and political rights were being stripped from them, blacks placed greater attention and importance on the home sphere. *In Their Own Interests,* 17.

114. Paved streets usually ended where black sections began. As Hylan Lewis noted, "The Negro looks forward to improved streets as one of the first signs of improved status—and incidentally, as a reward for political activity." *The Blackways of Kent* (New Haven, Conn.: College and University Press, 1955), 27.

115. *Graymont City Minutes,* November 16, 1909.

116. Carl V. Harris, *Political Power,* 239; Ordinance No. 42, p. 116, August 17, 1907, and Ordinance No. 184, p. 256, November 16, 1909, *Graymont City Minutes; Lien Record,* vol. 926, p. 544, and vol. 927, p. 570; Morris Knowles, "Water and Waste: The Sanitary Problems of a Modern Industrial District," *The Survey* 27 (January 6, 1912): 1487–89.

117. *Birmingham Voice of the People,* March 12, 19, 1921. If Smithfield services were lacking despite the presence of a large proportion of tax-paying property owners who were also community leaders, one can safely conclude that conditions in most other black districts were much worse.

118. *Birmingham Truth,* February 28, 1930.

119. *Graymont City Minutes,* September 22, 1908, 284–85. As noted earlier, T. C. Windham moved entire houses to other locations in Smithfield. Sam Finocchio, interview by the author, South Smithfield, June 24, 1994.

120. The conflict at Broad Street developed when a member was excluded from the church for misconduct. Fallin, "A Shelter in the Storm," 64.

121. He not only directed his congregation on religious matters, but he also instructed them on the importance of supporting black businesses when he declared that he held insurance policies with an African American company. Beyond his ministerial duties, Rev. Boyd was president of the Northwest Baptist Convention which had headquarters in Birmingham. *Sanborn Fire Insurance Maps,* 1911; Moorman and Barrett, *Leaders,* 25; *Birmingham City Directory,* 1918; *Birmingham Voice of the People,* October 16, 1920.

122. He edited the Birmingham *Weekly Review,* a black newspaper financed by TCI that "disseminated its anti-union propaganda within the black community." In 1930, his appeal for Thanksgiving donations were met with "glorious" responses from "big business men and businesses as well as civic, social and religious organizations. He was among many black ministers who responded to individual and community crises. He planned to operate

a lodging house for the homeless during the winter months and urged all churches to do the same. *Birmingham Truth*, November 7, 1930; Glenn T. Eskew, "But for Birmingham: The Local and National Movements in the Civil Rights Struggle" (Ph.D. diss., University of Georgia, 1993), 35.

123. Dr. D. E. Bradford, interview by the author, May 2, 1994; anonymous speaker, interview by the author, 1994.

124. However, James Borchert's innovative study *Alley Life in Washington*, illustrates how the alley dwellers used strategies to create their own communities. He found subtle signs that their actions were deliberate and fine-tuned to secure their survival within and beyond the boundaries of their neighborhood. Borchert, *Alley Life in Washington*.

125. Tarry, *The Third Door*, 14.

126. *Birmingham Truth*, August 3, 1907. *Birmingham City Directory*, 1908, 1916. Not until 1914 did blacks finally get the Tidewater Amusement Park at Fifth Avenue North at Thirtieth Street. In that year, the city awarded $300 for the playground, 2 percent of the city's $15,375 playground budget, and black volunteers were assigned responsibility for the maintenance and improvements to the small park. Edward Shannon LaMonte, *Politics and Welfare in Birmingham, 1900–1975* (Tuscaloosa: University of Alabama Press, 1995), 12.

127. Two years after the Episcopal Diocese of Alabama donated the site, the city, through the Parks and Recreation Board, finally moved to provide amusement and recreation facilities for African Americans. After the term expired, the city commissioners had to decide whether to purchase the site for a permanent park for African American patrons. *Birmingham Reporter*, March 8, July 26, 1919, October 9, 1920; *Birmingham Truth*, November 1, 1929.

128. Blacks also used this public space as a political platform. Oscar Adams urged black men to meet their duties as citizens and cooperate in liberating members of their race. "If I could get five hundred of you men to believe in yourselves, gather yourselves in faith, grasp the vision God has offered every sensible man today, without a single gun, without a bit of ammunition, without a sword, we would emancipate to the satisfaction of decent citizenry, every man and every woman of this race in the entire district." Both men and women attended this meeting, but only men were given the opportunity to speak. *Birmingham Reporter*, July 26, 1919.

129. Forrester B. Washington, "Recreational Facilities for the Negro," *Annals of the American Academy of Politics and Social Science* 140 (November 1928): 281. East Lake (amusement) Park, in contrast, was financed with city recreation monies. Carl V. Harris, *Political Power*, 166. *Birmingham Truth*, July 13, 1928, April 26, 1929; *Birmingham Truth*, July 12, 1928, July 5, 1929. Middle-class blacks gathered for parties at Tuxedo Park, and the Atlanta Life Insurance Company held its annual outing for the Birmingham District there as well. *Birmingham Truth*, July 12, 1928.

130. During the summers, the different playgrounds offered volleyball, music, swimming at Tuxedo Park, track, and baseball. Several baseball leagues competed in tournaments, including a junior and senior boys league and a men's league. Playground organizers arranged annual exhibits of the

children's handicrafts and art work, which were judged by community members. *Birmingham Truth,* July 12, 1928, June 28 and August 2, 1929.

131. Tarry, *The Third Door,* 7–8, 28. African Americans who attended white baseball games had to sit on the concrete bleachers along the extreme right and left sides, otherwise they could sit wherever they liked when the black teams played. Flynt, *Alabama,* 542. R. T. Jackson, a local entrepreneur who followed Oscar Adams as the club's president, was largely responsible for the seating improvements for blacks attending games at Rickwood Field. *Birmingham Truth,* March 2, April 3, 1928. Blacks also staged fundraisers at Rickwood Park: the Four Strangers Colored Teams donated the proceeds from a fundraiser to the Colored YWCA building fund and the Girls' Service League. *Birmingham Truth,* August 13, 17, 1928. In 1919, the Birmingham Black Barons, the city's professional Negro Southern League team, drew over "15,000 colored fans and 1,000 white people." Christopher Dean Fullerton, "Striking Out Jim Crow: The Birmingham Black Baron" (master's thesis, University of Mississippi, 1994), 71, 73, 75.

132. As noted in the introduction, conflict occurred when Dr. Saunders's play drew diverse classes of black patrons into a shared environment.

133. *Birmingham Ledger,* December 28, 1915.

134. Paul K. Edwards, *The Southern Urban Negro as a Consumer* (New York: Prentice-Hall, 1932), 8 (n. 7); *Birmingham City Directory,* 1920–21; *Birmingham Truth,* November 23, 1928; *Birmingham Reporter,* July 12, 1919; *Birmingham Voice of the People,* February 4, November 13, 1920. Race films played to audiences in cities with large black populations who were searching for more positive images of blacks than the negative stereotypes perpetuated in Hollywood films. For a detailed discussion of blacks and their relationship with the movie industry, see Thomas Cripps, *Slow Fade to Black: The Negro in American Film, 1900–1942* (London: Oxford University Press, 1977).

135. By 1925, Birmingham still failed to provide suitable leisure activities for its white residents. Brownell, "Birmingham, Alabama," 30–32. See also Harrison A. Trexler, "Birmingham's Struggle with Commission Government," *National Municipal Review* 14 (November 1925): 662.

CHAPTER 4. LEADERSHIP, THE BLACK ELITE, AND THE BUSINESS COMMUNITY

1. Benjamin was also a former educator and lawyer. Allen Woodrow Jones, "Alabama," in *The Black Press in the South, 1865–1979,* edited by Henry Lewis Suggs (Westport, Conn.: Greenwood Press, 1983), 33.

2. Jones, "Alabama," 33. Despite Benjamin's aggressive tactics and his forced departure from Birmingham, a group of one hundred black men from the city perceived him as a capable politician and drafted him to run for Congress in 1892. Brittain, "Negro Suffrage," 106.

3. National Negro Business League. *Report of the Fourteenth Annual Convention, 1913,* Philadelphia.

4. Nathan I. Huggins, "Afro-Americans," in *Ethnic Leadership in America* edited by John Higham (Baltimore: Johns Hopkins Press, 1979), 91–118.

5. Washington was a member of the Board of Trustees of the Alabama Colored Orphans and Old Folks Home. November 6, 1900, Booker T. Washington Papers; January 21, 1902; December 16, 1904; Leah Rawls Atkins, *The Valley and the Hills: An Illustrated History of Birmingham and Jefferson County* (Woodland Hills, Calif.: Windsor Publications, 1981), 100; *Birmingham Free Speech*, April 5, 1902. During Republican administrations, Washington was the primary dispenser of patronage positions in Alabama. Consequently, blacks such as Smithfield resident and postal carrier James Byrd, were given federal appointments.

6. Gaston recalled many years later: "[Washington] said opportunity was like a bald-headed man with only a patch of hair right in front. If you want to catch opportunity, you have to watch for it and face it head on." A. G. Gaston, *Green Power: The Successful Way of A. G. Gaston* (Troy, Ala.: Troy State University Press, 1968), 26.

7. Washington's refusal to take action against N. B. Smith and his Metropolitan Mercantile & Realty Company, moved E. A. Brown to castigate him: "Are you in favor of having men to continue their membership in the League who are plainly conducting a fraudulent business? I had thought that our League stood for business integrity, but frankly, Dr. Washington, . . . I find myself in doubt on this point." E. A. Brown to Booker T. Washington, August 22, 1906, box 28, folder 217, National Negro Business League Papers, Tuskegee University, Tuskegee, Ala.; *Birmingham City Directory*, 1905. As noted earlier, some blacks refused to support Washington's antiunion posture. Worthman, "Black Workers and Labor Unions," 386–87. See also Bond, *Negro Education in Alabama*, 217.

8. National Negro Business League. *Report of the Sixth Annual Convention, August 16, 17, and 18, 1905*, New York City.

9. Joseph A. Pierce, *Negro Business and Business Education* (New York: Harper & Brothers Publishers, 1947), 20; Rikard, "An Experiment in Welfare Capitalism," 110–11; *Negro American*, May 5, 1894.

10. Correspondence from Ellen Tarry to the author, January 22, 1995, in the author's possession.

11. At the time it was believed that Rameau received financial support from the coal operators and other Alabama industrialists. Consequently he highlighted the positive features of industrialists and their benevolent work practices. Spero and Harris, *The Black Worker*, 363–64.

12. Donald Comer was the general manager of Avondale Mills, the largest and ever-expanding textile company in Alabama, and son of the former governor, Braxton Bragg Comer. The Comers were an old Alabama family with political power and paternalistic instincts. Rogers et al., *Alabama*, 445. Robert Jemison Jr., was the son of Robert Jemison, Sr., a wealthy lawyer, prominent and successful businessman, and state senator from Tuscaloosa. John N. Ingham and Lynne B. Feldman, *African-American Business Leaders: A Biographical Dictionary* (Westport, Conn.: Greenwood Press, 1994), 404. In a letter of reference, Jemison stated that Rameau was "trying to do a constructive work in this community, is giving the colored people of the community proper ideas and viewpoints about their obligation to the community, their relations to their employers and to the white people of the community. So

far as I know, he has always been honest and fair in his dealings." P. Colfax Rameau to Jemison, April 3, 1925, and Robert Jemison to Whom It May Concern, October 28, 1914, Robert Jemison, Jr., Papers, Department of Archives and Manuscripts, Birmingham Public Library, Birmingham, Ala.

13. Letter from Carson Adams to James L. Davidson, May 24, 1923, with copies sent to Donald Comer and Frank Rushton, Donald Comer Business Papers, box 7.1.1.1.1–29, folder 7.1.1.1.1, Department of Archives and Manuscripts, Birmingham Public Library, Birmingham, Ala. U. G. Mason's wife and children had migrated to Chicago. There his children received an education that the Mason family believed was superior to that offered in Birmingham. Mason's son, Ira, became a leading surgeon in Chicago's black Provident Hospital.

14. *Birmingham Reporter,* May 10, 1919. The paper suggested that Driver had voted along with the "Lily Whites" and the regular Republicans, black and white. *Birmingham Voice of the People,* May 29, 1920.

15. Walker's dramatic preaching style did not appeal to all the members at Sixth Avenue Baptist. Amidst charges of arrogance and conceit, Walker left his position and briefly served at the First Baptist Church of Brighton in west Jefferson County before founding the Shiloh Baptist in Birmingham in 1891. Fallin, "A Shelter in the Storm," 114–15.

16. *Birmingham Voice of the People,* January 31, 1920.

17. Boothe, *Cyclopedia of the Colored Baptists of Alabama,* 212–13; Fallin, "A Shelter in the Storm," 113–14.

18. *Birmingham Truth,* June 11, 1903, June 9, and November 5, 1904.

19. *Birmingham Voice of the People,* January 31, 1920.

20. *Birmingham People's Weekly Tribune,* May 20, 1899; *Record of Incorporation,* I263, and T53.

21. Washington's donation to the Birmingham Grate Coal Mining Company was substantial enough to keep the company solvent. According to a letter from Pettiford to Washington in 1900, TCI agreed to allow them to "continue to operate the mines unmolested and as a result they have interested new parties who are bringing in capital sufficient to continue and extend the work." Pettiford to Washington, November 6, 1900, Reel #166, Booker T. Washington Papers; *Birmingham City Directory,* 1900, 1902, 1908; letter from Pettiford to Washington, November 6, 1900, Booker T. Washington Papers; Samuel William Bacote, ed., *Who's Who Among the Colored Baptists of the United States* (Kansas City, Mo.: Franklin Hudson, 1913; reprint, New York: Arno Press, 1980), 167–69.

22. W. E. B. Du Bois, ed., *The Negro in Business. Report of the social study made under the direction of Atlanta University; together with the proceedings of the Fourth Conference for the study of the Negro Problems held at Atlanta University, May 30–31, 1899,* Atlanta University Publications, no. 4 (1899; New York: Octagon Books, 1968).

23. W. R. Pettiford, "The Importance of Business to the Negro," address delivered at the Hampton Negro Conference, Hampton University, Va., July 1903.

24. Ibid.

25. *Birmingham Weekly Pilot,* August 18, 1883.

26. *Birmingham Weekly Voice*, June 23, 1917.

27. *Birmingham Voice of the People*, February 7, 1920.

28. In fact, Johnston's pharmacy was located at 601 S. 18th Street for seventeen years before it moved across the street to its new two-story building. *Birmingham Reporter*, October 23, 1920.

29. Traditional attitudes initially kept most women from aspiring to business-related careers. By the 1920s, women were hearing words of encouragement from a variety of sources, including race newspapers. The *Voice of the People* urged them to become involved: "We long to see some business venture or ventures in this district owned, operated, controlled and maintained by Negro women, especially through their club organizations." *Birmingham Voice of the People*, March 6, 1920. By the late 1920s, women not only ran businesses from their homes, but several women also owned businesses in the BBD. Hazel Carlton owned Carlton's Beauty Shoppe, while Mabel Hedgemon managed "Your Cafe," and Mrs. John Johnson ran the Grecian, a store that specialized in foundation garments. *Birmingham Truth*, April 20, June 1, 1928. The census report for 1890 revealed that nationally 514 black women worked as hairdressers; by 1920, their numbers increased to 12,660. This field offered many women the opportunity to operate independent businesses. Although the vast majority practiced their trade at home, a few women managed to set up businesses away from their home environments. Fewer even created large beauty empires including Madame C. J. Walker and Annie Turnbo Malone. Monroe N. Work, "The Negro in Business and the Professions," *Annals of the American Academy of Politics and Social Science* 140 (November 1928): 143.

30. *Birmingham Truth*, March 22, 1929.

31. Seretha Jackson, interview by the author, Smithfield, May 11, 1994.

32. *Proceedings of the Hampton Negro Conference*, July 1903. The concept of patronizing black business was articulated by Fred R. Moore, an organizer of the NNBL and editor of the *New York Age*, a political instrument of Washington's. At the 1904 NNBL proceedings, he strongly voiced his opinions regarding the concept of "buy black": "support all worthy enterprises managed by men and women of the race. . . . Jews support Jews; Germans support Germans; Italians support Italians until they get strong enough to compete with their brothers in the professions and trades; and Negroes should now begin to support Negroes." Cited in Meier, *Negro Thought in America*, 125–26. Moore later became very active in the Colored Merchants Association (CMA), an organization that was conceived on a local level in Montgomery, Alabama, in 1928. The CMA was essentially a cooperative of black-owned retail stores that paid weekly dues and bought from a wholesale dealer selected by the NNBL. Frazier, *Black Bourgeoisie*, 161–62.

33. *Birmingham Reporter*, March 30, 1918. This was a national cry that had appeared in local papers fifteen years earlier, the same time of Pettiford's address, when the *Truth* carried a letter from a Topeka resident who declared that "A Negro who will insist upon spending his money with mean and prejudiced white people is a fool, a deceiver, and is unfit for citizenship." *Birmingham Truth*, 1903, reprinted from the *Topeka Plaindealer*. Ministers often addressed the importance of supporting black business in their weekly sermons

and demonstrated their commitment to race businesses by personal example. Rev. Boyd of Trinity Baptist in Smithfield and Rev. Richardson of Harmony Street Baptist Church informed their congregations that they held policies with an African American insurance company. Fallin, "A Shelter in the Storm," 160–61.

34. *Birmingham Weekly Voice*, June 16, 1917.

35. Letter from Charles M. Moore (national organizer of the NNBL and newspaper correspondent) to Booker T. Washington, June 26, 1906, National Negro Business League Papers; *Birmingham Wide-Awake*, July 14, 1906. People's Drug Store served as the local headquarters for the Alabama Business League.

36. Franklin D. Wilson, "The Ecology of a Black Business District," *Review of Black Political Economy* 4 (Summer 1975): 358.

37. Ibid., 373 (n. 11), and *Birmingham City Directory, 1915; Birmingham Reporter,* January 11, 1919.

38. *Montgomery Colored Alabamian*, November 2, 1907. Two years later, as the Alabama Penny Savings Bank thrived, the paper continued to cite Birmingham as a fine example of business success. *Montgomery Colored Alabamian*, March 13, 1909.

39. In the first twenty years following the Civil War, the rapid expansion of fraternal insurance and burial societies were followed by the increase of independent black banking. Black banks flourished from 1888 to 1934, when the nation industrialized and the population became increasingly urbanized. There were no fewer than 134 banks that were organized by blacks, including both private institutions doing a general banking business and banks operating under state or national charters. Abram Harris, *The Negro As Capitalist: A Study of Banking and Business Among American Negroes* (Gloucester, Mass.: Peter Smith, 1968), 46–48.

40. National Negro Business League, *Report of the Eleventh Annual Convention, August 17, 18, and 19, 1910*, Nashville. African American business leaders across the nation recognized the importance of these anchor institutions. Anthony Overton, a well-respected Chicago insurance company pioneer who created a modest business empire, fully understood the importance of anchor institutions: "Life insurance organizations are the dominating forces in the production, distribution, consumption, and conservation of the wealth of our racial group. . . . Through the painstaking effort of our life insurance companies, these small sums have grown into millions of assets. . . . These millions are systematically and scientifically reinvested in the race." *Norfolk Journal and Guide*, April 26, 1930.

41. Before the creation of any black banks, the early black fraternal orders deposited money in white banks. However, the white institutions refused to provide loans to the fraternal orders, even when their deposits amounted to sizable savings accounts that enabled the white banks to realize a profit. The fraternal orders consequently were without a source of capital or credit.

42. The restrictions placed on public space did not inhibit all African Americans from exercising their freedom in important ways. Participation in parades provided an avenue for blacks to share public space with whites and to show that "they, too, had a right to the streets." Shane White, " 'It Was a

Proud Day': African Americans, Festivals, and Parades in the North, 1741–
1834," *Journal of American History* 81, no. 1 (June 1994): 50.

43. She recalled that "there were numerous parades around the time I was
in the fourth grade, because that was at the time of World War I. . . . The
biggest parade took place when the first Negro soldiers went away to war."
Tarry, *The Third Door*, 15–16. In 1919, the NAACP sponsored a parade to
welcome home returning soldiers. This parade was particularly significant because it allowed the soldiers to receive a hero's welcome, and it provided the
opportunity for young children to view role models up close. Furthermore, the
public showing demonstrated the contributions of black soldiers to the war
effort and demonstrated how African Americans shared a national patriotism
with whites. *Birmingham Voice of the People*, June 21, 1919.

44. Brown and Kimball, "Mapping the Terrain," 309–12.

45. Du Bois, *The Negro in Business*, 1:14; Paul K. Edwards, *The Southern
Urban Negro as a Consumer*, 133.

46. John Ingham, "African-American Business Leaders in the South—
1880–1945: Business Success, Community Leadership and Racial Protest,"
paper presented at the Business History Conference, Harvard Business School,
March 20, 1993; John Ingham, "Pride, Prejudice and Profits: African-American Business in the South, 1880–1933," paper presented at York University in
Toronto, February 1995; Franklin Wilson, "The Ecology of a Black Business
District," Institute for Research on Poverty Discussion Papers, University of
Wisconsin, Madison, 1975, 353; *Birmingham Wide-Awake*, December 22,
1906; Benjamin P. Fowlkes, *Co-operation the Solution of the So-Called Negro
Problem* (Birmingham, Ala.: Novelty Book Concern, 1908), 17–19, offers a
colorful description of I. B. Kigh's business.

47. In 1874, Browne arrived in Alabama and successfully established
many branches of the United Order of True Reformers, his temperance organization. To enhance his status, he was ordained in the AME Church and over
the next few years worked as a minister, temperance agitator, and fraternal
organizer in Selma and Montgomery. In 1880, his dreams of creating a grand
financial empire took him away from Alabama and on to Richmond, Virginia,
a city "tailor-made for his abilities and ambitions." Browne found fertile
ground. The True Reformers Bank made its appearance in 1888 and commenced operation in 1889. It was the cornerstone of the empire. From there,
Browne and the bank expanded outward into other fields: real estate, newspaper publishing, and hotel management. The Reformer's Mercantile and Industrial Association was established in the late 1890s to conduct a chain of
stores and to erect a 150-room hotel for blacks. Browne also founded an Old
Folks Home and the Westham Farm, where he set aside some of a 634-acre
property for agricultural production, while the remainder of the land was developed to create "Browneville," a new, all-black town. Browne had achieved
all this before his premature death in 1897, a time when black businesses were
struggling to establish a sure footing on very shaky ground. Browne exemplified the realization of ambitious dreams, and his influence was well known
among enterprising blacks across the nation but particularly in the South.
Ingham and Feldman, *African-American Business Leaders*, 112–20.

48. Booker T. Washington, *The Negro in Business* (1907; reprint, Chicago:

Afro-American Press, 1969), 129–32. The biographies in this volume were supplied by the subjects themselves. Washington urged Pettiford to furnish him with biographical information for the book, which he felt would be "incomplete" without Pettiford's inclusion. Letters from Washington to Pettiford, June 24, October 20, 1904, Booker T. Washington Papers. Boothe, *The Cyclopedia of the Colored Baptists of Alabama*, 183–84; William J. Simmons, *Men of Mark: Eminent, Progressive and Rising* (Cleveland: Rewell Publishing Co., 1887), 304–8.

49. Simmons, *Men of Mark*, 308; DuBose, *Jefferson County and Birmingham*. Pettiford's rise to prominence in the Negro Baptist State Convention can be followed in the Alabama Baptist State Convention Minutes, 1869–1899, microfilm, Special Collection, Samford University, Birmingham, Ala. The collection of minutes is incomplete.

50. Charles A. Brown, "W. A. Rayfield"; Sixteenth Street Baptist Church pamphlet (Birmingham, n.d.). In 1909, before the new building was completed, the city condemned the older building. The congregation was forced to comply with the city's order to raze the structure. Records are not available to determine whether, in fact, the thirty-year-old building had structural problems. Christopher M. Hamlin, *Behind the Stained Glass: A History of the Sixteenth Street Baptist Church* (Birmingham: Crane Hill Publishers, 1998), 14.

51. William R. Pettiford, *Guide of the Representative Council* (Birmingham: Willis Printing Co., n.d.), 2–6, as cited in a rough draft written by Rev. Wilson Fallin in author's possession; Charles A. Brown, "Alabama Blacks in Jones Valley," 10; Simmons, *Men of Mark*, 308; Boothe, *Cyclopedia of the Colored Baptists of Alabama; Birmingham City Directory*, 1887, *Record of Incorporation*, B82. The relationship among black business and civic leaders during Birmingham's infancy is difficult to comprehend. As blacks were actively establishing new business ventures, William Pettiford was well represented among their many boards as either a director or trustee. His presence as an officer in these newly incorporated companies went unmatched. Others, such as T. W. Walker, B. H. Hudson, and U. G. Mason, through their involvement in these enterprises also exhibited a commitment to the growth of new business, educational, and philanthropic ventures. No clear alliance emerges among the business leaders; the records of incorporation fail to help unravel the tangled web of relationships. The rosters of officers and board members changed with each new venture, although the names reveal that the incorporating officers were among the more elite members of Birmingham's black community.

52. The appeal had met with assurances from the governor, the speaker of the house, and members of the legislature from Jefferson County and the state at large that no opposition would be shown toward the bill seeking a charter for the school. The bill ultimately fell to deaf ears and the plans failed to materialize for lack of funding.

53. *Birmingham Ledger,* February 13, 16, 1903; Wayne Flynt, "Religion in the Urban South: The Divided Religious Mind of Birmingham, 1900–1930," *Alabama Review* 30 (April 1977): 108–35.

54. Their suspicion of the bank had its roots in the controversy over the Freedmen's Bank, which abandoned its black depositors during the panic of 1873.

55. National Negro Business League, *Report of the First Annual Convention, 1900,* Boston.

56. His success at banking in Richmond led him to Birmingham, where a growing African American population offered unlimited possibilities.

57. In 1888, the Capital Savings Bank of Washington, D.C., was the first bank established by blacks. Mobile, with its antebellum free black population, did not have a black-owned bank until 1911. Monroe N. Work, "The Negro in Business and the Professions," *Annals of the American Academy of Politics and Social Science* 140 (November 1928): 143; *New York Age,* January 1911. National Negro Business League, *Report of the Seventh Annual Convention, August 29, 30, and 31, 1906,* Atlanta.

58. Hudson was a school teacher, grocer, and cashier of the bank; N. B. Smith was a real estate broker, manager of the Metropolitan Mutual Benefit Association, and superior master of the Afro American Benevolent Society; and Diffay was a barber and proprietor, who later held the position of president of the Alabama Penny Savings Bank and the Peoples Mutual Aid Association. Others who lived outside of Birmingham also held shares and official positions within the company. Henry Boyd of Nashville's National Baptist Publishing Board served as vice-president of the Bank for a time as did W(ayne) W. Cox, of Indianola, Mississippi. Arnett B. Lindsay, "Negro in Banking," *Journal of Negro History* 14 (April 1929); *Birmingham City Directory,* 1900, 1905, 1907, 1911; Report of the People Investment & Banking Co, box 69, folder 395, National Negro Business League Papers; G. F. Richings, *Evidences of Progress Among Colored People* (Philadelphia: Geo. S. Ferguson Co., 1897), 340. See also Abram Harris, *The Negro As Capitalist,* 47–48; Pierce, *Negro Business,* 157; *Montgomery Colored Alabamian,* November 20, 1909.

59. The high profile of these officers was not unusual among founding members of African American banks. As Jesse Blayton noted, "An officer of the colored bank is the leader in the civic life of his group, and more often than not, every important social agency in the community where such a bank is located has on its board of directors one of more of the bank's officials." Jesse B. Blayton, "The Negro in Banking," *Banker's Magazine* 133, no. 6 (December 1936): 511–14. The bank's officers were individuals who had risen to prominence through various business interests as well as from their membership in carefully selected fraternal organizations and churches. The combined influence of the fraternal order, the church and the ministry stands out strikingly in the organization of the early black banks.

60. Gatewood, *Aristocrats of Color,* 25.

61. *New York Age,* January 11, 1914.

62. This occurred when the directors learned that a bank could not commence service without having $25,000 paid in and an equal amount subscribed. Rather than abandon the project and lose the confidence of African Americans, the directors operated the bank as a private company. National

Negro Business League, *Report of the Seventh Annual Convention, August 29, 30, and 31, 1906*, Atlanta.

63. Ibid.

64. *Birmingham Wide-Awake*, November 23, 1905; *Birmingham Age-Herald*, November 25, 1905; *Birmingham City Directory*, 1916; Charles A. Brown, "W. A. Rayfield"; letter from Rayfield to Emmett J. Scott, dated January 25, 1908, Booker T. Washington Papers, in which the former mentions his contract to design the Sixteenth Street Baptist Church. The real estate transactions were cited in Clement Richardson, "The Nestor of Negro Bankers," *Southern Workman* 43 (November 1914): 605–11.

65. The Peoples Investment and Banking Company also engaged in lending practices for mortgages, and realized impressive growth during its initial years of operation. Lauderdale's Great Southern Home Industrial Association provided the financial backing for the bank. To drum up business for his bank outside of Jefferson County, Lauderdale advertised his bank elsewhere in the state as the "Strongest Company South of the Ohio." He also founded the Royal Circle & Investment Company and the National Investment & Loan Company. "Peoples Investment & Banking Co. Report," box 69, folder 395, National Negro Business League Papers; *Birmingham Wide-Awake*, October 27, 1906; *Birmingham City Directory* 1901, 1905, 1908, 1911; *Montgomery Colored Alabamian*, October 26, 1907; *Birmingham Weekly Voice*, July 14, 1917. U. G. Mason and W. W. Hadnott, the Prudential's cashier, were former board directors of the Alabama Penny Savings and Loan Company. Other Board members included T. C. Windham and I. B. Kigh. Letterhead of the Prudential Savings Bank dated September 9, 1910, and letterhead of the Alabama Savings Bank dated September 4, 1906. A white-owned company known as the Afro-American Loan and Realty Company organized to serve Birmingham's rapidly growing black population. Other smaller cities that lay close to Birmingham had their own growing black communities. In Bessemer, the black organizers of the Consolidated Mercantile and Land Co, extended their operations to include a banking company in 1907. *Birmingham Truth*, November 30, 1907.

66. National Negro Business League, *Report of the Sixth Annual Convention, August 15, 17, 18, 1905*, New York City.

67. *New York Age*, December 22, 1909; National Negro Business League, *Report of the Eighth Annual Convention, 1907*, Topeka; *Montgomery Colored Alabamian*, June 28, 1913. In 1909, the Board of Directors voted to increase the bank's capital stock to $100,000. By issuing new stock, they sought to stimulate investment and thus "realize greater profits." They encouraged investment in the Bank and eased the process by encouraging deposits and subscriptions to the new stock by mail. Furthermore they enticed customers with their promise of paying 4 percent interest on time deposits and won the confidence of potential investors with their declaration that their officers and force were bonded and that the bank's monies were insured in the National Security Company in New York City. *Montgomery Colored Alabamian*, March 13, 1909. In 1910, Pettiford revealed the success of his campaign when he stated that stock was sold in fifteen states including Pennsylvania,

Minnesota, Maryland, and the District of Columbia. *Montgomery Colored Alabamian*, February 19, 1910.

68. National Negro Business League, *Report of the Seventh Annual Convention, August 29, 30, and 31, 1906*, Atlanta.

69. Ibid. The Bank's achievements earned praise from Fred Moore, recording secretary and national organizer of the NNBL, who reported that the bank was "doing a good business" when he visited Birmingham. Letter from Fred Moore to Washington, June 26, 1906, box 33, folder 238, Booker T. Washington Papers.

70. *Montgomery Colored Alabamian*, October 22, 1910.

71. Although the Alabama Penny Savings and Loan Company primarily served Birmingham's African American community, it did conduct business with a few white families. In 1899, J. M. Grady, a white grocer who owned a business in Ensley, and his wife Sallie took out a mortgage with the company for $329.25. *Mortgage Record*, vol. 616, p. 82.

72. Gaston, *Green Power*, 35.

73. *New York Age*, December 22, 1909; *Chicago Defender*, January 15, 1916; *Montgomery Colored Alabamian*, April 2, 1910.

74. Rev. T. W. Walker also had influence in banking and insurance outside of Alabama. When the first black-owned Georgia bank opened, Walker was elected to its board of directors. *Reformer*, March 7, 1908.

75. Pettiford's close relationship with Washington is revealed in their correspondence. Pettiford asked Washington to dispense patronage positions and to recommend such local blacks as Dr. A. M. Brown for the position of Surgeon-in-Chief of the Freedman's Hospital. He also invited Washington to sit on the Board of Trustees of the Alabama Orphans and Old Folks Home. November 6, 1900, October 5, 9, 1901, and January 21, 1902, Booker T. Washington Papers.

76. Louis R. Harlan, ed., *The Booker T. Washington Papers*, vols. 1:182, 3:480, 5:393, 6:233, 6:269, 5:388 (Urbana: University of Illinois Press, 1989).

77. Diffay had earned a reputation as a prominent business leader both in Birmingham and Alabama. His status also drew the attention of Charles Moore, the NNBL's national organizer, who recommended Diffay as a Birmingham representative at the 1910 NNBL meeting in New York City. Negro Business League of Greater Birmingham, Container 1055, folder 1907, #2, 1907; Local Birmingham NNBL, 1914; Alabama State Business League, box 1061, folder 1, 1914; Alabama State Business League meeting at Montgomery, April 21, 22, 23, 1914, container 1058, folder An, 1914, Booker T. Washington Papers.

78. One individual who was touched by the experience of attending an NNBL conference shared what he learned: "We had in mind the organization of a bank for many years, but it was not until some of our men visited the league and received the information and inspiration which it gives, were we able to affect an organization." J. R. E. Lee, "The Negro National Business League," *Voice of the Negro* (August 1904): 329. This refutes Louis Harlan's claim that the NNBL was nothing more than a vehicle that "provid[ed] Washington with an organized body of loyal, conservative followers in every

city with a substantial black population, North or South," with little constructive benefit to blacks seeking instruction on business strategies. Harlan, *Booker T. Washington: The Making of a Black Leader,* 266.

79. *Birmingham Truth,* September 2, 1905.

80. The National Banker's Association that was founded in 1906 was the precursor to an organization with the same name founded by Richard R. Wright in 1924. Both were offshoots of the NNBL and shared similar goals. Washington determined that the NNBA was founded to "encourage the establishment of negro banks, to unite the negro banks of the country for mutual support and to effect an organization that will exercise some sort of indirect control over the banks already in existence." *The Informer,* January 1907; Letter from William Pettiford to Booker T. Washington, August 18, 1906, box 33, folder 238, National Negro Business League Papers.

81. *Birmingham News,* September 21, 1914.

82. *Nashville Globe,* October 25, 1914.

83. *Montgomery Advertiser,* January 30, 1915.

84. *Birmingham Voice of the People,* May 21, 1915.

85. "Affidavit of A. E. Walker in re Consolidation of the Alabama Penny Savings Bank and the Prudential Savings Bank." Filed March 5, 1915, *Record of Incorporation,* Z489, and "Report of Consolidation Proceedings of Alabama Penny–Prudential Savings Bank," *Record of Incorporation,* Z554; *Searchlight,* November 28, 1915; "Negro Banks," *Howard University Record,* Commercial College Studies of Negroes in Business No. 1 Howard University Press (Dec. 1914); *Montgomery Advertiser,* December 23, 24, 1915.

86. *Birmingham Age-Herald,* December 23, 1915.

87. It is interesting to note that, when ministers of Birmingham and Bessemer convened to determine what their position should be concerning the bank's failure, the meeting took place at the African Methodist Episcopal Zion Church, the same church accused of withdrawing a large sum of money without notice. At the conclusion of the session, the ministers agreed that the welfare of blacks was dependent on a black-owned bank and that ministers "shall place themselves squarely and firmly behind the reorganization or organization of a Negro bank, contributing in the way of purchasing stock themselves, and urging upon their people, the necessity of purchasing stock and otherwise gaining their support to such a financial institution." *Birmingham Ledger,* January 8, 1916; *Birmingham Voice of the People,* January 22, 1916, and *Chicago Defender,* January 15, 1916.

88. The Selma branch had suffered a setback in 1913, when Randall W. Hunter, its cashier, disappeared with approximately $5,000. *Voice of the People,* January 24, 1916, and the *Montgomery Advertiser,* March 2, 1913.

89. It is important to note that the failure of the Alabama Penny Savings Bank and other black banks at this time was not a unique phenomenon. White banks also failed due to poor management, competition, and economic downturns. Aside from the few, well-capitalized white banks, including the First National Bank and the Steiner Brothers Bank, that survived from the late nineteenth century to well past 1930, numerous other white banks in Birmingham fared poorly. The Nickle Savings Bank and the Southside Savings Bank, which were both founded about the same time as the Alabama Penny

Savings Bank, foundered quickly and disappeared from record by 1895. *Birmingham City Directory,* 1891, 1896. As Butler notes, the banking industry is affected by the forces of the marketplace in any historical period, and his statement is supported by the number of bank closures during the early twentieth century. John Sibely Butler, *Entrepreneurship and Self-Help Among Black Americans: A Reconsideration of Race and Economics* (Albany: State University of New York Press, 1991), 141.

90. The term "fiscal agent" was taken from an article published in the *Journal of Negro History.* It is not clear what it means. However, it does suggest that the Penny Savings Bank had some financial arrangement with the Steiner Brothers Bank. No records are available which might reveal the type of relationship. When Pettiford addressed the NNBL meetings, he often referred to the support he received from white banks. In 1906, he recalled a time that several white banks and businesses rallied behind the Penny Savings Bank when Christmas withdrawals gave the public the impression that there was a run on the bank: "Three or four [banks] offered us their service to furnish whatever money we needed; several other business firms made similar proposals." Perhaps the Steiner Brothers Bank was one such bank that loaned money to the Penny Savings Bank. National Negro Business League, *Report of the Seventh Annual Convention, August 29, 30, and 31, 1906,* Atlanta. If, in fact, the Steiners somehow financially supported the Penny Savings Bank, they were not responsible for its failure. One other explanation that was offered was that the Bank was caught in the "backwash of steel and mining unemployement [*sic*] troubles" of the time. Although this may have contributed to the Bank's failure, it was not the defining factor. Harry Herbert Pace, "The Business of Banking Among Negroes," *Crisis* (February 1927): 184–88.

91. Letter from Pettiford to Washington, September 20, 1894, reel 15, Booker T. Washington Papers.

92. All the closing transactions were completed under the guidance of Peter F. Clarke. See Arnett G. Lindsay, "The Negro in Banking," *Journal of Negro History* 14 (April 29): 156–201; and "Economics," *Crisis* (February 1916): 166.

93. Ellen Tarry, interview, May 10, 1994; Gaston, *Green Power,* 35.

94. Ellen Tarry, interview, May 10, 1994; *Birmingham Reporter,* August 7, 1926. These terms differed from those settled in 1921, which stipulated that open account depositors were to receive dividends of 15 percent. *Birmingham Voice of the People,* May 28, 1921.

95. *Birmingham Ledger,* January 8, 1916. Smith and Freeman also were the founding members of the Afro-American Benevolent Society in 1908 — perhaps they intended to finance a new bank with resources from the benevolent organization. *Record of Incorporation,* R201.

96. Several of the same businessmen who sat on the executive committee to reorganize the Alabama Penny Savings Bank also sat on the special finance committee of this new venture. They were also the founding members and directors of the original Prudential Savings Bank. *Birmingham Reporter,* January 17, 29, 1920; *Birmingham Voice of the People,* January 31, 1920; *Birmingham Times Plaindealer,* June 4, 1921; *New York Age,* January 23, 1913. In 1929, officers of the Central Relief Insurance Company attempted to estab-

lish a bank, but their plans never materialized into anything concrete. *Birmingham Truth,* June 21, 1929.

97. *Birmingham Voice of the People,* January 24, 1920.

98. Oscar Adams, E. A. Brown, and Harriett S. Matthews were among the directors of the board of the Acme Finance Corporation. Harriett Matthews, Nora H. Martin, Oscar Adams, and E. A. Brown were among the company's fourteen original promoters. *Birmingham Truth,* June 29, December 21, 1928. In 1926, Windham was interested in the National Negro Finance Corporation, which Wanti Gomez founded in Durham, North Carolina, in 1924. Gomez, a man of questionable character, founded the corporation to provide capital and counsel for prospective black businessmen. Windham appealed to the Durham company via Robert Moton, president of Tuskegee, for financial assistance to avoid straining his credit with banks in Birmingham and in Nashville, where he financed and constructed the National Baptist Publishing House at a cost of $600,000. However, Gomez's sudden disappearance in 1926 and the subsequent restructuring and then final demise of the company suggests that Windham probably did not receive financial assistance. Nevertheless, he may have been inspired by the Durham-based company; his Acme Finance Corporation also was established to grant long-term loans at low interest to aspiring black entrepreneurs. Robert Moton to Wanti Gomez, March 25, 1926, box 124, folder 935, Robert Moton Papers; *Birmingham Reporter,* May 2, 1927; *Crisis,* 35, no. 1 (January 1928); letter from J. S. Jones, secretary of the Acme Finance Corporation to C. C. Spaulding, vice-president of the National Negro Finance Corporation, September 17, 1928, box 168, folder 1400, Robert Moton Papers. For additional information about Wanti Gomez, see Weare, *Black Business,* 120–21, 123, 148–49.

99. *Birmingham Reporter,* February 14, 1920; *Birmingham Truth,* January 17, 1930. The difficulty blacks faced in establishing another bank likely resulted from the lack of consumer confidence. The failure of the Alabama Penny Savings Bank and the other race bank sent a strong message to individuals and families who were reluctant to deposit money in a black-owned bank in the first place. According to the report of the president of the Negro Bankers' Association for 1928 and 1929, there were thirty-four black banks in U.S., and of these five, or 14.7 percent failed during 1929. Paul K. Edwards, *The Southern Urban Negro as a Consumer,* 143.

100. Insurance companies had their roots in beneficial or benevolent societies and mutual and fraternal organizations, which first offered blacks sick and death benefits and relief during extreme poverty. W. W. Browne took a groundbreaking step when his Richmond-based True Reformers united commercial practices with the traditional benevolent pursuits. Proceedings of the Hampton Negro Conference, July 1898. According to Weare, *Black Business,* 11–15, the True Reformers were "the first group to take cognizance of life contingencies in their effort to set rates that were based on crude estimates of mortality."

101. Essentially, white companies were handed permission to discriminate against blacks when, in 1896, Frederick L. Hoffman published *Race Traits and Tendencies of the American Negro.* Hoffman claimed that because of social diseases, living conditions and other undesirable circumstances, compa-

nies would be unwise to insure African Americans. Although the higher premiums (rationalized by higher mortality rates among blacks), and less comprehensive coverage were frustrating for many blacks, they often had no alternative than to take out a policy with a white-owned company.

102. As the industry grew, the need for a central organization became apparent. In 1921, the National Negro Insurance Association was founded to provide a parallel service to insurance companies that the Banker's Association offered to banks.

103. The charter, failing to recognize that the organization was actually operating as an insurance company, exempted the company from all city, county, and state license taxes. Every time new officers were elected to the State Insurance Department, they would attempt to destroy the charter with its exemptions. Walker's company spent large sums of money defending its charter but ultimately capitulated when the company's officers determined that it was cheaper to pay the taxes. Alexa Benson Henderson, *Atlanta Life Insurance Company: Guardian of Black Economic Dignity* (Tuscaloosa: University of Alabama Press, 1990), 9–11.

104. Walker's company entered the field of insurance before there were many men or women trained to work in the industry. The Union Central Relief was responsible for training inexperienced employees who then departed the company after a time to establish many of the competing insurance companies in Alabama and Georgia. Henderson, *Atlanta Life Insurance Company,* 9–10. White insurance companies that solicited black business were often fraudulent rackets run by whites looking to turn a quick profit. See Weare, *Black Business,* 16. The Metropolitan Life Insurance Company was a white-owned-and-operated organization that conducted business with blacks. Yet, the company never provided blacks with any employment opportunities. *Birmingham Truth,* December 7, 1928. Nevertheless, some white-owned companies were respectable. Former Congressman Jesse F. Stallings was, according to the *Birmingham Reporter,* a "well-known white citizen of Birmingham and Alabama and favorably known to the colored people throughout the country, and especially in the south." In 1912, Stallings was secretary of the Afro-American Life Insurance Company (formerly the Royal Life and Accident Association), and by 1919 he served as president of the Lincoln Reserve Life Insurance Company. His company served and employed members of Birmingham's black community, and Stallings acknowledged their contribution to the company's success in a speech delivered to his employees in 1919. Robert Taylor, editor of the *Birmingham American* and employee of Afro-American Insurance, expressed confidence in the company. He optimistically declared that beyond depositing money in black-owned banks, "It will have all colored agents and collectors, will employ colored physicians to examine applicants and where possible will hire colored lawyers to examine titles of property of those who seek to borrow." *Birmingham Reporter,* July 12, 1919; William J. Trent, Jr., "Development of Negro Life Insurance Enterprises" (master's thesis, University of Pennsylvania, 1932), 33–34; C. A. Spencer, "Benevolent Black Societies and the Development of Black Insurance Companies in Nineteenth Century Alabama," *Phylon* 46 (September 1985): 261; Weare, *Black Business,* 143; *Colored Montgomery Alabamian,* March 8, 1913.

105. *Birmingham Times Plaindealer,* June 4, 1921, and October 15, 1921. Atlanta Life ran an education program that trained young people in insurance sales. Many young men and women graduated from the Birmingham program, including Bertram Hudson, son of B. H. Hudson, Sr., and former employee of the Alabama Penny Savings Bank. *Birmingham Reporter,* March 19, 1923.

106. Charles M. Harris was one of the board members. *Birmingham Times Plaindealer,* June 4, 1921, October 15, 1921, June 10, 1922; *Birmingham Reporter,* November 14, 1925.

107. Mergers were not a new phenomenon among black-owned mutual aid associations and insurance companies in Birmingham. In 1913, the Mutual Aid Association of Mobile, which became the Union Mutual Insurance Company, purchased Dr. U. G. Mason's People's Mutual Aid Association. When two companies that served black interest merged, the response appeared to be optimistic. See *Voice of the People,* May 28, 1915, for an account of the formation of the American-Peoples Insurance Company through the consolidation of the American Health and Accident Insurance Company with the Peoples Insurance Company. *New York Age,* October 9, 1913; *Birmingham Reporter* July 5, 1930.

108. *Birmingham Truth,* January 17, 1930.

109. Although Adams had refrained from challenging the officers of the Alabama Penny Savings Bank when it closed its doors, he could not restrain himself from publicly castigating its officers when Mississippi Life fell into white control. This was the only time found that he or anyone else suggested that something deceitful caused the bank's failure. *Birmingham Reporter,* January 24, 1925.

110. V. L. Burnett managed to rise above the debacle when he quickly secured a management position with the National Benefit Life Insurance Company for a short time. For a detailed account of the political maneuvering behind the Mississippi Life–Southern Life takeover, see Ingham and Feldman, *African-American Business Leaders,* 418–19, 542, 659; *Birmingham Reporter,* June 21, 1918, July 19, 1919, and October 12, 1924; *Birmingham City Directory,* 1925.

111. Virgil Harris, oral history, interview by Otis Dismuke, January 6, 1981, Birmingfind files, Department of Archives and Manuscripts, Birmingham Public Library, Birmingham, Ala. *Birmingham Truth,* October 18, 1929. A. G. Gaston built his empire applying the same strategy used by Charles Harris. Gaston began with a burial society that laid the foundation for his Booker T. Washington Insurance Company in 1923. Moorman and Barrett, *Leaders,* 89; "The Other Side: The Story of Birmingham's Black Community," Brimingfind files, Department of Archives and Manuscripts, Birmingham Public Library, Birmingham, Ala.; *Birmingham Post-Herald,* July 14, 1987. *Birmingham Truth,* March 9, 1928.

112. *Birmingham Truth,* April 11, 1930. E. A. Bradford also operated a burial association that employed more than thirty people. *Birmingham Truth,* September 26, 1930. A. G. Gaston, like his competitors, also owned the Booker T. Washington Burial Society of Fairfield, Alabama, which had branch offices in several cities and towns in Alabama. After establishing a solid foun-

dation, it moved to expand its presence. In 1930 it purchased the Home Relief Burial Association of Pratt City. *Birmingham Truth,* September 12, 1930. The two types of businesses were interconnected and interdependent. As Smith and Gaston advertised: "Did You Know? We are issuing Group Insurance for the entire membership of Lodges and Societies all over the state? *Birmingham Truth,* January 4, July 6, 1928. In 1928, it was estimated that there was a weekly average of thirty-five deaths and funerals among Birmingham's African Americans. Although blacks represented less than 40 percent of the city's total population, black deaths constituted nearly 55 percent of all deaths in the city. *Birmingham Truth,* April 20, 1928. Smith and Gaston Funeral Services also adopted astute business practices that enabled it to continue operation into the twenty-first century.

113. *Birmingham Truth,* April 11, 1930.

114. Hylan Lewis, *Blackways of Kent,* 31. Although the influence of newspapers was slow to gain a loyal following, in 1899 W. E. B. Du Bois recognized the potential of black newspapers when he stated: "The Negro newspaper has not yet gained an assured footing, but it is rapidly becoming a social force. . . . there exists today no better means of forming, directing and crystalizing Negro public opinion than by means of the press." Du Bois, *The Negro in Business,* 1:77. By 1930, there were 114 black newspapers published in the U.S., half of which were published in the South. Bulletin published by the Domestic Commerce Division of the Bureau of Foreign and Domestic Commerce, cited in Paul K. Edwards, *The Southern Urban Negro as a Consumer,* 171.

115. P. Colfax Rameau, editor of the *Birmingham Workman's Chronicle,* was a self-styled leader who had no clear line of business or professional affiliation.

116. *Birmingham Truth,* March 24, 1902; Jones, "Alabama," 33–34.

117. *Birmingham Reporter,* August 28, 1920; Paul K. Edwards, *The Southern Urban Negro as a Consumer,* 173, 177.

118. In 1934, Adams suspended publication of the *Reporter* to give his time to the rehabilitation of the Grand Lodge Knights of Pythias when it was plagued by financial problems. Adams assumed the position of Supreme Chancellorship of the Supreme Lodge of Knights of Pythias in Chicago in 1940 and held the title through 1945. Mattie Rowe, "What Negroes Are Doing," undated typescript, Department of Archives and Manuscripts, Birmingham Public Library, Birmingham, Ala.; Gaston, *Green Power,* 25.

119. Moorman and Barrett, *Leaders,* 87.

120. Although some black businesses advertised in the *Reporter,* Adams faulted local businessmen who failed to see the benefit of advertising: "The Negro business man does not use enough printers' ink, for advertising is one of the very definite methods for educating the public as to the service offered by Negro business men. To know how to advertise is quite as important as knowing how to give service." *Forbes,* January 15, 1928. The benefits of advertising had been proven time and again; however, it is important to remember that the newspaper benefited financially from advertising dollars. Thus, Adams was as supportive of black enterprise as he was of his own business. Some black businesses advertised in papers outside of their district. I. B. Kigh's

Peoples Drug Company advertised in the *Selma Record*. In doing so, it reached a broader audience, some of whom might be potential customers upon a visit to the Magic City. *Selma Record*, March 1901.

121. *Birmingham Reporter*, September 13, 1919.

122. *Birmingham Voice of the People*, May 21, 1921, courtesy of the *Times-Plain Dealer*.

123. *Birmingham Reporter*, January 11, 1919; Autrey, "The National Association," 58–59.

124. The Four Minute Men Negro Organization evolved into the Jones Valley Booster Club, which in the late 1920s extended its reach into welfare work. *Birmingham Reporter*, January 5, 1918, and January 11, 1919. The Booster Club allowed women to participate: Fannie Blevins, Ola Bradford and Margaret Battle were among the female members. *Birmingham Truth*, March 16, 1928.

125. *Birmingham Truth*, February 17, 1928.

126. Jones, "Alabama," 42, 43; Moorman and Barrett, *Leaders*, 87; *Birmingham Reporter*, August 3, 1918.

127. *Birmingham Blade*, September 21, 1907; Rabinowitz, *Race Relations in the Urban South*, 235. *Birmingham Blade*, September 21, 1907.

128. Coar also became the owner of the Birmingham Black Barons baseball team. *Birmingham Reporter*, August 23, 1919.

129. On several occasions, the black press within Alabama made efforts to organize an association. In 1887, a convention was held in Selma, where the Alabama Colored Press Association was founded, and the participating editors adopted a constitution. The association was short-lived because three activist editors of the association were expelled from Alabama. The Afro-American Press Association of Alabama was founded in 1894, and its first convention was held in Birmingham in 1895. L. H. Harrison, editor of the *Wide-Awake*, was elected president, and he and his colleagues were hailed by Birmingham's white press as the new social, political, and educational leaders of their race. Moorman and Barrett, *Leaders*, 87.

130. Jones, "Alabama," 35, 42, 43, 58, and the quotation beginning "powerful forum" is from p. 51; see also various issues of the *Birmingham Reporter*, 1918, 1919. The earlier issues are non extant. The last quotation in the paragraph is from Rabinowitz, *Race Relations in the Urban South*, 232.

131. As August Meier notes, "Philosophies of economic chauvinism and separate institutions were part of a larger complex of ideas involving self-help, race pride, and group solidarity, though it must be emphasized that such ideas were usually regarded as being a tactic in the struggle for ultimate citizenship rights." *Negro Thought in America*, 50.

132. Mr. Williams participated in the League. He ran the O. K. French Cleaning business, "the largest business of its kind run by a member of the race anywhere." His presence at the NNBL and his well located plant in Birmingham's BBD ensured him recognition among the city's more prominent black leaders. *Birmingham Reporter*, March 2, 9, 1918. The local Business League met at the People's Drug Store (its local headquarters), where it discussed not only business-related issues but also education and religious con-

cerns, health conditions and literacy problems. *Montgomery Colored Alabamian*, April 10, 1915.

133. Although Birmingham's black businesses achieved some level of cooperation, up until 1930 they did not exhibit sufficient brotherhood to establish a retail organization like Selma's Colored Merchant's Association or Montgomery's black grocery merchants collective known as C. M. A. Stores. The model for these stores was the Colored Merchants Association of Winston-Salem. *Birmingham Truth*, June 21, 1929, February 7, 1930.

134. Meier, "Negro Class Structure," 266.

135. Ivan H. Light examined the atypical business tactics employed by W. W. Browne's True Reformers Savings Bank that resulted in the institution's collapse. He concluded that "mismanagement made excellent sense." One could make the same argument for the Alabama Penny Savings Bank. *Ethnic Enterprise in America: Business and Welfare among Chinese, Japanese, and Blacks* (Berkeley: University of California Press, 1972), 55.

CHAPTER 5. INSTITUTION BUILDING: THE CREATION OF SCHOOLS AND THEIR SIGNIFICANCE IN THE COMMUNITY

1. Grantham, *Southern Progressivism*, 246.

2. Peter Kolchin, *First Freedom, The Response of Alabama's Blacks to Emancipation and Reconstruction* (Westport, Conn.: Greenwood Press, 1972), 81–99; Joe M. Richardson, *Christian Reconstruction*, 42–46, 109–11, 187–209. See also Rabinowitz, *Race Relations in the Urban South*, 153. See Meier, *Negro Thought in America*, especially 88–89, for a discussion of the AMA's commitment to providing an industrial education to blacks.

3. For some comparative figures of white and black education in Alabama, see David Alan Harris, "Racists and Reformers," 359–60.

4. Graded schools also developed in Huntsville, Talladega, Selma, and Marion. Kolchin, *First Freedom*, 83–86.

5. Patricia Alberj Graham, *Community and Class in American Education, 1865–1918* (New York: John Wiley & Sons, 1974), 102.

6. McKiven, *Iron and Steel*, 119.

7. *Birmingham Board of Alderman Minutes*, October 4, 1876, 1:412–13, Birmingham City Hall, Birmingham, Ala., as cited in Bigelow, "Birmingham: Biography of a City," 223–24.

8. The fair at Iceland Park and the following supper supplemented an already existing though insufficient fund that together amounted to $70. Outside support was essential. *Iron Age*, May 25, 1882.

9. In Birmingham, only black teachers taught black students. This had not always been the case in Alabama during Reconstruction and post-Reconstruction, when northern white teachers instructed black students in many of the AMA schools. *Birmingham Board of Alderman Minutes*, May 16, 1883, 2:443, June 6, 1883, 2:449; *First Annual Report of the Birmingham Public Schools*, 1884, p. 10, as cited in Bigelow, "Birmingham: Biography of a City," 225–26.

10. Fallin, "A Shelter in the Storm," 120. In 1929, the president of Howard University, Mordecai W. Johnson, speaking to a Buffalo, New York, audience, recognized the contribution of local churches in filling in the gaps of public education: "The little insignificant colored churches which some big folk say are doing nothing, are actually spending upward of $3,000,000 per year on education." *Birmingham Truth,* January 18, 1929.

11. For a more detailed account of Carrie Tuggle's school, see chapter 7.

12. *Birmingham Age-Herald,* July 31, 1921.

13. The organization of the Board of Education, which was founded in 1884, was first provided for by the Legislature in the Acts of Alabama of 1873–74. *Report of Progress,* Birmingham Public Schools, September 1, 1921–August 31, 1931, Birmingham Board of Education, Birmingham, Ala., 15.

14. The city, through its Board of Alderman, continued to provide funds for the city's schools but no longer had a direct role in educational policy.

15. Margaret England Armbrester, *Samuel Ullman and "Youth": The Life, the Legacy* (Tuscaloosa: University of Alabama Press, 1993), 33–39.

16. The controversy over curriculum was not easily resolved. Many reformers who pushed for black education, including the Southern Education Board and the General Educational Board, favored industrial education to "prepare blacks for subordinate roles in the southern economy." James D. Anderson, *The Education of Blacks in the South, 1860–1935* (Chapel Hill: University of North Carolina Press, 1988), 92. For whites who rejected any kind of education for blacks, the idea of an industrial education did nothing to reverse or even quell their opposition. Carl Harris notes that this came at a time when Birmingham was prospering and that Phillips's reorganization reflected Progressive tenets: professionalization, bureaucratization, and centralization of authority. For a detailed account of the salary schedules and the comparison of white and black teachers' salaries, see Carl V. Harris, "Stability and Change," 375–401. Phillips took direct control of the system of education for blacks, and they seemed to respect his role in providing significant improvements to their schools and curriculum. With his influence, he also recruited many fine black teachers. Presently, many blacks continue to highly revere Superintendent Phillips.

17. In 1931, the Birmingham Board of Education reported on the progress of elementary schools for black children, including the Lincoln School and the Thomas School: "The course of study has been modified to meet the needs of boys and girls in the negro schools. Where possible more industrial work is offered; cooking, sewing, laundering, manual training, furniture repairing, chair caning, handicraft, shoe repairing, tailoring, gardening. These subjects are taught not so much in theory as in actual situations that will meet the daily needs of the child and at the same time give him or her a start toward a vocation. *Report of Progress,* Birmingham Public Schools, 132. See Bond, *Negro Education in Alabama,* 146–47, for Phillips's perception of blacks and their role in the economy.

18. Armbrester, *Samuel Ullman and "Youth,"* 43.

19. Harris, "Stability and Charge," offers an excellent analysis of the machinations of city politicians. It also provided the author with data essen-

tial for the writing of the part of the chapter addressing how blacks were able to obtain a high school in Birmingham when most other major southern cities were unwilling to cooperate with the black effort. Also see Bigelow, "Birmingham: Biography of a City," 229.

20. *Birmingham Board of Education Minutes,* January 3, February 8, March 5, April 3, and November 5, 1889, and November 6, 1905, Birmingham Board of Education, Birmingham, Ala. In 1898, the library opened, with funding from the black community supplemented with public funds awarded by Superintendent Phillips. It remained at Slater School until it disappeared from record. In contrast to the white library, which was opened to the public for fifty-four hours each week, the Washington Library was opened for just six. William T. Miller, "Library Service for Negroes in the New South: Birmingham, Alabama, 1871–1918," *Alabama Librarian* 27 (November/ December, 1975): 7; Map of Birmingham and Adjacent Suburbs, drawn, compiled, and published by George B. Kelley, 1903.

21. Nevertheless, when funding was curtailed, Birmingham's officials never diverted the state's black fund to the white schools as the Black Belt counties did. Bigelow, "Birmingham: Biography of a City," 234–35; Carl V. Harris, "Stability and Change," 390–92.

22. Yet, African Americans did pay more taxes than they were ever given credit for. Although blacks were underrepresented among property owners, they as renters often paid real estate taxes. One study concluded that "the vast number of homes rented by Negroes throughout the South have their assessed taxes paid by black renters rather than white owners. Further than this the Negro, as a consumer, pays an incalculable amount of indirect taxes. It is thus clear that in no sense of the word has the common school education in the South been a free gift to the Negro." W. E. B. Du Bois, ed., *The College-Bred Negro. Report of the social study made under the direction of Atlanta University; together with the proceedings of the Fifth Conference for the study of the Negro Problems held at Atlanta University, May 29–30, 1900,* vol. 1, Atlanta University Publications, no. 5 (1900; New York: Octagon Books, 1968), 88.

23. As Harris acknowledges, the explanation for Birmingham's fair allotment of state funds is complex. He suggests that white interest groups that dominated local government in Birmingham had a more favorable perspective on the value of education for blacks than did the planters who dominated local government in the Black Belt. See Carl V. Harris, "Stability and Change," 386–89, for a more detailed explanation; see also page 393 for a discussion on Birmingham property taxes and the funding of black education in the city.

24. *Birmingham Board of Education Minutes,* October 6, 1902, and March 26, 1903.

25. Although the Board had secured an option on a designated lot for $3,800 for the new school building in 1902, construction had not yet begun in 1905. Bigelow, "Birmingham: Biography of a City," 229–30; *Birmingham Board of Alderman Minutes,* May 17, 1899, to August 17, 1900, p. 62. See also *Birmingham News,* January 18, 1900; *Birmingham Herald,* November 16, 1905, and Carl V. Harris, "Stability and Change," 405. Overcrowding was a constant problem that plagued the black schools because of inadequate

funding allotted for new facilities. Strategies were developed to cope with the often impossible conditions. In 1920, when the Slater School was unable to accommodate all the students, a number of the children living in the vicinity were sent to the school at Acipco. *Birmingham Reporter,* October 2, 1920.

26. Phillips's statement reflects the white consensus on how property values respond (decline) to the presence of blacks in a district. Whether Phillips was merely stating the facts or sharing the white perception on property values is indeterminable. However, he probably was expressing some of his own perceptions as well as reflecting the attitude shared among white residents in Birmingham. Superintendent's Monthly Report, *Birmingham Board of Education Minutes,* November 4, 1907.

27. He presented an estimate of cost for the above mentioned improvements to both the white and black facilities: For both the building and for equipment, Phillips allotted a total of $205,000 for the white schools and $95,000 for the black schools, which were in more disrepair than the white schools. Ibid. In 1907, Ward's annual message revealed his commitment and his motivation: "The city authorities are not doing their duty to the colored population nor pursuing a wise or just course in holding colored schools down practically to a worse condition than they were in fifteen years ago. . . . The colored people are so intertwined in the life and traditions of the South that they must either be elevated by the whites or the whites will be affected injuriously by them through bad health and sanitary conditions." *Birmingham News,* May 1, 1909.

28. Twenty years later, a stark discrepancy persisted between the Graymont schools. In 1931, the Board of Education reported on the statement of Costs by Schools (including monies spent on administration, clerical service, teachers' salaries, educational supplies, and free textbooks and school library books). The Graymont School for white children spent a total of $24,431.03, whereas its black counterpart spent a total of $11,927.20. *Graymont City Minutes,* August 25, 1908; November 25, 1908. *Report of Progress,* Birmingham Public Schools, 181, 182.

29. The words were underlined as shown, and then the underlining was later deleted with a pencil. *Birmingham Board of Education Minutes,* June 13, 1904.

30. See also Anderson, *The Education of Blacks in the South,* 186. It was a question of money and employment needs. Alabama counties did not offer high school education until Governor Bibb Graves's education reforms in the 1920s, which began "consolidated county high schools." Graves made a significant contribution to education in Alabama when he introduced a reform package that was passed in 1927. Rogers et al., *Alabama,* 422–24.

31. These figures included junior high school enrollment. U.S. Government, *Department of the Interior,* as cited in *Birmingham Truth,* February 7, 1930. According to the *Crisis,* in 1908–9, one hundred and twelve public high schools (not including junior high school) served 6,806 black students. But, of the one million black children of high school age, only seven out of a thousand were enrolled, whereas a hundred out of a thousand white children attended high school. Mason A. Hawkins, "Colored High Schools," *Crisis* 2, no. 2 (June 1911): 73–75.

32. Cynthia Neverdon-Morton, *Afro-American Women of the South and the Advancement of the Race, 1895–1925* (Knoxville: University of Tennessee Press, 1989), 78.

33. Carl V. Harris, "Stability and Change," 403.

34. Arthur H. Parker's autobiography, *A Dream that Came True* (Birmingham, Ala.: Printing Department of Industrial High School, 1932–33), states that it was B. H. Hudson who was instrumental in initiating the campaign, rather than his wife. Other unidentified sources claim that it was Mrs. B. H. Hudson who played a significant role in the campaign. Perhaps, the importance lies less in whether it was Hudson or his wife and more in the fact that the Hudson family, one of the more prominent black families in Birmingham, supported the movement.

35. The *Wide-Awake* described Lauderdale College located in North Birmingham as a "high grade literary and industrial Christian school." The paper also reported that the school had a first-year enrollment of 750 students. *Birmingham Wide-Awake*, August 3, 24, 1905; *Birmingham City Directory*, 1887; *Incorporation Declaration of Lauderdale College*, vol. O, p. 467.

36. According to Margaret Armbrester, "Their battle for a black high school could hardly have occurred at a worse time. Efforts were made at this time to disfranchise blacks, and one of the easiest ways to discourage black voter participation was to require that voters be literate. Yet, Ullman pressed for a black high school during a time when disfranchisement dominated the order of business during the drafting of the new state constitution." Armbrester, *Samuel Ullman*, 40–42. Charles A. Brown, *The Origin and Development of Secondary Education for Negroes in the Metropolitan Area of Birmingham, Alabama* (Birmingham: Commercial Printing Co., 1959), 34.

37. Carl V. Harris, "Stability and Change," 388–89. The steel companies that dominated Birmingham's economy built schools for blacks in the company towns, such as Westfield and Fairfield. The superiority of the schools was evident. In 1930, when tests were administered to determine the quality of education, the children who attended TCI schools exhibited superior performance when compared to the scores of black children educated in the county and city schools and in the South overall. Nevertheless, the corporations determined that blacks only required a certain level of education to perform their jobs effectively; they offered education to black children only up to the high school level. Bond, *Negro Education in Alabama*, 243.

38. *Birmingham Alabamian*, January 16, 1902.

39. The thorny problem of taxation that plagued many of the state's decisions on education funding found a voice in Birmingham through a member of the Board of Education. Mr. Gray, a member of the Committee on Instruction, believed that blacks were receiving enough public monies, in comparison to the amount of taxes they were paying in their lower and grammar grades. The resolution put forth for a secondary school for blacks recorded that President Ullman thought "Negroes" would receive a high school education, and although it would cost the city nothing, the board should have the matter of paying the teachers in hand and conduct all affairs connected with the school. Mr. Gray represented the more reactionary view of the Board when he stated that he favored "giving 'Negroes' an education, if he paid for it, and that now

he was getting four times as much as he was paying in taxes." According to the *Birmingham News*, Gray suggested that all funds from the high school for the Negroes be given to the teacher therein, and if the amount was not as much as the fixed salary, then no appropriation be made therefor. His motion lost and the Board of Education assumed full charge of the affairs of the high school. *Birmingham News*, September 4, 1900.

40. Bond, *Negro Education in Alabama*, 257–58.

41. Quoted in Armbrester, *Samuel Ullman*, 42, 43.

42. Prior to the creation of the Industrial High School, Birmingham blacks aspiring to "higher learning" attended such nearby schools as Washington's Tuskegee Institute and the AMA's Talladega College. Whereas Tuskegee's emphasis was on industrial education, Talladega's initial objective was "to promote industrial, theological, normal, and collegiate training . . . [and] to train Christian teachers." Maxine D. Jones and Joe M. Richardson, *Talladega College: The First Century* (Tuscaloosa: University of Alabama Press, 1990), 9.

43. *Birmingham Board of Alderman Minutes*, February 7, 1900.

44. *Birmingham News*, June 11, 1900; *Birmingham Board of Education Minutes*, June 13, 1901. The quotation is from Charles A. Brown, *The Origin and Development of Secondary Education for Negroes in the Metropolitan Area of Birmingham, Alabama* (Birmingham: Commercial Printing Co., 1959), 35.

45. From Parker's autobiography, *A Dream that Came True*.

46. Ibid., 6 (quotation), 10.

47. This association pledged itself "to advance the interests of the profession of teaching along moral and intellectual lines . . . [and] to bring the teachers together in a social way." Booker T. Washington ran the STA during the late 1880s and early 1890s. Despite Washington's long tenure and the apparent support of fellow educators, his predecessors and successors in the STA emphasized liberal education over industrial education. Robert Sherer asserts that their emphasis on liberal education indicates that Washington was less influential in black education, even in Alabama, than was previously believed. Robert G. Sherer, *Subordination or Liberation? The Development and Conflicting Theories of Black Education in Nineteenth Century Alabama* (University, Ala.: University of Alabama Press, 1977), 19–21

48. One can only speculate that Pettiford's influence in the founding of the school may have allowed him to wield his influence in selecting a principal. In the early 1890s, Parker had become acquainted with Pettiford. Before Parker moved to Smithfield, for a time he resided next to the Sixteenth Street Baptist Church and held the position as Pettiford's private secretary. From 1910 to 1912, he opened the bookkeeping accounts for the branches of the Alabama Penny Savings Bank in Anniston, Montgomery, and Selma. Parker, *A Dream that Came True*, 26, 44.

49. Dr. Saunders E. Walker (a former student of Industrial High), interview by unnamed person, July 23, 1981, transcript, Birmingfind files, Department of Archives and Manuscripts, Birmingham Public Library, Birmingham, Ala.

50. Tarry chose to attend Talladega College. Tarry, *The Third Door*, 22.

Although not many graduates of Industrial High could afford to continue their education beyond the secondary level, some of the more affluent families sent their children away to university. There they fraternized with children who belonged to some of the most elite black families in America. Thelma Kigh attended Wilberforce, a school that was known for its classical curriculum taught in "an atmosphere of culture and refinement." Eunice and Vivian Mason attended Howard University, while Maggie Davis went to Atlanta to attend Spelman. Others went to Fisk, Columbia, and Northwestern universities. *Birmingham Reporter,* May 24, 1919; Gatewood, *Aristocrats of Color,* chap. 9 and p. 344, and Katzman, *Before the Ghetto,* 158. During the summer months, teachers often went elsewhere to teach summer school or to upgrade their education. Brunetta Hill taught summer classes at Florida A and M in Tallahassee while Nora Martin, instructor at Industrial High, was one of many teachers who migrated to New York City to take summer courses at Columbia University. *Birmingham Truth,* August 10, 1928, June 28, 1929.

51. Janette Thomas Greenwood, *Bittersweet Legacy: The Black and White "Better Classes" in Charlotte, 1850–1910* (Chapel Hill: University of North Carolina Press, 1994), 242.

52. Interview with anonymous speaker in 1993. The school, nonetheless, attempted to minimize the class differences and encourage democracy among the students by insisting upon uniforms. This was decided upon in 1914 at a Parent-Teachers Association meeting. *Christian Science Monitor,* October 11, 1932.

53. Charles E. King, "The Process of Social Stratification Among an Urban Southern Minority Population," *Social Forces* 31 (May 1953): 354; Norval D. Glenn, "Negro Prestige Criteria: A Case Study in the Bases of Prestige," *American Journal of Sociology* 68 (May 1963): 645–57.

54. Juliet R. Bradford, "The Industrial High School: A Brief History," (1925, n.p.), 21–23.

55. *Birmingham News,* May 30, 1903.

56. Ibid., 56.

57. Program of first graduation, "The History of Parker High School: From Its Beginning in 1900 to 1960," Birmingham Board of Education, May 1960, 4–5.

58. Mrs. Sidney [*sic*] M. Ullman, *Birmingham Age-Herald,* n.d., as reprinted in the *Uniontown News,* July 9, 1915.

59. Phillips and Ward collaborated in securing a new building for black students with a broader progressive campaign to upgrade the sanitation and health of Birmingham. Mayor Ward stated, "The colored people are so intertwined in the life and conditions of the South that they must either be elevated by the whites or the whites will be affected injuriously by them through bad health and sanitary conditions." *Birmingham News,* May 1, 1909.

60. *Birmingham City Directory,* 1916; *The History of Parker High School,* 3; *Birmingham Reporter,* March 30, 1918. See *The History of Parker High School* for a more detailed account of the new building and the subsequent additions over the decades.

61. These were, nevertheless, decades of genuine progress in black educa-

tion. Black teachers' salaries rose beyond the subsistence level, and black children moved out of severely dilapidated old frame buildings. Carl V. Harris, "Stability and Change," 410, 411, 413.

62. *Birmingham News,* May 30, 1903. Louise McCauley was a former teacher at Industrial High and she recalled that "[Parker] was well liked by the city (that is, Birmingham's white community) because they liked how he encouraged black children to work with their hands." Louise McCauley, interview by the author, Birmingham, Ala., February 1, 1993.

63. Louise McCauley, interview.

64. Sallye B. Davis, interview by Otis Dismuke, July 10, 1981, transcript, Birmingfind files, Department of Archives and Manuscripts, Birmingham Public Library, Birmingham, Ala.

65. Although Washington is credited with being the prime mover behind the trend of industrial education for blacks, he had not initiated the movement. It had been in place long before he rose to prominence. Meier, *Negro Thought,* 99.

66. Tarry, *The Third Door,* 25. Others found reason to criticize Parker's hiring practices.

67. The curriculum that Parker developed combined academic and industrial training. Like many other southern black educators, Parker preferred a varied curriculum, which deviated from the largely industrial Hampton-Tuskegee model. Anderson, *The Education of Blacks in the South,* 67.

68. Bradford, "The Industrial High School," 18. Industrial High School's achievements did not go unnoticed: In 1929 the Alabama Department of Education granted the school full accreditation. *Christian Science Monitor,* October 11, 1932.

69. These included gardening, tailoring, mechanical drawing, carpentry, sewing, laundering, cooking, household management, first aid, nursing, printing, millinery, beauty culture, auto-mechanics, shoe repairing, and upholstery. Students were required to devote a third of their time to two or more of these subjects. *Report of Progress,* Birmingham Public Schools, 140.

70. Carl V. Harris noted that in the 1920s white labor organizations and the Ku Klux Klan kept abreast of advancements in black education and protested against the construction of brick buildings for black students. "Stability and Change," 409; *Report of Progress,* Birmingham Public Schools, 137.

71. According to August Meier, "The Negro history movement had developed in the antebellum period out of two needs felt by blacks in their subordinate state in the American Social order: the need to assert and prove their equality with whites as one means of convincing whites of their worthiness for political and civil rights, and the need to give themselves a sense of dignity and pride of race to offset the inferiority doctrines of the whites and to stimulate a group solidarity." *Negro Thought in America,* 51.

72. The song *Lift Every Voice and Sing* was adopted as the Negro National Anthem. Meier, *Negro Thought in America,* 271.

73. Rosetta Clarke Young, interview by the author, Birmingham, Ala., January 18, 1993. During this interview Rosetta Clarke Young reminisced about how the school helped to nurture her siblings' musical talents: Her sister became the musical director of Industrial High School and her four brothers

migrated to New York to play with such legends as Duke Ellington, Johnny Hodges, Chick Webb, and Louis Armstrong. Other black schools also had music programs that performed annual concerts for the community. One year, grades six and seven of the Cameron School performed at the Sixth Avenue Baptist Church. For additional information on the Clarke's musical contributions and the jazz scene in Birmingham, see Jothan McKinley Callins, "'The Birmingham Jazz Community': The Role and Contribution of Afro-Americans (up to 1940)" (master's thesis, University of Pittsburgh, 1982).

74. The schools also reached out to the community when they sought parental support. Teachers at Cameron School entertained mothers of their students as a way to encourage their interest in their child's attendance and school work and their commitment to education. PTA meetings were organized and some schools offered prizes to stimulate interest among parents and children. *Birmingham Reporter*, October 11, 1919, and *Birmingham Truth*, November 1, 1929. Community support was extended to these other schools as well: Dr. Dave L. Johnston of Union Drug Company offered a $5 prize, which became known as the Margaret Johnston prize, for the best oration. The *Reporter* offered a gift of $2.50 for the 2nd prize. *Birmingham Reporter*, May 25, 1914.

75. *Birmingham Truth*, April 4, 1919.

76. Five months later, the *Reporter* noted that the "Community Sing" had once again outgrown its quarters "so eager has the public become to avail themselves of this form of innovation." *Birmingham Reporter*, March 29, August 30, 1919.

77. Hylan Lewis, *The Blackways of Kent*, 160.

78. Wallace Buttrick of the General Education Board, who took over the work of the Slater Fund after J. L. M. Curry's death, and Dr. Philander P. Claxton, former member of the Capon Springs coalition and U.S. Commissioner of Education, were responsible for the report. Buttrick was a staunch supporter of industrial education for blacks, which mirrored the views of his northern and southern colleagues in the Southern Education Board and the General Education Board. Industrial High School's curriculum seemed to fit Buttrick's perception of what was an appropriate education for black high school students. Anderson, *The Education of Blacks in the South*, 92; *Birmingham Reporter*, November 1, June 7, 1919; Bond, *Negro Education in Alabama*, 205, 340–41.

79. Jacqueline Jones notes that female teachers probably had to supplement their meager salaries with taking in laundry during the long summer vacations. Although several interviews with former teachers revealed that female teachers could not be married, which supports Jones's contention that "black female teachers were penalized for their marital status," the Manuscript Censuses of 1900, 1910, and 1920 reveal that several female teachers who resided in Smithfield were, in fact, wives and mothers—or at least they had been teachers and still identified themselves as such before they were married. Nevertheless, they still responded that they were employed as teachers. Jacqueline Jones, *Labor of Love, Labor of Sorrow: Black Women, Work and the Family, from Slavery to the Present* (New York: Vintage Books, 1985), 144–46.

80. Parker, *A Dream that Came True*, 20.

81. Louise McCauley, interview.

82. Marvine Bradford, interview by the author, Birmingham, January 18, 1993. Ms. Bradford came from a family of school teachers, all of whom emphasized the value of education.

83. *Birmingham Board of Education, Minutes,* March 6, 1894.

84. Louise McCauley, interview.

85. Parker, *A Dream that Came True*, 35.

86. The HI Y Club also taught the work ethic in practical ways. The club members built and painted huts at the Margaret Murray Washington Camp, and the boys used the camp's recreational facilities. *Birmingham Truth,* May 3, June 7, 1929.

87. Students ranging in age from sixteen to seventy received certificates upon completion of the prescribed courses. Although no credit was allowed for completing a course, certificates were eagerly sought as a source of accomplishment and pride. Furthermore, it was a means of securing better jobs. Their response was overwhelming: In 1927, 578 students attended the first evening class of that year. In 1927–28, the average attendance in the night classes for blacks was 819 students. *Christian Science Monitor,* October 11, 1932; *Birmingham Truth,* October 17, 1927, June 1, 1928; *Birmingham Reporter,* October 23, 1920. Night classes were also offered at other schools, including the Councill School in Ensley and the Hudson School in North Birmingham. *Birmingham Truth,* October 11, 1929. Cameron, Pratt, Washington and Industrial also offered literacy classes. The custodian of Industrial's building became a volunteer teacher after he completed night classes and wanted to share the gift of reading with others. *Birmingham Truth,* May 28, 1930.

88. Bradford, "The Industrial High School," 14. Also Parker, *A Dream that Came True*, 71. A school newspaper, the *Industrial High School Record* was later printed in these facilities. In subsequent decades the school extended its functions in the community. An example illustrating the close relationship between school and community is when students conducted a survey of Smithfield housing conditions in the twenty-four blocks surrounding the school. When results were finally tabulated, recommendations were offered to teach people of the need for better housing. *Birmingham News,* December 12, 1920, and *Birmingham Reporter,* December 18, 1920.

89. Hylan Lewis, *The Blackways of Kent,* 158–59.

90. There is no evidence that Parker conflicted with the black business leaders of the time, Pettiford being the most prominent. They had a rather unique working relationship that refutes Francis J. Grimké's argument that black entrepreneurs and managers followed a divergent path than that of preachers and educators since the 1890s, when the latter mounted their first sharp attacks upon the materialism and individualism of the black bourgeoisie. Parker did not discourage entrepreneurship, he merely offered an education that he determined would better prepare students for the reality of American society. See Francis Grimké, *The Things of Paramount Importance in the Development of the Negro Race* (Washington, D.C, 1903), 1–6, as cited in Timothy Smith's "Native Blacks and Foreign Whites: Varying Responses to

Educational Opportunity in America, 1880-1950," *Perspectives in American History* 6 (1972): 309-19.

91. Mary William Welborn, interview by unidentified person, January 13, 1981.

92. *Birmingham Reporter,* May 3, 1919.

93. According to Carl V. Harris, some people complained that Parker, who was light-skinned, hired only light-skinned teachers. Conversation with author.

94. Kelley, *Hammer and Hoe,* 116.

95. In 1912, the high school reportedly had 724 black students; of this number 201 were from Jefferson County. In 1926, 3,128 high school students hailed from Jefferson County; Industrial High School was making a difference, even though many high school age children were not receiving a high school education. In 1930, of 109,216 black children of high school age in Alabama, only 5.8 percent were in high school, as compared to 29.5 percent of whites. Clearly, a significant number of black children were benefiting from the improvements in public education, but many remained outside the system. Bond, *Negro Education in Alabama,* 257-58; Zane L. Miller, "*Urban Blacks in the South,*" 184-204. By 1920, there were 27,631 black students enrolled in public high schools. This figure reveals that twice as many students had made it to high school than in the ten years earlier. By 1928, there were 75,713 black high school students. Progress was being made, though most noticeably in the North and in the South's urban centers. U.S. Government, Department of the Interior, as cited in the *Birmingham Truth,* February 7, 1930.

96. A variety of Birmingham residents in all capacities shared these sentiments. Alma Anderson Dickinson offered a different perspective. She said it was a disgrace being called the largest black high school because it was only designated such because of the widespread practice of segregation.

97. Sallye B. Davis, interview.

98. Anderson, *The Education of Blacks in the South,* 197.

99. In 1940, the Executive Council of the Protestant Episcopal Church in the Diocese of Alabama closed the school when it recognized that Birmingham was offering higher education for blacks in the public school system. Brown, *The Origins and Development of Secondary Education,* 14-15; Fallin, "A Shelter in the Storm," 120.

100. In 1907, TCI, which held mineral rights to the land, wanted to open a mine there. TCI and the school's trustees negotiated a deal, and the school relocated to a thirty-acre lot that lay four miles outside of Birmingham. Fallin, "A Shelter in the Storm," 122.

101. Miles College also offered pedagogical courses during the summer sessions. In 1918, 107 teachers, mostly from the Birmingham area, received instruction. *Birmingham Reporter,* June 15, 1918.

102. Financial problems, internal conflicts, and the Great Depression resulted in the closure of Miles College. It reopened in 1939. Fallin, "A Shelter in the Storm," 164-65. One source states that the AME Church bought forty acres in Woodlawn for $25,000 for the school, whereas the *Weekly Voice* declared that Dr. Marcellus Freeman, Jr., donated forty acres to the

Methodists for Payne University. Fallin, "A Shelter in the Storm," 163; *Birmingham Weekly Voice,* July 21, 1917. White colleges also moved to Birmingham to take advantage of the city's progressive promise. Howard College (now Samford University) moved to Birmingham from Marion, Alabama, in 1886, and Southern University at Greensboro and North Alabama Conference College combined forces to become Birmingham-Southern College and relocated to Birmingham in 1918. Rogers et al., *Alabama,* 326–27.

103. Davis continued, "Those of us who recall twenty-five or thirty years ago can testify to the comparative insignificance of the proportions of Negro education, with only a few frame buildings and the basements of churches and they poorly equipped. Today there are twenty-four or more Negro schools in Birmingham, operated from public funds, with upwards of three hundred seventy five teachers." *Eagle-Truth,* December 1930.

CHAPTER 6. MEN SEEKING AN IDENTITY: INVOLVEMENT IN CHURCHES, CLUBS, AND CIVIC ASSOCIATIONS

1. Robert C. Smith and Richard Seltzer, *Race, Class, and Culture: A Study in Afro-American Mass Opinion* (Albany: State University of New York Press, 1992), 58.

2. As Jack Temple Kirby notes, "Jim Crow rescued the white South from the dark uncertainties of heterodoxy." *Darkness at the Dawning: Race and Reform in the Progressive South* (Philadelphia: Lippincott, 1972), 25.

3. The literature on women's clubs identifies race consciousness and social reform as the two fundamental goals of the organizations, which mirror the goals of men's clubs. See Beverly Washington Jones, *Quest for Equality: The Life and Writing of Mary Eliza Church Terrell, 1863–1954* (Brooklyn, N.Y.: Carlson Publishing, 1990); Jacqueline Anne Rouse, *Lugenia Burns Hope: Black Southern Reformer* (Athens: University of Georgia Press, 1989), 118; Kathleen C. Berkeley, " 'Colored Ladies Also Contributed': Black Women's Activities from Benevolence to Social Welfare, 1866–1896," in *The Web of Southern Social Relations: Women, Family, and Education,* edited by Walter J. Fraser et al. (Athens: University of Georgia Press, 1985), 184.

4. See the following chapter for a complete discussion of women's club and civic activities in Birmingham.

5. Consequently, "political rhetoric and ideology became more class and gender stratified." This quotation and the one in text are from Brown and Kimball, "Mapping the Terrain," 314.

6. William E. Montgomery, *Under Their Own Vine and Fig Tree: The African-American Church in the South, 1865–1900* (Baton Rouge: Louisiana State University Press, 1993). The black church was not simply a version of white churches. See Obie Clayton, Jr., "The Churches and Social Change: Accommodation, Moderation, or Protest, *Daedalus* 124 (Winter 1995): 101–117, for a discussion of the unique role of the black church and its place in the dominant community. Clayton agrees with Gunnar Myrdal's analysis of the role of the black church in Myrdal's *An American Dilemma: Volume 2, The Negro Social Structure* (New York: Harper & Row, 1944), chap. 40.

7. John Eighmy notes that blacks rejected any form of white paternal-

ism on the Christian front, and whites preferred separation because an integrated church suggested equality. John Lee Eighmy, *Churches in Cultural Captivity: A History of the Social Attitudes of Southern Baptists* (Knoxville: University of Tennessee Press, 1972), 31. As Wayne Flynt noted, "blacks organized their own schools, churches, and colleges. Some 600 blacks, who constituted two-thirds of Montgomery's First Baptist Church, withdrew under the leadership of the Rev. Nathan Ashby. . . . Methodists experienced similar withdrawals. . . . more than 90 percent of Alabama's black Christians enrolled in their own Methodist and Baptist churches." J. Wayne Flynt, "Alabama," in *Religion in the Southern States: A Historical Study,* edited by Samuel S. Hill (Macon, Ga.: Mercer University Press, 1983), 15. Rabinowitz, *Race Relations in the Urban South,* 223.

8. Black churches, like the white churches, "provided the institutional means to define acceptable behavior and . . . to mediate class distinctions." Mary Lethert Wingerd, "Rethinking Paternalism: Power and Parochialism in a Southern Mill Village," *Journal of American History* 83 (December 1996): 880.

9. Ellen Tarry, interview, May 10, 1994.

10. Lester M. Salamon, "Leadership and Modernization: The Emerging Black Political Elite in the American South," *Journal of Politics* 35 (August 1973): 623.

11. Although individuals who were selecting a church may have considered the congregants' skin color, there is no concrete evidence available to explore this possibility. Nevertheless, some older Birmingham residents recall some mention made of skin color and church affiliation. Mrs. Clevon Phillips, a member of Sixteenth Street Baptist, recalled that "Tales were told that Sixth Avenue Baptist Church, under Rev. Whilhite, had the white Negroes, those who were light-skinned, and Sixteenth Street had the professionals. Some said they made it hard for those who wanted to join Sixteenth Street, but it is not true." Mrs. Clevon Phillips, interview by Otis Dismuke, January 5, 1981, Birmingfind files, Department of Archives and Manuscripts, Birmingham Public Library, Birmingham, Ala.

12. See Fallin, "A Shelter in the Storm," for a detailed account of the birth and development of the different churches in the Birmingham area.

13. In 1890 Edward Brawley, a prominent black minister who had participated in the creation of the Baptist Women's State Convention of Alabama, commented on the growth of religious organizations, ministers, and related associations and their impact on the greater black community. He attributed much of the advancements among blacks to their affiliation with the Baptist church. Edward M. Brawley, ed., *The Negro Baptist Pulpit: A Collection of Sermons and Papers by Colored Baptist Ministers* (1890; reprint, Freeport, N.Y.: Books for Libraries Press, 1971), 287–89.

14. The Baptists predominance in Birmingham reflected its southern presence and influence. Benjamin Elijah Mays and Joseph William Nicholson, *The Negro's Church* (Institute of Social and Religious Research, 1933; reprint, New York: Negro Universities Press, 1969), 312. Generally, blacks did not embrace Catholicism, and blacks in Birmingham were no different. Gradually a few joined the Catholic church and initially attended white churches. Ellen

Tarry was raised in the Congregational church but converted to and became an early member of the Catholic Church in Birmingham. Miss Tarry recalled: "[Papa's] family had been Congregationalists as far back as he knew and he reminded me that if I broke my promise [to never become a Catholic] to him everybody would blame him for allowing me to go to a Catholic school." *The Third Door*, 30. She committed her life to the church, and she defended it against charges of racism: "And though my life has been spent in 'Jim Crow Land' I have never seen the church practice Jim Crowism and segregation as charged." *Birmingham Truth*, March 23, 1928.

15. The services at the AME churches were *somewhat* emotional though more restrained than those held at working-class churches. Fallin, "A Shelter in the Storm," 153.

16. St. Mark's, Miller Memorial, and First Congregational were founded by white missionary groups who gave continuous support. Each of these churches operated large and long-standing schools that received financial support from the respective white agencies. Clearly a form of white paternalism was present at these churches that thus refutes John Eighmy's claim that blacks rejected any form of white paternalism on the Christian front. The black working-class churches were not connected to white agencies that comprised their control. Rather, these churches exhibited greater autonomy and independence. Ibid., 120, 149, and Eighmy, *Churches in Cultural Captivity*, 31.

17. See also Fallin, "A Shelter in the Storm," 152. Talladega, a Congregational school supported by the American Missionary Association, was the primary source of the church's membership. Congregationalists had a reputation for possessing dignity and reservedness, "both in their social lives and in their church services. Members of the denomination tended to be more wealthy and better educated than their counterparts in other denominations." David Fort Godshalk, "In the Wake of Riot: Atlanta's Struggle for Order, 1899–1919" (Ph.D. diss., Yale University, 1992), 274.

18. Parker's decision to change his religious affiliation to a church of potentially higher prestige came at a time when he was moving up the social ladder. Although this phenomenon was not uncommon among blacks and whites seeking greater status, it was not widely practiced among Birmingham's black elites. James E. Blackwell, *The Black Community: Diversity and Unity* (New York: Harper & Row, 1975), 86.

19. The annual sessions of the Colored Missionary Baptists Convention of Alabama drew Baptists from across the state, who shared ideas, established rules, and developed networks with other prominent Baptists. Here they also learned and refined leadership skills that they then applied in their local environments. *Proceedings of the 27th Annual Session of the Colored Missionary Baptists State Convention*, Mt. Zion Baptist Church, Anniston, Ala., November 21–25, 1895, microfilm, in the Alabama Baptist State Convention Minutes, Special Collection, Samford University, Birmingham, Ala.; *Proceedings of the 29th Annual Session of the Colored Missionary Baptists State Convention*, Birmingham, November 18–22, 1896.

20. Bacote, *Who's Who Among the Colored Baptists*, 167–69; Boothe, *Cyclopedia of the Colored Baptists of Alabama*, 212–13; Robert Henry Walker,

Jr., *The Trumpet Blast* (Washington, D.C.: The R. H. Walker Publishers, 1902), 43–51, as cited in Fallin, "A Shelter in the Storm," 114–15.

21. *Birmingham Truth*, May 13, 1905, and *Birmingham Wide-Awake*, May 26, 1906. Several other ministers traveled to other locales where they nurtured institutional ties and professional relationships. Rev. C. T. Robinson of Birmingham conducted services and organized meetings in McDowell County, West Virginia. Joe William Trotter, Jr., *Coal, Class, and Color: Blacks in Southern West Virginia, 1913–1932* (Urbana: University of Illinois Press, 1990), 191.

22. The Church of the Living God was in the Pentecostal-Holiness tradition. Fallin, "A Shelter in the Storm," 199.

23. A minority of congregants tended to assume the financial burden of constructing the church and the daily operating expenses. Mays and Nicholson, *The Negro's Church*, 279.

24. No other single objective in the history of African Americans has commanded the degree of personal commitment expressed through financial support from its members than the church buildings. Fallin, "A Shelter in the Storm," 66.

25. *Direct Index to Records of Deeds and Mortgages*, vol. 542, p. 257.

26. One month later, they sold the lot to Joe Levy for $9,000.00. *Mortgage Record*, vol. 1661, p. 185.

27. In 1920, as one of the church's twelve clubs, it pledged to raise $2,500 of the $12,000 needed to pay the entire indebtedness of the church or a little more than one-fifth of the needed amount. *Birmingham Voice of the People*, July 31, 1920. Joe Trotter is only one of many historians who have illustrated the predominance of women among church fund-raisers; see his *Coal, Class, and Color*, 185.

28. Goodgame had strong ties to Rev. James E. Dillard. He was a white pastor of the Southside Baptist Church, a white church and the leading church in Birmingham.

29. *Birmingham Voice of the People*, July 31, 1920. For a detailed profile of Rev. John Goodgame, see Fallin, "A Shelter in the Storm," 166–72.

30. Census figures reveal that as early as 1890, all black churches owned property worth $26.6 million, which increased to a total value of $56.6 million by 1906. *U.S. Census of Religious Bodies: 1916*, Washington, D.C., 1919, 1:134, as cited in Montgomery, *Their Own Vine and Fig Tree*, 342.

31. The larger and most visible African American churches that were located in the city of Birmingham shared the role of community institution with smaller churches scattered throughout the area. These churches served their local communities. Their community outreach efforts and their significance to their local communities mirrored, on a smaller scale, the work of the larger Baptist and Methodist churches located in the heart of the city.

32. The churches probably submitted their respective weekly agendas.

33. *Birmingham Reporter*, March 16, 23, 1918. The Periclean Club among other social clubs, also sponsored some of the most outstanding black speakers. James L. Lowe, interview by the author, May 25, 1994.

34. *Birmingham Truth*, December 24, 1915. The *Birmingham Ledger*, a white-operated paper, also featured society news in the column "News and

Notes of Negro Affairs About Birmingham," which was written by Rev. T. S. Johnson.

35. They regarded this as "a serious corruption of the morals of our youth, and a menace to the welfare of our homes." Unidentified newspaper article found in the George Ward Scrapbook, 1899–1901. This meeting may have represented a class struggle within the black community; however, when taken as a whole, the orators' own congregations reflected a cross section of Birmingham's black community.

36. Fallin, "Shelter in the Storm," 170. Although the city threatened to close every black poolroom, it did not follow through; in 1907, five black-owned billiard and pool halls were listed in the city directory. And in 1919, when the city again threatened to close black poolrooms and dance halls, the city did not take action against all black pool halls: In 1920, there were eleven, and in 1930, there were ten. The city's threats against black saloons moved editors of race papers to speak out against the discriminatory behavior, even though they largely opposed these forms of entertainment. Despite the seeming inconsistency in their reactions, African American editors were business people first; they recognized the importance of supporting race businesses. Also, they were race men who promoted social equality. Race leaders demanded fair treatment: "It is reassuring that if this law is inacted upon white and colored amusement halls alike much good will be the outcome, but where it falls only upon the black man, there can be nothing more than a streak of prejudice." *Birmingham Reporter,* February 8, 1919.

37. Charles L. Fisher, *Social Evils: A Series of Sermons* (Jackson, Mississippi: Truth Publishing, 1899), 23–35, as cited in Fallin, "A Shelter in the Storm," 92.

38. *Birmingham Ledger,* January 3, 1916; *Birmingham Reporter,* January 7, 1928. Emancipation Day celebrations also took place in the State Fair Grounds where entertainment was provided and prominent white and black guest speakers appeared. In 1899, T. W. Walker had obtained permission from the mayor to celebrate Emancipation Day complete with activities that included parades. *Birmingham Voice of the People,* August 9, 1919. Birmingham's African Americans did not celebrate Emancipation Day annually. In fact, in 1909, when they did not observe the day, the *Colored Alabamian* saw fit to comment: "We wonder why, are the people in Birmingham less patriotic than in other cities?" January 9, 1909.

39. As was typical among Baptists, the black churches were constantly in a state of flux. In 1920, Sixteenth Street Baptist Church experienced conflict when the members divided into two factions who disputed the effectiveness of Pastor A. C. Williams as their leader. He ultimately resigned his position and moved to Philadelphia. Nearly a decade later, Pastor C. L. Fisher found himself similarly charged. The church provided male members with a forum where they could exercise their influence and authority, and disagreements were part of the process of asserting their political interests. Disfranchisement had summarily excluded blacks from the political process, but it did not quell their quest for avenues of political expression. Brown and Kimball, "Mapping the Terrain of Black Richmond," 313; *Birmingham News,* December 20, 1895; Fallin, "A Shelter in the Storm," 113 and 143.

40. Its members included Revs. T. W. Coffee, T. W. Walker, G. L. Thornton, and R. N. Hall. Oscar Adams and A. H. Parker were also members. Two women, Mrs. R. B. Maclin and Mrs. Hattie C. Davenport, were part of the organization, but they were relegated to serving on the reception committee. *Birmingham Reporter,* April 13, 1918. Male members of the churches tended to hold positions of power within the church; all ministers and deacons were men. Women members, despite their secondary status in the black church, initiated and implemented the majority of fund-raising, outreach, and self-help programs.

41. *Birmingham Reporter,* March 30, 1918. The Colored Citizens' League of Bessemer, a local civic group, also challenged the disorderly conduct of conductors on public streetcars. *Birmingham Reporter,* April 13, and June 27, 1918.

42. C. O. Booth, *Colored Baptists of Alabama,* 225.

43. Flynt, "Religion in the Urban South," 133.

44. During a national tour, the Fisk Jubilee Singers performed a concert at the First Congregational. *Birmingham Reporter,* March 1, 1919.

45. Fallin, "A Shelter in the Storm," 145.

46. *Birmingham Reporter,* February 16, 1918.

47. As cited in Litwack, *Trouble in Mind,* 382; Fallin, "A Shelter in the Storm," 68.

48. Both quotations are from the *Birmingham Truth,* April 25, 1930. W. E. B. Du Bois noted in 1899, that second only to the church, the fraternal orders and mutual aid and benevolent societies were "the most popular organization among Negroes." W. E. B. Du Bois, *The Philadelphia Negro* (New York: Stockmen Books, 1967), 224.

49. There were 124 beneficial fraternal orders, and between 1890 and 1901, blacks founded 366 additional ones. The mutual aid societies and self-help groups with their traditions of social and economic cooperation laid the foundations for black insurance companies, black banks, and other commercial enterprises. Charles Harris Wesley, *History of the Improved Benevolent and Protective Order of Elks of the World, 1898–1954* (Washington, D.C.: Association for the Study of Negro Life and History, 1955), 20; Lawrence W. Levine, *Black Culture and Black Consciousness: Afro-American Folk Thought from Slavery to Freedom* (Oxford: Oxford University Press, 1977), 268–69; Kelley, *Race Rebels,* 38; Betty M. Kuyk, "The African Derivation of Black Fraternal Orders in the United States," *Comparative Studies in Society and History* 25 (October 1983): 581, 585, 591; Charles Williams, Jr., and Hilda J. B. Williams, "Mutual Aid Societies and Economic Development: Survival Efforts," in *African Americans in the South: Issues of Race, Class, and Gender,* edited by Hans A. Baer and Yvonne Jones, Southern Anthropological Society Proceedings, no. 25 (Athens: University of Georgia Press, 1992), 28; Edward Nelson Palmer, "Race, Cultural Groups, Social Differentiation," *Social Forces* (December 1944): 210; and James A. Jackson, "Fraternal Societies and Race Progress," *Crisis* 45 (1938): 244.

50. Rabinowitz, *Race Relations in the Urban South,* 227.

51. Frazier, *Black Bourgeoisie;* Myrdal, *An American Dilemma,* 952–55.

52. Betty Kuyk, in her comparative study of African and African Ameri-

can fraternal orders, noted that "The benevolent society became an institution of belonging and a badge of status. It served the black American psyche through the trauma of Reconstruction and through the disillusionment of disfranchisement and Jim Crowism." Kuyk, "African Derivation," 581.

53. Fowlkes, *Co-operation*, 133–35.

54. Ellen Tarry, interview, May 10, 1994. Blacks placed great importance on a proper burial, and membership in an order ensured them a respectable departure. After the funeral services were completed for A. J. Arrington, his body was turned over to the Triune Lodge No. 430 of the Masonic order, which performed the last rites at the Grace Hill cemetery. *Birmingham Voice of the People,* January 29, 1921.

55. Muraskin, *Middle-Cass Blacks,* 58; Angel Kwoleck-Folland, "The African American Financial Industries: Issues of Class, Race, and Gender in the Early 20th Century," paper prepared for Business and Economic History, ed. William J. Hausman, May 12, 1994, pp. 13–14; Mary Ann Clawson, *Constructing Brotherhood: Class, Gender, and Fraternalism* (Princeton: Princeton University Press, 1989); David M. Fahey, *The Black Lodge in White America: "True Reformer" Browne and His Economic Strategy* (Dayton, Ohio: Wright State University, 1994), 8.

56. Drake and Cayton concluded in their study of the African American community in Chicago: "The voluntary association functions in much the same way as the church to provide the Negro not only with an opportunity for self-expression and status recognition but also with an avenue to compete for prestige, to hold office, to exercise power and control, to win applause and acclaim." St. Clair Drake and Horace R. Cayton, *Black Metropolis: A Study of Negro Life in a Northern City,* vol. 2 (New York: Harper Torchbooks, 1961; reprint, New York: Harper & Row, 1962), 423–24.

57. The organizations attracted individuals who sought affiliation with others who reflected their achievements and/or shared their values. According to Joe Trotter, the orders also "offered a substantial institutional framework for the expansion of the black elite." Trotter, *Coal, Class, and Color,* 198.

58. *Birmingham Reporter,* July 26, 1919.

59. *Birmingham City Directory,* 1916.

60. Davis's activities were also cited in the *Reporter,* where he was noted for his "faithful service and interest in humanity and his civic activities among people of Birmingham." *Birmingham Reporter,* April 27, 1918; Moorman and Barrett, *Leaders,* 88; *Birmingham Truth,* December 20, 1929. Variations on Davis's numerous affiliations were replicated by elite African Americans.

61. *Birmingham Truth,* December 20, 1929.

62. Muraskin, *Middle-Class Blacks,* 26; Loretta J. Williams, *Black Freemasonry;* S. W. Green et al., *History and Manual of the Knights of Pythias,* 14–15, 463; Charles H. Brooks, *The Official History and Manual of the Grand United Order of Odd Fellows in America* (1902; reprint, Freeport, N.Y.: Books for Libraries Press, 1971), 6.

63. Between 1866 and 1880, Alabama and 13 other states founded their first Prince Hall Lodges. When compared to the growth of the Free Masons

in other southern states, the growth realized in Alabama is particularly noteworthy. For example, African Americans in Georgia organized their first lodge in 1865, and had 130 lodges with 2,686 members. Despite its larger membership, Georgia's Masons could boast ownership of property worth only $50,000, and cash and securities totaling $34,892. William H. Grimshaw, *Official History of Freemasonry among the Colored People in North America* (1903; reprint, New York: Negro Universities Press, 1969), 304; Loretta J. Williams, *Black Freemasonry,* 45; Grimshaw, *Official History,* 288–90. By 1928, the real and personal property holdings of the U.S. black Masonic order totaled $3,000,000. Harry A. Williamson, "A Masonic Digest for Free Masonry in the Prince Hall Fraternity," Harry A. Williamson Collection, Schomburg Center for Research in Black Culture, New York Public Library, N.Y.

64. *Birmingham Weekly Pilot,* August 25, 1883, and *Birmingham City Directory,* 1887.

65. Prominent middle-class blacks sat on the board, including Peter F. Clarke, Charles Handley, H. C. Binford, Grand Master, and C. H. Harris. *Birmingham Wide-Awake,* January 5, 1907. The Alabama Endowment Department of the Masons became very wealthy because it did not annually distribute its money to its branch lodges. Muraskin, *Middle-Class Blacks,* 138; Clawson, *Constructing Brotherhood,* 96.

66. Alexis de Tocqueville observed that "in no country in the world has the principle of association been more successfully used, or applied to a greater multitude of objects than in America."

67. Because the Knights of Pythias was established later than the Masons, their total membership in Alabama did not challenge the success of the Masons until after the turn of the century. S. W. Green et al., *History and Manual of the Knights of Pythias,* 14–15, 463; *Birmingham City Directory,* 1887, 1890, 1892. John Tuggle, a letter carrier and a Mason, was the husband of Carrie Tuggle.

68. Under Tuggle's direction, the Order increased from seven to sixty-five lodges in Alabama. In 1895, he was elected Supreme Worthy Councillor of the Calanthe, the Order's women's auxiliary, and declined to serve as Grand Chancellor after 1901. When Blount assumed the title, he oversaw fifty-one lodges, after fourteen had closed. State Deputy W. H. Ward challenged the competence of Tuggle. When Ward addressed an audience of Pythians during a meeting held in the Masonic hall in Auburn, he stated: "At the time that [Blount] was elected to [Grand Chancellor], the order was penniless and unable to pay its claims promptly. We were paying $25.00 every four and six months in an effort to keep the pledge and promises of the Grand Lodge, under a contract held by each individual member. When R. A. Blount was elected we did not have thirty lodges in good and regular standing but today, we have more than three hundred lodges that were brought into being through the leadership of R. A. Blount." *Birmingham Truth,* October 3, 1930. S. W. Green, Joseph L. Jones, and E. A. Williams, *History and Manual of the Knights of Pythias* (Nashville: National Baptist Publishing Board, 1917), 592–93, 906.

69. When a receiver was appointed by the courts to temporarily take

charge of all assets of the society, including the custody and control of the seals, jewels, and rituals, the Order was assured that the receiver was not interested in gaining control of the "secret works of the society." Secrecy was a vital aspect of the Knights of Pythias, as well as of the Masons, Elks, and other similar organizations.

70. Some dissension occurred, for example, when Masons disagreed on the appropriate manner in which to conduct business. *Birmingham Truth*, August 30, 1929; Moorman and Barrett, *Leaders*, 87, 89, 92. For information on the conflicts within the Alabama Knights of Pythias see the following articles: *Birmingham Truth*, January 28, June 15, July 27, 1928; October 11, 1929; May 2 and 30, 1930; August 1, 1930; September 5, 12, and 26, 1930; October 24, 1930; November 7, 1930; *Birmingham Reporter*, October 25, 1930. For information on other suits that were filed see S. W. Green et al., *History and Manual of the Knights of Pythias*. Blount's leadership did not go unchallenged. In 1904, hundreds of Pythians from all parts of Alabama called for his resignation, "whom they claim has made himself a dictator of the order." Blount handily managed the criticisms and remained in office for several more decades. *Hot Shots*, March 26, 1904; *Birmingham Truth*, July 22, 1905.

71. Quoted in Harry Herbert Pace, "The Case of the Negro Elks," *The Voice* 4 (June 1907): 253–55; *Birmingham Reporter*, December 27, 1919.

72. Brooks, *Odd Fellows in America*, 6.

73. Wesley, *Improved Order of Elks*, 25, 40–46, 53–55; *Birmingham Truth*, March 16, 1928.

74. The quotation is from the *Birmingham Weekly Voice*, July 21, 1917. Before opening his own business, Robert Mabry worked for the white-owned American Tailoring Company. For a time he and J. W. Taylor were proprietors of American Tailoring Company at 103 North Eighteenth Street. By 1905, he operated his successful Mabry Bros. at Second Avenue and Eighteenth Street. *Birmingham City Directory*, 1900, 1901, 1906.

75. Robert Mabry also served as the Grand Director of the Alabama Knights and Ladies of Honor of America. *Birmingham Weekly Voice*, July 21, 1917.

76. *Birmingham Truth*, September 21, 28, 1907.

77. Masons were a more elite organization than some of the other orders and only allowed Masters and those holding higher ranking positions to vote. The Odd Fellows operated a more egalitarian order. According to Charles H. Brooks: "Its fundamental principles and distinguishing characteristics are as different from those of Masonry as chalk is from cheese. The rich and poor, the high and low, the Prince and Peasant, men of every rank and station in life are and always have been admitted to Odd Fellowship on equal footing. Not so with Free Masonry." Brooks, *Odd Fellows in America*, 6.

78. Loretta J. Williams, *Black Freemasonry*, 9, 50, 48. William Muraskin concluded that Prince Hall Freemasonry performed significant psychological and social functions for its members and that it helped to estrange members from the mass of black people. *Middle-Class Blacks*, 74.

79. This edict also reflected the conservatism of *Hot Shots* editor, William McGill, who was responsible for printing the statement. Henry C. Binford, quoted in *Hot Shots*, August 26, 1908.

80. P. D. Davis's address to the Jasper Hill Baptist Church in Walker County. *Birmingham Truth*, July 6, 1928.

81. Muraskin, *Middle-Class Blacks*, 152–53; *Birmingham Truth*, quoted in March 22, 1929, issue; see also April 5, 1929, issue.

82. The plan to organize an endowment or pension department was declared "the first movement of its kind ever launched in the history of the order and if culminated will prove quite beneficial to its members if fostered." *Birmingham Truth*, August 3, 1907, October 3, 1908, March 22, April 5, and September 13, 1929.

83. The Elks had a picnic for themselves at Tuxedo Park, but they also held a banquet at the Elks Rest that was open to the public. *Birmingham Reporter*, November 29, 1919; February 14, July 1, 1920; *Birmingham Truth*, June 8, July 19, 1929.

84. LaMonte, *Politics & Welfare in Birmingham*, 44, 45.

85. *Birmingham Reporter*, June 4, 1921.

86. It was not uncommon for the various white Orders to attempt to halt the progress of black organizations, which resulted in the white Elks, the white Masons and so forth filing lawsuits and injunctions against the various black orders. *Birmingham Reporter*, June 4, 1921; Wesley, *Protective Order of Elks*, 68–69, 86–87. The quotation is from Pace, "The Case of the Negro Elks," 255.

87. *Birmingham Reporter*, July 10, August 14, November 6, 1920.

88. *Birmingham Voice of the People*, August 19, 1922.

89. *Birmingham City Directory*, 1915, 1916; *Birmingham Weekly Voice*, June 30, 1917; *Birmingham Truth*, July 26, 1929, and June 12, August 8, 1930; *Birmingham Wide-Awake*, January 5, 1907; and *Birmingham Reporter*, November 6, 1920. Williamson, "A Masonic Digest for Free Masons in the Prince Hall Fraternity," box 21–23, Harry A. Williamson Collection; *Birmingham Truth*, October 3, 1930.

90. Du Bois, *The Philadelphia Negro*, 222.

91. *Birmingham Reporter*, February 2, 1918, and November 6, 1920.

92. Green et al., *Knights of Pythias*, 374, 422; *Birmingham Truth*, October 3, 1930.

93. Wesley, *Protective Order of Elks*, 157, 178. All the black orders suffered a substantial decline in membership between 1929 and 1940, as members were struggling financially and many were unable to pay weekly and monthly dues. Harry A. Williamson, "A Masonic Digest for Free Masonry in the Prince Hall Fraternity," Harry A. Williamson Collection. As David Fahey notes, collectively the local and regional societies probably had more members than did the national organizations. Fahey, *The Black Lodge in White America*, 10

94. In Birmingham, the Prince Hall Masons continues to command respect and exert influence. Helen Shores Lee, an attorney in Birmingham, declared that the Prince Hall Grand Lodge of Masons is an "institution" that has "huge assets." The Masons' central headquarters is in Birmingham, and it continues to serve the community in a variety of ways: it makes loans for home mortgages; it ensures a proper burial of a member; through the collection of small dues, the organization, upon death of a member, pays over from

their endowment to their heirs; and its social component offers members a sense of belonging and an opportunity to network. Its vitality is testament to its place in the black community. Helen Shores Lee, interview by the author, Birmingham, Ala., May 2, 1995. Ms. Lee is the daughter of Arthur D. Shores, a leading civil rights attorney and activist and a Mason.

95. *Birmingham Truth,* June 27, 1930.

96. Drake and Cayton, *Black Metropolis,* 688; *Birmingham Reporter,* March 29, 1919.

97. *Birmingham Reporter,* December 27, 1919.

98. Bigelow, "Birmingham: Biography of a City," 256.

99. Optimism may have been nurtured by developments happening elsewhere in the South. In 1915, the NAACP won a battle when the Supreme Court struck down Oklahoma's grandfather clause in *Guinn v. the United States,* which clearly violated the Fifteenth Amendment's ban on racial tests for voting. Although Oklahoma immediately passed another law that re-registered previously eligible whites but barred blacks from voting, the case offered hope for future efforts to dismantle discrimination. It was just about the only "glimmer of hope" for blacks in 1915. John Milton Cooper, Jr., *Pivotal Decades: The United States, 1900–1920* (New York: W. W. Norton, 1990), 208–9.

100. *Birmingham Reporter,* January 17, 1920. The League may have been the successor to the Colored Citizens' Club, which was in operation as early as 1904. *Birmingham Truth,* November 5, December 3, 1905; *Birmingham Reporter,* March 9, 1918, March 1, 1919.

101. *Birmingham Voice of the People,* January 25, 1919.

102. The quotation is from Autrey, "The National Association," 59. Overall, the most influential members belonged to the black middle class, many of whom were also affiliated with the Interdenominational Ministerial Alliance and the Colored Citizens' League. True to the pattern of black membership that had emerged between 1890–1930, prominent NAACP members also belonged to civic, religious, fraternal, and social clubs in the city. W. B. Driver, J. O. Diffay, and other local businessmen often directed the proceedings; and their professional interests dominated the earliest meetings, where business women also had a presence. At least as early as the fall of 1918, individuals were discussing the possibility of starting a Birmingham branch of the NAACP. *Birmingham Voice of the People,* May 3, 1919.

103. In 1919, it sponsored a parade for returning World War I soldiers.

104. Even the national office of the NAACP came down hard on the local officers who had failed to maintain the branch. Charles McPherson was the sole individual who was committed to the local organization, yet he alone could not rally support, and by the late 1920s, the local branch was in an irreversible tailspin from which it did not recover until the Scottsboro crisis and a local murder trial in the early 1930s.

105. Autrey, "The National Association," 59.

106. It took ten years for African Americans to reorganize and benefit from the favorable political sentiment created by the "Indiana Little Affair." (See chapter 7 for a description of the "Indiana Little Affair.")

107. Members of the black middle class were moved to react to civil injustices during the "Indiana Little Affair."

108. *Birmingham Voice of the People,* March 22, 1919.

109. *Hot Shots,* March 26, 1904; George C. Wright, *Life Behind a Veil: Blacks in Louisville, Kentucky, 1865–1930* (Baton Rouge: Louisiana State University Press, 1985), 144; Meier, *Negro Thought in America,* 133.

110. *Birmingham Reporter,* October 11, 1919; *Birmingham Weekly Voice,* May 5, 1917; *Birmingham Truth,* April 9, 1903.

111. During Reconstruction, segregated branches of the YMCA had appeared in both the North and the South. A permanent organization was founded to establish local black branches in response to a petition from Richmond's African American pastors in 1875. In 1890, William A. Hunton, the first black employed officer of the YMCA, was instrumental in creating a permanent black organization. The great movement in building local YMCA's came in 1911, when Julius Rosenwald, president of Sears, Roebuck and Company, made a financial commitment to assist in the erection of buildings. C. H. Tobias, "The Work of the Young Men's and Young Women's Christian Associations with Negro Youth," *Annals of the American Academy of Politics and Social Science,* 140 (November 1928): 283–84.

112. E. H. Beardsley, "Dedicated Servant or Errant Professional: The Southern Negro Physician Before World War II," in *The Southern Enigma: Essays on Race, Class, and Folk Culture,* edited by Walter J. Fraser, Jr., and Winfred B. Moore, Jr. (Westport, Conn.: Greenwood Press, 1983), 144.

113. For a more detailed and comparative account of the segregated wards, see LaMonte, *Politics & Welfare in Birmingham,* 45, 52–53; Wright, *Life Behind a Veil,* 141; Weare, *Black Business,* 53.

114. *Birmingham Ledger,* January 8, 1916. Drs. U. G. Mason, M. H. Freeman, F. D. Bradford, A. M. Brown, and Sadie Grant, a female physician at Tuggle Institute, were among the organization's members. They and others participated in the annual meetings of the Alabama Medical, Dental, and Pharmaceutical Association. Brown served as president of the National Medical Association in the 1910s, and during this time, Negro Health Week was inaugurated. National Negro Health Week was intended to educate African Americans on health issues and reverse the ravages of illnesses infesting the black neighborhoods. It originated in Virginia in 1910 but was nationalized shortly thereafter by Booker T. Washington through the auspices of the NNBL. Robert Moton noted that "Although the movement has the fullest support and cooperation of the medical profession, it is an interesting fact that it was not originated in that group, and that every type of organization from business firms to fraternal societies shares in the effort." R. R. Moton, "Organized Negro Effort for Racial Progress," *Annals of the American Academy of Politics and Social Science* 140 (November 1928): 262; *Birmingham Truth,* March 22, 1929.

115. Around 1907, Superintendent John H. Phillips led a successful movement to establish a free library system. Birmingham Board of Education, *Report of the Birmingham Public Schools: 1913,* 62–63, as cited in Miller, "Library Service for Negroes," 8.

116. U. G. Mason to Andrew Carnegie, May 5, 1913, Library Building Records, Microfilm Edition (Reel 89), Carnegie Corporation of New York, New York City, as cited in Miller, "Library Service for Negroes," 7.

117. U. G. Mason to Andrew Carnegie, May 24, 1917, Library Building Record, Microfilm Edition (Reel 89), as cited in Miller, 7.

118. Carl V. Harris, *Political Power,* 167; *Birmingham Age Herald,* October 21, 1918; *Birmingham Voice of the People,* December 21, 1918.

119. Lottie M. Hood, an "ardent friend of the Booker Washington Library," expressed her pride with a gift of three engravings that she had framed at her own expense to decorate the wall of the new library. The pictures were of Martha Washington, of Dr. Frizzell, who was the late president of Hampton Institute, and of African American artist Henry Tanner. *Birmingham Voice of the People,* December 21, 1918. Librarian Mattie Herd, the daughter of a railroad switchman, received her training at the black branch of the Louisville Public Library, "admittedly, the best colored library in the country." *Birmingham Age Herald,* October 21, 1918. By 1914, Louisville blacks could boast that they had the first black branch library in the United States. Although they too had their own library before that time it was not publicly funded. Unlike the Washington branch in Birmingham, Louisville's library building was constructed with Carnegie money. Wright, *Life Behind a Veil,* 167 (n. 22).

120. Especially during this week, schools emphasized the contributions of African Americans. Speakers presented papers on such topics as "The Negro in Literature and Art," "The New Progress of a Race," and "The Black Man's Gift." The staff also gave out diplomas to patrons who read the required number of books and who submitted written reports of their readings, which gave the recipients a sense of pride in their accomplishments. They became role models for others. *Birmingham Truth,* October 19, 1928. In 1928, blacks in Charleston, West Virginia, won the right to share with whites the Charleston Public Library. Despite their notable victory, the Charleston Board of Education continued segregating black and white patrons within the building. Trotter, *Coal, Class, and Color,* 137; *Birmingham Truth,* December 14, 1928. This was a far superior state of affairs than what was practiced in Birmingham well into the 1960s: The public library operated a segregated system and refused black patrons access to its main downtown facility. LaMonte, *Politics & Welfare in Birmingham,* 163. By 1943, the Washington branch had a collection of 14,530 volumes and 15,033 members. It was in need of a new building where it could accommodate its growing collection and serve its enthusiastic patrons. When it finally received adequate funding, it relocated to its present location on Eighth Avenue in Smithfield.

121. Moton, "Organized Negro Effort," 263.

CHAPTER 7. WOMEN SEEKING AN IDENTITY:
IMPROVING THE SOCIAL AND POLITICAL ENVIRONMENT

1. Cooper, quoted in bell hooks, *Ain't I A Woman: Black Women and Feminism* (Boston: South End Press, 1981), 168.

2. They did more than "contribute to the development of an institu-

tional infrastructure within their local communities (an admirable accomplishment in and of itself). More important, black women were often in the vanguard in founding and sustaining autonomous organizations designed specifically to improve social conditions within their respective communities." Berkeley, " 'Colored Ladies Also Contributed,' " 184.

3. *Birmingham Voice of the People,* January 29, 1921; *Birmingham Truth,* October 28, 1927, March 2, August 3, 1928, October 3, 1930. Brown was among elite company as a recipient of the Jones Valley award. Other recipients included Carrie Tuggle, Arthur H. Parker, Carrie B. McQueen (a city missionary and welfare worker), P. D. Davis, and James J. Pearson (a social and welfare worker). *Birmingham Truth,* February 22, 1929.

4. U.S. Bureau of the Census, *Thirteenth Census of the United States: 1910—Population.*

5. Historian Beverly Guy-Sheftall identified the pervasiveness of the conflict: "Black women were more painfully aware than any other segment of the population of the peculiar burden of race and sex under which they struggled. *Daughters of Sorrow: Attitudes Toward Black Women, 1880–1920* (Brooklyn, N.Y.: Carlson Publishing, 1990), 162.

6. Cooper was a strong advocate of higher learning and insisted that black women were entitled to an advanced education, which would equip them with the necessary tools to fight for and achieve equality. Anna Julia Cooper, *A Voice from the South, by a Black Woman of the South* (1892; reprint, New York: Oxford University Press, 1988), 134.

7. Some middle-class women had their resourcefulness called upon during difficult times. Dr. Bradford recalled that his "at-home" mother started a peanut and potato chip business to see the family through hard times. Women who otherwise did not work outside the home accepted their new roles and used innovative ways to endure an economic crisis. Dr. D. E. Bradford, interview by the author, January 18, 1993.

8. Rosalyn Terbor-Penn, "Discrimination Against Afro-American Women in the Woman's Movement, 1830–1920," in *The Afro-American Woman: Struggles and Images,* edited by Sharon Harley and Rosalyn Terborg-Penn (Port Washington, N.Y.: National University Publications, Kennikat Press, 1978), 26.

9. Dorothy Salem, *To Better Our World: Black Women in Organized Reform, 1890–1920* (Brooklyn, N.Y.: Carlson Publishing, 1990), 76. Deborah Gray White identified "chastity [as] the litmus test of middle-class respectability." Deborah Gray White, "The Cost of Club Work, the Price of Black Feminism," in *Visible Women: New Essays on American Activism,* edited by Nancy A. Hewitt and Suzanne Lebsock (Urbana: University of Illinois Press, 1993), 258.

10. The NACW was not the first coordinating body that black women established. It had resulted from the merging of two independent organizations—the Colored Women's League and the Federation of Afro-American Women. The establishment of the NACW, the systematizing and unifying of independent women's clubs, was done under the aegis of the Woman's Era Club of Boston. Beverly Washington Jones, *Quest for Equality,* 19; Charles Harris Wesley, *The History of the National Association of Colored Women's*

Clubs: A Legacy of Service (Washington, D.C.: National Association of Colored Women's Clubs, 1984), 24–39.

11. "The burden of giving knowledge and bringing about the practice of the laws of hygiene among a people ignorant of the laws of nature and common decency, is not a slight one. But this, too, the intelligent women can and must help to carry." Lucy C. Laney, "The Burden of the Educated Colored Woman," *Southern Workman* 28 (September 1899): 341–44.

12. *Birmingham Truth*, October 27, 1906.

13. Evelyn Brooks Higginbotham, *Righteous Discontent: The Women's Movement in the Black Baptist Church, 1880–1920* (Cambridge: Harvard University Press, 1993), 47.

14. As black activist Fannie Barrier Williams noted, black clubwomen, through their affiliation in the church, "learned the meaning of unity of effort for the common good, [where] the development of social sympathies grew into women's consciousness." Cited in Salem, *To Better Our World*, 8.

15. Ibid., 9–10.

16. Mays and Nicholson, *The Negro's Church*, 100–101.

17. Although other religious denominations organized women's associations, the women of the Baptist church have received the most attention from scholars.

18. Higginbotham, *Righteous Discontent*, 7; Boothe, *Cyclopedia of the Colored Baptists of Alabama*, 80. The Sanctified Church experienced growth in Birmingham and by 1930 there were over twenty holiness churches in the city. Unfortunately, their activities were not well documented in the race papers. Mays and Nicholson, *The Negro's Church*, 312. Some general statements can been made about the role of women in the Sanctified church. In contrast to the rigid hierarchical structure in the Baptist Church, the Sanctified Church allowed women to rise through the ranks and assume positions of leadership. Cheryl Townsend Gilkes, "'Together and in Harness': Women's Traditions in the Sanctified Church," *Signs* 10 (Summer 1985): 680.

19. Brawley recognized the value of women in the church and urged others to accept them as irreplaceable assets. He was moved to declare that "the women of Alabama are thoroughly organized, and ready and willing to make any sacrifice the work demands." Brawley, *The Negro Baptist Pulpit*, 282, 285. In 1902, after decades of completely ignoring blacks, the State Baptist Convention (white) voted to appropriate funds for the ministerial students at the school. Wayne Flynt, "The Negro and Alabama Baptists During the Progressive Era," *Journal of the Alabama Academy of Science* 39 (April 1968): 165.

20. Selma University was a fertile environment in which women immersed themselves in the Baptist teachings and where they created valuable networks of professional relationships with other Baptist women. Using their own devices, the women initially raised $4,000 of the necessary $10,000 to construct a hall for young women on the grounds of Selma University. They founded their own monthly newspaper, the *Baptist Women's Era*, and used it to extend their influence in the church. Higginbotham, *Righteous Discontent*, 167.

21. Members congregated in churches scattered about the Birmingham

District. The association adopted its own program of cooperation that placed emphasis on the home and on racial progress, and it became a major supporter of Birmingham Baptist College. Boothe, *Cyclopedia of Colored Baptists,* 79–80; Fallin, "A Shelter in the Storm," 124–25.

22. Mrs. R. B. Maclin and Mrs. B. H. Hudson had presented that paper. These women were active in community affairs and had earned reputations notable enough to draw large audiences.

23. Higginbotham, *Righteous Discontent,* 202.

24. Boothe, *Encyclopedia of Colored Baptists,* 233.

25. Without their effort, the pastor would have had to buy his own groceries, which he had not had to do for seven months. *Birmingham Weekly Voice,* August 4, 1917.

26. *Birmingham Truth,* December 9, 1927.

27. Bigelow, "Birmingham: Biography of a City," 155; *Birmingham Reporter,* November 27, 1920.

28. *Birmingham Reporter,* March 23, 1918.

29. Club meetings were also held in the homes of members to reduce the expense for lighting, heating, and cleaning the church building. Mays and Nicholson, *The Negro's Church,* 155; *Birmingham Reporter,* April 13, 1918, October 15, 1919, May 1, October 2, 1920.

30. For an analysis of the oppression black women experienced in the church, see Jacquelyn Grant, "Black Women and the Church," in *All the Women Are White, All the Blacks Are Men, but Some Of Us Are Brave,* edited by Gloria T. Hull, Patricia Bell Scott, and Barbara Smith (Old Westbury, N.Y.: Feminist Press, 1982), 141–52.

31. Mamie Tuggle died in 1915. Oscar Adams married his second wife, Ella Eaton, in 1922. *Montgomery Colored Alabamian,* April 2, 1910, and February 27, 1915; Mattie B. Rowe, "What Negroes Are Doing," transcript in the Mattie B. Rowe Papers, 1918–1953, Department of Archives and Manuscripts, Birmingham Public Library, Birmingham, Ala.

32. *Birmingham Truth,* August 28, 1931.

33. *Birmingham Weekly Voice,* June 30, 1917.

34. It was founded upon the same principles of benevolence, charity, and fraternity; and it cited among its goals the establishment of a Widow and Orphan Fund, as well as a fund for the relief of sick and distressed members. Green et al., *Knights of Pythias,* 843.

35. Ibid., 724–25, 786; Elsa Barkley Brown, "Womanist Consciousness: Maggie Lena Walker and the Independent Order of Saint Luke," *Signs* 14 (Spring 1989): 616; *Birmingham Truth,* May 8, 1909.

36. *Birmingham Truth,* May 8, 1909.

37. May Teressa Holder, "Carrie A. Tuggle," Hill-Ferguson Collection, Department of Archives and Manuscripts, Birmingham Public Library, Birmingham, Ala.; Moorman and Barrett, *Leaders,* 55.

38. *Birmingham Wide-Awake,* August 24, 1905; *Birmingham Truth,* May 27, 1905, and May 23, 1930; and Arthur G. Gaston, interviews by Ann Elizabeth Adams, Birmingham, Ala., November 17, 1976, and June 1, 1977, Sterne Library, University of Alabama at Birmingham. Kathleen Berkeley sug-

gested that women assumed the responsibility for social welfare because of their "socioculturally defined duties as the mothers and wives of the race." See Berkeley, " 'Colored Ladies Also Contributed,' " 188.

39. Gaston, interview, June 1, 1977.

40. LaMonte, *Politics and Welfare in Birmingham*, 45. Mrs. C. P. Orr was particularly instrumental in helping Carrie Tuggle build the Institute. She served as Chairman of the White Advisory Board for many years and recruited other white women who donated money and time to the school. Orr, an active charity worker, also supported the Alabama Colored Orphans and Old Folks Home and the Birmingham Colored Kindergarten Association. LaMonte, *Politics and Welfare in Birmingham*, 44–45; *Birmingham Weekly Voice*, July 16, 1917; *Birmingham Truth*, October 10, 1930.

41. Gaston, *Green Power*, 22–23. The quotation is from the *Birmingham Truth*, May 16, 1908.

42. Gaston, interview, June 1, 1977. Black women who were involved in the school wanted the children not only to receive an academic and industrial education but also "to improve the children's racial awareness." Salem, *To Better Our World*, 84.

43. *Birmingham Reporter*, September 27, December 13, 1919. The new building committee was composed of all members of the advisory board, including the chairperson Mrs. Orr and William B. Driver, who had charge of war work among blacks. *Birmingham Voice of the People*, October 4, 1919.

44. *Birmingham Reporter*, December 6 and 13, 1919; February 28, 1920; *Times Plain Dealer*, September 27, 1919.

45. Gaston, *Green Power*, 24.

46. As cited in Rogers et al., *Alabama*, 448.

47. *Birmingham Truth*, December 16, 1927. According to A. G. Gaston, "It wasn't much of a hospital, mostly just part of the school." Gaston, interview, June 1, 1977.

48. Moorman and Barrett, *Leaders*, 55; *Birmingham Truth*, October 19, 1928; April 4 and September 12, 1930; Holder, *Carrie A. Tuggle*, 2. Only Tuggle Institute's orphanage, chartered under the Welfare Department of the State of Alabama, received public funding from Birmingham's Community Chest. *Birmingham Truth*, December 7, 1928.

49. LaMonte, *Politics and Welfare in Birmingham*, 46.

50. Black secret societies supported not only Tuggle Institute but also the Alabama Colored Orphans and Old Folks Home. LaMonte, *Politics and Welfare in Birmingham*, 44. Carrie Tuggle, herself, organized the Daughters of the Rising Sun "solely for the support of Tuggle [Institute]." Gaston, interview, June 1, 1977.

51. Black women in other cities created orphanages similar to the Tuggle Institute through their cooperative efforts. One such home was located in Atlanta, where Minnie Perry worked. She shared Fannie Blevins' sentiments when she reflected on the work of the Carrie Steele Orphanage in her city: "These young people who would otherwise be useless and possibly dangerous, will become peaceful, law-abiding, industrious, Christian citizens." W. E. B. Du Bois, ed., *Some Efforts of American Negroes for Their Own Social Better-*

ment. Report of the investigation under the direction of Atlanta University; together with proceedings of the Third Conference for the study of the Negro Problems, held at Atlanta University, May 25–26, 1898, Atlanta University Publications, no. 3 (Atlanta, Ga.: Atlanta University Press, 1898), 60–61; *Birmingham Truth,* October 28, 1927.

52. Gaston, interview, June 1, 1977.

53. Salem, *To Better Our World,* 67.

54. Throughout Alabama, women were meeting and sharing ideas about how to improve conditions for blacks. Some of the programs they initiated directly served the African American female population, whereas others served both men and women. Regions where colleges and schools were located were often centers of social activity. In 1893, Georgia Washington founded the People's Village School in Mt. Meigs Village, a private school for black children that also benefited the entire community. In the same vicinity, in 1889 Cornelia Bowen founded the Mt. Meigs Institute. Women had a particularly integral role in the Tuskegee Conferences prior to 1900. Margaret Murray Washington directed many Tuskegee programs intended to serve women. She organized the Tuskegee Woman's Club, and she was the principal organizer and first president of the Alabama State Federation of Colored Women's Clubs (ASFCWC). Neverdon-Morton, *Afro-American Women,* 95–99, 123–27, 134. The oldest federated club in Alabama was the "Ten Times One Is Ten Club" founded in 1888. Wesley, *The History of the National Association of Colored Women's Clubs,* 279. Addie Waits Hunton, the president of the Atlanta Woman's Club, recalled that clubwomen formed the Southern Federation of Colored Women "to make the colored woman her own emancipator, from conditions and customs bequeathed her by a bitter past, and by a mighty desire to help in the warfare against vice and ignorance wherever it might abound." She emphasized the role of the home in the work of the clubwomen and encouraged homeownership. This "home work" had deep roots in Alabama where the majority of active clubwomen affiliated with the Southern Federation lived. Hunton, "The Southern Federation of Colored Women," 850–52.

55. The state Senate, in 1903 passed the Boys Home Bill (for white boys) in East Lake. *Birmingham Ledger,* February 12, 21, 1903.

56. In 1911, there were only eleven reformatories in the South, out of 105 such facilities nationally. The national club network disseminated information about the activities of the state federations. The Arkansas Federation developed a reformatory using Mt. Meigs as the model. Salem, *To Better Our World,* 109–10; Neverdon-Morton, *Afro-American Women,* 137–38; *Birmingham Truth,* July 9, 1903; *Birmingham Reporter,* July 12, 1919.

57. Before the City Federation met regularly at the First Congregational Church, it held its meetings in either private homes of Smithfield or Enon Ridge residents or in the Booker T. Washington Library or the YMCA.

58. In 1901, the Colored Women's Mission Congress Hospital Association planned to build a hospital to serve the black community, but one was never built. *Birmingham Reporter,* May 3, 17, 24, November 8, December 13, 1919; *Birmingham Truth,* February 28, 1930. Berkeley, " 'Colored Ladies Also Con-

tributed,'" 195; Anne Firor Scott, "Most Invisible of All: Black Women's Voluntary Associations," *Journal of Southern History* 56 (February 1990): 16–17; *Birmingham Reporter,* March 1, November 8, 1919.

59. Pettiford headed the all-black board of directors, which was composed of businessmen, doctors, and ministers. *Birmingham Weekly Voice,* June 16, 1917. Although public assistance came as a $25 monthly subsidy from the city, it appears that by 1920, it no longer received city or county funding. LaMonte, *Politics and Welfare in Birmingham,* 45; *Birmingham Reporter,* November 20, 1920. Louis Pizitz, the same merchant who donated substantial sums of money to the Tuggle Institute, also demonstrated his support for this facility when he donated twenty-three Thanksgiving dinners to the residents of the home. *Birmingham Truth,* December 2, 1927.

60. *Birmingham Voice of the People,* November 20, 1920.

61. In the early twentieth century, black women in Alabama supported woman suffrage before their white counterparts did. Black women had been involved in woman suffrage from the early nineteenth century. Rosalyn Terborg-Penn, "Discrimination Against Afro-American Women in the Woman's Movement, 1830–1920," in *The Afro-American Woman: Struggles and Images,* edited by Sharon Harley and Rosalyn Terborg-Penn (Port Washington, N.Y.: Kennikat Press, 1978), 24–26. See Rosalyn Terborg-Penn, "Black Male Perspectives on the Nineteenth-Century Woman," in *The Afro-American Woman,* 35–42, for information on early black women's movements and the cooperation they received from black males. Although the national WTCU voted to support suffrage in 1881, the Alabama unions could not bring themselves to support the issue until 1914. And it was not until 1918 that the white Alabama Federation of Women's Clubs was able to mobilize enough women to endorse the suffrage amendment. Mary Martha Thomas, "The 'New Woman' in Alabama, 1890–1920," *Alabama Review* 43 (July 1990): 174. The Selma Suffrage Association, founded in 1910, merged with the Equal Suffrage League of Birmingham (1911). Together they created the Alabama Equal Suffrage Association in 1912, which joined with the National American Woman Suffrage Association. Pattie Ruffner Jacobs of Birmingham was a driving force for woman suffrage in the state and was a respected orator and strategist within the National American Woman Suffrage Association. Mary Martha Thomas, "The 'New Woman,'" 172; Rogers et al., *Alabama,* 433

62. Mary Martha Thomas, "White and Black Alabama Women during the Progressive Era, 1890–1920," in *Stepping Out of the Shadows: Alabama Women, 1819–1990,* edited by Mary Martha Thomas (Tuscaloosa: University of Alabama Press, 1995), 91.

63. *Birmingham Reporter,* September 4, 1920; *Birmingham Voice of the People,* October 23, 30, 1920. Other states exhibited similar patterns of discrimination when black women tried to register. For comparative purposes, see Suzanne Lebsock, "Woman Suffrage and White Supremacy: A Virginia Case Study," in *Women's America,* 4th edition, edited by Linda K. Kerber and Jane Sherron De Hart (New York: Oxford University Press, 1995), 330.

64. *Birmingham News,* September 8, 1920.

65. *Birmingham Reporter,* October 23, 1920.

66. Some states allowed black women to vote, but the vast majority of southern black women were not allowed to exercise their right. Neverdon-Morton, *Afro-American Women*, 205–6.

67. Ten years later, sympathetic public sentiment created by the Indiana Little Affair mobilized blacks to take more aggressive and unified action. Little did not become a registered voter until she was fifty-five years old, thirty-one years later. Among the black organizations founded in Alabama to challenge disfranchisement after 1930 were the Negro Voters League, the Metropolitan Council of Negro Women, and the Abraham Lincoln Suffrage League of Alabama. Brittain, "Negro Suffrage," 177–78, 208, and his "Some Reflections on Negro Suffrage and Politics in Alabama—Past and Present," *Journal of Negro History* 47 (April 1962), 128. For black-organized challenges to disfranchisement in Birmingham after 1930, see Brittain, 178–214, and Autrey, "The National Association," 137–38, and Kelley, *Hammer and Hoe*, 182–84, 212–14.

68. The City Federation of Colored Women's Clubs in Birmingham represented "the combined thinking and efforts of its affiliated members in connection with basic issues." In years beyond the scope of this study, the City Federation sponsored the Federation Day Nursery and a junior federation, which provided community training for girls. Geraldine Moore, *Behind the Ebony Mask* (Birmingham: Southern University Press, 1961), 54.

69. It taught Christian principles that were at the core of black religion. Salem, *To Better Our World*, 207.

70. The national organization did nothing to deter the discrimination in local branches, because it practiced the same brand of racism at the national level. The national organization did not allow black women to have an Association "except as a branch of the white Association and that they must be governed by the will of the white women in initiating such an organization." See Rouse, *Lugenia Burns Hope*, 91–118, for a detailed account of the conflict between black women and the white-controlled YWCA. The Young Men's Christian Association, on the other hand, had enjoyed an earlier success organizing branches through the generosity of Julius Rosenwald and his financial commitment. Eva Bowles summarized their ordeal and their confidence in directing their own affairs: "We are asking that in all work affecting Colored people, full recognition of leadership be given Colored women because we wish to develop initiative and leadership in our own group." Eva Bowles, YWCA Manuscript, Neighborhood Union Papers, Trevor Arnett Library, Atlanta University, as cited in Gerda Lerner, *Black Women in White America*, 481.

71. Lerner, *Black Women in White America*, 477–78.

72. *Birmingham Weekly Voice*, May 12, June 9, 1917.

73. *Birmingham Voice of the People*, May 3, 1919. See Salem, *To Better Our World*, 207–22, for the development of YWCA among black women.

74. *Birmingham City Directory*, 1916; *Birmingham Truth*, August 3, 1928.

75. W. E. B. Du Bois, "The Black Soldier," *Crisis* (June 1918) as cited in Jack D. Foner, *Blacks and the Military in American History* (New York: Praeger Publishers, 1974): 109–10.

76. Several of Birmingham's young men served in France. *Birmingham Reporter,* March 15, 1919.

77. *Birmingham Reporter,* January 19, 1918.

78. Hannah Jane Patterson to Alice Dunbar Nelson, August 14, 1918, in the Central Correspondence File of the Committee on Women's Defense Work, 13A-A2, box 512, file 131, as cited in William J. Breen, "Black Women and the Great War: Mobilization and Reform in the South," *Journal of Southern History* 44 (August 1978): 425. Separation was the practice in the South, although there were variations in the form. *To Better Our World,* 206. Black women in Birmingham were not allowed to do canteen service but were allowed to knit garments and prepare kits, which they did with pride. *Birmingham Reporter,* January 4, 1919.

79. *Birmingham Reporter,* March 16, 23, 1918, and quotation from May 25, 1918. Black women throughout Alabama were organizing at different rates to support the war effort. In Bessemer, they worked through an active Council of Defense, supplying comfort kits and Bibles for soldiers and infant layettes for their spouses. The Women's Committee of the Council of National Defense detailed how women could help the war effort. Among the suggestions were food conservation, buying Liberty Bonds, and assisting the Red Cross. Salem, *To Better Our World,* 219; Neverdon-Morton, *Afro-American Women,* 218.

80. In 1918, Hattie Davenport, former president of the organization, was hired by ACIPCO to teach cooking and sewing to the black employees' wives and daughters. McKiven, *Iron and Steel,* 146. After the war ended, women continued to urge frugality as a means of countering the high rates of inflation that were plaguing the entire country. *Birmingham Reporter,* February 16, 1918.

81. Nelson to Patterson, August 14, 1918, as cited in Breen, "Black Women and the Great War," 432.

82. Salem, *To Better Our World,* 214; *Birmingham Reporter,* July 6, 1918.

83. Women in Birmingham generated interest in public health, specifically the high infant mortality rate among black babies. The workers organized facilities in three different sections of the city to weigh and measure babies, but their efforts lacked coordination and sufficient knowledge to take full advantage of the program. Alice Nelson addressed a large audience of Birmingham's African American residents about the importance of the nurses' drive, the need for adequate playgrounds for the children, and the need to take measures to safeguard women in industry. Blacks were aware of these problems and worked in subsequent years to remedy the social ills that plagued their community. Breen, "Black Women in World War I," 438.

84. *Birmingham Truth,* December 23, 1927.

85. *Birmingham Truth,* December 23, 1927, June 21, August 2, September 6, 1929.

86. During the 1920s, the movement to centralize social services that had characterized northern cities moved south. Birmingham's move to create such an agency was long overdue as its annual budget for welfare services had fallen far short when its funding was compared to that of other southern cit-

ies. LaMonte, *Politics and Welfare in Birmingham*, 96–98. For information on the history of the chest and its operations during the time period in this study, see especially 96–122 in LaMonte.

87. The Red Cross Family Service, a chest agency, secured funding that modestly benefited the black community. Ibid., 105. The funds they raised through their own initiative via the Colored Division of the Community Chest were passed on to the broader organization, which then earmarked the recipients and the amounts of disbursements back to black charities. In 1927, chest monies were granted to the following black organizations among others: Alabama Association for the Colored Blind, the Tuggle Institute, the Children's Home Hospital, the black YWCA, and the Girls' Service League. *Birmingham Truth*, November 11, 1927. The Jefferson County Anti-Tuberculosis Association, which had a ward that served black patients, also received funding. Blacks also benefited from funding contributed through the Salvation Army, the Travelers Aid Society, the Tuberculosis Sanitorium, and the American Red Cross for Ex-soldiers. *Birmingham Truth*, October 18, 1929.

88. According to one report, the Stockham Pipe and Fitting Company's eight hundred employees contributed more than $30,000. *Birmingham Truth*, November 18, 1927, October 11, 1929. The *Truth* published an incomplete list of contributions. The amounts varied from $9.25 donated by the Colored Employees, Brittling Cafeteria No. 1, to $190.00 from the Colored Postmen of Birmingham. Employees from different black- and white-owned businesses, members of women's clubs, and individuals such as P. Colfax Rameau who gave $20 and Mr. and Mrs. M. W. Goodson who donated $100, all supported the campaign. *Birmingham Truth*, December 6, 1929.

89. Lucile Higgins, "A History of Charity in Birmingham" (bachelor's thesis, Howard College, 1928), appendix B, as cited in LaMonte, *Politics and Welfare in Birmingham*, 106; *Birmingham Truth*, January 27, August 2, 1928.

90. *Birmingham Truth*, July 18, 1930.

91. In 1929, among many other donations, the Sinovadad Club, the Semper Fidelis, and the Cosmos Circle each donated $25; in 1930 E. A. Brown and T. C. Windham both contributed $100 to the drive, and among the $50 and over donors were Smith and Gaston Undertakers, Dr. U. G. Mason, and the employees of Bethlehem House. *Birmingham Truth*, December 6, 1929, November 21, 1930. As the decade progressed, donations dwindled as did disbursements. See LaMonte, *Politics and Welfare in Birmingham*, 106. For parallels between black and white women's clubs in Alabama and how their activities mirrored each other, see Mary Martha Thomas, "White and Black Alabama Women during the Progressive Era, 1890–1920," in *Stepping Out of the Shadows*, 75–95.

92. *Birmingham Truth*, November 11, 1927.

93. *Birmingham Truth*, April 4, 1930. See LaMonte, *Politics and Welfare in Birmingham*, 106, for the nature of the Chest's work during the Great Depression.

94. Most of the members in the women's clubs were the spouses of prominent men, and some, like Nellie Brown, had achieved recognition apart from their husband's accomplishments. The quotation is from Joe William Trotter,

Jr., *Black Milwaukee: The Making of an Industrial Proletariat, 1915–1945,* Blacks in the New World series (Urbana: University of Illinois Press, 1985), 131.

95. Tarry, *The Third Door,* 76.

96. *Birmingham Reporter,* October 16, 1920.

97. Drake and Cayton, *Black Metropolis,* 688–89, 698.

98. Jack C. Ross and Raymond H. Wheeler, *Black Belonging: A Study of the Social Correlates of Work Relations among Negroes* (Westport: Greenwood Publishing, 1971), 116.

99. *Birmingham Reporter,* February 7, 14, 1920.

100. Terrell praised the progressive spirit of Birmingham but criticized the poor conditions of public schools. *Birmingham Wide-Awake,* February 16, 1907.

101. Women living in Eufala, Greensboro, and in other parts of Alabama also organized official NACW clubs. *Birmingham Truth,* February 7, 1903; Wesley, *History of the National Association of Colored Women's Clubs,* 50; Cynthia Neverdon-Morton, "The Black Woman's Struggle," in *Afro-American Women,* 49.

102. Each club identified pet charities. The Cosmos Circle in 1928 donated $25 to each of the following organizations: the YWCA building fund, the Tuggle Institute, the Children's Home Hospital Cripple Clinic, and the Community Chest. *Birmingham Truth,* October 19, 1928.

103. Wesley, *History of the National Association of Colored Women's Clubs,* 51. Members of the Sojourner Truth Club included Mrs. William Pettiford, Mrs. Peter Clarke, and Mrs. B. H. Hudson. *Birmingham Reporter,* May 17, 1919; *Birmingham Truth,* February 7, 1903.

104. *Birmingham Truth,* December 14, 1928, February 15, 1929, March 14, 1930.

105. *Birmingham Reporter,* October 24, November 8, 1919.

106. The Anti-Tuberculosis Society's services fell far short of reaching the large numbers of blacks who suffered from the disease. Blacks, in fact, comprised three-quarters of the deaths from TB each year. LaMonte, *Politics and Welfare in Birmingham,* 54.

107. Salem, *To Better Our World,* 107. White clubwomen who originally gathered to socialize with friends also launched civic reform programs to benefit the broader society. See Estelle Freedman for an important article on this theme. "Female Institution Building and American Feminism, 1870–1930," *Feminist Studies* 5, no. 3 (Fall 1979): 512–29.

108. *Birmingham Wide-Awake,* August 10, 1905. In 1902, when the *Alabamian* (white) advertised the Alabama State Fair it encouraged patrons to visit the numerous attractions, including the Cattle Show, the Poultry Show, the Art Show and the "Nigger Shows." Blacks were acutely aware of their status in the fair and eventually moved to organize one of their own. *Birmingham Alabamian,* August 29, 1902.

109. This particular event was organized by the Semper Fidelis Club. Unidentified source, August 10, 1928.

110. Gerda Lerner, "Early Community Work of Black Club Women," *Journal of Negro History* 59 (April 1974): 160.

CONCLUSION

1. "Negro Class Distinctions," *Southern Workman* 28 (October 1899): 372. This brief self-congratulatory article also recognized the mutable boundaries of this class that "stands for all that is best."

2. Muraskin, *Middle-Class Blacks,* 26.

3. These types of associations were, in fact, the foundations upon which the black civic leagues of following decades were founded.

4. Banner-Haley, *To Do Good and To Do Well,* xiii.

5. As Kenneth Kusmer noted, these facilities were strange hybrids: "they represented on the one hand the impulse toward black separatism, but were neither controlled completely by nor always in the best interests of the black community." Kenneth L. Kusmer, *A Ghetto Takes Shape: Black Cleveland, 1870–1930* (Urbana: University of Illinois Press, 1976), 259.

6. *Birmingham Voice of the People,* February 14, 1920. It appears that members of Birmingham's Jewish community were overrepresented among those who assisted blacks. Although they were few in number, some prominent Jews, such as Louis Pizitz, Carl Steiner, Rabbi Morris Newfield, and Samuel Ullman, exhibited a social conscience when they joined forces with blacks in their effort to uplift the community.

7. When Ward served as president of the City Commission, the first public park opened to African Americans was established. Edward Shannon LaMonte, "George B. Ward: Birmingham's Urban Statesman" (Birmingham, Ala.: Birmingham Public Library, 1974), 43.

8. John Eagan, a Birmingham industrialist living in Atlanta, founded the CIC in 1919 to solve racial problems. As Glenn Eskew noted, Eagan "did what he could to advance the welfare of African Americans except enfranchise them and end segregation because he, like other businessmen, knew that these two demands actually threatened the colonial economy." Glenn T. Eskew, *But for Birmingham: The Local and National Movements in the Civil Rights Struggle* (Chapel Hill: University of North Carolina Press, 1997), 176. Some white power brokers did try to change some injustices committed against blacks, but their challenges often fell on deaf ears. Jewish activist Irving Engel spoke out against the conflict lease system and the KKK, but his verbal attacks were ignored. In 1925, Engel left the city and migrated north to escape his unhappiness "living in a community that accepted complete domination by the Klan." Robert G. Corley, *Paying "Civic Rent": The Jews of Emanu-El and the Birmingham Community* (Birmingham: A. H. Cather Publishing, 1982), n.p.

9. Not one white person supported the local branch of the NAACP, which had significant white involvement in its national organization. In 1943, Birmingham's traditional black leaders and a few white liberals had attempted to organize a local branch of the National Urban League, but white opposition moved it to fold in 1950. In 1951, an Interracial Council was established, which lasted until 1956, when it disbanded under the pressure of racist politicians and like-minded white residents. Interracial cooperation was a hard sell in Birmingham. See Kelley, *Race Rebels,* 82–83.

Bibliography

PRIMARY SOURCES

MANUSCRIPT COLLECTIONS

Afrika, Kamau, Collection. Civil Rights Institute Archives, Birmingham, Ala.

Alabama Baptist State Convention Minutes, 1868–1884, 1888–1899, 1917. Microfilm. Special Collection, Samford University, Birmingham, Ala.

Behind the Veil Oral History Project Collection. Civil Rights Institute Archives, Birmingham, Ala.

Birmingfind Photograph Collection. Department of Archives and Manuscripts, Birmingham Public Library, Birmingham, Ala.

Birmingfind Project Interviews. Department of Archives and Manuscripts, Birmingham Public Library, Birmingham, Ala.

Birmingham Civil Rights Institute Oral History Project. Birmingham, Ala.

Birmingham Historical Society—Journal, Photographs. Department of Archives and Manuscripts, Birmingham Public Library, Birmingham, Ala.

Birmingham—Neighborhood—Smithfield. Clipping File. Tutwiler Collection of Southern History and Literature, Department of Archives and Manuscripts, Birmingham Public Library, Birmingham, Ala.

Birmingham Real Estate Association Minute Book, December 19, 1899–October 1900, and June 1905–July 2, 1907, except October 1900 to May 1905. Department of Archives and Manuscripts, Birmingham Public Library, Birmingham, Ala.

Comer, Donald. Business Papers. Department of Archives and Manuscripts, Birmingham Public Library, Birmingham, Ala.

Hill-Ferguson Collection. Tutwiler Collection of Southern History and Literature, Department of Archives and Manuscripts, Birmingham Public Library, Birmingham, Ala.

Jemison, Robert, Jr. Papers. Department of Archives and Manuscripts, Birmingham Public Library, Birmingham, Ala.

Knights of Pythias Collection. Department of Archives and Manuscripts, Birmingham Public Library, Birmingham, Ala.

Moton, Robert. Papers. Tuskegee University, Tuskegee, Ala.

National Negro Business League. Papers. Tuskegee University, Tuskegee, Ala.

Newfield, Rabbi Morris. Papers. Department of Archives and Manuscripts, Birmingham Public Library, Birmingham, Ala.

Peabody Collection. Clipping File, Hampton University, Va.

Rowe, Mattie B. Papers, 1918–1953. Department of Archives and Manuscripts, Birmingham Public Library, Birmingham, Ala.

Smith, Dr. Joseph R. Papers. Department of Archives and Manuscripts, Birmingham Public Library, Birmingham, Ala.

Smith, Henley Jordan. Private Collection. Birmingham, Ala.

Smith Family File. Southern History Collection, Department of Archives and Manuscripts, Birmingham Public Library, Birmingham, Ala.

Steiner Bank Records (incomplete). Department of Archives and Manuscripts, Birmingham Public Library, Birmingham, Ala.

Ward, George. Scrapbook, 1899–1901, March 15, 1913–January 10, 1915. Southern History Collection, Department of Archives and Manuscripts, Birmingham Public Library, Birmingham, Ala.

Washington, Booker T. Papers. Library of Congress, Washington, D.C.

Williamson, Harry A. Collection. Schomburg Center for Research in Black Culture, New York Public Library, N.Y.

GOVERNMENT DOCUMENTS AND REPORTS

Alabama Schedules, 1860, Slave Population, Augauga—Madison Counties. Microfiche. Auburn University, Ala.

Birmingham Board of Alderman Minutes, May 16, 1883, June 6, 1883, May 17, 1899–August 17, 1900. Birmingham City Hall, Birmingham, Ala.

Birmingham Board of Education Minutes, 1889, 1902, 1903, 1904, 1905, 1907. Birmingham Board of Education, Birmingham, Ala.

Block Book Survey, 1905–11, Roll #47, Alpha Start: J. M. Morgan End: Walker City; 1st Add. Tax Assessor's Office, Jefferson County Court House, Birmingham, Ala.

Block Book Survey, 1912–15, Roll #44, Start at South Side Land Co., Block 4. Tax Assessor's Office, Jefferson County Court House, Birmingham, Ala.

Block Book Survey, 1916–19, Roll #37, Alpha Queenstown—Block 40 To: Waverly Terrace. Tax Assessor's Office, Jefferson County Court House, Birmingham, Ala.

Block Book Survey, 1920–24, Roll #30, Alpha Russell Heights Lot 18 Block 14 To: Wilkes J. W. Tax Assessor's Office, Jefferson County Court House, Birmingham, Ala.

Board of Equalization Appraisal Files. Department of Archives and Manuscripts, Birmingham Public Library, Birmingham, Ala.

Direct Index to Deeds and Mortgages, Jefferson County, 1898–1915, Probate Court Record Room, Jefferson County Court House, Birmingham, Ala.

1850 Agricultural and Manufacturing Census Records, Dale—Marengo, Schedule—Agricultural; 1860 Alabama, Dekalb—Morgan, Agricultural. Microfiche. Auburn University, Ala.

1860 Census—Population Schedule (Free Inhabitants in Greene Precinct), P. O.—Elyton, Ala., Jeff.—Lawrence. Microfiche. Auburn University, Ala.

1880 Agricultural and Manufacturing Census Records, Ala., Jeff.—Limestone, Agricultural. Microfiche. Auburn University, Ala.

The General Code of the City of Birmingham Alabama: The General Ordinances of the City. Published by Order of the City Commission. Charlottesville, Va.: Michie, 1944. Copy located in the Birmingham Public Library, Birmingham, Ala.

General Laws (and Joint Resolutions) of the Legislature of Alabama, Special Session 1909. Brown Printing Co., 1909. Copy located in the Birmingham Public Library, Birmingham, Ala.

Graymont City Minutes, 1907–9. Birmingham City Hall, Birmingham, Ala.

Indirect Index to Deeds and Mortgages, Jefferson County, vols. 16–52 (even numbers only), 1898–1915. Probate Court Record Room, Jefferson County Court House, Birmingham, Ala.

Marriage Records, Jefferson County Marriage Licenses, 1818–present. Probate Court Record Room, Jefferson County Court House, Birmingham, Ala.

1900 Federal Population Census. A catalog of microfilm copies of the schedules. Washington, D.C.: National Archives Trust Fund Board, 1979.

Probate Records, 1890–1930. Probate Court Record Room, Jefferson County Court House, Birmingham, Ala.

Record of Incorporation, Jefferson County, 1880–1930. Probate Court Record Room, Jefferson County Court House, Birmingham, Ala.

Report of Progress, Birmingham Public Schools, September 1, 1921–August 31, 1931. Birmingham Board of Education, Birmingham, Ala.

Tax Return List—Real and Personal Property, 1904–23. Tax Assessor's Office, Jefferson County Court House, Birmingham, Ala.

U.S. Bureau of the Census. *Abstract of the Fourteenth Census of the United States, 1920.* Washington, D.C.: Government Printing Office, 1923.

U.S. Bureau of the Census. *Federal Population Censuses, 1790–1890.* A catalog of microfilm copies of the schedules. Washington, D.C.: National Archives Trust Fund Board, 1979.

U.S. Bureau of the Census. *Fourteenth United States Census: 1920—Population.* Washington, D.C.: Government Printing Office, 1920.

U.S. Bureau of the Census. *Negroes in the United States, 1920–1932.* Washington D.C.: Government Printing Office, 1935.

U.S. Bureau of the Census. *Negro Population, 1790–1915.* Washington, D.C.: Government Printing Office, 1918.

U.S. Bureau of the Census. *The Statistical History of the United States from Colonial Times to the Present.* Washington, D.C.: Government Printing Office, 1965.

U.S. Bureau of the Census. *Thirteenth United States Census: 1910—Population.* Washington, D.C.: Government Printing Office, 1910.

U.S. Bureau of the Census. *Twelfth United States Census: 1900—Population.* Washington, D.C.: Government Printing Office, 1900.

U.S. Census of Religious Bodies: 1906. Vol. 1. Washington, D.C., 1909.

U.S. Census of Religious Bodies: 1916. Vol. 1. Washington, D.C., 1919.

United States Department of the Interior, National Park Service. *National*

Register of Historic Places, Inventory—Nomination Form. Joseph Riley Smith Historic District. Department of Archives and Manuscripts, Birmingham Public Library, Birmingham, Ala.

United States Department of the Interior, National Park Service. *National Register of Historic Places,* Inventory—Nomination Form. Smithfield Historic District. Department of Archives and Manuscripts, Birmingham Public Library, Birmingham, Ala.

MAPS

Baist's Property Atlas of the City of Birmingham and Suburbs, Alabama. Philadelphia: G. W. Baist, 1902.

Birmingham, Alabama, 1898. George Franklin Cram, Chicago, Ill., 1898.

Birmingham and Adjacent Suburbs. Drawn, compiled, and published by George B. Kelley, 1903. Tutwiler Collection of Southern History and Literature, Birmingham Public Library, Birmingham, Ala.

Elyton Map of City of Birmingham, Alabama, and Suburbs. H. Schoel, Produced by Rand McNally, Chicago, Ill., 1888.

Fire Insurance Maps of Birmingham, Alabama. Vol. 3. New York: Sanborn Map Co., 1928.

Insurance Maps: Birmingham, Jefferson, Alabama. New York: Sanborn-Perris Map Co., 1891.

Insurance Maps of Birmingham, Alabama. Vol. 3. New York: Sanborn Map Co., 1911.

Kelley's Map of Birmingham Alabama. Birmingham, Ala.: Kelley Co. Engineers, 1911.

NEWSPAPERS, DIRECTORIES, AND REPORTS

Anniston Baptist Leader, 1900
Anniston Union-Leader, 1900
Birmingham Age-Herald, 1886, 1895, 1902, 1905, 1907, 1915, 1916, 1918, 1919, 1921, 1922, 1927.
Birmingham Alabamian, 1902.
Birmingham Blade, 1907–9.
Birmingham City Directory, 1880–1930.
Birmingham Free Speech, 1901–2.
Birmingham Ledger, 1902, 1903, 1906, 1915, 1916.
Birmingham News, 1895, 1900, 1903, 1907, 1909, 1914, 1920, 1922, 1923, 1926, 1927.
Birmingham People's Weekly Tribune, 1894, 1896, 1898–1900.
Birmingham Reporter, 1914, 1918–23, 1925–28, 1930.
Birmingham Silent Eye, 1901–6.
Birmingham Truth, 1902–9, 1919, 1927–31.
Birmingham Weekly Pilot, 1883.
Birmingham Weekly Voice, later *Birmingham Voice of the People,* 1915–22.
Birmingham Wide-Awake, 1905–7, 1909.

Birmingham Workman's Chronicle, 1918.

Chicago Afro-American Union Analytic Catalog. Boston: G. K. Hall and Co., 1972. At Vivian G. Hirsh Collection of Afro-American History and Literature at George Cleveland Hall Branch Library now Carter G. Woodson Branch Library, Chicago, Ill.

Chicago Defender, January 15, 1916.

Christian Science Monitor, October 11, 1932.

Colored Alabamian, 1907, 1909–11, 1913, 1915.

Dallas Express, 1923.

Huntsville Gazette, 1891

Huntsville Journal, later the *Journal,* 1895–1912.

Journal of the 61st Annual Session of the Alabama Colored Baptist State Convention, Fairfield, Ala., November 20–23, 1928.

Jubilee Volume of the Fifteenth Annual Session of the Alabama Colored Baptist State Convention, Birmingham, Ala., November 22–26, 1917.

Memphis City Directory, 1904.

Montgomery Advertiser, June 1, 1905; March 2, 1913; April 22, 1914; December 23, 24; January 30, 1915; May 3, June 2 and 7, September 4 and 8, 1922; August 2, January 25, March 13, 14, 21, April 13, 1923.

Montgomery Colored Alabamian, 1907–16.

Proceedings of the Hampton Negro Conference, Hampton University, Va., 1898, 1903.

Proceedings of the National Negro Business League, Hampton University, Va.

Report of the First Colored Baptist Church, Montgomery, Ala., December 17–20, 1869.

Savannah Tribune, 1921.

Selma Record, 1901–2.

Uniontown News, 1901–16.

SECONDARY SOURCES

Aaron, Henry. *I Had a Hammer: The Hank Aaron Story.* New York: Harper-Collins, 1991.

Agresti, B. F. "Household Composition, The Family Cycle and Economic Hardship in a Post-bellum Southern County, Walton, Florida, 1870–1885." *International Journal of Sociology of the Family* 2 (1982): 245–55.

Alexander, Will W. "The Negro in the New South." *Annals of the American Academy of Politics and Social Science* 140 (November 1928): 145–52.

Allen, Isabel Dangaix. "The Savings Bank Militant." *Outlook* 77 (May 1904): 118–22.

——. "Negro Enterprise: An Institutional Church." *Outlook* 88 (September 17, 1904): 179–83.

Anderson, James D. *The Education of Blacks in the South, 1860–1935.* Chapel Hill: University of North Carolina Press, 1988.

Armbrester, Margaret England. *Samuel Ullman and "Youth": The Life, the Legacy.* Tuscaloosa: University of Alabama Press, 1993.

———. "Samuel Ullman: Birmingham Progressive." *Alabama Review* 47 (January 1994): 29–43.

Armes, Ethel. *The Story of Coal and Iron in Alabama.* 1910. Reprint, New York: Arno Press, 1973.

———. "The Spirit of the Founders." *The Survey* 27 (January 6, 1912): 1453–63.

Aronovici, Carol. *Housing the Masses.* New York: John Wiley & Sons, 1939.

Atkins, Leah Rawls. *The Valley and the Hills: An Illustrated History of Birmingham and Jefferson County.* Woodland Hills, Calif.: Windsor Publications, 1981.

———. *Nineteenth Century Club: Celebrating 100 Years of "Mutual Mental Improvement," 1895–1995.* Birmingham, Ala.: Nineteenth Century Club, 1995.

Autrey, Dorothy. "The National Association for the Advancement of Colored People in Alabama, 1913–1952." Ph.D. diss., University of Notre Dame, 1985.

———. "Can These Bones Live?: The National Association for the Advancement of Colored People in Alabama, 1918–1930." *Journal of Negro History* 82 (Winter 1997): 1–12.

Ayers, Edward L. *The Promise of the New South: Life After Reconstruction.* New York: Oxford University Press, 1992.

Babchuk, Nicholas, and Ralph V. Thompson. "The Voluntary Association of Negroes." *American Sociological Review* 27 (October 1962): 647–55.

Bacote, Samuel William, ed. *Who's Who Among the Colored Baptists of the United States.* Kansas City, Mo.: Franklin Hudson, 1913. Reprint, New York: Arno Press, 1980.

Banner-Haley, Charles Pete T. *To Do Good and To Do Well: Middle-Class Blacks and the Depression, Philadelphia, 1929–1941.* New York: Garland Publishing, 1993.

———. *The Fruits of Integration: Black Middle-Class Ideology and Culture, 1960–1990.* Jackson: University of Mississippi Press, 1994.

Barrows, Robert G. "Beyond the Tenement: Patterns of American Urban Housing, 1870–1930." *Journal of Urban History* 9 (August 1983): 395–420.

Bauman, John F. "Housing the Urban Poor." *Journal of Urban History* 6 (February 1980): 211–19.

Beale, Frances. "Double Jeopardy: To Be Black and Female." In *The Black Woman: An Anthology.* Edited by Toni Cade. New York: New American Library, 1970.

Beardsley, E. H. "Dedicated Servant or Errant Professional: The Southern Negro Physician Before World War II." In *The Southern Enigma: Essays on Race, Class, and Folk Culture.* Edited by Walter J. Fraser, Jr., and Winfred B. Moore, Jr., 143–52. Westport, Conn.: Greenwood Press, 1983.

Beavers, Theresa Aguglia. "The Italians of the Birmingham District." Master's thesis, Samford University, 1969.

Beck, Carolyn Stickney. "Our Own Vine and Fig Tree: The Persistence of an Historic Afro-American Community." Ph.D. diss., Bryn Mawr College, 1980.

Bell, Wendell, and Ernest M. Willis. "The Segregation of Negroes in American Cities." *Social and Economic Studies* 6 (1957): 59–75.

Berkeley, Kathleen C. " 'Colored Ladies Also Contributed': Black Women's Activities from Benevolence to Social Welfare, 1866–1896." In *The Web of Southern Social Relations: Women, Family, and Education,* edited by Walter J. Fraser et al., 181–203. Athens: University of Georgia Press, 1985.

Berman, Paul, ed. *Blacks and Jews: Alliances and Arguments.* New York: Delacorte Press, 1994.

Bethel, Elizabeth Rauh. *Promiseland: A Century of Life in a Negro Community.* Philadelphia: Temple University Press, 1981.

Bigelow, Martha Mitchell. "Birmingham: Biography of a City of the New South." Ph.D. diss., University of Chicago, 1946.

——. "Birmingham's Carnival of Crime." *Alabama Review* 3 (April 1950): 123–33.

Billingsley, Andrew. *Climbing Jacob's Ladder: The Enduring Legacy of African-American Families.* New York: Simon & Schuster, 1992.

Biographical Sketches of Citizens of Birmingham and Jefferson County. Indianapolis, Ind.: Citizens Historical Association, 1936–44.

"Black Belt Settlement Work." *Southern Workman* 31 (July 1902): 383–88.

Blackwell, James E. *The Black Community: Diversity and Unity.* New York: Harper & Row, 1975.

Blassingame, John W. *The Slave Community: Plantation Life in the Antebellum South.* New York: Oxford University Press, 1979.

Blayton, Jesse B. "The Negro in Banking." *Banker's Magazine* 133, no. 6 (December 1936): 511–14.

Blum, Terry, and Paul W. Kingston. "Homeownership and Social Attachment." *Sociological Perspectives* 27 (April 1984): 159–80.

Bodnar, John, Roger Simon, and Michael P. Weber. *Lives of Their Own: Blacks, Italians, and Poles in Pittsburgh, 1900–1960.* Urbana: University of Illinois Press, 1982.

Boles, W. J. *Romance and Realty: Story of Real Estate Transactions in Birmingham Since the First Land Sale in 1871 to the Latest Recorded Sale.* Birmingham, Ala.: Roberts and Sons, 1928.

Bond, Horace Mann. *Negro Education in Alabama: A Study in Cotton and Steel.* Washington, D.C.: Associated Publishers, 1939. Reprint, Tuscaloosa: University of Alabama Press, 1994.

——. "Negro Attitudes Toward Jews." *Jewish Social Studies* 27 (January 1965): 3–9.

Boothe, Charles Octavius. *Cyclopedia of the Colored Baptists of Alabama: Their Leaders and Their Work.* Birmingham: Alabama Publishing Co., 1895.

Borchert, James. *Alley Life in Washington: Family, Community, Religion, and Folklife in the City, 1850–1970.* Urbana: University of Illinois Press, 1980.

Boris, Eileen, and Cynthia Daniels, eds. *Homework: Historical and Contemporary Perspectives on Paid Labor at Home.* Urbana: University of Illinois Press, 1989.

Bowsher, Alice M., et al. "An Index to the Name or Number Designations of Changes of Alleys, Avenues, Circles, Courts, Places, Streets, Terraces, and

Ways on the Southside Made by Ordinance of the Commission of the City of Birmingham, Alabama, June 10, 1914." *Journal of the Birmingham Historical Society* 6 (July 1980): 24–51.

Bracey, John, and August Meier. "Towards a Research Agenda on Blacks and Jews in United States History." *Journal of American Ethnic History* (Spring 1993): 60–76.

Bracey, John H., Jr., August Meier, and Elliott Rudwick, eds. *Black Nationalism in America.* Indianapolis: Bobbs-Merrill, 1970.

Bradford, Juliet R. "The Industrial High School: A Brief History." N.p., 1925. 8–30.

Brawley, Edward M., ed. *The Negro Baptist Pulpit: A Collection of Sermons and Papers by Colored Baptist Ministers.* 1890. Reprint, Freeport, N.Y.: Books for Libraries Press, 1971.

Breedlove, Michael A. "Donald Comer: New Southerner, New Dealer." Ph.D. diss., The American University, Washington, D.C., 1990.

Breen, William J. "Black Women and the Great War: Mobilization and Reform in the South." *Journal of Southern History* 44 (August 1978): 421–40.

Brittain, Joseph M. "Negro Suffrage and Politics in Alabama Since 1870." Ph.D. diss., Indiana University, 1958.

———. "Some Reflections on Negro Suffrage and Politics in Alabama—Past and Present." *Journal of Negro History* 47 (April 1962): 127–38.

Brooks, Charles H. *The Official History and Manual of the Grand United Order of Odd Fellows in America.* 1902. Reprint, Freeport, N.Y.: Books for Libraries Press, 1971.

Brooks, Sarah. *You May Plow Here: The Narrative of Sarah Brooks.* Edited by Thordis Simonsen. Touchstone edition. New York: Simon and Schuster, 1987.

Broussard, Albert. "Organizing the Black Community in the San Francisco Bay Area." *Arizona and the West* 23 (1981): 335–54.

Brown, Charles A. "W. A. Rayfield: Pioneer Black Architect of Birmingham, Ala." Birmingham: Gray Printing Company, n.d.

———. *The Origin and Development of Secondary Education for Negroes in the Metropolitan Area of Birmingham, Alabama.* Birmingham: Commercial Printing Co., 1959.

Brown, Elsa Barkley. "Womanist Consciousness: Maggie Lena Walker and the Independent Order of Saint Luke." *Signs* 14 (Spring 1989): 610–33.

Brown, Elsa Barkley, and Gregg D. Kimball. "Mapping the Terrain of Black Richmond" *Journal of Urban History* 21 (March 1995): 296–346.

Brown, James Seay, Jr. *Up before Daylight: Life Histories from the Alabama Writers' Project, 1938–1939.* University, Ala.: University of Alabama Press, 1982.

Brown, William H., Jr. "Access to Housing: The Role of the Real Estate Industry." *Economic Geography* 47 (January 1972): 66–78.

Brownell, Blaine A. "Birmingham, Alabama: New South City in the 1920s." *Journal of Southern History* 38 (February 1972): 21–48.

———. "The Notorious Jitney and the Urban Transportation Crisis in Birmingham in the 1920's." *Alabama Review* 25 (April 1972): 105–18.

———. "The Urban South Comes of Age, 1900–1940." In *The City in Southern History: The Growth of Urban Civilization in the South,* edited by Blaine A. Brownell and David R. Goldfield. Port Washington, N.Y.: National Universities Publications, 1977.

Bullock, Henry Allen. *A History of Negro Education in the South: From 1619 to the Present.* Cambridge, Mass.: Harvard University Press, 1967.

Bullough, Bonnie. *Social-Psychological Barriers to Housing Desegregation.* Berkeley, Calif.: Center for Real Estate and Urban Economics, 1969.

Burgess, Ernest W. "Residential Segregation in American Cities." *Annals of the American Academy of Politics and Social Science* 140 (November 1928): 105–15.

Burkhardt, Ann McCorquodale. *House Detective: A Guide to Researching Birmingham Buildings.* Birmingham, Ala.: Birmingham Historical Society, 1988.

Butler, John Sibley. *Entrepreneurship and Self-Help Among Black Americans: A Reconsideration of Race and Economics.* Albany: State University of New York Press, 1991.

Caldwell, H. M. *History of the Elyton Land Company and Birmingham, Alabama.* Birmingham, 1892.

Callins, Jothan McKinley. "'The Birmingham Jazz Community': The Role and Contributions of Afro-Americans (up to 1940)." Master's thesis, University of Pittsburgh, 1982.

Chestnut, J. L., Jr., and Julia Cass. *Black in Selma, The Uncommon Life of J. L. Chestnut, Jr.* New York: Farrar, Straus and Giroux, 1990.

Chudacoff, Howard P. "A Reconsideration of Geographical Mobility in American Urban History." *The Virginia Magazine of History and Biography* 102, no. 4 (October 1994): 501–18.

Citizens Historical Association. *Biographical Sketches of Citizens of Birmingham and Jefferson County.* Birmingham, 1965.

Clark, Clifford Edward, Jr. *The American Family Home, 1800–1960.* Chapel Hill: University of North Carolina Press, 1986.

Clark, Kenneth B. *Dark Ghetto.* New York: Harper Torchbooks, 1965.

Clark-Lewis, Elizabeth. "This Work Had an End." In *"To Toil the Livelong Day": America's Women at Work, 1780–1900,* edited by Carol Groneman and Mary Beth Norton. Ithaca, N.Y.: Cornell University Press, 1987.

Clawson, Mary Ann. *Constructing Brotherhood: Class, Gender, and Fraternalism.* Princeton, N.J.: Princeton University Press, 1989.

Clayton, Obie, Jr. "The Churches and Social Change: Accommodation, Moderation, or Protest." *Daedalus* 124 (Winter 1995): 101–17.

Cochran, Lynda Dempsey. "Arthur Davis Shores: Advocate for Freedom." Master's thesis, Georgia Southern College, Statesboro, Ga., 1977.

Cohen, Abraham. "Birmingham." *The Universal Jewish Encyclopedia.* Vol. 40. New York: Universal Jewish Encyclopedia, 1940.

Cohen, William. "Negro Involuntary Servitude in the South, 1865–1940: A Preliminary Analysis." *Journal of Southern History* 42 (February 1976): 56.

Comer, James P. *Maggie's American Dream: The Life and Times of a Black Family.* New York: New American Library, 1988.

The Common School and the Negro American. Atlanta University Publications, 16. Atlanta: Atlanta University Press, 1911.

Connerly, Charles, E. "One Great City: Birmingham's Struggle for Greatness Through Suburban Annexation and Consolidation, 1890 to the Present." Paper presented at the ACSP-AESOP Joint International Congress, Oxford, England, July 1991.

Conzen, Kathleen Neils. "Patterns of Residence in Early Milwaukee." In *The New Urban History: Quantitative Explorations by American Historians,* edited by Leo F. Schnore, 145–83. Princeton: Princeton University Press, 1975.

Cooper, Anna Julia. *A Voice from the South, by a Black Woman of the South.* 1892. Reprint, New York: Oxford University Press, 1988.

Cooper, Gary Douglas. "The Economics of Ghetto Expansion: A Study of Residential Segregation." Ph.D. diss., Florida State University, 1974.

Cooper, John Milton, Jr. *Pivotal Decades: The United States, 1900–1920.* New York: W. W. Norton, 1990.

Corley, Robert G. "The Quest for Racial Harmony: Race Relations in Birmingham, 1947–1963." Ph.D. diss., University of Virginia, 1979.

——. *Paying "Civic Rent": The Jews of Temple Emanu-El and the Birmingham Community.* Birmingham, Ala.: A. H. Cather Publishing Company, 1982.

Cowett, Mark. *Birmingham's Rabbi: Morris Newfield and Alabama, 1895–1940.* University, Ala.: University of Alabama Press, 1986.

Cripps, Thomas. *Slow Fade to Black: The Negro in American Film, 1900–1942.* London: Oxford University Press, 1977.

Cruikshank, G. M. *History of Birmingham and its Environs: a Narrative Account of Their Historical Progress, Their People and Their Principal Interests.* Chicago: Lewis Pub. Co., 1920.

Daniels, Douglas Henry. *Pioneer Urbanites: A Social and Cultural History of Black San Francisco.* Philadelphia: Temple University Press, 1980.

Darden, Joe T. "The Significance of Race and Class in Residential Segregation." *Journal of Urban Affairs* 8, no. 1 (Winter 1986): 49–55.

Davis, Angela Y. *Women, Race and Class.* New York: Vintage Books, 1983.

Davis, Dernoral. "Against the Odds: Postbellum Growth and Development in a Southern Black Urban Community, 1865–1900." Ph.D. diss., State University of New York at Binghamton, 1987.

Dean, John P. *Home Ownership: Is It Sound?* New York: Harper & Brothers Publishers, 1945.

Deetz, James. *In Small Things Forgotten: The Archeology of Early American Life.* Garden City, N.Y.: Anchor Press/Doubleday, 1977.

DeVigne, Sadie E. Beach. "St. Mark's School, Birmingham, Alabama." *Colored American Magazine* 13 (December 1907): 417–20.

Dickson, Lynda F. "Toward a Broader Angle of Vision in Uncovering Women's History: Black Women's Clubs Revisited." *Frontiers* 9, no. 2 (1987): 62–68.

Dill, Bonnie Thornton, "Race, Class, and Gender: Prospects for an All-Inclusive Sisterhood." *Feminist Studies* 9 (Spring 1983): 131–50.

Diner, Hasia R. *In the Almost Promised Land: American Jews and Blacks, 1915–1935.* Westport, Conn.: Greenwood Press, 1977.

DiPasquale, Denise, and Langley C. Keyes, eds. *Building Foundations: Housing and Federal Policy.* Philadelphia: University of Pennsylvania Press, 1990.

Dittmer, John. *Black Georgia in the Progressive Era, 1900–1920.* Urbana: University of Illinois Press, 1977.

Dollard, John. *Caste and Class in a Southern Town.* New Haven: Yale University Press, 1937.

Doucet, Michael, and John Weaver. *Housing the North American City.* Montreal: McGill-Queen's University Press, 1991.

Doyle, Don H. "The Social Functions of Voluntary Associations in a Nineteenth-Century American Town." *Social Science History* 1, no. 3 (Spring 1977): 333–55.

———. *The Social Order of a Frontier Community.* Urbana: University of Illinois Press, 1978.

———. *New Men, New Cities, New South: Atlanta, Nashville, Charleston, Mobile, 1860–1910.* Chapel Hill: University of North Carolina Press, 1990.

Drake, St. Clair, and Horace R. Cayton. *Black Metropolis: A Study of Negro Life in a Northern City.* Vol. 2. New York: Harper Torchbooks, 1961. Reprint, New York: Harper & Row, 1962

Du Bois, W. E. B., ed. *Some Efforts of American Negroes for Their Own Social Betterment. Report of the investigation under the direction of Atlanta University; together with proceedings of the Third Conference for the study of the Negro Problems, held at Atlanta University, May 25–26, 1898.* Atlanta University Publications, no. 3. Atlanta, Ga.: Atlanta University Press, 1898.

———, ed. *The Negro in Business. Report of the social study made under the direction of Atlanta University; together with the proceedings of the Fourth Conference for the study of the Negro Problems held at Atlanta University, May 30–31, 1899.* Vol. 1. Atlanta University Publications, no. 4. 1899. New York: Octagon Books, 1968.

———. *The Philadelphia Negro: A Social Study.* New York: Stockmen Books, 1967.

———. "The Negro in the Black Belt, A County Seat: Marion, Perry County, Alabama." *Bulletin of the Department of Labor,* no. 22 (May 1899): 411–13.

———, ed. *The College-Bred Negro. Report of the social study made under the direction of Atlanta University; together with the proceedings of the Fifth Conference for the study of the Negro Problems held at Atlanta University, May 29–30, 1900.* Vol. 1. Atlanta University Publications, no. 5. 1900. New York: Octagon Books, 1968.

———, ed. *The Negro Artisan. Report of the social study made under the direction of Atlanta University; together with the proceedings of the Seventh Conference for the study of the Negro Problems held at Atlanta University, May 27th, 1902.* Atlanta University Publications, no. 7. Atlanta, Ga.: Atlanta University Press, 1902.

———. *The Negro American Family.* Atlanta, Ga.: Atlanta University Press, 1908.

———, ed. *The Negro Church: Report of a Social Study Made Under the Direction of Atlanta University.* Atlanta, 1903.

DuBose, John Witherspoon. *Jefferson County and Birmingham, Alabama, Historical and Biographical.* Birmingham: Caldwell Printing Works, 1887.

"The Duty of the National Association of Colored Women to the Race." *AME Church Review* 96 (January 1900): 346–47.

Edel, Matthew, Elliot D. Sclar, and Daniel Luria. *Shaky Palaces: Homeownership and Social Mobility in Boston's Suburbanization.* New York: Columbia University Press, 1984.

Edwards, Paul K. *The Southern Urban Negro as a Consumer.* New York: Prentice-Hall, 1932.

Edwards, William J. *Twenty-Five Years in the Black Belt.* 1918. Reprint, Westport, Conn.: Negro Universities Press, 1970.

Eighmy, John Lee. *Churches in Cultural Captivity: A History of the Social Attitudes of Southern Baptists.* Knoxville: University of Tennessee Press, 1972.

Ellison, Ralph. *Shadow and Act.* New York: Random House, 1964.

Elovitz, Mark H. *A Century of Jewish Life in Dixie: The Birmingham Experience* University, Ala.: University of Alabama Press, 1974.

Eskew, Glenn T. "Black Elitism and the Failure of Paternalism in Postbellum Georgia: The Case of Bishop Lucius Henry Holsey." *Journal of Southern History* 58 (November 1992): 637–66.

———. "But for Birmingham: The Local and National Movements in the Civil Rights Struggle." Ph.D. diss., University of Georgia, Athens, 1993.

———. *But for Birmingham: The Local and National Movements in the Civil Rights Struggle.* Chapel Hill: University of North Carolina Press, 1997.

Fahey, David M. *The Black Lodge in White America: "True Reformer" Browne and His Economic Strategy.* Dayton, Ohio: Wright State University, 1994.

Fairbanks, Robert B. *Making Better Citizens: Housing Reform and the Community Development Strategy in Cincinnati, 1890–1960.* Urbana: University of Illinois Press, 1988.

Fallin, Wilson, Jr. "A Shelter in the Storm: The African-American Church in Birmingham, Alabama, 1815–1963." Ph.D. diss., University of Alabama, Tuscaloosa, 1995.

Farley, Reynolds. "The Changing Distribution of Negroes within Metropolitan Areas: the Emergence of Black Suburbs." *American Journal of Sociology* 75, no. 4 (January 1970): 512–29.

Feldman, Glenn. "Research Needs and Opportunities: Race, Class, and New Directions in Southern Labor History." *Alabama Review* 51 (April 1998): 96–106.

Festinger, Leon, Stanley Schacter, and Kurt Back. *Social Pressures in Informal Groups: A Study of Human Factors in Housing.* New York: Harper & Brothers Publishers, 1950.

Fitch, James A. "The Human Side of Large Outputs: Steel and Steel Workers in Six American States: IV, The Birmingham District." *The Survey* (January 6, 1912), 1532–37.

Flynt, Wayne. "The Negro and Alabama Baptists During the Progressive Era." *Journal of the Alabama Academy of Science* 39 (April 1968): 163–67.

———. "Dissent in Zion: Alabama Baptists and Social Issues, 1900–1914." *Journal of Southern History* 35 (November 1969): 523–42.

———. "Religion in the Urban South: The Divided Religious Mind of Birmingham, 1900–1930." *Alabama Review* 30 (April 1977): 108–35.

———. "Alabama." In *Religion in the Southern States: A Historical Study*, edited by Samuel S. Hill, 4–26. Macon, Ga.: Mercer University Press, 1983.

———. "Southern Protestantism and Reform, 1890–1920." *Varieties of Southern Religious Experience*, edited by Samuel S. Hill, 135–55. Baton Rouge: Louisiana State University Press, 1988.

Foner, Jack D. *Blacks and the Military in American History*. New York: Praeger Publishers, 1974.

Foner, Philip S. "Black-Jewish Relations in the Opening Years of the Twentieth Century." *Phylon* 36 (Winter 1975): 359–67.

Forrest, Ray, and Alan Murie. "Transformation through Tenure? The Early Purchasers of Council Houses, 1968–1973." *Journal of Social Policy* 20 (January 1991): 1–25.

Fowlkes, Benjamin P. *Co-operation the Solution of the So-Called Negro Problem*. Birmingham, Ala.: Novelty Book Concern, 1908.

Franklin, Jimmie Lewis. *Back to Birmingham: Richard Arrington, Jr., and His Times*. Tuscaloosa: University of Alabama Press, 1989.

Franklin, John Hope, and Alfred A. Moss, Jr. *From Slavery to Freedom*. 6th ed. New York: McGraw-Hill, 1988.

Fraser, Walter J., Jr., ed. *The Web of Southern Social Relations: Women, Family and Education*. Athens: University of Georgia Press, 1985.

Frazier, E. Franklin. "Occupational Classes Among Negroes in Cities," *American Journal of Sociology* 35 (July 1929–May 1930): 718–38.

———. *Black Bourgeoisie: The Rise of the New Middle Class in the United States*. New York: Free Press, 1957.

———. *The Negro Church in America*. Liverpool: Liverpool University Press, 1964.

———. *The Negro Family in the United States*. 1948. Revised and abridged edition. Chicago: The University of Chicago Press, 1966.

Freedman, Estelle. "Female Institution Building and American Feminism, 1870–1930." *Feminist Studies* 5, no. 3 (Fall 1979): 512–29.

Fried, Joseph P. *Housing Crisis U.S.A.* Baltimore: Kingsport Press, 1971.

Fullerton, Christopher Dean. "Striking Out Jim Crow: The Birmingham Black Barons." Master's thesis, University of Mississippi, 1994.

Furstenberg, Frank F., Jr., et al. "The Origins of the Female-Headed Black Family: The Impact of the Urban Experience." *Journal of Interdisciplinary History* 6, no. 2 (Autumn 1975): 211–34.

Gaines, Kevin K. *Uplifting the Race: Black Leadership, Politics, and Culture in the Twentieth Century*. Chapel Hill: University of North Carolina Press, 1996.

———. "Rethinking Race and Class in African-American Struggles for Equality, 1885–1941." *American Historical Review* 102 (April 1997): 378–87.

Gaston, A. G. *Green Power: The Successful Way of A. G. Gaston*. Troy, Ala.: Troy State University Press, 1968.

Gatewood, Willard B. *Aristocrats of Color: The Black Elite, 1880-1920*. Bloomington: Indiana University Press, 1990.

Genovese, Eugene D. *Roll, Jordan, Roll: The World the Slaves Made*. New York: Vintage Books, 1976.

Giddings, Paula. *When and Where I Enter: The Impact of Black Women on Race and Sex in America*. New York: Bantam Books, 1984.

Gilkes, Cheryl Townsend. " 'Together and in Harness': Women's Traditions in the Sanctified Church." *Signs* 10 (Summer 1985): 678-99.

Gillette, Howard, Jr. "The Evolution of Neighborhood Planning: From the Progressive Era to the 1949 Housing Act." *Journal of Urban History* 9 (August 1983): 421-44.

Glazer, Nathan, and Davis McEntire, eds. *Studies in Housing and Minority Groups*. Berkeley: University of California Press, 1960.

Glenn, Norval D. "Negro Prestige Criteria: A Case Study in the Bases of Prestige." *American Journal of Sociology* 68 (May 1963): 645-57.

Godshalk, David Fort. "In the Wake of Riot: Atlanta's Struggle for Order, 1899-1919." Ph.D. diss., Yale University, 1992.

Goodman, James. *Stories of Scottsboro*. New York: Vintage Books, 1994.

Gordon, Eugene. "The Negro Press." *Annals of the American Academy of Politics and Social Science* 140 (November 1928): 248-56.

Gottlieb, Peter. "Migration and Jobs: The New Black Workers in Pittsburgh, 1916-1930," *The Western Pennsylvania Historical Magazine* 61 (January 1978): 1-15.

———. *Making Their Own Way: Southern Blacks' Migration to Pittsburgh, 1916-30*. Urbana: University of Illinois Press, 1987.

Gowans, Alan. *The Comfortable House*. Cambridge, Mass.: MIT Press, 1986.

Graham, Joseph B. "Current Problems in Alabama." *Annals* 22 (September 1903): 280-83.

Graham, Patricia Albjerg. *Community and Class in American Education, 1865-1918*. New York: John Wiley & Sons, 1974.

Grant, Jacquelyn. "Black Women and the Church." In *All the Women Are White, All the Blacks Are Men, But Some Of Us Are Brave*, edited by Gloria T. Hull et al., 141-52. Old Westbury, N.Y.: Feminist Press, 1982.

Grantham, Dewey W. *Southern Progressivism: The Reconciliation of Progress and Tradition*. Knoxville: University of Tennessee Press, 1983.

Green, S. W., Joseph L. Jones, and E. A. Williams. *History and Manual of the Knights of Pythias*. Nashville: National Baptist Publishing Board, 1917.

Greenwood, Janette Thomas. *Bittersweet Legacy: The Black and White "Better Classes" in Charlotte, 1850-1910*. Chapel Hill: University of North Carolina Press, 1994.

Griffith, Lucille. *Alabama: A Documentary History to 1900*. University, Ala.: University of Alabama Press, 1968.

Grimké, Francis. *The Things of Paramount Importance in the Development of the Negro Race*. Washington, D.C., 1903.

Grimshaw, William H. *Official History of Freemasonry among the Colored People in North America.* 1903. Reprint, New York: Negro Universities Press, 1969.

Gross, Jimmie Frank. "Alabama Politics and the Negro, 1874–1901." Ph.D. diss., University of Georgia, 1969.

Groves, Paul A., and Edward K. Muller. "The Evolution of Black Residential Areas in Late Nineteenth Century Cities." *Journal of Historical Geography* 1, no. 2 (April 1975): 169–91.

Gutman, Herbert G. "Persistent Myths About the Afro-American Family." *Journal of Interdisciplinary History* 6, no. 2 (August 1975): 181–210.

——. *The Black Family in Slavery and Freedom, 1750–1925.* New York: Random House, 1976.

Guy-Sheftall, Beverly. *Daughters of Sorrow: Attitudes Toward Black Women, 1880–1920.* Brooklyn, N.Y.: Carlson Publishing, 1990.

Hackney, Sheldon. *Populism to Progressivism in Alabama.* Princeton, N.J.: Princeton University Press, 1969.

Haeberle, Steven H. *Planting the Grassroots: Structuring Citizen Participation.* New York: Praeger, 1989.

Hair, William Ivy. *Carnival of Fury: Robert Charles and the New Orleans Race Riot of 1900.* Baton Rouge: Louisiana State University Press, 1976.

Halbert, Blanche, ed. *The Better Homes Manual.* Chicago: University of Chicago Press, 1931.

Hamilton, Tulia K. B. "The National Association of Colored Women, 1896–1920." Ph.D. diss., Emory University, 1978.

Hamlin, Christopher M. *Behind the Stained Glass: A History of the Sixteenth Street Baptist Church.* Birmingham, Ala.: Crane Hill Publishers, 1998.

Hanchett, Thomas Walter. "Sorting Out the New South City: Charlotte and Its Neighborhoods." Ph.D. diss., Chapel Hill: University of North Carolina, 1993.

Handlin, David P. *The American Home: Architecture and Society, 1815–1915.* Boston: Little, Brown, 1979.

Handlin, Oscar. *The Newcomers: Negroes and Puerto Ricans in a Changing Metropolis.* Garden City, N.Y.: Harvard University Press, 1962.

Hannerz, Ulf. *Soulside: Inquiries into Ghetto Culture and Community.* New York: Columbia University Press, 1969.

Hareven, Tamara K., ed. *Anonymous Americans: Explorations in Nineteenth-Century Social History.* Englewood Cliffs, N.J.: Prentice-Hall, 1971.

Harlan, Louis R. *Booker T. Washington: The Making of a Black Leader, 1856–1901.* London: Oxford University Press, 1972.

——. ed. *The Booker T. Washington Papers.* 14 vols. Urbana: University of Illinois Press, 1989.

Harley, Sharon. "For the Good of Family and Race: Gender, Work, and Domestic Roles in the Black Community, 1880–1930." In *Black Women in America: Social Science Perspectives,* edited by Micheline R. Malson, Elisabeth Mudimbe-Boyi, Jean F. O'Barr, and Mary Wyer, 159–72. Chicago: University of Chicago Press, 1990.

Harley, Sharon, and Rosalyn Terborg-Penn, eds. *The Afro-American Woman:*

Struggles and Images. Port Washington, N.Y.: National University Publications, Kennikat Press, 1978.

Harris, Abram. *The Negro As Capitalist: A Study of Banking and Business Among American Negroes.* Gloucester, Mass.: Peter Smith, 1968.

Harris, Carl V. "Reforms in Government Control of Negroes in Birmingham, Alabama, 1890–1920." *Journal of Southern History* 38 (November 1972): 567–600.

———. "Annexation Struggles and Political Power in Birmingham, 1890–1910." *Alabama Review* 27 (July 1974): 163–84.

———. *Political Power in Birmingham, 1871–1921.* Knoxville: University of Tennessee Press, 1977.

———. "Stability and Change in Discrimination Against Black Public Schools: Birmingham, Alabama, 1871–1931." *Journal of Southern History* 51 (August 1985): 375–416.

Harris, David Alan. "Racists and Reformers: A Study of Progressivism in Alabama, 1896–1911." Ph.D. diss., University of North Carolina, Chapel Hill, 1967.

Harris, Richard. "Working-Class Home Ownership in the American Metropolis." *Journal of Urban History* 13 (November 1990): 26–69.

———. "Self-Building in the Urban Housing Market." *Economic Geography* 67 (January 1991): 1–21.

Harris, Richard, and Chris Hammett. "The Myth of the Promised Land: The Social Diffusion of Home Ownership in Britain and North America." *Annals of the Association of American Geographers* 77 (1987): 173–90.

Hauser, Philip M. "Demographic Factors in the Integration of the Negro," *Daedalus* 94 (Fall 1965): 847–77.

Hawkins, Mason A. "Colored High Schools," *Crisis* 2, no. 2 (June 1911): 73–5.

Hawks, Joanne V., and Sheila L. Skemp, eds. *Sex, Race, and the Role of Women in the South.* Jackson: University of Mississippi Press, 1983.

Haynes, George Edmund. "Conditions Among Negroes in the Cities." *The Annals of the American Academy* 49 (September 1913): 109–12.

———. "The Church and Negro Progress." *Annals of the American Academy of Politics and Social Science* 140 (November 1928): 264–71.

Hemphill, Paul. *Leaving Birmingham: Notes of a Native Son.* New York: Viking Penguin, 1993.

Henderson, Alexa Benson. *Atlanta Life Insurance Company: Guardian of Black Economic Dignity.* Tuscaloosa: University of Alabama Press, 1990.

Henri, Florette. *Black Migration: Movement North, 1900–1920.* Garden City, N.Y.: Anchor Press, 1975.

Hertzberg, Steven. *Strangers Within the Gate City: The Jews of Atlanta, 1845–1915.* Philadelphia: Jewish Publication Society of America, 1978.

Higginbotham, Evelyn Brooks. "African-American Women's History and the Metalanguage of Race." *Signs* 17 (Winter 1992): 251–74.

———. *Righteous Discontent: The Women's Movement in the Black Baptist Church, 1880–1920.* Cambridge: Harvard University Press, 1993.

Higham, John, ed. *Ethnic Leadership in America.* Baltimore: Johns Hopkins University Press, 1978.

Hill, Ruth. "Lifting As We Climb: Black Women's Organizations, 1890–1930." *Radcliffe Quarterly* 70, no. 1 (March 1984): 24–26.

Hill, Samuel S., ed. *Religion in the Southern States: A Historical Study.* Macon, Ga.: Mercer University Press, 1983.

——, ed. *Varieties of Southern Religious Experience.* Baton Rouge: Louisiana State University Press, 1988.

Hiller, E. T. "The Community as a Social Group." *American Sociological Review* 6 (October 1941): 189–202.

Hillery, George A., Jr. "Definitions of Community: Areas of Agreement." *Rural Sociology* 20 (June 1955): 111–23.

Hine, Darlene Clark. *The State of Afro-American History: Past, Present, and Future.* Baton Rouge: Louisiana State University Press, 1986.

Hines, Darlene Clark. "The Housewives' League of Detroit: Black Women and Economic Nationalism." In *Visible Women: New Essays on American Activism,* edited by Nancy A. Hewitt and Suzanne Lebsock, 221–41. Urbana: University of Illinois Press, 1993.

Historic Sites of Jefferson County, Alabama. Prepared for the Jefferson County Historic Commission by Carolyn Green. Birmingham: Gray Printing Co., 1976. Reprint, Birmingham: Loury Printing, 1985.

"The History of Parker High School: From Its Beginning in 1900 to 1960." Birmingham Board of Education, May 1960.

hooks, bell. *Ain't I a Woman: Black Women and Feminism.* Boston: South End Press, 1981.

Hornaday, John Randolph. *The Book of Birmingham.* New York: Dodd, Mead, 1921.

Howard-Pitney, David. "Calvin Chase's Washington Bee and Black Middle-Class Ideology, 1882–1900." *Journalism Quarterly* 63 (Spring 1986): 89–97.

"How to Keep Women at Home." *Colored American Magazine* 14, no. 1 (January 1908): 7–8.

Howze, Henry R. "A Friend's Tribute to and a Short History of the Steiner Family and The Steiner Bank." Unpublished transcript. September 20, 1963.

Hudson, Alvin W., and Harold E. Cox. *Street Railways of Birmingham.* Forty Fort, Pa: Harold E. Cox, 1976.

Hull, Gloria T., Patricia Bell Scott, and Barbara Smith. *All the Women Are White, All the Blacks Are Men, but Some of Us Are Brave.* Old Westbury, N.Y.: Feminist Press, 1982.

Hunter, Andrea G. "Making a Way: Strategies of Southern Urban African-American Families, 1900 and 1936." *Journal of Family History* 18, no. 3 (Summer 1993): 231–48.

Hunton, Addie Waits. "The Southern Federation of Colored Women." *Voice of the Negro* (December 1905): 850–52.

Ingham, John N. *Biographical Dictionary of American Business Leaders.* Westport, Conn.: Greenwood Press, 1983.

——. *Making Iron and Steel: Independent Mills in Pittsburgh, 1820–1920.* Columbus: Ohio State Press, 1991.

——. "African-American Business Leaders in the South—1880–1945: Business Success, Community Leadership and Racial Protest." Paper presented at the Business History Conference, Harvard Business School, March 20, 1993.

——. "African-American Business in the South, 1880–1945." *Business and Economic History* 22, no. 1 (Fall 1993): 1–11.

——. "Pride, Prejudice and Profits: African-American Business in Ten Southern Cities, 1880–1929." Presented at the Seminar Series, Hagley Museum, March 19, 1994.

——. "Pride, Prejudice and Profits: African-American Business in the South, 1880–1933." Presented at York University, Toronto, February 1995.

Ingham, John N., and Lynne B. Feldman. *African-American Business Leaders: A Biographical Dictionary.* Westport, Conn.: Greenwood Press, 1994.

Jackson, Anthony. *A Place Called Home: A History of Low-Cost Housing in Manhattan.* Cambridge: MIT Press, 1977.

Jackson, James A. "Fraternal Societies and Race Progress." *Crisis* 45 (1938).

Jackson, Kenneth T. *The Ku Klux Klan in the City, 1915–1930.* New York: Oxford University Press, 1967.

——. *Crabgrass Frontier: The Suburbanization of the United States.* New York: Oxford University Press, 1985.

Jaynes, Gerald David, and Robin M. Williams, Jr., eds. *A Common Destiny: Blacks and American Society.* Washington, D.C.: National Academy Press, 1989.

Johnson, Charles S. "The Changing Economic Status of the Negro." *Annals of the American Academy of Politics and Social Science* 140 (November 1928): 128–37.

——. *Negro Housing.* Report of the Committee on Negro Housing, The President's Conference on Home Building and Home Ownership, Washington, D.C., 1932.

——. *Shadow of the Plantation.* Chicago: University of Chicago Press, 1934.

——. *Growing Up in the Black Belt: Negro Youth in the Rural South.* 1941. Reprint, New York: Schocken Books, 1967.

Johnson, Daniel Milo. "Black Return Migration to a Southern Metropolitan Community: Birmingham, Alabama." Ph.D. diss., University of Missouri, Columbia, 1973.

Jones, Allen Woodrow. "Alabama." In *The Black Press in the South, 1865–1979*, edited by Henry Lewis Suggs, 23–61. Westport, Conn.: Greenwood Press, 1983.

Jones, Beverly Washington. *Quest for Equality: The Life and Writing of Mary Eliza Church Terrell, 1863–1954.* Brooklyn, N.Y.: Carlson Publishing, 1990.

Jones, Jacqueline. *Labor of Love, Labor of Sorrow: Black Women, Work and the Family, from Slavery to the Present.* New York: Vintage Books, 1985.

Jones, Maxine D., and Joe M. Richardson. *Talladega College: The First Century.* Tuscaloosa: University of Alabama Press, 1990.

Jones, Terry. "Attitude of Alabama Baptists." Master's thesis, Samford University, 1968.

Jordan, Weymouth T. *Ante-Bellum Alabama, Town and County.* 1957. Reprint, Tuscaloosa: University of Alabama Press, 1986.

Kaganoff, Nathan M., and Melvin I. Urofsky. *"Turn to the South"*: *Essays on Southern Jewry*. Charlottesville: University Press of Virginia for the American Jewish Historical Society, Waltham, Mass., 1979.

Katz, Michael B., ed. *Education in American History: Readings on the Social Issues*. New York: Praeger Publishers, 1973.

Katzman, David M. *Before the Ghetto: Black Detroit in the Nineteenth Century*. Urbana: University of Illinois Press, 1973.

———. *Seven Days a Week: Women and Domestic Service*. New York: Oxford University Press, 1978.

Keller, Suzanne. *The Urban Neighborhood: A Sociological Perspective*. New York: Random House, 1968.

Kelley, Robin D. G. *Hammer and Hoe: Alabama Communists during the Great Depression*. Chapel Hill: University of North Carolina Press, 1990.

———. *Race Rebels: Culture, Politics, and the Black Working Class*. New York: Free Press, 1994.

Kellogg, John. "Negro Urban Clusters in the Postbellum South." *Geographical Review* 7 (July 1977): 310–21.

———. "The Evolution of Black Residence Areas in Lexington, Ky., 1865–1887." *Journal of Southern History* 48 (February 1982): 21–52.

King, Charles E. "The Process of Social Stratification Among an Urban Southern Minority Population." *Social Forces* 31 (May 1953): 352–55.

King, Jere C., Jr. "The Formation of Greater Birmingham." Master's thesis, University of Alabama, 1936.

Kirby, Jack Temple. *Darkness at the Dawning: Race and Reform in the Progressive South*. Philadelphia: Lippincott, 1972.

Kirk, Carolyn T., and Gordon K. Kirk. "The Impact of the City on Home Ownership." *Journal of Urban History* 7 (August 1981): 471–98.

Kleinberg, S. J. *The Shadow of the Mills: Working-Class Families in Pittsburgh, 1870–1907*. Pittsburgh: University of Pittsburgh Press, 1989.

Knight, Charles Louis. *Negro Housing in Certain Virginia Cities*. Publications of the University of Virginia Phelps-Stokes Fellowship Papers No. 8. Richmond: William Byrd Press, 1927.

Knowles, Morris. "Water and Waste: The Sanitary Problems of a Modern Industrial District." *The Survey* 27 (January 6, 1912): 1485–1500.

Kohn, Sylvia Blascoer. *By Reason of Strength: The Story of Temple Emanu-El's Seventy Years, 1882–1952*. Birmingham, Ala.: Temple Emanu-El, 1952.

Kolchin, Peter. *First Freedom: The Responses of Alabama's Blacks to Emancipation and Reconstruction*. Westport, Conn.: Greenwood Press, 1972.

Kramer, John, ed. *North American Suburbs: Politics, Diversity, and Change*. Berkeley: The Glendaressary Press, 1972.

Kremer, Gary R. "The World of Make-Believe: James Milton Turner and Black Masonry." *Missouri Historical Review* 74, no. 1 (October 1979–July 1980): 50–71.

Kronus, Sidney. *The Black Middle-Class*. Merrill Sociology Series. Columbus, Ohio: Merrill, 1971.

Kusmer, Kenneth L. *A Ghetto Takes Shape: Black Cleveland, 1870–1930*. Urbana: University of Illinois Press, 1976.

——. "The Black Urban Experience in American History." In *The State of Afro-American History: Past, Present, and Future,* edited by Darlene Clark Hine, 91–122. Baton Rouge: Louisiana State University Press, 1986.

Kuyk, Betty. "The African Derivation of Black Fraternal Orders in the United States" *Comparative Studies in Society and History* 25 (October 1983): 559–92.

Kwolek-Folland, Angel. "The African American Financial Industries: Issues of Class, Race, and Gender in the Early 20th Century." Paper presented at the Business History Conference, Williamsburg, Virginia, March 11–13, 1994.

LaMonte, Edward Shannon. *George B. Ward: Birmingham's Urban Statesman.* Birmingham, Ala.: Birmingham Public Library, 1974.

——. "The Mercy Home and Private Charity in Early Birmingham." *Journal of the Birmingham Historical Society* 5, no. 4 (July 1978): 3–15.

——. *Politics and Welfare in Birmingham, 1900–1975.* Tuscaloosa: University of Alabama Press, 1995.

LaMonte, Ruth Bradbury. "The Origins of an Urban School System: Birmingham, 1873–1900." *Journal of the Birmingham Historical Society* 5, no. 2 (July 1977): 5–17.

Landry, Bart. *The New Black Middle-Class.* Berkeley: University of California Press, 1987.

Laney, Lucy C. "The Burden of the Educated Colored Woman." *Southern Workman* 28 (September 1899): 341–44.

Lanier, Martha Louise. "Alabama Methodists and Social Issues, 1900–1914." Master's thesis, Samford University, 1969.

Lebsock, Suzanne. "Woman Suffrage and White Supremacy: A Virginia Case Study." In *Women's America: Refocusing the Past,* 4th edition, edited by Linda K. Kerber and Jane Sherron De Hart, 320–34. New York: Oxford University Press, 1995.

Lee, M. E. "The Home-Maker." *AME Church Review* (July 1891): 63–66.

Leighton, George R. "Birmingham, Alabama: The City of Perpetual Promise." *Harper's Magazine,* August 1937.

——. *Five Cities: The Story of Their Youth and Old Age.* New York: Harper & Brothers Publishers, 1939.

Lerner, Gerda, ed. "Early Community Work of Black Club Women." *Journal of Negro History* 59 (April 1974): 158–67.

——, ed. *Black Women in White America: A Documentary History.* New York: Vintage Books, 1973.

Lerner, Jack Leonard. "A Monument to Shame: The Convict Lease System in Alabama." Master's thesis, Samford University, 1969.

Letwin, Daniel. "Race, Class, and Industrialization in the New South: Black and White Coal Miners in the Birmingham District of Alabama, 1878–1897." Ph.D. diss., Yale University, 1991.

——. "Interracial Unionism, Gender, and 'Social Equality' in the Alabama Coalfields, 1878–1908." *Journal of Southern History* 61 (August 1995): 519–54.

Levine, Lawrence W. *Black Culture and Black Consciousness: Afro-American*

Folk Thought from Slavery to Freedom. Oxford: Oxford University Press, 1977.

Lewis, Earl. "The Beginnings of a Renaissance: Black Migration, the Industrial Order, and the Search for Power." *Journal of Urban History* 17 (May 1991): 296–302.

———. *In Their Own Interests: Race, Class, and Power in Twentieth-Century Norfolk, Virginia*. Berkeley: University of California Press, 1991.

Lewis, Hylan. *The Blackways of Kent*. New Haven, Conn.: College and University Press, 1955.

Lewis, W. David. *Sloss Furnaces and the Rise of the Birmingham District: An Industrial Epic*. Tuscaloosa: University of Alabama Press, 1994.

Light, Ivan H. *Ethnic Enterprise in America: Business and Welfare among Chinese, Japanese, and Blacks*. Berkeley: University of California Press, 1972.

"Like It Ain't Never Passed: Remembering Life in Sloss Quarters, 1930s–1950s." Sloss Furnaces Association and the Oral History Project of the University of Alabama at Birmingham, April 12, 1985, p. 16.

Lindsay, Arnett B. "The Negro in Banking." *Journal of Negro History* 14 (April 29): 156–201.

Litwack, Leon F. *Been in the Storm So Long: The Aftermath of Slavery*. New York: Random House, 1979.

———. *Trouble in Mind: Black Southerners in the Age of Jim Crow*. New York: Alfred A. Knopf, 1998.

Logan, Adella Hunt. "Colored Women as Voters." *Crisis* 4 (September 1912): 242–43.

Logan, John R., and Glenna D. Spitze. "Family Neighbors." *American Journal of Sociology* 100, no. 2 (September 1994): 453–76.

Luria, Daniel D. "Wealth, Capital, and Power: The Social Meaning of Home Ownership." *Journal of Interdisciplinary History* 7 (Autumn 1976): 261–82.

Mays, Benjamin Elijah, and Joseph William Nicholson. *The Negro's Church*. Institute of Social and Religious Research, 1933. Reprint, New York: Negro Universities Press, 1969.

McClymer, John E. "Late Nineteenth-Century American Working-Class Living Standards." *Journal of Interdisciplinary History* 17, no. 2 (Autumn 1986): 379–98.

McCrae, Lee. "Birmingham's Probation Plan for the Little Negro." *Charities and Commons* 19 (March 14, 1908): 1729.

McDaniel, Antonio. "Historical Racial Differences in Living Arrangements of Children." *Journal of Family History* 19, no. 1 (1994): 57–77.

McDavid, Mittie Owen. "The Smith Family of Smithfield," Birmingham, October 1944, unpublished transcript, Hill-Ferguson Collection, Tutwiler Collection of Southern History and Literature, Department of Archives and Manuscripts, Birmingham Public Library, Birmingham, Ala.

———. *John Smith, Esquire, His Ancestors and His Descendants: A Story of the Pioneers*. Birmingham, Ala.: Birmingham Publishing Co., 1948.

McGrath, W. M. "Conservation of Health." *The Survey* 27 (January 6, 1912): 1508–14.

McKelway, A. J. "Conservation of Childhood." *The Survey* 27 (January 6, 1912): 1515–26.

McKiven, Henry M., Jr. *Iron and Steel: Class, Race, and Community in Birmingham, Alabama, 1875–1920.* Chapel Hill: University of North Carolina Press, 1995.

McMillan, Malcolm Cook. *Constitutional Development in Alabama, 1798–1901: A Study in Politics, the Negro, and Sectionalism.* 1955. Reprint, Spartanburg, S.C.: Reprint Co., 1978.

McMillen, Neil R. *Dark Journey: Black Mississippians in the Age of Jim Crow.* Urbana: University of Illinois Press, 1989.

Meier, August. "Vogue of Industrial Education." *Mid-West Journal* 7 (Fall 1955): 241–66.

———. "Negro Class Structure and Ideology in the Age of Booker T. Washington." *Phylon* 23 (Fall 1962): 258–66.

———. *Negro Thought in America, 1880–1915.* Ann Arbor: University of Michigan Press, 1963.

Meier, August, and David Lewis. "History of the Negro Upper Class in Atlanta, Georgia, 1890–1958." *Journal of Negro Education* 28 (Spring 1958): 128–39.

Meier, August, and Elliott Rudwick. "Attitudes of Negro Leaders Toward the American Labor Movement from the Civil War to World War I." In *The Negro and the American Labor Movement,* edited by Julius Jacobson. Garden City, N.Y.: Anchor Books, 1968.

———. "The Boycott Movement Against Jim Crow Streetcars in the South, 1900–1906." *Journal of American History* 55 (March 1969): 756–75.

Menzer, Mitch, and Mike Williams. "Images of Work: Birmingham, 1894–1937." *Journal of Birmingham Historic Society* 6 (July 1980): 10–36.

Michelson, William. *Man and His Urban Environment.* Reading, Mass.: Addison-Wesley Publishing, 1970.

Miller, William T. "Library Service for Negroes in the New South: Birmingham, Alabama, 1871–1918." *Alabama Librarian* 27 (November/December 1975): 6–8.

Miller, Zane L. "Urban Blacks in the South, 1865–1920: An Analysis of Some Quantitative Data on Richmond, Savannah, New Orleans, Louisville, and Birmingham." In *The New Urban History: Quantitative Explorations by American Historians,* edited by Leo F. Schnore, 184–204. Princeton, N.J.: Princeton University Press, 1975.

Mitchell, J. Paul, ed. *Federal Housing Policy & Programs: Past and Present.* New Brunswick, N.J.: Center for Urban Policy Research, 1985.

Mixon, Gregory. "Henry McNeal Turner versus the Tuskegee Machine: Black Leadership in the Nineteenth Century." *Journal of Negro History* 79 (Fall 1994): 363–80.

Modell, John, and Tamara K. Hareven. "Urbanization and the Malleable Household: An Examination of Boarding and Lodging in American Families." *Journal of Marriage and the Family* 35 (1973): 467–79.

Montgomery, William E. *Under Their Own Vine and Fig Tree. The African-American Church in the South, 1865–1900.* Baton Rouge: Louisiana State University Press, 1993.

Moore, Albert Burton. *History of Alabama*. Tuscaloosa: Alabama Book Store, 1951.

Moore, Geraldine. *Behind the Ebony Mask*. Birmingham: Southern University Press, 1961.

———. "Editorial." *The Ferrous Journal* 8, no. 6 (March 1976).

Moorman, J. H., and E. L. Barrett, eds. *Leaders of the Colored Race In Alabama*. Mobile, Ala.: News Publishing, 1928.

Morgan, S. Philip, Antonio McDaniel, Andrew T. Miller, and Samuel H. Preston. "Racial Differences in Household and Family Structure at the Turn of the Century. *American Journal of Sociology* 98 (January 1993): 798–828.

Moss, Florence Hawkins Wood. *Building Birmingham and Jefferson County*. Birmingham, Ala.: Birmingham Printing Co., 1947.

Mossell, N. E. *The Work of the Afro-American Woman*. New York: Oxford University Press, 1988.

Moton, Robert R. "Signs of Grocery Cooperation." *Southern Workman* 43 (October 1914).

Moton, R. R. "Organized Negro Effort for Racial Progress." *Annals of the American Academy of Politics and Social Science* 140 (November 1928): 257–63.

Munger, Rose McDavid, comp. *Pioneer Scrapbook*. Birmingham, Ala.: Birmingham Publishing Co., 1967.

Muraskin, William A. *Middle-Class Blacks in a White Society: Prince Hall Freemasonry in America*. Berkeley: University of California Press, 1975.

Myrdal, Gunnar. *An American Dilemma: Volume 2, The Negro Social Structure*. New York: Harper & Row, 1944.

National Housing Association. *Housing Problems in America: Proceedings of the Second National Conference on Housing, Philadelphia, December 4, 5, 6, 1912*. Cambridge: Harvard University Press, 1913.

National Negro Business League. *Report of the First Annual Convention, 1900*. Boston.

National Negro Business League. *Report of the Sixth Annual Convention, 1905*. New York City.

National Negro Business League. *Report of the Seventh Annual Convention, 1906*. Atlanta.

National Negro Business League. *Report of the Eighth Annual Convention, 1907*. Topeka.

National Negro Business League. *Report of the Eleventh Annual Convention, 1910*, Nashville.

National Negro Business League. *Report of the Thirteenth Annual Convention, 1912*. Chicago.

National Negro Business League. *Report of the Fourteenth Annual Convention, 1913*. Philadelphia.

"Negro Class Distinctions." *Southern Workman* 27 (October 1899): 372.

"Negro Womanhood Defended." *Voice of the Negro* 1 (July 1904): 280–81.

Neverdon-Morton, Cynthia. *Afro-American Women of the South and the Advancement of the Race, 1895–1925*. Knoxville: University of Tennessee Press, 1989.

Newbill, Robert S. "A Study of the Growth of the City of Birmingham's Corporate Boundaries from 1871 to the present." Unpublished manuscript. April 1980. Department of Archives and Manuscripts, Birmingham Public Library, Birmingham, Ala.

Newbold, N. C. "Common Schools for Negroes in the South." *Annals of the American Academy of Politics and Social Science* 140 (November 1928): 209–23.

Newfield, Morris. "The History of the Jews of Birmingham." *Reform Advocate,* November 4, 1911, 5–33.

Newman, Debra Lynn. "Black Women Workers in the Twentieth Century." *Sage,* 3 (Spring 1986): 10–15.

Newstelle, George M. "A Negro Business League at Work." *Southern Workman* 44 no. 1 (January 1915): 43–47.

Nieman, Donald G., ed. *Church and Community Among Black Southerners, 1865–1900.* New York: Garland Publishing, 1994.

Nisbet, Robert A. *The Sociological Tradition.* New York: Basic Books, 1966.

Norrell, Robert J. *Reaping the Whirlwind: The Civil Rights Movement in Tuskegee.* New York: Alfred A. Knopf, 1985.

——. "Caste in Steel: Jim Crow Careers in Birmingham, Alabama." *Journal of American History* 73 (December 1986): 669–94.

——. "The Other Side: The Story of Birmingham's Black Community." [1981?] Birmingfind files. Department of Archives and Manuscripts, Birmingham Public Library, Birmingham, Ala.

Northrup, Herbert R. "The Negro and Unionism in the Birmingham, Ala., Iron and Steel Industry." *Southern Economic Journal* 10 (July 1943): 27–40.

Norton, Mary Beth, ed. *Major Problems in American Women's History.* Lexington, Mass.: D. C. Heath, 1989.

Odum, Howard W. "Social and Mental Traits of the Negro." Ph.D. diss., Columbia University, New York, 1910.

Oliver, Leavy W. "Zoning Ordinances in Relation to Segregated Negro Housing in Birmingham, Alabama." Master's thesis, Department of Government, Indiana State University, 1951.

Owen, Thomas McAdory. *History of Alabama and Dictionary of Alabama Biography.* 4 vols. 1921. Reprint. Spartanburg, S.C.: Reprint Co., 1978.

Pace, Harry Herbert. "The Case of the Negro Elks." *The Voice* 4 (June 1907): 253–55.

——. "The Business of Banking Among Negroes." *Crisis* 33, no. 4 (February 1927): 184–88.

Painter, Nell I. *The Narrative of Hosea Hudson.* Cambridge, Mass.: Harvard University Press, 1979.

Palmer, Edward Niles. "Negro Secret Societies." *Social Forces* 23 (December 1944): 207–12.

Pannell, Anne Gary, and Dorothea E. Wyatt. *Julia S. Tutwiler and Social Progress in Alabama.* University, Ala.: University of Alabama Press, 1961.

Parker, Arthur Harold. *A Dream that Came True.* Birmingham, Ala.: Printing Department of Industrial High School, 1932–33.

Parris, Guichard, and Lester Brooks. *Blacks in the City: A History of the National Urban League.* Boston: Little, Brown, 1971.

Patton, June O. "The Black Community of Augusta and the Struggle for Ware High School, 1880–1899." In *New Perspectives on Black Educational History,* edited by V. P. Franklin and James D. Anderson, 45–59. Boston: G. K. Hall, 1978.

Payne, John Howard. *Clari, The Maid of Milan,* London: T. H. Lacy, 1823.

Perin, Constance. *Everything in Its Place: Social Order and Land Use in America.* Princeton: Princeton University Press, 1977.

Pettiford, W. R. "How to Help the Negro to Help Himself." In *Twentieth-Century Negro Literature: Or A Cyclopedia of Thought,* edited by D. W. Culp, 468–72. Atlanta: J. L. Nichols, 1902.

———. "The Importance of Business to the Negro." *Hampton Negro Conference* 7 (July 1903): 38–40.

Pierce, Joseph A. *Negro Business and Business Education.* New York: Harper & Brothers Publishers, 1947.

Porter, Michael Leroy. "Black Atlanta: An Interdisciplinary Study of Blacks on the East Side of Atlanta, 1890–1930." Ph.D. diss., Emory University, 1974.

Pratt, Geraldine. "Housing Tenure and Social Cleavages in Urban Canada." *Annals of the Association of American Geographers* 76 (1986): 366–80.

Praytor, Robert Earl. "From Concern to Neglect: Alabama Baptists' Religious Relationship to the Negro, 1823–1870." Master's thesis, Samford University, 1971.

Proceedings of the 27th Annual Session of the Colored Missionary Baptists State Convention. Mt. Zion Baptist Church, Anniston, Ala., November 21–25, 1895. Microfilm, in the *Alabama Baptist State Convention Minutes,* Special Collection, Samford University, Birmingham, Ala.

Proceedings of the 29th Annual Session of the Colored Missionary Baptists State Convention, Birmingham, November 18–22, 1896. Microfilm, in the *Alabama Baptist State Convention Minutes,* Special Collection, Samford University, Birmingham, Ala.

Pruitt, Paul M., Jr. "Julia S. Tutwiler." *Alabama Heritage* 22 (Fall 1991): 37–44.

Rabinowitz, Howard N. "Half a Loaf: The Shift from White to Black Teachers in the Negro Schools of the Urban South, 1865–90." *Journal of Southern History* 40 (November 1974): 565–94.

———. *Race Relations in the Urban South, 1865–1890.* Urbana: University of Illinois Press, 1978.

Radford, John P. "Race, Residence, and Ideology: Charleston, South Carolina, in the Mid-Nineteenth Century." *Journal of Historical Geography* 2, no. 4 (October 1976): 329–46.

Ransom, Roger, and Richard Sutch. *One Kind of Freedom: The Economic Consequences of Emancipation.* New York: Cambridge University Press, 1977.

Reiss, Albert J. "The Sociological Study of Communities." *Rural Sociology* 24 (June 1959): 118–30.

Reuse, Ruth Beaumont. *Molton, Allen & Williams: The First One Hundred Years.* Birmingham, Ala.: Birmingham Publishing Co., 1988.

Rice, Roger L. "Residential Segregation by Law, 1910–1917." *Journal of Southern History* 34 (May 1968): 179–99.

Richardson, Clement. "The Nestor of Negro Bankers." *Southern Workman* 43 (November 1914): 605–11.

Richardson, Joe M. *Christian Reconstruction: The American Missionary Association and Southern Blacks, 1861–1890.* Athens: University of Georgia Press, 1986.

Richings, G. F. *Evidences of Progress Among Colored People.* Philadelphia: Geo. S. Ferguson Co., 1897.

Rikard, Marlene Hunt. "An Experiment in Welfare Capitalism: The Health Care Services of the Tennessee Coal, Iron and Railroad Company." Ph.D. diss., University of Alabama, 1983.

——. "A Case Study on Welfare Capitalism and Industrial Communities: The Tennessee Coal, Iron and Railroad Company of Birmingham, Alabama, 1907–1950." Paper presented at the Conference on Steel and Coal Communities in Comparative Perspective, 1900–1990: United States and Germany. Pittsburgh, April 20–22, 1990.

Riley, B. F. *The White Man's Burden.* Chicago: Regan House, 1910. Reprint, New York: Negro Universities Press, 1969.

Rogers, William Warren, et al. *Alabama: The History of a Deep South State.* Tuscaloosa: University of Alabama Press, 1994.

Rose, Harold M. "Social Processes in the City: Race and Urban Residential Choice." Resource paper No. 6, Association of American Geographers, Commission on College Geography, Washington, D.C., 1969.

Rosengarten, Theodore. *All God's Danger: The Life of Nate Shaw.* New York: Vintage Books, 1974.

Ross, J. P. "Notes on Birmingham's Public Utilities." Unpublished manuscript. Birmingham Public Library, Birmingham, Ala.

Ross, Jack C., and Raymond H. Wheeler. *Black Belonging: A Study of the Social Correlates of Work Relations among Negroes.* Westport, Conn.: Greenwood Publishing Corp., 1971.

Rouse, Jacqueline Anne. *Lugenia Burns Hope: Black Southern Reformer.* Athens: University of Georgia Press, 1989.

Ruggles, Steven. "The Origins of the African-American Family Structure." *American Sociological Review* 59 (February 1994): 136–51.

Salamon, Lester M. "Leadership and Modernization: The Emerging Black Political Elite in the American South." *Journal of Politics* 35 (August 1973): 615–46.

Salem, Dorothy. *To Better Our World: Black Women in Organized Reform, 1890–1920.* Brooklyn, N.Y.: Carlson Publishing, 1990.

Scherzer, Kenneth A. *The Unbounded Community: Neighborhood Life and Structure in New York City, 1830–1875.* Durham: Duke University Press, 1992.

Schnore, Leo F., ed. *The New Urban History: Quantitative Explorations by American Historians.* Princeton, N.J.: Princeton University Press, 1975.

Scott, Anne Firor. *The Southern Lady: From Pedestal to Politics 1830–1930.* Chicago: University of Chicago Press, 1970.

———. "Most Invisible of All: Black Women's Voluntary Association." *Journal of Southern History* 56 (February 1990): 3–22.

Scroggins, Raymond. "A Cultural and Religious History of Birmingham, Alabama, 1871–1931." A.B. thesis, Howard College, 1939.

Settle, George T. "Good Reading for Negroes." *Southern Workman* 44, no. 7 (July 1915).

Sharpless, John, and Ray M. Shortridge. "Biased Underenumeration in Census Manuscripts: Methodological Implications." *Journal of Urban History* 1 (August 1975): 409–39.

Sherer, Robert G. *Subordination or Liberation? The Development and Conflicting Theories of Black Education in Nineteenth Century Alabama.* University, Ala.: University of Alabama Press, 1977.

Shifflett, Crandall A. "The Household Composition of Rural Black Families: Louisa County, Virginia, 1880." *Journal of Interdisciplinary History* 6, no. 2 (Autumn 1975): 235–60.

Silver, Christopher. "The Racial Origins of Zoning: Southern Cities 1910–1940." *Planning Perspectives* 6, no. 2 (May 1991): 189–205.

Simmons, William J. *Men of Mark: Eminent, Progressive and Rising.* Cleveland: Rewell Publishing Co., 1887.

Simonsen, Thordis, ed. *You May Plow Here: The Narrative of Sara Brooks.* New York: W. W. Norton, 1986.

Sisk, Glenn N. "Social Aspects of the Alabama Black Belt, 1875–1917." *Mid-America* 37 (January 1955): 31–47.

Skotnes, Andor. " 'Buy Where You Can Work': Boycotting for Jobs in African-American Baltimore, 1933–1934." *Journal of Social History* 27 (Summer 1994): 735–61.

Smith, Robert C., and Richard Seltzer. *Race, Class, and Culture: A Study in Afro-American Mass Opinion.* Albany: State University of New York Press, 1992.

Smith, Timothy. "Native Blacks and Foreign Whites: Varying Responses to Educational Opportunity in America, 1880–1950." *Perspectives in American History* 6 (1972): 309–19.

"Smithfield: An Historic Birmingham Neighborhood." Birmingham Historical Society, 1986. Copy found in the Hill-Ferguson Collection, Department of Archives and Manuscripts, Birmingham Public Library.

Snell, William R. "Fiery Crosses in the Roaring Twenties: Activities of the Revised Klan in Alabama, 1915–1930." *Alabama Review* 23 (October 1970): 256–76.

———. "Masked Men in the Magic City: Activities of the Revised Klan in Birmingham, 1916–1940." *Alabama Historical Quarterly* 34, no. 3–4 (Fall and Winter 1972): 206–27.

———. "The Ku Klux Klan in Jefferson County, Alabama, 1916–1930." Master's thesis, Samford University, 1977.

Sparks, John. "American Negro Reaction to Disenfranchisement, 1901–1904." Master's thesis, Samford University, 1973.

Spear, Allan H. *Black Chicago: The Making of a Negro Ghetto, 1890–1920.* Chicago: University of Chicago Press, 1967.

Spencer, C. A. "Benevolent Black Societies and the Development of Black Insurance Companies in Nineteenth Century Alabama," *Phylon* 46 (September 1985): 251–61.

Spero, Sterling D., and Abram L. Harris. *The Black Worker: The Negro and the Labor Movement.* 1931. Reprint, New York: Atheneum Press, 1968.

Spotswood, James E. *Crossroad to Service: The Birmingham Area Red Cross, 1917–1976.* Birmingham, Ala.: Birmingham Red Cross, 1976.

Stack, Carol. *All Our Kin: Strategies for Survival in a Black Community.* New York: Harper & Row, 1974.

Stein, Judith. "Steelworkers and their Union in Birmingham, Alabama." Paper presented at the Conference on Steel and Coal Communities in Comparative Perspective 1900–1990: United States and Germany. Pittsburgh, April 20–22, 1990.

Sterner, Richard, et al. *The Negro's Share: A Study of Income, Consumption, Housing and Public Assistance.* New York: Harper & Brothers Publishers, 1943.

Straus, Nathan. *Two-Thirds of a Nation.* New York: Alfred A. Knopf, 1952.

Straw, Richard A. "The Collapse of Biracial Unionism: The Alabama Coal Strike of 1908." *Alabama Historical Quarterly* 37 (Summer 1975): 92–114.

———. "This is Not a Strike, It is Simply a Revolution: Birmingham Miners Struggle for Power, 1894–1908." Ph.D. diss., University of Missouri, 1980.

Stuckey, Sterling. *The Ideological Origins of Black Nationalism.* Boston: Beacon Press, 1972.

———. *Slave Culture: Nationalist Theory and the Foundations of Black America.* New York: Oxford University Press, 1987.

Sulzby, James F. *Birmingham Sketches.* Birmingham, Ala.: Birmingham Printing Co., 1945.

Sundstrom, William A. "The Color Line: Racial Norms and Discrimination in Urban Labor Markets, 1910–1950." *Journal of Economic History* 54, no. 2 (June 1994): 382–96.

Sweeney, Charles P. "Bigotry Turns to Murder." *The Nation* 113 (August 31, 1921): 232–33.

Taeuber, Karl E., and Alma F. Taeuber. *Negroes in Cities: Residential Segregation and Neighborhood Change.* Chicago: Aldine Publishing Co., 1965.

Tarry, Ellen. *The Third Door: The Autobiography of an American Negro Woman.* New York: D. McKay Co., 1955. Reprint, Tuscaloosa: University of Alabama Press, 1992.

Taylor, Arnold H. *Travail and Triumph: Black Life and Culture in the South Since the Civil War.* Westport, Conn.: Greenwood Press, 1976.

Taylor, Graham Romeyn. "Birmingham's Civic Front." *The Survey* 27 (January 6, 1912): 1464–84.

Taylor, Henry L. "Spatial Organization and the Residential Experience: Black Cincinnati in 1850." *Social Science History* 10, no. 1 (Spring 1986): 45–69.

Teeple, W. F., and N. Davis Smith. *History of Jefferson County and Birmingham, Alabama.* Birmingham: Teeple and Smith, 1887.

Terborg-Penn, Rosalyn. "Discrimination Against Afro-American Women in the Woman's Movement, 1830–1920." In *The Afro-American Woman: Struggles and Images,* edited by Sharon Harley and Rosalyn Terborg-Penn, 17–27. Port Washington, N.Y.: National University Publications, Kennikat Press, 1978.

————. "Black Male Perspectives on the Nineteenth-Century Woman." In *The Afro-American Woman: Struggles and Images,* edited by Sharon Harley and Rosalyn Terborg-Penn, 28–42. Port Washington, N.Y.: National University Publications, Kennikat Press, 1978.

Terrell, Mary Church. "Club Work of Colored Women." *Southern Workman* 30 (August 1901): 435–38.

Thernstrom, Stephan. *Poverty and Progress: Social Mobility in a Nineteenth Century City.* Cambridge: Harvard University Press, 1964.

Thomas, Mary Martha. "The 'New Woman' in Alabama, 1890–1920." *Alabama Review* 43 (July 1990): 163–80.

————, ed. *Stepping Out of the Shadows: Alabama Women, 1819–1990.* Tuscaloosa: University of Alabama Press, 1995.

Thomas, Rebecca. "John J. Eagan and Industrial Democracy at Acipco." *Alabama Review* 43 (October 1990): 270–88.

Thomas, Richard W. *Life for Us Is What We Make It: Building Black Community in Detroit, 1915–1945.* Bloomington: University of Indiana Press, 1992.

Thompson, Daniel C. *The Negro Leadership Class.* Englewood Cliffs, N.J.: Prentice-Hall, 1963.

Tobias, C. H. "The Work of the Young Men's and Young Women's Christian Associations with Negro Youth." *Annals of the American Academy of Politics and Social Science* 140 (November 1928): 283–93.

Trent, William J., Jr. "Development of Negro Life Insurance Enterprises." Master's thesis, University of Pennsylvania, 1932.

Trexler, Harrison A. "Birmingham's Struggle with Commission Government." *National Municipal Review* 14 (November 1925): 662–63.

Trotter, Joe William, Jr. *Black Milwaukee: The Making of an Industrial Proletariat, 1915–1945.* Blacks in the New World series. Urbana: University of Illinois Press, 1985.

————. *Coal, Class, and Color: Blacks in Southern West Virginia, 1913–1932.* Urbana: University of Illinois Press, 1990.

————, ed. *The Great Migration in Historical Perspective: New Dimensions of Race, Class, and Gender.* Bloomington: Indiana University Press, 1991.

Tucker, Susan. "A Complete Bond: Southern Black Domestic Workers and Their White Employers." *Frontiers* 11, no. 3 (1982): 6–13.

Tyler, Elizabeth Ann. *Research in Black History: A Guide to Resources in the Birmingham Public Library.* Birmingham, Ala.: A. H. Cather Publishing Co., 1981.

Valch, John M. "Shotgun Houses." *Natural History* 86 (February 1977): 51–57.

Warner, Sam B., Jr. *Streetcar Suburbs: The Process of Growth in Boston*

1870-1900. Cambridge: Harvard University Press and The M. I. T. Press, 1962.

Warren, Roland L. *Studying Your Community.* New York: Russell Sage Foundation, 1955.

——. *The Community in America.* Chicago: Rand McNally & Co., 1963.

——, ed. *Perspectives on the American Community.* Chicago: Rand McNally & Co., 1966.

Washington, Booker T. *The Future of the American Negro.* Boston: Small, Maynard & Co., 1899, 1902.

——. *The Negro in Business.* 1907. Reprint, Chicago: Afro-American Press, 1969.

Washington, Forrester B. "Recreational Facilities for the Negro." *Annals of the American Academy of Politics and Social Science* 140 (November 1928): 272–82.

Weare, Walter B. *Black Business in the New South: A Social History of the North Carolina Mutual Life Insurance Company.* Urbana: University of Illinois Press, 1973.

Weiner, Jonathan. *Social Origins of the New South: Alabama, 1860–1885.* Baton Rouge: Louisiana State University Press, 1978.

Weisberger, William. "Fraternalism in America." *Pittsburgh History* (Spring 1993): 39–42.

Weisbord, Robert G., and Arthur Stein. *Bittersweet Encounter: The Afro-American and the American Jew.* Westport, Conn.: Negro Universities Press, 1970.

Wesley, Charles Harris. *History of the Improved Benevolent and Protective Order of Elks of the World, 1898–1954.* Washington, D.C.: Association of the Study of Negro Life and History, 1955.

——. *The History of the National Association of Colored Women's Clubs: A Legacy of Service.* Washington, D.C.: National Association of Colored Women's Clubs, 1984.

White, Deborah Gray. "The Cost of Club Work, the Price of Black Feminism." In *Visible Women: New Essays on American Activism,* edited by Nancy A. Hewitt and Suzanne Lebsock, 247–69. Urbana: University of Illinois Press, 1993.

——. "Private Lives, Public Personae: A Look at Early Twentieth-Century African-American Clubwomen." In *Talking Gender: Public Images, Personal Journeys, and Political Critiques,* edited by Nancy Hewitt, Jean O'Barr, and Nancy Rosebaugh, 106–23. Chapel Hill: University of North Carolina Press, 1996.

White, John. *Black Leadership in America: From Booker T. Washington to Jesse Jackson.* 2nd edition. London: Longman, 1985.

White, Marjorie Longenecker. *The Birmingham District: An Industrial History and Guide.* Birmingham, Ala.: Birmingham Historical Society, 1981.

——. "Images of Smithfield." *Journal of the Birmingham Historical Society* 9 (December 1985).

White, Shane. " 'It Was a Proud Day': African Americans, Festivals, and Parades in the North, 1741–1834." *Journal of American History* 81, no. 1 (June 1994): 13–50.

Wiebe, Robert. *The Segmented Society*. New York: Oxford University Press, 1975.

Wiener, Jonathan M. *Social Origins of the New South, Alabama 1860–1885*. Baton Rouge: Louisiana State University Press, 1978.

Wiese, Andrew. "Places of Our Own: Suburban Black Towns Before 1960." *Journal of Urban History* 19 (May 1993): 30–54.

Williams, Charles, Jr., and Hilda J. B. Williams. "Mutual Aid Societies and Economic Development: Survival Efforts." In *African Americans in the South: Issues of Race, Class, and Gender,* edited by Hans A. Baer and Yvonne Jones. Southern Anthropological Society Proceedings, no. 25. Athens: University of Georgia Press, 1992.

Williams, Emily H. "The National Association of Colored Women." *Southern Workman* 43 (September 1914): 481–83.

Williams, Fanny Barrier. "The Club Movement among the Colored Women." *Voice of the Negro* 1 (1904): 99–100.

Williams, Loretta J. *Black Freemasonry and Middle-Class Realities*. Columbia: University of Missouri Press, 1980.

Wilson, Bobby M. "Black Housing Opportunities in Birmingham, Alabama." *Southeastern Geographer* 17 (May 1977): 49–57.

———. "Racial Segregation Trends in Birmingham." *Southeastern Geographer* 25 (May 1985): 30–43.

Wilson, Franklin. D. "Ecology of a Black Business District." *Review of Black Political Economy* 4 (Summer 1975): 353–75.

———. "The Ecology of a Black Business District: Sociological and Historical Analysis," Institute for Research on Poverty Discussion Papers, University of Wisconsin, Madison, November 1975.

Wingerd, Mary Lethert. "Rethinking Paternalism: Power and Parochialism in a Southern Mill Village." *Journal of American History* 83 (December 1996): 872–902.

Wood, Edith Elmer. *Recent Trends in American Housing*. New York: Macmillan, 1931.

Woodson, Carter G. "Insurance Business Among Negroes." *Journal of Negro History* 14 (April 1929): 202–26.

Woodward, C. Vann. *Origins of the New South, 1877–1913*. Baton Rouge: Louisiana State University Press, 1951.

———. *The Strange Career of Jim Crow*. 2nd rev. edition. New York: Oxford University Press, 1966.

Woofter, T. J. *Negro Problems in Cities*. New York: Doubleday Doran, 1928.

Work, Monroe N. "The Negro in Business and the Professions." *Annals of the American Academy of Politics and Social Science* 140 (November 1928): 138–44.

Worthman, Paul. "Black Workers and Labor Unions in Birmingham, Alabama, 1897–1904." *Labor History* 10 (Summer 1969): 375–407.

———. "Working Class Mobility in Birmingham, Alabama, 1880–1914." In *Anonymous Americans: Explorations in Nineteenth Century Social His-*

tory, edited by Tamara K. Hareven. Englewood Cliffs, N.J.: Prentice-Hall, 1971.

Wright, Gavin. *Old South, New South: Revolutions in the Southern Economy Since the Civil War.* New York: Basic Books, 1986.

Wright, George C. *Life Behind a Veil: Blacks in Louisville, Kentucky, 1865–1930.* Baton Rouge: Louisiana State University Press, 1985.

Wright, Gwendolyn. *Building the Dream: A Social History of Housing in America.* New York: Pantheon Books, 1981.

Zimmerman, Jane. "The Penal Reform Movement in the South During the Progressive Era, 1890–1917." *Journal of Southern History* 17 (November 1951): 462–92.

Zunz, Olivier. *The Changing Face of Inequality: Urbanization, Industrial Development, and Immigrants in Detroit, 1880–1920.* Chicago: University of Chicago Press, 1982.

Index

About the Author

Lynne B. Feldman is an independent scholar living in Toronto. She was educated at the University of Toronto and at Florida State University. Her other works include *African-American Business Leaders: A Biographical Dictionary* (1994), and *Contemporary American Business Leaders: A Biographical Dictionary* (1990), both co-written with John N. Ingham, as well as entries in *American National Biography* (forthcoming), *Encyclopedia of African American Associations* (forthcoming), and *Encyclopedia of World Biography* (1990).